The Behavioral Science of Leadership

The Behavioral Science of Leadership

An Interdisciplinary Japanese Research Program

Jyuji Misumi

General Editor: Mark F. Peterson

Ann Arbor The University of Michigan Press

Published in the United States of America by
The University of Michigan Press and simultaneously
in Rexdale, Canada, by John Wiley & Sons Canada, Limited
Manufactured in the United States of America

1988 1987 1986 1985 4 3 2 1

This work received a Grant-in-aid for the Publication of Scientific Research Results, Grant-in-aid for Scientific Research from the Ministry of Education, Science and Culture, Japan.

Library of Congress Cataloging in Publication Data

Misumi, Jūji, 1924–
The behavioral science of leadership.

Translation of: Rīdashippu Kōdō no kagaku.
Bibliography: p.
Includes index.
1. Leadership. 2. Social groups. 3. Management.
4. Management—Japan. I. Peterson, Mark (Mark F.)
II. Title.
HM141.M4813 1985 303.3′4 85-1068
ISBN 0-472-10060-2

Preface

Soon after World War II ended, Professor Kanae Sakuma of Kyushu University received a letter from Professor Kurt Lewin, then the director of the Research Center for Group Dynamics at the Massachusetts Institute of Technology. I was a graduate student at the time, but I still vividly remember Professor Sakuma sharing the communication with me. In his letter, Professor Lewin made reference to Ronald Lippitt and Ralph White's comparative study of democratic, autocratic, and laissez-faire leadership styles, and furthermore proposed a joint research effort on the subject to be conducted in Japan. This letter undoubtedly served as the motivating force behind my subsequent devotion to the study of leadership.

When we began our study of leadership, Japanese cities and towns were still wild stretches of burnt ruins as a result of the war. The occupation forces soon moved into Japan, however, and as a part of the occupation policy, the general headquarters of the supreme commander for the Allied powers carried out a series of programs at universities in major Japanese cities under the title of "The Institute for Educational Leaders (IFEL)." It was through these IFEL programs that I became familiar with the procedures and results of Lippitt and White's research. As a student who participated in the program, I had some doubts as to whether or not the results obtained in the experiments conducted in the United States could be duplicated in Japan. Thus, I decided to undertake a follow-up study in Fukuoka. This is how I began my study of leadership. Recognizing the fact that Japanese children of that time had not been accustomed to democratic leadership, I did not anticipate obtaining any result indicating democratic style leadership to be as effective as it is in the United States. To our surprise, however, we found that the major part of our findings were very similar to the findings of the United States study. While we allow for sociohistorical and cultural differences in human social behavior, we cannot help but recognize the general and universal nature of group dynamics.

Our study of leadership began as a study of group dynamics. When the IFEL program was completed in 1949, the Japanese Group Dynamics Association was formed at Kyushu University. Our first study on leadership was conducted over a period of several years using fifth- and sixth-grade school children as subjects. However, as teachers' union activities intensified in the late fifties, we found it increasingly difficult to conduct surveys in the elementary and junior high schools. As a result, we found it necessary to phase out the surveys in the schools, and seizing upon an unexpected opportunity, we shifted our efforts to a leadership study at a coal mine. At this coal mine, and later at such diverse institutions as steel mills, shipyards, chemical factories, banks, and railroad and bus companies, we conducted surveys designed to evaluate leadership behavior, diagnostic work, and counseling and training sessions with first-line supervisors, middle management, and project managers. We first classified each supervisor into one of four categories based upon leadership scores obtained through ratings given by subordinates. We then examined the validity of the resultant categorization in relationship to such variables as group performance, accident rate, teamwork, communication, mental hygiene, and workplace meeting scores, as well as subordinate satisfaction with work, wages, promotions, and sense of belonging to company and labor unions. As a result, we found that regardless of the industry or type of job, rankings of the four categories based on relative leadership effectiveness nearly always produced the same order.

Using the results of this survey research as reference, we embarked upon a study of administrative leadership in government in 1974. We prepared PM leadership scales from samples obtained from government offices in the Kanto (including Tokyo), Kansai, and Kyushu areas. Then, using those scales, we evaluated the leadership of the government office section and subsection chiefs. We found, to our surprise, that the effectiveness of the four PM leadership types ranked in almost the same order that had resulted from the surveys conducted in the industrial organizations. Following this study, we have been engaged in the preparation and evaluation of scales and surveys to be used in appraising leadership in such areas as college sports, Japanese political parties, teachers' leadership in the classroom, and parents' leadership in the home. Many of these studies, with the notable exception of the political leadership studies and some of our earliest studies which preceded the PM theory, are presented in the pages that follow.

Business and industrial organizations, government offices, schools, sports groups, and family groups are all representative of the type of institutions in which people spend their social lives. However, because they all differ from one another, the leadership phenomena found in each of these organizations should exhibit corresponding differences. In this sense, there may be different leadership theories that befit different leadership situations. However, in all the many widely different occupational and professional disciplines covered by our studies, rankings of the PM leadership types according to effectiveness always produced essentially the same order. Of course, the phrasing of P and M items used in the questionnaires differed somewhat contingent upon the nature of the particular organization under evaluation. These different professional organizations and groups are each handled by their respective disciplinary field of the social sciences. Nevertheless, in spite of the differences under which these various organizations operate, our studies consistently produced strikingly similar tendencies.

These results have led us to believe that we can, in meaningful terms, describe and explain a theory of leadership that transcends all the differences of environment under which it may operate. In the course of our studies we have come to believe that the present system of classifying the various disciplinary areas of the social sciences according to differences present in the social environment often stands in the way of any interdisciplinary studies dealing with leadership. It is for this reason that we have proposed the four new paradigms of disciplinary areas in the social sciences that are used in this book.

The traditional concepts and methods of the study of leadership have not necessarily been applicable to all contexts of experimental psychology. Methods used in previous studies have generally been limited to questionnaire studies that, by nature, are incapable of dealing directly with independent variables such as experimental conditions. Moreover, even when experimental studies have been conducted, concepts have often been expressed in nebulous terms familiar to the public such as *democratic* or *authoritarian*. In contrast, the concepts and methods of the PM leadership theory that we have developed in this book are applicable to both field and laboratory study.

We have conducted some experimental studies concerning an individual's motives for learning, sensorimotor learning, problem-solving processes, and memory reproduction. These studies suggest that leadership in these particular fields has something to do with experimental and general psychology.

We would like to make it clear at this point that our studies have been inspired by leadership studies conducted not only in Japan but in other countries as well, particularly the United States. We would like to express our sincere thanks to all our friends and colleagues for their support and guidance.

The studies discussed in this book have been conducted at Kyushu University located in Fukuoka City. The secretariat of the Japanese Group Dynamics Association, established in 1949 at Kyushu University, is now located at the Institute for Group Dynamics, headquartered in the Nishinippon Shinbun Kaikan Building, Tenjin 1-chome, Fukuoka City, Japan. The Institute for Group Dynamics was founded in 1969 through motivation provided by Dr. Rensis Likert, then the director of the Institute for Social Research at the University of Michigan, who visited Fukuoka at the time.

In 1961, the Chair of Group Dynamics was established at the Faculty of

Education in Kyushu University as the first and only Chair of Group Dynamics in Japan. This book has grown out of the studies sponsored by that Chair of Group Dynamics and the Institute for Group Dynamics.

Most of the empirical and experimental studies discussed in this book are the results of joint research efforts made with students, particularly graduate students in group dynamics, at Kyushu University. Needless to say, our studies would not have been possible had it not been for the energy that these highly motivated young students devoted to the effort. We kept working hard on our project even when the faculty buildings were "occupied" by those radical students who disrupted Japanese campuses throughout the country in the 1960s.

We are deeply indebted to Dr. Chikio Hayashi for information and reference on the analysis approach that we used in several of our field studies. For our study on leadership in government offices, we received tremendous cooperation from the research department of the College of Local Government. We conducted a study on political leadership with the help of the Local Government Section of the Fukuoka Prefectural Government. The assistance received from the Industrial Machinery Association was instrumental in our task of developing the scales for measuring the leadership of project managers in engineering companies. We are sincerely grateful to all these people and institutions for their help and cooperation.

Professor Rensis Likert and Professor Robert Kahn have been instrumental in facilitating the English publication of the PM research program and the initiation of PM research in the United States. Professor Likert fulfilled an important cross-national "linking pin" function for many years by acting as a personal adviser and collaborator. Our thanks also go to Professors Cartwright, Zander, Zajonc, and all the staff members of the Institute for Social Research at the University of Michigan for their valuable guidance. I would like to single out for special thanks Professors Leon Festinger, Morton Deutsch, and Harold Kelley, who have always been personal sources of inspiration to me. Our studies have extended beyond national boundaries, and our overseas research activities would not have been possible if it had not been for the assistance of Mr. James Marshall to whom I extend my heartfelt thanks. I would also like to gratefully acknowledge that many of the basic research studies described in this book were done with the financial support of the Japanese Ministry of Education, Science, and Culture. The English translation of this book was supported by a Grant-in-Aid for the Publication of Scientific Research Results from the Japanese Ministry of Education, Science, and Culture. Publication has been supported by a grant from the Suntory Foundation.

I am indebted to many people who have cooperated with us in the English translation of the manuscript. I thank Mr. Hiromichi Ito for having helped us with the translation. I deeply value his long-standing friendship. Special mention must be made of the contributions of Associate Professor Masaru Kurokawa of Hiroshima University; Associate Professor Seiichi Sato of Kumamoto University; Associate Professor Hirofumi Shinohara of Kumamoto University; Professor Fumiyasu Seiki, director of the Institute of Group Dynamics in Fukuoka City; and particularly Mr. Omura, chairman of the Institute of Group Dynamics. Last but not least, I would like to thank Mr. Toshio Sugiman of Osaka University. Mr. Sugiman has been instrumental in analyzing, sorting out, and editing the material used in this book. Our thanks also go to Mr. Teisuke Koh, Mrs. Emiko Misumi, and Mrs. Yuki Kubota who have devoted much of their time to the planning and publication of this book, and the consolidation and proofreading of the manuscripts. Mr. Katsuhisa Hashiguchi and Mr. and Mrs. Fujita were also very helpful in proofreading the manuscripts. It must be noted that certain parts of this book were taken directly from others of the author's writings, namely, *New Leadership* (Diamond Publishing Co., 1967), *Leadership: Anthology of Modern Management,* edited by Susumu Takamiya (Diamond Publishing Co., 1972), and *Group Dynamics* (Kyoritsu Publishing Co., 1976). In having this book published, we are indebted to Mr. Koji Jinushi, president of Parusu Publishing Company, Isamu Takashima of Yuhikaku Publishing Company, and the University of Michigan Press. We also express our special thanks to Mrs. Keiko Tajima and Miss Nobuko Misumi.

Jyuji Misumi
November, 1983

Editor's Preface

The Behavioral Science of Leadership makes a timely contribution to two topics being discussed outside Japan. One topic is comparative management, particularly what characterizes effective management in Japan and how effective Japanese management differs from effective management elsewhere. The second topic is leadership, particularly as it is discussed and studied by academic organizational researchers. The contribution made in both areas is quite distinctive. On the one hand, the work reflects a process of empirical and conceptual development that is conversant with Western paradigms of social science research and which reflects the same basic values of empiricism. On the other hand, it has developed without being dominated by the particular fads and fashions in Western social science.

Social science in the United States has been strongly affected by an academic versus pragmatic dialectic. Social science departments, professional societies (including divisions within the same society), and professional journals tend to either wholly embrace or wholly reject either basic or applied social science research. No visible, currently active leadership research program in the United States gives the equal emphasis to both laboratory experimentation and field study that characterizes the PM research program. It is possible that a strong, integrated leadership research program like that reported here could not be developed in the current subculture of United States social science. Thus, the PM leadership theory has the potential to contribute to discussions of leadership by indicating what might have been and, conceivably, what might still be if basic and applied research can be coordinated in the leadership area. Realistically, however, even within the currently atomized social sciences in the West, specific studies reported in the present book can provide additional directions for research concerning learning, stress, politics, and organization change.

To the issue of comparative management, the PM theory of leadership contributes otherwise unavailable data. Although other very competent research has been carried out to compare management practices depending on different combinations of Japanese and United States ownership and location, such research is not fully suited to a focused treatment of a more discrete phenomenon like leadership. At present, the appropriate comparative application of PM research is to identify reasonably similar research programs conducted elsewhere, evaluate the extent of their methodological similarity, and compare their results. It is hoped that some of the subjectivity required in such an analysis will be reduced as PM research is conducted outside Japan. Pending such work, PM research bears at least some superficial resemblance to the Ohio State, Michigan, and path-goal leadership models as well as others emphasizing two basic leadership functions, each of which may have particular expressions. Considering the results of these research programs as a group, the distinctive, consistent finding in Japan that a combined emphasis on both performance and maintenance is generally constructive is not consistent with the results of United States research. This difference in results may reflect the emphasis placed in PM research on a laboratory paradigm and the interactive combination of performance and maintenance. However, the difference may also reflect a greater dependence of Japanese organizations than U.S. organizations on formal leaders.

The latter interpretation, although not certain, is consistent with several models of organizational function as they are applied to differences between the contingencies facing large Japanese and United States organizations. Katz and Kahn (1978) suggest, in part, that leadership and formal rules tend to supplement or substitute for one another. Western organization design has been strongly influenced by a technological imperative in which the purely impersonal causal events of physical processes have been imitated by a rule-centered approach to management as reflected in bureaucratic and scientific management models. While Japanese organizations have been affected by such ideas, it is possible that a greater emphasis is placed on personal guidance by particularly competent and experienced individuals than in the United States. Quantitative approaches to management in Japan have been implemented often through quality circle groups working under the leadership of either a formal supervisor or another employee. Quantitative approaches to management in the West have been implemented through staff systems analysts whose recommendations are either accepted or rejected at relatively high management levels and then imposed on others in the form of rules and procedures. United States employees may even respond differently to the maintenance function than do Japanese employees. Those United States employees who are alienated from their work or who accept bureaucratic ideals of impersonal professionalism may be unresponsive to any personal concern or support their supervisor shows. In general, there are forces that may make leadership more consequential in Japan than in the United States.

Personally, the opportunity to collaborate in preparing the English edition of *The Behavioral Science of Leadership* has provided an incentive to puzzle through some of these issues concerning leadership and comparative social science. I was introduced to the PM theory of leadership as a graduate student when Dr. Dorwin Cartwright assigned me to present a review and critique of an early PM study in his group dynamics seminar. It was clear to me then that the PM research program had a unique contribution to make to the leadership field. Dr. Robert Kahn and Dr. Rensis Likert were instrumental in arranging the collaboration that has produced the English edition. Many faculty and staff of the University of Miami School of Business have contributed in preparing the English manuscript. These include especially Dr. Carl E. B. McKenry, chairman of the Department of General Business, Management, and Organization, who has provided considerable encouragement and support throughout the process. Lourdes Diaz, Sheila Mihoubi, Sharon Hinson, and Linda Sinkes have put particular effort into preparing the manuscript. The cultural sensitivity of Dr. Misumi, Dr. Sugiman, and the graduate students and other Japanese authors of the original work have facilitated the completion of the many revisions necessary in preparing the English edition.

Mark F. Peterson
March, 1984

Contents

PART I

The PM Perspective on Leadership

CHAPTER 1

Introduction

Since leadership has existed wherever human groups have existed, observations and theories about leadership are almost as old as the history of social thought. The Christian Bible includes an excellent example of a leadership theory. According to the Bible, Christ on a beach in Galilee told fishermen drawing in their nets to tell other people about God and in this way to become "fishers of men." Thus, early Christian leaders—the Apostles—went about their task of preaching the Gospel and in this way fishing exclusively for human souls. Absolute devotion to religious leaders is also encouraged in the Islamic Koran, in the writings of otherwise life-abnegating Buddhism, and probably in all religions. Another theory of leadership can be found in Plato's *Republic*. One of the noteworthy thoughts in the *Republic* is the idea of the "philosopher-king" based upon Plato's famous dictum that the ideal leader must be a philosopher. Machiavelli's *Prince* in the Renaissance period presents a classic political leadership theory emphasizing power and coercion that continues to influence modern theories of leadership. Max Weber's (1947) theory of leadership is equally well known in the fields of sociology and management. Weber classified leadership into three ideal types—legal, traditional, and charismatic—according to different bases for legitimizing authority. As modern bourgeois society matured during the mid-nineteenth century, numerous theories about elites appeared in the writings of social philosophers in Europe. Some examples are the "great men" and "genius" theories proposed by Carlyle (1841), Emerson (1850), and Nietzsche (1885). A biologically oriented theory with an elitist theme is the "Genetic Study of Genius" proposed by F. Galton (1870). A bibliography of leadership theory would be a long one indeed, especially if it included biographies and memoirs of prominent corporate and business leaders.

Although behavioral science research on leadership has been influenced by these traditional theories, scientific research must go beyond them. Behavioral science research must be rooted in a clear conceptualization of clearly specified social phenomena. The present volume presents an approach to leadership that attempts to meet the requirements of empirical behavioral science.

As a result of the massive social changes that have occurred throughout history, the meaning of the term *leadership* has often been questioned. The concept of "democratization" in Japanese society required a reorientation from a previous social perspective on leadership. Democracy calls for each individual's freedom and equality. It emphasizes equality of power and the direct participation of every citizen in decision-making processes having consequences that affect them. People in Japan who interpret leadership as an exercise of power are uncomfortable with democratization because they believe that democratization negates leadership itself. However, leadership cannot be negated by democracy, only transformed. People in a highly complex modern society are necessarily members of groups and complex organizations with either formal or informal leaders. Participation in some form of organized behavior is inescapable, no matter how free or equal a person may feel.

During the 1960s and 1970s the issue of leadership quality was raised with special intensity in Japanese institutions. Previously well established groups and formerly stable organizational hierarchies were shaken to their foundations. Widespread student rebellions at universities throughout Japan and the phenomena of "dropping out" and "copping out" from the Establishment occurred. Moreover, the "disappearance of leadership" has been reported in private enterprises, labor unions, government bureaucracies, universities, hospitals, and even family groups. The problem of leadership is one of the major social problems facing Japan today.

Despite the evident difficulties facing Japanese leaders, the criticisms leveled against them are difficult to study. The traditional, popular concepts of leadership held in Japan, like those held in the West, are ambiguous. First, they have multiple meanings and do not correspond precisely to specific phenomena. Second, they are often built around simple bipolar conceptual dichotomies (e.g., "right" versus "left," "democratic" versus "autocratic," "employee" versus "production" centered). Third, they often have a strong social desirability component. Fourth, they typically confound historical and functional concepts.

The traditional concepts of leadership types have multiple meanings and lack precision in their operational definitions. Consider for example the concept of democratic leadership. In the first place, the definition of democracy itself has many meanings. White and Lippitt, in their book *Autocracy and Democracy* (1960), analyzed the many meanings of democracy and identified four common elements in its numerous definitions. They are (*a*) rule by the masses, (*b*) liberty, (*c*) responsibility, and (*d*) human dignity. Even within the first concept, rule by the masses, Lenin and Stalin took one well-known perspective. Lincoln's definition of democracy as "government of the people, by the people, and for the people" reflects a very different view. Opinion also varies about how directly the masses should rule. Some people believe that the extent to which the people should rule hinges on the level of growth and maturity of the people. With regard to liberty and responsibility, arguments go on and on as to the precise nature and practical outworking of these attributes. It is certainly very important to discuss how democracy should operate, but in order to scientifically determine the effects of democratic leadership, research is necessarily confined to those leadership conditions that can be clearly measured or controlled.

Many conceptualizations of leadership types are built around dichotomies in which leadership types are polarized according to a single dimension rather than being based on a multidimensional classification. The following represent some of the leadership types that have been traditionally classified according to such dichotomies: democratic–dictatorial/autocratic, conservative-progressive, participative–one-man-rule, liberal-authoritarian, pupil-centered–teacher-centered, nondirective-directive, dovish-hawkish, employee-centered–production-centered, modern-premodern.

However, the leadership types that are actually found in human society cannot be adequately described according to such unidimensional dichotomies. Even the Lippitt and White experiment (1943) reflected a rudimentary departure from a dichotomous formula by distinguishing among democratic, autocratic, and laissez-faire leadership types. They argued that democratic leadership is not a median or average position between the poles of the autocratic and laissez-faire leadership types. Lippitt and White's research marks an acceptance that the dichotomous method that social scientists once resorted to is not fully adequate for classifying leadership types.

A third problem of traditional leadership concepts, an operational problem, must also be considered. Early conceptualizations of leadership types have a strong value basis that impedes the dispassionate scientific study of leadership functions. For instance, if the outcome of a study indicates that democratic leadership is positive, the result is likely to be considered trivially obvious. If the outcome is negative, the public response might be, "Well, maybe what was studied was not really democratic leadership," "Maybe the subjects used for the study were not accustomed to democratic leadership," or "If the study were conducted over a longer period of time, then a positive outcome would have been obtained." Conversely, if the outcome of a study on autocratic leadership proves positive, the response might be, "If the study was conducted over a longer term, the outcome would be negative," and so on.

True, there is nothing wrong with social scientists evaluating social phenomena by consciously applying democratic ideologies. But if such an inclination toward democratic values were to play a part, if only on a subconscious level, in the supposedly neutral process of gathering, selecting, and interpreting data, the results thus obtained and conclusions drawn would be warped. There is no denying that some of the previous studies on leadership were accompanied by such a democratic bias.

Traditional conceptualizations of leadership types involve a combination of historical concepts and functional concepts. For example, when people criticize supervisors or top managers in a Japanese company or office, they often say, "they are feudalistic." The confounded nature of the concepts being used becomes clear when it is asked, "What makes feudalistic leadership different from authoritarian or autocratic one-man-rule leadership?

The concept of feudalism is a very complex one. Under the feudal system, the lord of the manor provides his retainers with an estate ex gratia. In return, the retainers are required to pledge personal allegiance to the lord and become subordinate to him. The historical conditions surrounding the lord-retainer relationship are included in the concept of feudalism making it a historical concept. The master-subordinate relationships that depended upon the ownership of estate do not exist in industrial or business organizations, government offices, hospitals, or schools today. However, human relations practices reminiscent of the master-subordinate relations associated with the feudal system can still be found. Such practices often are referred to as *feudalistic*. Since the historical conditions involving estate ownership under which these practices arose no longer exist, the term *feudalistic* should not be used in its strict sense. When the leaders in industrial organizations or government offices are described as feudalistic, types of leadership are being referred to which have no causal relation to the historical condition of feudalism. Since it is a term given to the leader's behavior in a specific social situation, it is being used not as a historical concept but as an imprecise functional concept.

The traditional concepts of leadership types have arisen out of historically important ideas in the fields of history, political science, and sociology. The concepts are all-embracing, equivocal, dichotomous, and confounded by ideology and social desirability. Many of these concepts, like feudalism, combine historical conditions with the behavioral types brought about by the historical conditions. Many combine historical and functional meanings with no sharp conceptual distinction being made between situations causing behavior and the behavior that is caused. Therefore, traditional conceptualizations of leader types cannot provide the basis for a behavioral science of leadership. Concepts suitable for leadership research should be unequivocally measurable so that independent variables can be operationally controlled in experimental settings. They should also be ideologically neutral and not heavily value-laden, and defined in a way that makes multidimensional analysis possible. Although traditional leadership concepts have been used for a long time, basing experimental and field studies on these concepts is like building a hill of sand. When the hill reaches a certain height, it crumbles. In order to lay a firmer groundwork, the PM leadership theory has been developed around concepts of basic group functions.

Theories of Leadership in the Social Sciences

All branches of social science are essentially scientific approaches to the study of human groups. The study of leadership is thus relevant to all branches of social science because leadership occurs wherever groups are found. For example, leadership is one of the central problems of political science because it is closely related to authority. Likewise, leadership is an important subject in the management and administrative sciences because it involves the relationship between supervisors and subordinates in work organizations. In education, the process by which a teacher influences students can be viewed as a form of leadership. In sociology and social psychology, parental leadership in the family exercises a crucial influence on the basic character formation of children. Research has also been conducted to identify the form that leadership takes in religious groups. Cross-cultural anthropological studies allow leadership processes to be compared between primitive societies and more advanced cultures. In animal ethology and primate research, the emergence of leaders and "bosses" has been investigated among monkeys, chimpanzees, and gorillas. Leadership is also one of the major subjects studied in those areas of sociology, social psychology, and group dynamics that focus on social systems. Viewed in the light of its broad implications, leadership clearly warrants the serious concern of many branches of social science.

A Perspective on the Behavioral Science of Leadership

The proposed approach to the study of leadership is based on a more fundamental perspective on scientific research than is typically found within any single discipline. One purpose of the research program has been to develop a "morphology" of leadership. The process of developing such a "behavioral morphology" has involved describing and classifying the types and forms of leadership behavior. A second theme has been to develop a theory of the causal relationships or "behavioral dynamics" of leadership. This line of work has aimed at systematizing knowledge about laws governing the causes and consequences of leadership behavior.

The research program has now developed to the point where these areas can each be further divided into two subareas. These subareas differ according to whether characteristics of leadership broadly applicable to many settings are being investigated, or whether the implications of specific circumstances for leadership are being considered. In other words, ''general'' studies can be distinguished from ''specific'' studies depending on the degree of abstraction being considered—universal or setting-specific. Thus, ''behavioral morphology'' can be divided into the subareas of ''general behavioral morphology'' when leadership behavior is being considered under circumstances and situations common to all leadership events, and ''specific behavioral morphology'' when the implications of more specific and concrete circumstances for leadership behavior are being studied. Likewise, ''behavioral dynamics'' can also be divided into ''general behavioral dynamics'' and ''specific behavioral dynamics.'' Thus, ''behavioral morphology'' is primarily concerned with the description and classification of leadership behavior either in general or in specific situations, whereas ''behavioral dynamics'' is concerned with causal explanations of the antecedents and consequences of leadership either in general or under specific conditions. The distinctions among the four perspectives on leadership are summarized in the paradigm shown in table 1.

An overview of the main concepts and hypotheses of PM leadership theory will facilitate the detailed description of related research. Various definitions of leadership have been developed that emphasize a recognized role, influence processes, particular behaviors, or a contribution to group functioning or goal achievement (Stogdill 1974, 7–13). In the present model, formal leadership is understood as the role behavior of a specific group member who, more than other members, exerts some kind of outstanding, lasting, and positive influence in fulfilling the group's functions of problem solving or goal achievement and group maintenance. In a more comprehensive sense, however, leadership can be attributed to the group member who influences a group's course of action at a particular time. From this point of view, all members can share in providing different degrees of leadership.

TABLE 1. Paradigm for the Science of Leadership Behavior

	Situation	
Dimension	General Characteristics	Specific Situational Expressions
Behavioral Forms (Morphology dimension)	General behavioral morphology	Specific behavioral morphology
Behavioral Causes (Dynamics dimension)	General behavioral dynamics	Specific behavioral dynamics

The PM Leadership Type

In view of the limited validity of popular leadership concepts, such as "feudalistic," a framework has been sought that would have less ambiguous operational dimensions, would be more emotionally neutral, and would make multidimensional analysis more possible than do popular commonsense concepts. The PM concept centers around the idea of basic group functions. Numerous studies of small groups and hierarchical organizations indicate that group functions can be broadly divided into two components. One is the function of contributing toward a group's goal achievement or problem solving, and the other is that of promoting a group's self-preservation or of maintaining and strengthening the group process itself. The problem-solving or goal achievement function may be referred to as P, for performance, and the self-preservation function may be referred to as M, for maintenance.

From an operational point of view, leadership conditions are independent variables. Clear-cut distinctions were rarely made between methods of fulfilling group functions as independent variables and the fulfillment of group functions as dependent variables in prescientific and early scientific leadership studies (e.g., Carlyle 1841; Emerson 1850; Galton 1870; Nietzsche 1885). Since leadership is a normative, value-laden phenomenon that supports values associated with goal achievement and group preservation, P and M behaviors should first be studied as independent variables that move and reinforce a group in the "desirable" direction. Theoretically, "negative" P or M leadership can also exist. Negative P leadership is leadership that moves a group in a direction away from the desirable outcome, while negative M leadership is leadership that reduces the social stability of a group. The study of leadership has importance only to the extent that leadership affects valued outcomes.

The reasons for selecting the PM conceptualization of leadership types parallel the reasons for the limited validity of traditional leadership types. First, leadership is a "corollary" of the functions which must be fulfilled in group situations. Since leadership is not simply the behavior of an isolated individual but involves the process of influencing another person or group, it is essentially a group phenomenon. Second, compared with prescientific and popular concepts of leadership types, the PM concept is more precise in its operational rules and has fewer confounded meanings. The lack of confounded meanings does not imply that the PM concept includes only a single dimension. Third, the PM concept is a more emotively neutral concept than are most popular leadership concepts, and contains no inherent transcendental social values. Because leadership is a normative phenomenon, PM leadership does have implications for value-related outcomes. However, the PM concept itself is not a value-based concept. The effectiveness of different leadership behaviors is evaluated according to criteria independent of the PM concept itself. Fourth, the PM concept allows at least two dimensions of leadership to be identified and studied. Fifth, it is a functional, scientific concept that makes experimental and field studies easier than do popular concepts. The following discussion covers in greater detail the meaning of the PM leadership types.

P Leadership Behavior

Leadership behavior that prompts and motivates group goal achievement is called P leadership. Any group, be it a "group" of two persons, or a hierarchical organization, a race, or a nation, has some set of goals, and engages in a process to achieve goals. Basic governmental goals are to provide people with services. The primary goals of manufacturing companies are to maintain high productivity and make profits. The goal of schools is to promote educational accomplishments. The goal of research institutes is to solve problems and progress in science through the results of research.

However, these goals are generally not as clearly defined as the white tape marking the finish line of a race. In many cases, the work process of groups may be better described not so much as the process of goal achievement but as the process of problem solving. There are differences between performing relatively specific, routine tasks such as crossing a finish line and accomplishing complex tasks such as solving difficult unstructured problems. Despite these differences, some form of P leadership can be identified in both situations because leadership is necessary in both cases for achieving a group's goal.

Even in a situation where no leader has been appointed, P leadership must appear to some extent as long as any kind of leadership is provided at all. As the differentiation of status and role in a group or hierarchical organization becomes firmly established, these differences affect how the P function is distributed among group members. As the status and role of supervisor becomes distinguished from that of subordinates, the P leadership function converges in the supervisor's role. Even then, however, it would be wrong to believe that no P leadership behavior can be provided by subordinates. Considerable P behavior can be shown by subordinates in the System 4 management climate described by Likert (1967) and also in the Japanese decision-making process involving the "ringi" procedure. ("Ringi" is a traditional decision-making procedure in Japan. It is a "bottom-up" formula, in which a plan is first drafted by the supervisor at the lowest level of the hierarchy, as opposed to the top-down formula practiced in Western countries [Misumi 1983].) However, the supervisor's P behavior is more crucial in a hierarchical organization than in a fluid leadership situation because supervisors are expected to provide leadership.

P leadership behavior is defined as behavior oriented toward goal achievement and problem solving. Although this is the basic form of P leadership behavior, its specific contents vary among different experimental and field situations.

M Leadership Behavior

Once a group or hierarchical organization has been formed, it tends to preserve or maintain itself. M leadership behavior is oriented toward promoting and reinforcing the tendency toward self-preservation. Maintenance-oriented behavior is directed toward dispelling excessive tensions that arise in interpersonal relations within a group or organization, promoting the resolution of conflict and strife, giving encouragement and support, providing an opportunity for minority opinions to be expressed, inspiring personal need fulfillment and promoting an acceptance of interdependence among group members. Like the P function, the M function is provided in groups or organizations of all sizes. Maintenance-oriented leadership can be observed in government offices, industrial organizations, school groups, sports groups, and in a nation as a whole as efforts are made to prevent each kind of social system from disintegrating.

When a person joins a group or organization, the desire for self-expression inherent in human beings, that is, the desire for self-rule, autonomy, spontaneity, and independence, is impeded or restrained to some extent. Therefore, any group or organization must always manage problems which arise from the frustration of its members' self-expression. Even when such frustrations do not become alienating, a group or organization always faces the danger of disintegration and collapse. Avoiding disintegration is made easier because people have desires that can be satisfied only by belonging to the group. Satisfying members' desires has the effect of keeping a group or organization in existence and bringing about its social integration. Thus, there are conflicting forces at work that can serve to disintegrate or integrate a group or organization. The M function involves preventing any tendency toward disintegration from being catalyzed and at the same time energizing, accelerating, and strengthening the tendency toward integration.

The M function, like the P function, is also found in group situations where there is no chairman or leader. For instance, suppose opinions are divided and emotional confrontations develop in a leaderless meeting to the point where the group is in danger of disintegrating. If one of the members of the group plays a role in reconciling the conflicts, the M function is fulfilled by this person. Sometimes a difference of opinion can result in creative ideas or actions. However, if confrontations become more intense than necessary, up maintenance may be jeopardized. If group maintenance is destroyed, P function—group performance—also comes to an end.

Interaction of P and M

In this chapter, the meaning and aspects of P and M leadership behaviors have been discussed. However, the PM leadership theory does not deal with P and M separately. The theory is premised on the proposition that although any leadership behavior may emphasize either P or M functions, every leadership behavior contains some degree of both P and M at the same time. Therefore, leadership behavior is not discussed on an ''either P or M'' basis, as it is in many other leadership research programs.

According to the PM leadership theory, there are four basic types of leadership behavior—PM, Pm, pM, and pm. P and M are both contained to different degrees in each of these leadership types. As is argued in this book, the results of field surveys and laboratory studies in Japan consistently indicate that the PM type is generally the best and most desirable of the four types of leadership. What are the causal reasons for the finding that the PM type is consistently associated with the most positive levels of criterion variables? Can the effect of the PM type be explained as an additive effect of P and M combined, or can it be better understood as the interactive or multiplicative effect of P and M behavior? A central theme in the PM research program has been to test the hypothesis that an interactive interpretation of the effects of P and M leadership is more appropriate than an additive interpretation.

PART II
General Behavioral Morphology of Leadership

CHAPTER 2

Studies of the Validity of PM Leadership Types

The establishment of a new behavioral morphology requires that the validity of the behavior types be demonstrated by (1) showing their convergence with other variables which should be associated with them for conceptual reasons and (2) showing their divergence from one another in their association with other variables. Several experimental and field studies were conducted to evaluate the validity of the P, M, PM, and pm types as applied to both first-line and second-line supervisors.

These studies parallel to some extent those conducted to assess the validity of the consideration and initiating structure measures developed by the Ohio State group (Fleishmann 1953; Stogdill 1963; Stogdill and Coons 1957). However, there are a few distinct differences between the approaches taken in the two research programs. Although the Ohio State researchers pursued an extensive validation program for their measures, their emphasis was on validating survey measures for use in field research. The approach taken in the PM leadership research program has been to demonstrate the validity of the four proposed leadership types and to establish consistent, complementary methods for manipulating these types in experimental settings and assessing their effects in field settings.

While the basic purpose of the studies reported in the present chapter was to test the validity of the PM types, causal relations with other value-related outcomes were necessarily considered. Thus, the focus of these studies is on developing a general morphology of leadership behavior while their implications for the study of general leadership dynamics is left in the background. Issues of leadership dynamics are brought to the forefront in subsequent chapters.

Study 1: An Experimental Study of Postal Trainees

Problem and Method

In the initial experimental study to assess the validity of PM leadership types (Misumi and Shirakashi 1963, 1966), first-line and second-line supervisors providing the P, M, and PM types of leadership supervised groups of three subjects as they worked on the simple job of counting holes punched in IBM cards. First-line supervisors are those who directly supervise workers. Second-line supervisors are the immediate supervisors of the first-line supervisors and thus supervise workers indirectly.

The experimental hypotheses were as follows.

1. Group productivity under P-type supervision will be greater than under M-type supervision.
2. Group morale under M-type supervision will be greater than under P-type supervision.
3. Group productivity and group morale under PM-type supervision will be greater than under P- and M-type supervision.
4. Productivity and morale will be greater when P and M functions fulfilled by first-line and second-line supervision complement each other (e.g., when one provides P-type leadership and the other M-type leadership) than when they duplicate each other (e.g., when both provide P-type leadership).

Subjects

Subjects for this experiment were fifteen students (men; average age twenty-two) enrolled in the Kyushu Postal Administration Employees' Training Center. Five graduate students and research assistants from Kyushu University were recruited to play the role of supervisors. Five experimental groups were formed.

Each group was made up of three subjects plus one first-line supervisor, and one "hidden" second-line supervisor. Supervision by the second-line supervisor took the form of messages written in advance on a piece of paper, which were conveyed by the first-line supervisor of each group. The second-line supervisor was not physically present at the place of the experiment.

Supervisory Behavior Types

First-line Supervisor

Three leadership types were introduced as independent variables.

First type. This is described as the performance-centered type (referred to as P). Under the conditions of this experiment, the performance-centered type is a style of supervisory behavior directly oriented toward the achievement of group goals. A supervisor of this type, urging his group to expedite the work, would say, for example: "Work more quickly," "You are slow," "Hurry up, hurry up," "We haven't much time left," "Don't fool around, get to work." In order to put pressure on the subjects to do their work accurately, he might say: "Count more accurately," "Keep the cards in better order.'' He might compare one group with others to encourage competition by saying: ''You are behind other groups,'' ''This group is the worst.''

Second type. This is the group maintenance–centered type (referred to as M). Under the conditions of this experiment, the group maintenance–centered type is a style of supervisory behavior directly oriented toward maintaining and strengthening the group itself. To encourage the subjects, a supervisor of this type would say things like: ''Let's be pleasant and merry,'' ''Let's be more friendly.'' To show feelings of sympathy toward the subject, he might say: ''That's a big job, isn't it?'' ''Stick it out a little longer.'' This type of supervisor sees to it that interpersonal tensions are eased by cracking jokes and laughing as is appropriate to maintain a pleasant group atmosphere.

Third type. This is the combined task performance/group maintenance–centered type (referred to as PM for short). It is a style of supervisory behavior emphasizing maintaining and strengthening the group while also achieving group performance goals. A supervisor of this type not only puts pressure on the subjects to expedite their work and do their work accurately, but also attempts to develop good interpersonal relations within the group by offering encouragement or showing sympathy toward the workers. In other words, this is a style of supervision that combines both the first and second leadership functions.

Each first-line supervisor directed his three workers by using the supervisory behavior (P or M or PM) in which he had been trained beforehand.

Second-line Supervisor

The second-line supervisor was not physically present in the group. Instead, his ''presence'' was impressed on the subjects by what were supposed to be his instructions written on a card. The instructions on the instruction card were given through the first-line supervisor once or twice during the experimental working period of fifty minutes a day. As in the case of the first-line supervisors, the second-line supervisors were divided into three types, P, M, and PM. Examples of their written instructions that were read to the groups are:

P. ''I want you to supervise in such a way as to increase efficiency more.'' ''The workers are still making many mistakes. Be sure that they do not make mistakes.''

M. ''It seems to me that you are tired with the monotonous work. I want the supervisor to take the workers' feelings into consideration in supervising them.'' ''Please take good care of anyone who complains of eye strain or fatigue.''

PM. (Give the P and M instructions alternately.)

Task

The job assigned to the teams of three subjects was to count as quickly and accurately as possible the number of holes in IBM punch cards. Their productivity was measured by the number of punch cards they finished counting accurately during the fifty-minute working period. The procedure was as follows.

1. The three subjects sit side by side at a table in front of the first-line supervisor.
2. Subject A pulls out one of the IBM cards and counts the number of holes between the first line and the twenty-ninth line on the card. He then records the number on a piece of tabulation paper. Upon finishing the process, he passes the card and tabulation paper to subject B, seated next to him.
3. Subject B counts the number of holes between the thirtieth line and the fifty-ninth line, writes it on the tabulation paper, and passes card and paper to subject C.
4. Subject C counts the holes between the sixtieth line and the eightieth line and puts the number down on the tabulation paper. He then calculates the total number of holes in the card, and puts the card in the place assigned for cards with that particular number of holes.

Measurement of Group Productivity

The productivity of the group is measured by the total number of cards in which the holes had been counted accurately in fifty minutes. To detect errors in the number of holes counted, a special checking procedure was developed. The cards were designed in such a way that the number of holes each contained could be determined by the location of a hole on a specific line of the card. For example, a card with forty-two holes could be identified by a hole punched at spot 2 on the thirtieth line; a card with forty-three holes was identified by a hole at 3 in that line. In this way, a card which had been inaccurately counted could be easily identified from among those punch cards the workers had classified as having a certain number of holes.

Observation of Group Member Behavior

Observers recorded the behavior of the subjects and the first-line supervisor during the course of their work using an observation sheet prepared beforehand. A questionnaire survey was administered twice to measure group atmosphere, friendship toward the supervisor, and morale. The first survey was conducted upon completion of the fifth session, and the second at the end of the thirteenth session.

Procedure

A total of thirteen work sessions were conducted, each session lasting fifty minutes. Each first-line supervisor had been fully trained in the method of supervision during a four-week preliminary experiment conducted beforehand. The first-line supervisor was to supervise three subjects located one meter in front of him.

A bell rang fifteen minutes after the task began. The first-line supervisor collected the punch cards counted by the subjects and the tabulation paper which showed the results of the work done. He left the room and proceeded to the place where he was supposed to receive instructions from the second-line supervisor. Even when the first-line supervisor had left the room, the subjects were to continue to work. A second bell rang thirty minutes after the work began and a third bell rang upon termination of the fifty-minute working period. Every time the bell rang, the first-line supervisor left the room in the same manner. He then came back to the work room, having received instructions from the second-line supervisor. He orally conveyed the second-line supervisor's instructions to the subjects by reading out the message. It took the first-line supervisor less than two minutes to leave the room and return with the instructions.

Results

Validity of Supervisory Behavior Types

Results of Observation
Table 2 shows the observed behavior of the first-line supervisors whose actions were intended to reflect the three behavioral types which comprised the

TABLE 2. Observers' Reports of First-line Supervisors' Behavior

Group No.	Leadership Condition	P Behavior Observed	M Behavior Observed	F (Frustration, Complaints)	O (Other Actions)	Behavior Observed
1	P	216(82.8)	31(11.8)	0	14 (5.4)	261
2	P	147(85.0)	12 (6.9)	2(1.2)	12 (6.9)	173
3	PM	56(25.6)	105(48.2)	1(0.5)	56(25.6)	219
4	PM	85(40.5)	87(41.4)	0	38(18.1)	210
5	M	51(24.6)	96(46.0)	1(0.5)	60(28.9)	208

Notes: Figures not in parentheses represent the frequency of behavior observed in each category. Figures in parentheses represent the percentage of total leader behaviors falling within each category.

These data show the results of the experiment from the second through the thirteenth session. The first session is the only session that involved no experimental conditions of P, M, and PM leadership.

experimental conditions (independent variables). As shown in table 2, observers verified that the first and second groups were provided with P leadership while the third and fourth groups were provided with PM leadership by their first-line supervisors. However, although the first-line supervisor for the fifth group was supposed to behave as an M leader, the observers described his behavior as not being significantly different from that of the PM-type leader. Only when supported by the workers' perceptions and the supervisor's own records based on his self-judgement (self-descriptive records prepared upon the completion of each session) could the leadership in this fifth group be classified as M supervision.

Perceptions by the Subjects

The subjects were asked to provide their perceptions of the first- and second-line supervisors' behavior types using a questionnaire. The questionnaire included two questions that asked for responses using seven-point scales ranging from "Not at All" to "Very Much."

1. "How much is the supervisor of your group concerned with an increase of productivity?"
2. "How much is the supervisor of your group concerned to create an amicable atmosphere so that the three of you can work comfortably?"

Table 3 presents the results of the questionnaire. The PM type was clearly different from the P type based on subjects' perceptions. Although the

TABLE 3. Experimental Subjects' Perceptions of First-line and Second-line Supervisors' Behavior

Survey Measure	Experimental Conditions[a] P	M	PM	Significant Difference among Conditions[b]
First-line supervisor	(N = 6)	(N = 3)	(N = 6)	
P scale (1st survey)	6.17	4.67	4.17	P > PM
P scale (2d survey)	6.33	2.33	4.17	P > PM, P > M
M scale (1st survey)	2.00	4.33	4.67	PM > P
M scale (2d survey)	2.17	3.00	5.33	PM > P
Second-line supervisor	(N = 8)	(N = 3)	(N = 3)	
P scale (1st survey)	5.44	3.00	3.67	n.s.
P scale (2d survey)	4.67	3.00	4.67	n.s.
M scale (1st survey)	2.11	5.00	2.67	n.s.
M scale (2d survey)	2.22	6.00	4.33	n.s.

[a]Figures indicate mean scores of subjects' perceptions.

[b]The significance test was not conducted by comparing mean scores shown in this table but by using a U test or sign test. The low scores of reactions by individual members of each group were used. A "greater than" sign (>) indicates a significant difference at the .05 level; none of the other results are significant.

differences between the M type and the other two types were less distinct, they were consistent with the intended conditions and with observers' ratings. The levels of P and M behavior provided by the second-line supervisors were not found to be significantly different among the experimental conditions although they tended to differ in the way originally intended. The effects of second-line supervisors' behavior on subjects' perceptions do not seem to have been as strong as the effects of first-line supervisors' behavior.

Productivity of Experimental Groups

The following formula was used to measure the productivity of the experimental groups:

$$Pn = \frac{fn - f1}{f1} \times 100$$

Pn = productivity index at the time of the nth session
fn = number of cards accurately counted at the time of the nth session
$f1$ = number of cards accurately counted at the time of the first session. (The first session was conducted as a base session: no supervisory types [P, M, PM] were assigned, and all the supervisory behaviors were "neutral.")

The performance results are presented in table 4. No significant difference is found between the first and second groups, but significant differences do appear among the other groups. Of the three types of first-line supervisory behavior, the results show that PM comes first, followed by P and finally by M in terms of group productivity.

TABLE 4. Differences in Productivity among the Experimental Groups

<table>
<tr><td rowspan="2">Productivity Indices</td><td colspan="10">Experimental Conditions, Second-line and First-line Supervisory Types (by group number)</td></tr>
<tr><td colspan="2">4 (PM-PM)</td><td colspan="2">3 (P-PM)</td><td colspan="2">1 (P-P)</td><td colspan="2">2 (M-P)</td><td colspan="2">5 (P-M)</td></tr>
<tr><td>Mean</td><td colspan="2">74.73</td><td colspan="2">54.42</td><td colspan="2">34.05</td><td colspan="2">32.14</td><td colspan="2">17.15</td></tr>
<tr><td>SD</td><td colspan="2">28.08</td><td colspan="2">23.29</td><td colspan="2">19.62</td><td colspan="2">19.74</td><td colspan="2">9.54</td></tr>
<tr><td rowspan="3">Results of sign test</td><td></td><td colspan="2">3.24**</td><td colspan="2">3.24**</td><td colspan="2">0.58</td><td colspan="2">0.02*</td><td></td></tr>
<tr><td colspan="3"></td><td colspan="4">3.24**</td><td colspan="3"></td></tr>
<tr><td colspan="5"></td><td colspan="5">3.24**</td></tr>
</table>

Note: Significance tests were conducted using a sign test rather than by using the mean scores reported above.

$*p < .05$, $**p < .01$

Morale in Experimental Groups

The survey of subjects' attitudes toward their supervisors, and their work motivation, group cohesiveness, group attractiveness, and feelings of fatigue was used to measure various aspects of morale. Subjects under a first-line supervisor of the PM type showed a greater interest in their work than did subjects under P- or M-type supervisors ($p < .05$).

Subjects under a PM type of first-line supervisor showed a more favorable attitude toward their supervisor than did subjects under the P or M types of supervision ($p < .05$). No significant differences in group cohesiveness, group attractiveness, or feelings of fatigue were found among the P, M, and PM types of first-line supervision. No significant differences among the three types of second-line supervision were found in subjects' attitudes toward their second-line supervisors or in any of their other attitudes.

Discussion

Although leadership research had already been conducted by the Japanese Group Dynamics Association at Kyushu University, the postal trainee study was the first study based on the PM leadership theory. Although the experiment has several obvious weaknesses that have been corrected in subsequent laboratory studies, it is presented because of its key role in shaping the PM leadership research program. It contributed to the conceptualization of PM types in a way that is amenable to experimental operationalization perhaps to an even greater degree than to field measurement. It also supported the interactive conceptualization of M-oriented behavior as catalyzing the performance-inducing function of P-oriented behavior. The lack of support for the complementarity hypothesis concerning the provision of P and M behavior from different sources moved the PM theory away from the complementarity perspective being postulated by Bales (1953) at about the same time.

Study 2: A Field Study of a Coal Mine

Problem and Method

Another study conducted in a Japanese coal mine was designed to determine the generalizability of the experimental results to the social situation of an ongoing hierarchical organization. This study was conducted to determine which supervisory patterns would correspond to the highest levels of group productivity and morale. As in the experimental study, the implications of the behavior of both first-line and second-line supervisors were studied.

Subjects

Subjects for this study were members of eight work groups including a total of 215 workers who were engaged in digging coal in the pit of Fukushima Coal Mine operated by the Chuko Coal Mine Co. Ltd., Nagasaki prefecture. Each group was made up of 20 to 30 coal miners. The survey was conducted originally with nineteen work groups involving a total of 500 workers. As explained later, only those work groups that could be clearly classified as either high producing groups or low producing groups were included in the data analysis.

The first-line supervisor for a work group is called the *Sekinin,* or work leader. The Sekinin is elected once a year in each group from among members. He, like every other member, is paid on a contractual basis but is authorized to supervise all other coal miners in the group.

The Sekinin's superior—the second-line supervisor—is referred to as *Kakari-in,* or officer-in-charge. The Kakari-in is a qualified engineer who has passed a national certifying examination. He is on the regular payroll of the company and receives a fixed salary. The Sekinin is a miner while the Kakari-in is a professional manager.

The responsibilities of the Sekinin include (1) assigning jobs at the coal face, (2) determining the work procedure, (3) determining the daily work quota, and (4) rating the proficiency of each worker. The wage for each worker is decided on the basis of this rating.

The main function of the Kakari-in is (1) to assume overall responsibility for safety in the pit, (2) to provide technical guidance to all the coal miners including the Sekinin, and (3) to check on all the decisions made by the Sekinin. In particular, any decision concerning proficiency ratings is subject to approval by the Kakari-in.

The survey was conducted in July, 1963, using questionnaires administered to groups.

Measurement of Supervisory Behaviors

Measures were designed to reflect the job-centered supervisory function (P) and the human relations–centered supervisory function (M) fulfilled by supervisors at both levels. Supervisory behaviors were measured using descriptions by their subordinates. Each subject was asked to rate the supervisory behaviors of their Sekinin and Kakari-in by answering the following questions using a five-point Likert scale. Questions concerning the P function were:

1. Is your Sekinin (or Kakari-in) a stickler about obeying the rules?
2. Does your Sekinin (or Kakari-in) ask about your progress in reaching your production quota?

3. Does your Sekinin (or Kakari-in) suggest new ways to solve work-related problems?
4. How important does your Sekinin (or Kakari-in) believe it is to increase the efficiency and productivity of your work group?
5. Does your Sekinin (or Kakari-in) urge you to finish your daily production quota by the specified time?
6. When you do a poor job, does your Sekinin (or Kakari-in) criticize the poor work which was done rather than you as a person?
7. Does your Sekinin (or Kakari-in) try to make you work as hard as you possibly can?
8. Does your Sekinin (or Kakari-in) emphasize that you should use established work methods?

Questions concerning the M function were:

1. Do you believe your Sekinin (or Kakari-in) is willing to listen to your opinions and suggestions?
2. When your Sekinin (or Kakari-in) disagrees with you about something, does he impose his opinion upon you?
3. Does your Sekinin (or Kakari-in) treat you and your co-workers equally?
4. Does your Sekinin (or Kakari-in) tend to ask your opinion about important matters concerning the work?
5. Can you speak freely to your Sekinin (or Kakari-in) about your work?
6. Are there times when your Sekinin (or Kakari-in) makes you work without concern for your feelings?
7. Can you understand why your Sekinin (or Kakari-in) speaks and acts the way he does?
8. Are there times when your Sekinin (or Kakari-in) arbitrarily changes work assignments without consulting with you?

A five-point response scale was used for each question. The value 5 was assigned for the most job-centered (or the most human relations–centered) responses while 1 was assigned for the least job-centered (or human relations–centered) responses. Consequently, each supervisor could get between eight and forty points each for the P and M functions.

Measures of Work Group Productivity

The productivity of the two or three groups working at each workplace were compared on the basis of the following three indices.

1. Monthly output during the one-year period preceding the survey.
2. Monthly attendance rate during the one-year period preceding the survey.
3. Work efficiency as rated by subsection chief, section chief, and manager.

High-producing groups and low-producing groups were identified on the basis of the three indices. Only those groups which could be clearly classified either as high- or low-producing groups were studied. In workplaces having three work groups, only those two were used which were clearly either high-producing or low-producing. Thus eight of the original nineteen working groups were selected for study, two in each of the four workplaces.

The four workplaces are referred to as I, II, III, and IV respectively. The corresponding high-producing and low-producing groups at each of the four workplaces are referred to as A-A′, B-B′, C-C′, and D-D′.

Opinions and Attitudes toward the Work, Working Groups, and Supervisors

Questionnaires were used to measure satisfaction with the work, group cohesiveness or attractiveness, and satisfaction with and trust in first-line and second-line supervisors using the following questions.

1. (Job satisfaction) "Are you satisfied with your present job?"
2. (Group cohesiveness) "Can you work comfortably with other workers on the same shift?"
3. (Satisfaction with supervisors) "Are you satisfied with working under your present Sekinin (or Kakari-in)?"
4. (Confidence in supervisors) "Do you think your Sekinin (or Kakari-in) is an excellent Sekinin (or Kakari-in) compared with the one for the other group working in the same workplace?"

Results

Data were analyzed to identify differences between the high- and low-producing groups in the behavior patterns of the first-line and second-line supervisors at the four workplaces. It was first necessary to set a criterion to distinguish between high and low levels of emphasis on the P and M functions in order to operationally identify the four PM leadership types. Since each of the supervisory behavior questions was answered according to a five-point scale, the index midpoints could have been used to distinguish between high and low levels of each form of leadership. In this study, however, the mean scores of P and M were used as the dividing line. As stated before, eight out of the nineteen work groups were clearly identified as either high-producing or low-producing groups on the basis of the productivity indices. However, it was considered more appropriate to use scores obtained from all nineteen groups to determine the average levels of P and M supervisory behaviors in this coal mine as a whole.

Table 5 shows the scores based on perceptions of the five hundred workers for the supervisory behaviors of the first-line and second-line supervisors. P and M scores were derived by summing each person's responses to the items comprising the P and M scales, respectively. The averages reported for P and M supervisory behavior of the first-line supervisor are 25.9 and 27.3, respectively. A high level of perceived P behavior is indicated when a first-line supervisor is described as over 25.9 points in P behavior by subordinates.

Supervisory patterns of the eight groups are classified as P, M, PM, or pm depending on the percentage of employees who describe their supervisor's behavior as above or below the mean on the P and M dimensions. First, the percentage of workers in each group who described their supervisor as providing more than average P-oriented or M-oriented leadership was calculated. When the number of workers who gave more than the mean P scores to their first-line supervisors was greater than that of those workers who gave less than the mean scores, a high level of P behavior was inferred. A similar method was used to identify a high level of M behavior. The same approach was used for assessing the leadership of both first-line and second-line supervisors. When more than half of the workers gave more than the mean scores on both the P and M functional dimensions, the supervisory behaviors were classified as PM. When the majority of workers gave less than the mean scores on both dimensions, the supervisors were classified as providing pm leadership. Shown in table 6 are the results of this survey. Results showing differences in supervisor behavior between the high-producing groups and the low-producing groups are presented in table 7.

According to table 7, both first-line and second-line supervisors in all the low-producing groups except in workplace I were P-type supervisors. In the high-producing groups, however, no first-line or second-line supervisors were P leaders. Instead, PM leadership was often provided by either first-line or second-line supervisors.

The combinations of first-line and second-line supervisors' behavior was

TABLE 5. Mean Scores of P and M Supervisory Behavior Functions in Coal Mining Groups

	First-line Supervisors		Second-line Supervisors	
	P	M	P	M
Mean	25.9	27.3	26.2	28.2
SD	1.8	2.7	2.7	2.3

more varied for the high-producing groups than for the low-producing groups. The first-line supervisors in the high-producing group at workplace II showed PM leadership while second-line supervisors provided pm leadership. In the high-producing group at workplace IV the situation was reversed. In the high-producing group at workplace III, first-line supervisors were M-type leaders and the second-line supervisors were PM leaders. By contrast, both first-line and second-line supervisors in all low-producing groups except in workplace I provided P-type supervision.

The leadership patterns in workplace I differed somewhat from the other workplaces. Both first-line and second-line supervisors in the low-producing group exhibited the pm pattern of leadership. In the high-producing group, however, first-line supervisory behavior tended to be of the M type. The presence of M-type leadership was the main difference between the high-producing group and the low-producing group.

Analyses were also conducted to determine the difference between the high-producing groups and the low-producing groups in workers' job satisfaction, their group cohesiveness, and their satisfaction with and confidence in their first-line and second-line supervisors. When pairs of high- and low-producing groups from the same workplace were compared, not all of the differences were significant nor were they uniformly in the expected direction.

Discussion

In the laboratory study of postal trainees, second-line supervision was expressed to workers only indirectly. All instructions representing the statements of a second-line supervisor were conveyed by the first-line supervisors. Consequently, the results indicated a stronger effect of the first-line supervisor's leadership than the second-line supervisor's leadership. However, second-line supervisors in the coal mine were often in direct contact with the miners. As a result, there is no sharp distinction between first- and second-line supervisors as long as at least one of the two provides either PM-type or M-type leadership. Even though employees in the coal mine hold different hierarchical positions, the organization seems to operate as an integrated unit.

Generally speaking, the PM supervisory pattern was the most typical in the high-producing mining groups, while P-type supervision was the most typical of the low-producing groups. Work attitudes or "morale" was also higher under PM-type than under P-type leadership. These findings dovetail with the results of the previous experimental study.

In workplace I, the difference between the more productive and the less productive group was the presence of M-type leadership from one supervisor

TABLE 6. Subordinates' Descriptions of First-line and Second-line Supervisors' P and M Behaviors in Coal Mining Groups

		Working Group						
	A	A′	B	B′	C	C′	D	D′
Second-line (Kakari-in)								
Supervisory pattern determined	pm	pm	pm	P	PM	P	PM	P
P: Percentage of workers who gave more than the mean scores shown in table 5	20.6	58.8	53.1	92.3**	68.9*	75.0*	72.4*	75.0*
P: Percentage of workers who gave less than the mean scores shown in table 5	79.4	41.2	46.9	7.7	31.1	25.0	23.6	25.0
M: Percentage of workers who gave more than the mean scores shown in table 5	58.6	35.2	65.6	53.8	68.9*	45.0	76.4*	25.0
M: Percentage of workers who gave less than the mean scores shown in table 5	41.4	64.8	34.4	46.2	31.1	55.0	23.6	75.0

First-line (Sekinin)									
	Supervisory pattern determined	M	pm	PM	P	M	P	pm	P
P	Percentage of workers who gave more than the mean scores shown in table 5	31.0	41.2	75.0*	69.2*	41.3	75.0*	41.1	75.0*
	Percentage of workers who gave less than the mean scores shown in table 5	69.0	58.8	25.0	30.8	58.7	25.0	58.9	25.0
M	Percentage of workers who gave more than the mean scores shown in table 5	72.4*	64.8	68.7*	61.5	75.8*	40.0	11.7	0.0
	Percentage of workers who gave less than the mean scores shown in table 5	27.6	35.2	31.3	38.5	24.2	60.0	88.3	100.0

Note: Significance tests are student t-tests comparing means for the high and low levels of P and M behavior for first- and second-line supervisors in each work group.

$^{*}p < .05$

$^{**}p < .01$

in the more productive group compared to pm-type leadership by both supervisors in the less productive group. This finding that productivity and morale are lower under P-type than under M-type leadership contrasts with the experimental results. Since this difference in the results of laboratory and field studies was found repeatedly in later research, it will be discussed at other points (e.g., chap. 16). It was tentatively interpreted after the early studies to mean that some degree of P-oriented leadership may always be present in field settings, even for leaders who provide below-average amounts of it.

A working hypothesis following the experimental study was that when the M function and the P function are combined, thus enabling the former to catalyze the latter, productivity and morale are optimally stimulated. Although the coal mining study was not designed to permit clear causal inferences, the results were consistent with those of the previous experiment. Furthermore, the finding of the first field study that productivity and morale are lower under pm than under M leadership contrasts with the experimental results. This finding may indicate that in field settings where some degree of both P and M leadership are almost always likely to be present, the intensity of the P and M leadership provided may be important.

In early empirical studies of leadership, a bipolar continuum with P and M poles was often assumed. Most studies concerning the effect of leadership prior to the early PM studies in Japan and the Ohio State studies in the United States tended to dichotomize leadership patterns. Contrasts were made between democratic, employee-centered, and consideration-oriented leadership on the one hand and despotic, authoritarian, production-centered leadership on the other. More often than not, the former was regarded as a "good" leadership pattern, and the latter as a "bad" one. The results of the initial PM studies, however, indicated that the effects of certain leadership patterns, in particular the effects of democratic, employee-centered, and consideration-oriented leadership, which were supposed to be "good," were not always

TABLE 7. Relationship between Productivity and Supervisory Patterns of First-line and Second-line Supervisors in Coal Mining Groups

	High-producing Group			Low-producing Group		
Workplace	Work Group	Second-line Supervisor	First-line Supervisor	Work Group	Second-line Supervisor	First-line Supervisor
I	A	pm	M	A′	pm	pm
II	B	pm	PM	B′	P	P
III	C	PM	M	C′	P	P
IV	D	PM	pm	D′	P	P

superior to despotic, production-centered, and initiating structure–oriented leadership. But by the same token, no evidence was found to show that the latter is superior to the former. These considerations point to the conclusion that research treating leadership and supervisory patterns on a dichotomous basis had come to an impasse.

In the frame of reference of our study, the pm supervisory pattern is somewhat similar to laissez-faire leadership, the M pattern approaches an employee-centered or consideration-oriented supervisory pattern, and P leadership approximates a job-centered, despotic, and initiating structure–oriented supervisory pattern. But what is the closest equivalent to the PM leadership pattern? It might be called a democratic leadership pattern. However, there is no definite way to show that M is not a democratic leadership pattern. As a matter of fact, when democratic leadership is referred to in common parlance, the pattern of M is often emphasized.

At any rate, whatever colloquial labels are given to the various supervisory styles—laissez-faire, democratic, autocratic, employee-centered, consideration-oriented, or initiating structure–oriented—it is important to remember that all these are merely descriptive terms that have no unified, consistent meaning in their operational usage. By replacing such colloquial terms with the PM morphology, research dealing with leadership behavior can more easily avoid the tendency toward dichotomous stereotyping. A conceptual base can be created which orders and relates the various classification models that traditionally have been used. Our studies were conducted with that purpose in mind.

As previously stated, the research described in this chapter represents the early attempts to verify in the field the earlier laboratory results of Misumi and Shirakashi. The PM leadership theory has since been verified further through a number of field surveys. After completing our survey research at the Chuko Coal Mine, full-scale efforts were begun to develop PM leadership behavior scales. The next chapter deals with that project.

CHAPTER 3

Measuring and Rating PM Leadership

Selection of Items to Measure PM Leadership Behavior

Developing adequate survey measures has been the central issue in many modern leadership research programs. The first presentations of the "consideration" and "initiating structure" concepts in the Ohio State studies are dominated by the factor-analytic procedure used to develop survey measures (Fleishman 1953; Stogdill and Coons 1957). The same emphasis on defending survey measures on statistical grounds is evident in the first presentation of the "four-factor theory of leadership" (Bowers and Seashore 1966). The central concern to design universally valid survey measures appropriate for most if not all work situations is reflected in nearly all subsequent research in these two research traditions (Schriesheim and Kerr 1977).

The process of developing PM measures for industrial organizations is described below. This process has contributed greatly to an understanding of the leadership behaviors that subordinates in many work situations typically experience as being associated with the P and M functions.

However, the basic conceptualization and initial laboratory experiments involving the four PM types had occurred prior to survey measure development. The primary purpose of survey development was to design measures that would allow these four types to be represented in field research. As will be described in the studies of "General Dynamics," the fundamental experimental research using the PM concepts continued during the period of survey research. Although the value of survey research to test the generalization of PM theory in field application is not to be minimized, the basic causal hypotheses and theoretical formulations rested on other grounds. Thus, in evaluating the survey research component of PM theory, readers familiar with survey-dominated United States leadership research traditions will need to evaluate PM survey research in the context of PM experimental research, presented in later chapters.

The core PM survey measures are presented in the present chapter, while measures adapted to several specific populations follow. Other measures continue in use that are adapted either to particular functional specialties (e.g., engineers) or particular organization types (e.g., banks).

Preparation of Questionnaire Items

Preparation of questionnaire items designed to measure and evaluate first-line supervisors' leadership and various dimensions of group members' attitudes was begun in November, 1967 (Misumi et al. 1970). Questionnaire items prepared by F. C. Mann of the University of Michigan (form A including 122 items, form B including 154 items), particularly those items concerning immediate supervisors, were used for reference. Eventually, 41 of these items were adopted.

Second, about 800 items used in questionnaires that the laboratory of Group Dynamics, Faculty of Education, Kyushu University, distributed to twenty-eight organizations (such as manufacturing factories, mines, banking institutions, hospitals, etc.) during the period from 1961 to 1968 were screened. After eliminating duplicated items, 385 items were adopted. (Those items used in our previous questionnaires concerning PM leadership were included in the final selection). Third, 290 new items were prepared concerning job satisfaction and 24 of these items were adopted. A total of 450 items were selected.

The initial version of the questionnaire consisted of thirteen a priori factors identified by analyzing 232 items using Jiro Kawakita's (1967) KJ method of qualitative analysis. This initial version was carefully examined by graduate students in group dynamics from Kyushu University, staff members of the Institute for Group Dynamics, and supervisors and workers from several industrial organizations. Industrial employees were consulted to see if the questions made sense from the point of view of members of the industrial organizations concerned and if the situations assumed by these questions actually were found in their organizations. Based on comments by these different parties, some of the questionnaire items were reworded. The initial survey version was checked for accuracy over and over again, and after having been revised three times, was finalized into a questionnaire comprising fourteen factors and 164 items in July, 1968.

Administration of Survey

The survey was tested by distributing the questionnaire in eighteen organizations (including five manufacturing companies, one power company, one gas company, one water supply company, two wholesalers and retailers, government offices, and several others) selected according to the industrial classification established by the Statistics Bureau of the Prime Minister's Office. This sample represents a wider variety of organizations than those used to first develop the Ohio State (Halpin and Winer 1957) or Four-Factor Theory (Bowers and Seashore 1966) measures in the United States. The survey began in August, 1968, and ended in January, 1969. Fifty-two hundred people were covered by this survey. These people were employees (not holding any supervisory positions) who were working under first-line supervisors. They were asked to assemble in a room in groups of ten to fifty, and the interviewer (a staff member of the Institute for Group Dynamics) administered the questionnaires to the group. The questionnaire was distributed to each person and the questions were read aloud one at a time along with the five possible alternative answers for each question. The interviewees were asked to answer by circling the response they selected. Respondents returned the completed questionnaires signing their names. The entire process took forty to seventy minutes for each group including a five-minute intermission.

Factor Analyses of Leadership Items

Of the 164 items that made up the questionnaire, 63 concerned leadership behavior. These 63 items were factor analyzed. The factor analysis was conducted using data from four hundred persons picked at random from among the fifty-two hundred completing the questionnaire. Six factors were obtained using the centroid method where communalities are 1.00. These factors were rotated using the iterative varimax method. The factor loadings are by far the highest on three factors.

Showing high loadings on Factor I are items involving the extent to which the supervisor makes subordinates work to their maximum capacity, is strict about the amount of work subordinates do, and gives instructions and orders. These items concern supervisory behavior regarding strict observance of regulations and pressure for production. Therefore, Factor I was labeled "Pressure for Performance."

Items with high loadings on Factor II concern the extent to which the superior supports his subordinates, understands his subordinates' viewpoint, can be spoken with freely, and helps remove any unpleasantness that may develop in the workplace atmosphere. These items concern mutual trust, consideration for personal problems, and relaxation of tension prevailing within a group. Factor II was labeled "Group Maintenance."

High factor loadings on Factor III are found for the items "How precisely does your superior work out plans for goal achievement each month," "No work time is wasted because of poor planning and organization," "Lets you know about plans concerning the work you are to do each day," and "Sets time limits for completing the work." These items concern the planning and processing of work. This factor, Factor III, is referred to as "Planning."

The first and third of these factors are associated with the P function, while the second is associated with the M function. Independent measures of P and M leadership were developed by selecting items with strong loadings only on the P factors or only on the M factor.

Reanalyzing Items Selected to Measure PM Behavior

Based on the results of the factor analyses, twelve items were selected to measure P behavior and twelve items were selected to measure M behavior as shown in table 8. Misumi, Seki, and Shinohara (1974) reanalyzed these twenty-four items, using the same data that were used for the factor analyses described in the preceding section.

Three factors were obtained using communalities of 1.00 when principal components factor analysis was applied to these twenty-four items. The factors were then rotated using the varimax method. The factor loadings when just these twenty-four items are used is shown on the left in table 8. Shown on the right are the factor loadings for these same items obtained in the previous factor analysis when they are included with the larger set of items. With the exception of a few items, the results of the two factor analyses turned out to be very much the same, despite differences in the number of items used in the analysis and the techniques used. Therefore, the factors obtained as a result of the reanalysis are given the same names as they were in the initial analysis.

From the results of the reanalysis, the twenty-four items can be divided into the following three groups: those items closely related to the factor of "Group Maintenance (Factor I)" Q14, 15, 16, 17, 18, 19, 20, 21, 22, 23, 24; those items closely related to the factor of "Pressure for Performance (Factor II)" Q1, 2, 4, 5, 6, 7; and those items closely related to the factor of "Planning (Factor III)" Q3, 8, 9, 11, 12. Q10 and Q13 do not fit unambiguously into any one of these groups. The group principal axes method using the Procrustes program (Hurley and Cattell 1962; Shiba 1967) was used to obtain the composite variables most highly correlated with each of the three groups of items. Correlations among the composite variables and also between each composite variable and each item were calculated. The results are shown in table 9 and table 10. The α-coefficients for all the composite variables in table 9 are quite high. This attests to the homogeneity of the items in each of the groups. Table 10, showing the correlations among the three composite variables, indicates that the variable composed of items closely related to the factor of "Planning" is considerably correlated ($r = .537$) with the factor of "Maintenance." In general, these results are similar to those obtained in the studies used to develop the Ohio State measures (Halpin and Winer 1957).

TABLE 8. Factor Loadings in Initial Factor Analysis and in Reanalysis

Item	Reanalysis (1974)				Initial Factor Analysis (1970)		
	I	II	III	h^2	I	II	III
1. Is your superior strict about observing regulations?	−.116	.649	−.213	.4804	.664	−.072	.001
2. To what extent does your superior give you instructions and orders?	.134	.518	−.429	.4689	.546	.207	.198
3. When your superior gives you assignments, does he set clear time limits for completing the work?	.236	.202	−.696	.5812	.319	.299	.554
4. Is your superior strict about the amount of work that you do?	−.184	.743	−.144	.6067	.670	−.172	.029
5. Does your superior urge you to complete your work by the time he has specified?	.050	.684	−.201	.5104	.639	.070	.065
6. Does your superior try to make you work to your maximum capacity?	.028	.744	.170	.5832	.687	−.017	.203
7. When you do an inadequate job, does your superior focus on the inadequate way the job is done instead of on your personality?	.108	.613	.054	.3907	.528	.113	−.121
8. Does your superior know anything about the machinery and equipment you operate?	.245	.220	−.565	.4281	.255	.304	.458
9. Does your superior let you know about the plans concerning the work you are to do each day?	.211	.119	−.678	.5188	.278	.254	.607
10. Does your superior ask you for reports about the progress of your work?	.297	.395	−.291	.3286	.466	.303	.175
11. Are there times when your working time is wasted because of inadequate planning and organization on the part of your superior?	.311	−.144	−.611	.4910	.038	.333	.614

Item							
12. How precisely does your superior work out plans for goal achievement each month?	.128	.063	−.771	.6152	.229	.212	.635
13. When an unpleasant atmosphere develops in the workplace, does your superior do anything to remove it?	.497	.140	−.461	.4797	.233	.538	.338
14. Can you talk freely with your superior about your work?	.712	−.048	−.130	.5263	−.026	.722	.059
15. When you ask your superior to improve the facilities needed for your work, does he try to fulfill your request?	.633	.063	−.366	.5385	.110	.606	.333
16. Generally, does your superior support you?	.799	.068	−.175	.6710	.071	.780	.085
17. Is your superior concerned about your personal problems?	.664	.097	−.272	.5237	.132	.705	.150
18. Do you think your superior trusts you?	.788	.046	−.042	.6248	.024	.753	−.003
19. Does your superior give you recognition when you do your job well?	.675	.004	−.176	.4869	.058	.651	.129
20. When a problem arises in your workplace, does your superior ask your opinion about how to solve it?	.597	.023	−.241	.4154	.049	.643	.121
21. Does your superior try to understand your viewpoint?	.753	−.006	−.347	.6874	.079	.775	.229
22. Is your superior concerned about your future benefits like promotions and pay raises?	.682	.087	−.246	.5332	.147	.713	.134
23. Does your superior treat you fairly?	.696	−.196	−.166	.5508	−.143	.644	.164
24. Is your superior friendly toward you?	.796	.063	.000	.6374	.067	.742	−.050
Variance explained	6.258	3.015	3.406	12.679			
Percentage of variance explained	26.1	12.6	14.2	52.9			

Source: Misumi et al. 1970 for Initial Factor Analysis figures; Misumi, Seki, and Shinohara 1974 for Reanalysis figures.

TABLE 9. Results of Group Principal Axes Analysis (Three Composite Variables)

Item	Group Weighting			Factor Structure		
	I	II	III	I	II	III
1. Is your superior strict about observing regulations?	1	0	0	.701	.208	−.016
2. To what extent does your superior give you instructions and orders?	1	0	0	.617	.463	.256
3. When your superior gives you assignments, does he set clear time limits for completing the work?	0	1	0	.312	.774	.409
4. Is your superior strict about the amount of work that you do?	1	0	0	.763	.162	−.104
5. Does your superior urge you to complete your work by the time he has specified?	1	0	0	.722	.278	.122
6. Does your superior try to make you work to your maximum capacity?	1	0	0	.689	.005	−.010
7. When you do an inadequate job, does your superior focus on the inadequate way the job is done instead of on your personality?	1	0	0	.582	.103	.080
8. Does your superior know anything about the machinery and equipment you operate?	0	1	0	.306	.682	.390
9. Does your superior let you know about the plans concerning the work you are to do each day?	0	1	0	.213	.735	.383
10. Does your superior ask you for reports about the progress of your work?	0	0	0	.339	.372	.345
11. Are there times when your working time is wasted because of inadequate planning and organization on the part of your superior?	0	1	0	.029	.671	.447
12. How precisely does your superior work out plans for goal achievement each month?	0	1	0	.201	.769	.336
13. When an unpleasant atmosphere develops in the workplace, does your superior do anything to remove it?	0	0	0	.204	.523	.569
14. Can you talk freely with your superior about your work?	0	0	1	−.021	.347	.718
15. When you ask your superior to improve the facilities needed for your work, does he try to fulfill your request?	0	0	1	.134	.516	.719
16. Generally, does your superior support you?	0	0	1	.088	.427	.821

TABLE 9—*Continued*

Item	Group Weighting			Factor Structure		
	I	II	III	I	II	III
17. Is your superior concerned about your personal problems?	0	0	1	.128	.426	.722
18. Do you think your superior trusts you?	0	0	1	.052	.317	.772
19. Does your supervisor give you recognition when you do your job well?	0	0	1	.043	.385	.701
20. When a problem arises in your workplace, does your superior ask your opinion about how to solve it?	0	0	1	.064	.366	.649
21. Does your superior try to understand your viewpoint?	0	0	1	.061	.522	.816
22. Is your superior concerned about your future benefits like promotions and pay raises?	0	0	1	.116	.431	.734
23. Does your superior treat you fairly?	0	0	1	−.135	.347	.707
24. Is your superior friendly toward you?	0	0	1	.056	.283	.760
Eigen value				2.790	2.647	6.018
Percentage of variance explained (in group items)				46.5	52.9	54.7
α-coefficient				.770	.778	.917

These same twenty-four items were also divided into two groups, one group to measure P leadership and a second to measure M, and the group principal axes method was applied again. The results (data not shown) indicated that no item had correlations over .50 with both variables. The α-coefficients were high for both composite variables, thus confirming their homogeneity. However, three of the items intended to measure P behavior (Q6, Q7, and Q11 from table 11) had only low correlations in the .35 to .45 range on the P dimension. Several of the other items (Q3, Q8, Q9, Q11, Q13,

TABLE 10. Correlations among the Three Composite Variables Obtained Using Group Principal Axes Analysis

Composite No.	I	II	III
I (Pressure)	1.000		
II (Planning)	0.294	1.000	
III (Maintenance)	0.073	0.537	1.000

TABLE 11. Results of Group Principal Axes Analysis Using Eight P Items and Eight M Items

Item	Group Weighting I	Group Weighting II	Factor Structure I	Factor Structure II
1. Is your superior strict about observing regulations?	1	0	.674	−.029
2. To what extent does your superior give you instructions and orders?	1	0	.642	.241
3. When your superior gives you assignments, does he set clear time limits for completing the work?	0	0	.393	.402
4. Is your superior strict about the amount of work that you do?	1	0	.736	−.093
5. Does your superior urge you to complete your work by the time he has specified?	1	0	.722	.109
6. Does your superior try to make you work to your maximum capacity?	1	0	.646	−.014
7. When you do an inadequate job, does your superior focus on the inadequate way the job is done instead of on your personality?	1	0	.557	.061
8. Does your superior know anything about the machinery and equipment you operate?	0	0	.369	.373
9. Does your superior let you know about the plans concerning the work you are to do each day?	0	0	.308	.374
10. Does your superior ask you for reports about the progress of your work?	1	0	.509	.340
11. Are there times when your working time is wasted becaue of inadequate planning and organization on the part of your superior?	0	0	.091	.413
12. How precisely does your superior work out plans for goal achievement each month?	1	0	.354	.316
13. When an unpleasant atmosphere develops in the workplace, does your superior do anything to remove it?	0	0	.287	.544
14. Can you talk freely with your superior about your work?	0	1	.041	.748
15. When you ask your superior to improve the facilities needed for your work, does he try to fulfill your request?	0	0	.206	.649
16. Generally, does your superior support you?	0	1	.161	.824
17. Is your superior concerned about your personal problems?	0	1	.204	.733

TABLE 11—*Continued*

Item	Group Weighting I	Group Weighting II	Factor Structure I	Factor Structure II
18. Do you think your superior trusts you?	0	1	.108	.778
19. Does your superior give you recognition when you do your job well?	0	1	.102	.711
20. When a problem arises in your workplace, does your superior ask your opinion about how to solve it?	0	1	.137	.661
21. Does your superior try to understand your viewpoint?	0	0	.156	.756
22. Is your superior concerned about your future benefits like promotions and pay raises?	0	1	.186	.749
23. Does your superior treat you fairly?	0	1	−.060	.709
24. Is your superior friendly toward you?	0	0	.105	.689
Eigen value			3.039	4.387
Percentage of variance explained (in group items)			38.0	54.8
α-coefficient			.767	.882

(Correlation between two composite variables was −.184)

Q15, Q21, Q24) had higher correlations on the dimension they were *not* intended to measure than was desirable. As a result, the correlation between the P and M composite variables was .420, undesirably high given that statistical independence was being sought for analytic purposes.

Consequently, the data were reanalyzed yielding the results shown in table 11. Factor scores were determined based on those sixteen of the twenty-four items in table 11 that are noted under the "Group Weighting" columns as defining Factor I or Factor II. Seven of the eight "P" items are those most highly associated with the "Pressure" factor in the three-factor solution. The eighth "P" item had a high loading on the "Planning" factor and a relatively low loading on the "Maintenance" factor compared to other "Planning" items. The correlation between the two resulting composite variables was .184. These sixteen items have subsequently been used to measure P and M leadership in many field studies. The "P" measure in the sixteen-item form probably comes closer to reflecting the "Pressure for Production" factor identified but not studied extensively in the Ohio State program than "Initiating Structure."

The Validity of PM Leadership Types

The results of factor analytic studies of questionnaire items indicate that perceived leadership behavior at lower levels in Japanese work organizations is typically represented by three factors. The factor of pressure for performance and the factor of planning are related to the P behavior concept, and the factor of group maintenance is related to the M behavior concept. Consequently, twelve items were selected to measure P behavior which were highly correlated with the factor of pressure for performance and the factor of planning but not with the factor of group maintenance. Another twelve were selected to measure M behavior which were highly correlated with the factor of group maintenance but not with the other two factors. These items are the twenty-four items used for the reanalysis discussed in the preceding section.

Each of the questionnaire items was rated on a five-point scale. A method was devised to use the composite index derived from these items to reflect the four leadership types of PM theory. The P and M scores for each leader were obtained using the average of ratings by his immediate subordinates. P scores were obtained by adding up the twelve P behavior scores, and M scores were obtained in a similar way. If the leader of a group had a P score higher than the average of P scores for all respondents and also had an M score higher than the average M score for all respondents, then he was classified as a PM-type leader. A leader who only had an above average score in P leadership was classified as a Pm type leader (or simply P-type leader), and one who had a higher than average score only in M behavior was classified as pM (or simply M-type). A leader whose score was below average in both P and M scores was classified as a pm-type leader. All leaders were classified as either PM-, P-, M-, or pm-type leaders using this procedure.

To examine the validity of these leadership types, criterion variables were selected such as productivity indices, accident rates, group members' satisfaction with work, and other "morale" variables. A questionnaire was prepared that included items concerning job satisfaction, satisfaction with compensation, satisfaction with the company/teamwork, group meeting quality, communication adequacy, mental health, and performance norms.

Over 150,000 persons were surveyed in coal mines, steel mills, electric power companies, gas companies, shipyards, machinery manufacturing companies, petrochemical companies, railroad companies, bus companies, and banks. Since it was difficult to obtain productivity measures, accident rates, and other objective indices in all the organizations surveyed, the validity of the PM leadership types could only be evaluated against objective indices in some of the organizations. However, morale variables were measured in all of the surveys. Because the surveys showed similar results, a survey conducted at the Mitsubishi Heavy Industries' Nagasaki Shipyard in 1973 will be discussed as an example. The survey covered 186 working groups of about ten members each, including a total of 2,257 rank and file workers.

Leadership Types and Job Satisfaction

The following five questionnaire items were used to measure satisfaction with "motivator" aspects of the job (Herzberg et al. 1957). Each item was rated on a five-point scale as were the questionnaire items concerning leadership.

1. "Are you interested in your present work?"
2. "Do you find your day-to-day work worthwhile?"
3. "Do you feel that you have mastered your present job?"
4. "Are you proud of the job you are responsible for?"
5. "Do you want to gain greater knowledge and skill in the job you are responsible for?"

Each respondent's job satisfaction (or "motivator") scores were derived by summing the scores on the five questionnaire items. Each work group's scores were obtained by calculating the average of its members' scores. (Respondents' scores and work groups' scores for all the satisfaction and morale variables were determined in the same way as they were for job satisfaction.)

Levels of job satisfaction differed as expected among the four leadership types. The percentage of groups with job satisfaction levels higher than the average is largest under PM-type leaders with 73.1 percent, followed by M-type leaders with 67.8 percent, P-type leaders with 37.5 percent, and pm-type leaders with 28.3 percent. However, in terms of average scores, the difference between PM-type and M-type leadership is not very large—the average job satisfaction score for the PM type is 17.42 and for M type is 17.34, followed by P type 16.42, and pm type 15.91.

Leadership Types and Satisfaction with Compensation

Relationships were also studied between leadership types and the degree of satisfaction with variables such as salaries and promotions. The following five questionnaire items were used to measure satisfaction with compensation and extrinsic rewards.

1. "What do you think of the promotion system in your company?"
2. "Are you satisfied with your present salary considering the nature of your job and the effort required of you?"
3. "What do you think of the bonus system in your company?"

4. "Do you think promotions in your company are given on a fair and equitable basis?"
5. "How do you feel about your company's fringe benefits by and large?"

As for job satisfaction, no striking difference appears between PM-type and M-type leadership. The average pay satisfaction score under PM-type leadership was 11.59 while under M-type leadership it was 11.52, followed by P-type leadership with 10.97 and pm-type leadership with 10.48. Even small differences among leadership types in satisfaction with salaries and promotions is noteworthy because these variables are likely to be hard for a leader to influence.

Leadership Types and Satisfaction with the Company

The implications of leadership for another factor—satisfaction with the company and work setting—were also studied. The following five questionnaire items were used to measure satisfaction with the company.

1. "Are you glad you joined this company?"
2. "Do you believe the company is genuinely concerned with its employees' welfare?"
3. "Do you believe the company is committed to improving its employees' working conditions (facilities, salaries, etc.)?"
4. "How do your family members feel about your working for this company?"
5. "Generally, how does your company compare with other companies?"

Satisfaction with the company was highest under leaders of the PM type (mean = 16.54), followed by M-type (mean = 16.05), P-type (mean = 15.75), and pm-type (mean = 15.23) leaders.

Leadership Types and Teamwork

Teamwork concerns the sense of cohesion within the group or the sense of identity with the group. Used to measure teamwork were the following five questions.

1. "Do your co-workers help you when you need help with your work?"
2. "Do your co-workers have a good sense of teamwork?"
3. "Do you get along well with your co-workers?"
4. "Do you want to remain a member of your present group?"
5. "Do your co-workers encourage one another to give their best effort in doing a job?"

The results show that teamwork tended to be best under PM-type leaders (mean = 17.90), followed by M-type (mean = 16.79), P-type (mean = 15.64), and pm-type (mean = 15.21) leaders.

Leadership Types and Evaluation of Group Meeting Quality by Subordinates

The quality of group meetings concerns group members' evaluations of and satisfaction with the meetings a leader calls at the workplace. The following five questions were used to measure the quality of group meetings.

1. "Do you think the discussions during these meetings are practically useful?"
2. "How satisfied are you with these meetings?"
3. "By and large, do you think these meetings are well run?"
4. "Is there an atmosphere in which you can freely discuss things at those meetings?"
5. "Does your superior seriously consider the suggestions and opinions you bring up at those meetings?"

Evaluations of group meetings were most positive under PM-type leaders (mean = 17.49), followed by M-type (mean = 16.45), P-type (mean = 15.30), and pm-type (mean = 14.51) leaders.

Leadership Types and Communication Adequacy

Communication adequacy concerns the channel of communication to and from the company's top management and the free flow of information among workplaces. Communication adequacy was measured using the following five questions.

1. "Does your company keep you posted on the company's plans and its management conditions?"
2. "Does your superior keep in close touch with other workplaces?"
3. "Does the company management sometimes fail to let you know things that you should know about?"
4. "Are your immediate superior and his superior in close contact with one another?"
5. "Are there times when the suggestions and opinions that you had submitted seem to have evaporated somewhere along the line and never reached top management?"

Communication was most adequate under PM-type leaders (mean = 17.50), followed by M-type (mean = 16.38), P-type (mean = 16.07), and pm-type leaders (mean = 14.73).

Leadership Types and Mental Health

The questionnaire included items concerning the extent to which group members feel tension, stress, and anxiety in the workplace. The following six questions were asked.

1. "Do you usually feel under unreasonably strong pressure from your superior?"
2. "Do you feel that your area of responsibility is clearly defined?"
3. "Do you feel that you are given more responsibility and authority than is appropriate for the position you now hold?"
4. "Do you feel somewhat uneasy when you consider what the future holds in store for you?"
5. "Are there times when you feel like quitting your present company?"
6. "Are there times when you feel restless?"

The higher the mental health scores were, the less tension, stress, and anxiety a worker feels. Mental health scores were highest under PM-type leaders (mean = 19.89), followed by M-type (mean = 19.56), P-type (mean = 18.30), and pm-type (mean = 18.12) leaders.

Leadership Types and Group Performance Norms

Performance norms concern attitudes shared among group members about how high a level of performance the group should achieve. The following five items comprised the measure of group performance norms.

1. "Are there times when your co-workers criticize the way things are done in your workplace?"
2. "Is there an atmosphere among your co-workers of placing strong pressure on one another to work hard?"
3. "To what extent do your co-workers hate to be outperformed by any other work group?"
4. "How much importance do you yourself place on achieving work goals?"
5. "How much importance do the majority of your co-workers place on achieving work goals?"

Performance norms were the highest under leaders of the PM type (mean = 17.34), followed by M-type (mean = 16.54), P-type (mean = 16.34), and pm-type leaders (mean = 15.77).

The relationship of leadership types to eight variables—job satisfaction, satisfaction with compensation, satisfaction with the company, teamwork, group meeting quality, communication adequacy, mental health, and group performance norms—have been summarized. The results indicate that the scores on these eight variables were the highest under leaders of PM type, followed by M-type, P-type, and pm-type leaders. Very similar results have been obtained in surveys conducted in many other business and industrial organizations in Japan.

Analysis of Intercorrelations among Variables Using Hayashi's Method of Quantification

In the preceding sections, the bivariate relationship of leadership type to each of eight other variables was described. In this section, the intercorrelations among all nine variables—the above eight variables plus the leadership types—will be considered from a multivariate perspective.

This analysis makes use of the "Quantification of Pattern Classification (Quantification Theory III)" advanced by C. Hayashi. The analytic procedure involved in the Quantification of Pattern Classification is described in the following discussion as various portions of its application are presented. The data used for this analysis are the data obtained from the 186 groups (2,257 respondents) at the Mitsubishi Heavy Industry's Nagasaki Shipyard already described. The format of the data used as the point of departure for the analysis is shown in table 12. As shown in table 12, the nine variables were analyzed after dividing them into a table of twenty categories comprising the twenty columns of the table. Four categories are used to represent the four PM leadership types while two categories ("high" and "low") are used to represent each of the eight criterion variables. In the Quantification of Pattern Classification, each of the categories is now quantified by assigning similar values to variable categories which tended to characterize the same work groups and giving different values to variable categories that tend to characterize different work groups. For instance, suppose most of the groups that were marked ○ in table 12 for category "Leadership PM-type" (i.e., had PM-type leaders) were also marked ○ for the category "High Communication Adequacy." If so, then similar values were given to the category "Leadership PM-type" and the category "High Communication Adequacy." By the same token, if most of the groups marked ○ for the category "Leadership pm-type" were not marked ○ for the category "High Teamwork," then different values were assigned to these two categories.

The Quantification of Pattern Classification is designed to quantify the similarities and differences among a set of variable categories (in this case, twenty categories) measured for a set of objects (in the present case, 186 groups). It is, in effect, a type of categorical multidimensional scaling method. (In the Quantification of Pattern Classification, all the categories are quantified according to the above principles and at the same time; the subjects [in this case, work groups] are also quantified. So, the unique characteristic of

TABLE 12. Format of Data Input to the "Quantification of Pattern Classification" Program

	Leadership Type				Job Satisfaction		Satisfaction with Compensation		Satisfaction with Company		Teamwork		Group Meeting Quality		Communication Adequacy		Mental Health		Performance Norms	
Group no.	PM	P	M	pm	High	Low	High	Low	High	Low	High	Low	High	Low	High	Low	High	Low	High	Low
001	o				o			o	o		o		o		o		o		o	
002		o				o		o		o	o			o		o		o	o	
003		o				o	o		o			o	o			o	o			o
004			o		o		o		o		o		o		o		o			o
005				o	o		o			o	o			o		o		o		o
006	o				o		o		o		o		o		o		o		o	
007		o			o			o		o		o	o		o		o		o	
008				o		o		o		o		o		o		o		o		o
.																				
.																				
.																				
.																				
.																				
.																				
.																				
182			o			o		o	o		o			o	o			o	o	
183			o		o		o		o			o		o		o	o			o
184				o		o		o		o		o		o		o	o			o
185				o	o		o		o			o		o		o	o			o
186			o			o		o			o			o	o		o			o

Note: "High" of each variable means that the average score of a group is above the total average, while "Low" means it is below the total average. For instance, in group No. 005, the leader is a pm-type leader, and job satisfaction is above average (High), satisfaction with compensation is above average (High), satisfaction with the company below average (Low), teamwork above average (High), group meeting quality below average (Low), mental health below average (Low), and performance norms below average (Low).

the Quantification of Pattern Classification lies in the fact that the categories and subjects are quantified simultaneously. In other words, if those categories which apply to Subject A also apply to Subject B, similar values are given to both Subject A and Subject B. See Hayashi, Higuchi, and Komazawa [1970, 244–49] for further details concerning the Quantification of Pattern Classification.)

The number of sets of values or "components" used in the analysis is determined in a similar way to that which would be used if continuous variables were being factor analyzed. In factor analysis, various numbers of factors are typically computed and the solution with the largest number of interpretable factors possible is selected. In the present analysis, two sets of values or "components" were derived.

The Quantification of Pattern Classification was chosen over other available mutivariate procedures for several reasons. First, a multivariate procedure was needed which allowed interactive combinations of P and M leadership to be considered. Procedures such as factor analysis or component analysis would only allow the P and M dimensions to be studied as independent factors. Second, a procedure was required which allowed the cross-sectional data to be represented in a way which did not reflect a causal assumption not justified by the research design. Although the laboratory studies indicate that leadership types can affect the kinds of criteria being studied, the field studies themselves do not strictly allow this causal hypothesis to be tested. Therefore multiple regression procedures were considered inappropriate. Third, a procedure was needed which would treat the various attitudinal criteria simultaneously. Although for simplicity and clarity the preceding discussion has presented analyses which treat them separately, they are themselves interrelated. Given these three considerations, the Quantification of Pattern Classification is the most appropriate available method for summarizing the associations between the four leadership types and the criterion variables.

Two "components" (in this case, the first and second quantification) were used. The values assigned to each variable category for the first and second component are presented in table 13.

The relationship of leadership types to the other variables can be summarized by simultaneously plotting the first and second components on a two-dimensional plane as illustrated in figure 1. The category "PM-type leadership" is located at the extreme left near the categories "High Performance Norms," "High Teamwork," "High Group Meeting Quality," and "High Communication Adequacy." Groups under PM-type leaders are thus shown to have the highest levels on all these variables, particularly those related to group activities such as performance norms, teamwork, group meeting quality, and communication adequacy. The "M-type leadership" category is on

TABLE 13. Values Given to the Variable Categories as a Result of the "Quantification of Pattern Classification"

Variable	Categories	Component I	Component II
Leadership type	PM type	−.145	−.176
	M type	−.049	.345
	P type	.086	.021
	pm type	.164	−.012
Job satisfaction	High	−.096	.003
	Low	.110	−.003
Satisfaction with compensation	High	−.067	.199
	Low	.066	−.195
Satisfaction with the company	High	−.090	.129
	Low	.103	−.147
Teamwork	High	−.111	−.065
	Low	.114	.066
Group meeting quality	High	−.118	−.057
	Low	.148	.072
Communication adequacy	High	−.127	−.016
	Low	.133	.017
Mental health	High	−.112	.053
	Low	.117	−.055
Performance norms	High	−.098	−.092
	Low	.100	.094
η^2		.443	.132

the left side of the graph as is the category "PM-type leadership." Also located on the left are the categories "High Satisfaction with Compensation," "High Satisfaction with Company," and "High Mental Health." Groups under M-type leaders are thus found to be the second highest in all the outcome variables, particularly those variables which are personally oriented. The category "P-type leadership" is on the right side of the graph, close to the category "pm-type leadership." Located near them are the "Low" categories of "Teamwork," "Group Meeting Quality," and "Performance Norms." Although groups under P-type leaders are found to be low in all the outcome variables (particularly in satisfaction with communication adequacy, teamwork, group meeting quality, and performance norms), they are slightly higher than groups under pm-type leaders. The category

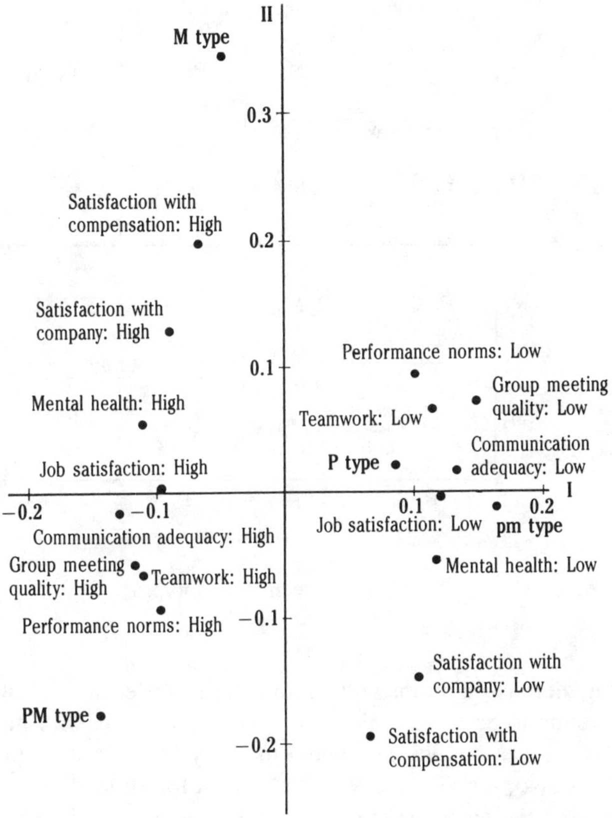

Fig. 1. Values given to the variable categories as a result of applying "Quantification of Pattern Classification" (Component I and Component II)

"pm-type leadership" is the farthest to the right of all the four leadership types. Near it are those same variable categories located near the category "P-type leadership" as well as the category "Low Mental Health." Thus groups under pm-type leaders are found to be the lowest in all the variables.

The Validity of Sixteen PM Leadership Types

Purpose of the Study

In the preceding section, four PM types, PM, P, M, and pm, were identified by comparing an individual leader's P and M scores with the average P and M scores of all leaders in the organization. Their validity was evaluated by

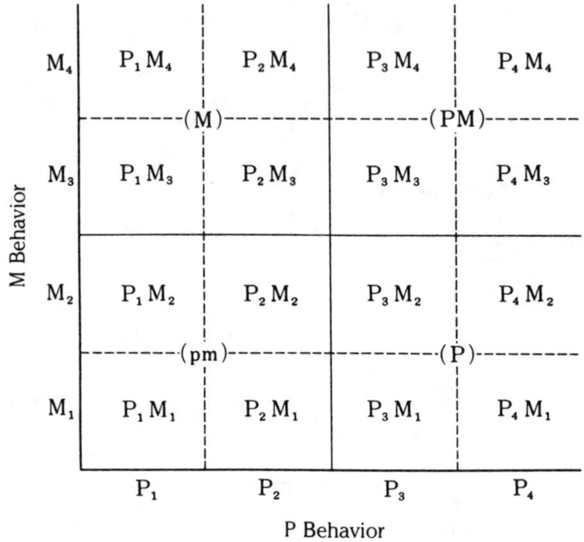

Fig. 2. Sixteen PM subtypes

determining their associations with eight external criterion variables. Not only were they found to be valid in the setting described here, they have also been found to be valid in studies conducted in many other organizations. In other organizations also, the average P and M scores for all leaders in each organization was used to determine the leadership category into which an individual leader fell. The standard used for classifying leaders differs from organization to organization. Despite this difference, however, very similar results have been obtained for the validity of the four PM types. Thus, a common standard applicable to all organizations throughout Japan is not necessary. The average scores of each organization serve very adequately as the standard for classifying individual leaders. The consistency of results also suggest that the PM leadership types are likely to be valid even when the four PM types are further subdivided. In the present section, the validity of the PM types will be examined further by subdividing them into sixteen subtypes.

The sixteen subtypes of leadership are designated using the notation shown in figure 2. Nine "areas" consisting of four types each can be identified in figure 3.

Area 1. P_2M_2, P_2M_1, P_1M_2, P_1M_1 (this area corresponds to pm of the four PM types)
Area 2. P_3M_2, P_3M_1, P_2M_2, P_2M_1
Area 3. P_4M_2, P_4M_1, P_3M_2, P_3M_1 (this area corresponds to P of the four PM types)

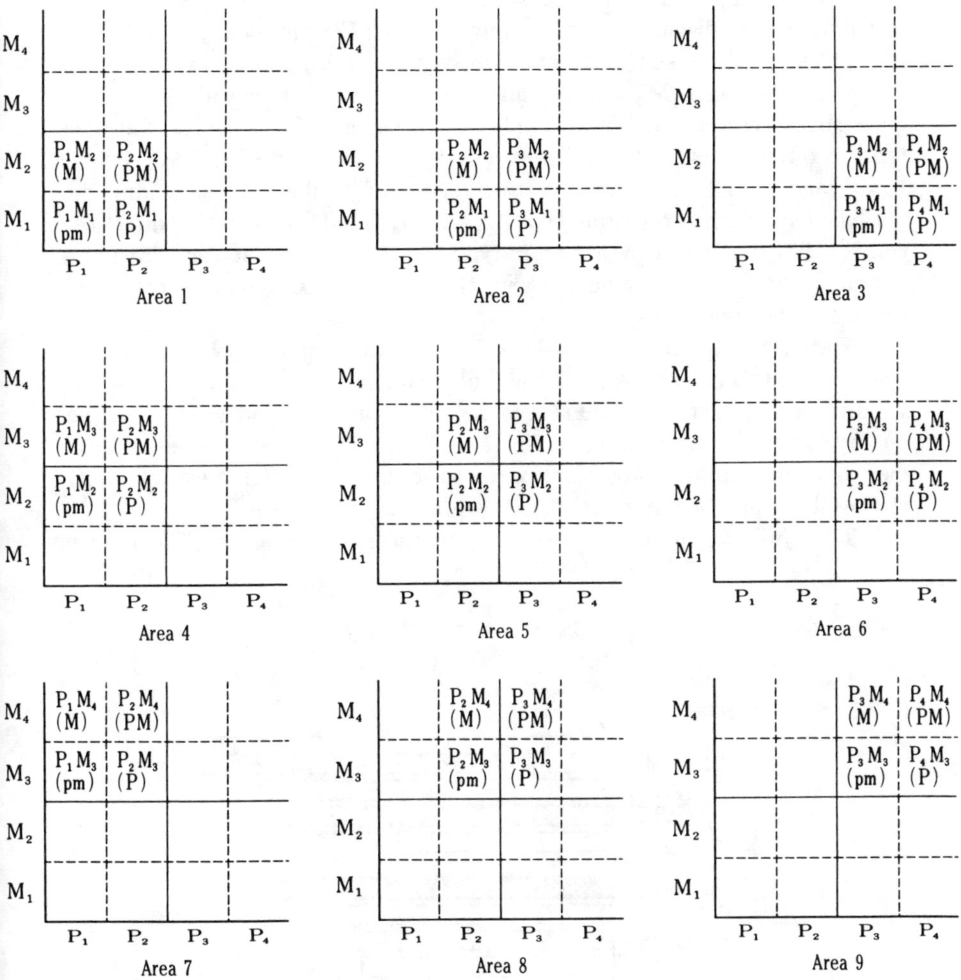

Fig. 3. Nine areas within the sixteen PM subtypes

Area 4. P_2M_3, P_2M_2, P_1M_3, P_1M_2
Area 5. P_3M_3, P_3M_2, P_2M_3, P_2M_2
Area 6. P_4M_3, P_4M_2, P_3M_3, P_3M_2
Area 7. P_2M_4, P_2M_3, P_1M_4, P_1M_3 (this area corresponds to M of the four PM types)
Area 8. P_3M_4, P_3M_3, P_2M_4, P_2M_3
Area 9. P_4M_4, P_4M_3, P_3M_4, P_3M_3 (this area corresponds to PM of the four PM types)

As noted, certain groups of these sixteen types correspond to the four types which have been discussed in preceding sections. For instance, P_4M_4, P_3M_4, P_4M_3, and P_3M_3, taken as a set, correspond to the PM type while P_2M_2, P_1M_2, P_2M_1, and P_1M_1 correspond to the pm type. However, the sixteen types should not only be understood as subdivisions of each of the four PM types into four parts. Instead, *within* each set of four cells (e.g., P_4M_4, P_3M_4, P_4M_3, and P_3M_3), the four PM types can be identified. Thus, within the cluster of four cells consisting of P_3M_4, P_2M_4, P_3M_3, and P_2M_3, the P_3M_4 cell is a PM type and P_2M_4 is a pm type. The validity of the four PM types within this area can be evaluated by identifying differences in their correspondence to other outcomes.

The first study concerning the validity of these sixteen types was conducted by Misumi, Kurokawa, and Shinohara (1973). They examined the validity of each set of four PM types using teamwork and group meeting quality as external criterion variables. These two criteria were chosen because they were the variables found in previous research to differ most markedly among the four PM types.

The results of these analyses are shown in figures 4 and 5. The sixteen

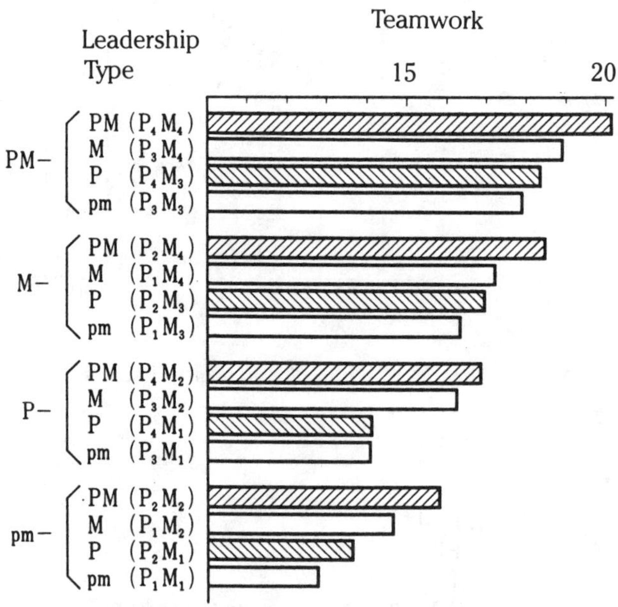

Fig. 4. Teamwork for sixteen PM subtypes

PM types shown in these figures correspond to the subtypes in Areas 1, 3, 7, and 9 of figure 3. Figures 4 and 5 show the averages of teamwork scores and group meeting quality scores for each of the sixteen leadership subtypes. Within each of these areas, the subtypes of leadership which correspond most to PM leadership are also associated with the highest teamwork and group meeting quality scores followed by M, P, and pm leadership in that order. Thus the four basic leadership types appear to be valid even within areas 1, 3, 7, and 9. In order to verify these results in other settings and using other criteria, surveys were conducted in two different types of organizations—a steel mill and a bank.

Sixteen PM Types in a Steel Mill

Method

The first study involved 1,309 white-collar employees of a steel mill. Fully completed questionnaires were returned by 1,005 respondents. Seven questionnaire items were used to measure P behavior.

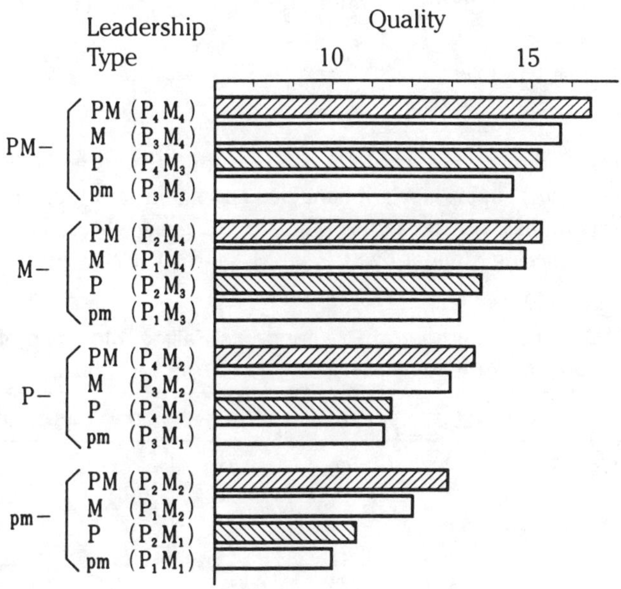

Fig. 5. Group meeting quality for sixteen PM subtypes

1. "Strict about observing regulations."
2. "Sets clear time limits for completing work."
3. "Strict about the amount of work that you do."
4. "Urges completion by the specified time."
5. "Criticizes poor work instead of your personality."
6. "Tries to make you work to your maximum capacity."
7. "Asks for reports about the progress of your work."

The seven items to measure M behavior were:

1. "Asks for subordinates' opinions about how to solve problems."
2. "Does not impose his own opinion on others."
3. "Does not make changes in your job without consulting you."
4. "Can be approached without reservation."
5. "Considers your preferences when assigning tasks."
6. "Informs you in advance about important changes."
7. "Generally supports you."

Five criterion variables similar to those used in prior studies were measured: willingness to work (two items), teamwork (five items), sense of belonging to the company (six items), sense of belonging to the labor union (six items), and group meeting quality (four items). All these items were rated using five-point response scales with higher values representing more favorable attitudes than lower values.

Results

Individual respondents were divided once into four groups according to their descriptions of their supervisor's P behavior and again into four groups based on their descriptions of M behavior. The "low" groups were constructed to include people having standardized P or M scores 0.67 or more below the

TABLE 14. Number of Respondents Falling into Each of the Sixteen PM Subtypes

Category	P_1	P_2	P_3	P_4	Total
M_4	53	50	73	77	253
M_3	69	79	74	101	323
M_2	34	47	39	38	158
M_1	81	47	63	80	271
Total	237	223	249	296	1,005

average (P_1 and M_1). The next level included individuals with P or M scores between the average and 0.67 below the average (P_2 and M_2). The third level included people with standardized scores between the average and 0.67 above the average. The "high" groups were comprised of individuals with standardized scores greater than 0.67 above the mean. Table 14 shows the number of respondents in each of the sixteen categories based on the P and M scores

TABLE 15. Rank Order of the Effects of Sixteen PM Subtypes

1. Teamwork

	P_1	P_2	P_3	P_4
M_4	7	5	3	1
M_3	10	6	4	2
M_2	14	11	9	8
M_1	16	13	15	12

2. Job satisfaction

	P_1	P_2	P_3	P_4
M_4	9	7	3	1
M_3	12	6	4	2
M_2	14	11	8	5
M_1	16	15	13	10

3. Sense of belonging to company

	P_1	P_2	P_3	P_4
M_4	7	5	3	1
M_3	10	9	4	2
M_2	14	13	8	6
M_1	16	12	15	11

4. Sense of belonging to labor union

	P_1	P_2	P_3	P_4
M_4	13	7	3	1
M_3	12	5	4	2
M_2	11	8	6	10
M_1	15	14	16	9

5. Group meeting quality

	P_1	P_2	P_3	P_4
M_4	6	3	2	1
M_3	7	9	5	4
M_2	12	11	8	10
M_1	16	15	14	13

they gave to their first-line supervisors. The P and M scores are independent of each other ($r = .075$).

Table 15 shows the sixteen types ranked according to the levels of the five external criterion variables. Three basic rankings of the leadership behaviors can be discerned. For some criteria, the rank from most effective to least effective is PM > M > P > pm. This order will be labeled "Type A." For other criteria, the rank from most to least effective also places the PM type highest and the pm type lowest, however the order of P type and M type leadership are reversed compared to "Type A." This order—PM > P > M > pm—is labeled "Type B" in table 15. In both the "Type A" order and the "Type B" order, the PM leadership type ranks highest and the pm type is lowest; the only difference between these two orders is in the rank of P-type and M-type leadership. Any other order, those rankings in which either the PM type is not highest or the pm type is not lowest, are categorized as a "Type C" order.

Table 15 shows the sxiteen PM types ranked according to the levels of five criterion variables. As in other studies, criterion variable scores were first calculated according to the criterion average score for the respondents who place their leader into each PM type. However, the data in table 15 are presented as the ranks of each of the sixteen types with respect to the five criteria rather than the mean criterion scores for each type. Within each of the nine areas described in figure 3, the four PM types can be identified as representing either a "Type A," "Type B," or "Type C" order based on the data from table 15. Thus, for each criterion, the number out of the nine areas showing each of the "Type A," "Type B," and "Type C" orders can be identified.

With respect to the "teamwork" criterion, areas 3, 4, 5, and 6 belong to Type A, areas 1, 7, 8, and 9 belong to Type B, and area 2 belongs to Type C. In Types A and B, PM ranks first and pm fourth in that pattern that is typically found when leadership is grouped into four instead of sixteen types. The finding that the leadership subtypes in eight out of nine areas fits either the A or B patterns further supports the validity of studying four basic leadership types.

Similar analyses were conducted to determine the relationship between the PM subtypes in each area and the variables of willingness to work, sense of belonging to the company, sense of belonging to the labor union and group meeting quality. Table 16 shows the number of areas for which the rank order of PM types follows the pattern of Type A, B, or C as described above and A + B (PM first and pm last) for each criterion variable. The rankings of leadership types according to the criteria of teamwork, willingness to work, sense of belonging to company, and sense of belonging to labor union tend to follow either the Type A or Type B pattern. Thus the results for the sixteen areas tend to be consistent with the four leadership types. However, PM leadership does not consistently rank first or pm last in relation to sense of belonging to labor unions.

A Survey of the Sixteen PM Subtypes in Banks

The steel mill study was based on subordinates' perceptions of their first-line supervisors' leadership behavior as individuals rather than as group members. The bank study was designed to determine the effects of leadership types on subordinate groups rather than individuals. Leadership behavior was divided into sixteen types by using work group averages of the ratings given to first-line supervisors by their subordinates.

Method

Data were collected from 2,489 groups in sixteen banks by the Japan Institute for Group Dynamics between 1969 and 1972. Each group included between three and thirteen employees. The same questionnaire items used in the study of eighteen organizations were used to measure eight criterion variables—job satisfaction, satisfaction with compensation, satisfaction with company, teamwork, group meeting quality, communication adequacy, mental health, and performance norms—as well as supervisors' P and M behavior.

TABLE 16. Number of Areas Showing A, B, C, and A+B Rank Orders

External Criterion Variable	Types of Rank Order					Total
	A	B	C	A+B	C	
Teamwork	4	4	1	8	1	9
Willingness to work	5	3	1	8	1	9
Belonging to company	4	3	2	7	2	9
Belonging to labor union	2	1	6	3	6	9
Group meeting quality	7	0	2	7	2	9
Total	22	11	12	33	12	45

Note: The types of rank order are as follows: Type A = PM > M > P > pm; Type B = PM > P > M > pm; Type C = Other than Type A and B; Type A+B = PM first and pm last.

Results

Averages were calculated for the leadership behavior and criterion variables in each group led by a first-line supervisor. Next, the group averages for each variable were compared with the average for the entire bank. Each criterion variable was divided into two parts depending on whether a group's score was higher or lower than the average for the bank. The percentage of groups under each type of leader that were above average or below average on each criterion was calculated. These percentages provide a slightly different basis for ranking the sixteen PM types than the mean scores used in the preceding study. P and M leadership scores were each divided into four parts as before using each bank's average and the average plus and minus 0.67 as the three dividing points to form the sixteen PM types.

The number of groups whose first-line supervisor fell into each of the sixteen PM types is shown in table 17. The data were analyzed to identify the percentage of groups with above average scores on the various criterion variables for each of the sixteen PM subtypes. The results are very similar to those shown in figures 4 and 5 even though the analyses are based on the percentage of groups with above average scores while the previous analyses are based on mean scores for each criterion.

The variables "satisfaction with compensation" and "mental health" show no striking differences either among the four PM types or among the sixteen subtypes. However, PM leadership did rank the highest and pm the lowest for each of the other six criterion variables. This particular analysis was designed to evaluate the validity of the subtypes in areas 1, 3, 7, and 9. The following discussion considers the validity of each set of four subtypes in the nine areas.

Table 18 shows the number of areas in which Type A, Type B, and Type C rankings were found for each of the eight criterion variables. For six of the eight criteria—job satisfaction, satisfaction with company, teamwork, group

TABLE 17. Number of Work Groups Falling into Each of the Sixteen PM Subtypes

	P_1	P_2	P_3	P_4	Total
M_4	33	115	188	353	689
M_3	109	177	169	158	613
M_2	151	199	153	103	606
M_1	275	147	89	70	581
Total	568	638	599	684	2,489

meeting quality, communication adequacy, and performance norms—either Type A or Type B rank orders are found in almost all the areas. However, the pattern in which PM ranks highest and pm ranks lowest can hardly be found in any area for satisfaction with salary or mental health. Even for these two variables, PM ranks highest and pm ranks lowest when comparison is among the four main PM types rather than among different areas of the sixteen subtypes.

Three studies have now been discussed in which the validity of sixteen PM subtypes was demonstrated by showing their association with several criterion variables in a shipyard, a steel mill, and a set of banks. Overall, these studies tend to verify the validity of the subtypes. Although the sixteen subtypes are not associated in any clear way with respondents' sense of belonging to their labor union, satisfaction with compensation, or level of mental health, they are associated with a number of other variables which leadership should affect even more than these three. This conclusion also holds for the nine sets of four adjacent subtypes. Thus, the four PM types appear to be basic leadership types which can be found when leadership is subdivided into sixteen, and perhaps more, subordinate types. Given the wide generalizability of the four fundamental types, the various laboratory and field results based on them can clearly be compared in the way that is necessary for developing an interdisciplinary leadership theory. Even though the average levels of P and M leadership used to establish the four types vary among different settings, the results of studies based on the four-part PM leadership

TABLE 18. Number of Areas Showing Type A, B, and C Rank Orders

External Criterion Variable	Types of Rank Order			Total
	A	B	C	
Job satisfaction	5	1	3	9
Satisfaction with salary	2	0	7	9
Satisfaction with company	7	2	0	9
Teamwork	7	0	2	9
Group meeting quality	7	2	0	9
Communication adequacy	5	2	2	9
Mental health	3	0	6	9
Performance norm	5	4	0	9
Total	41	11	20	72

Note: Type A = PM > M > P >pm; Type B = PM > P > M > pm; Type C = Order other than A or B morphology can meaningfully be compared. The generalizability of the four PM types has made it possible to develop a coherent research program using both laboratory studies and field studies covering such varied settings as organizations, political parties, family groups, and sports groups.

CHAPTER 4

Implications of General PM Leadership Morphology for Other Research Programs

The development of a general PM morphology of leadership behavior began with a review of the place held by leadership concepts and theories in the history of social thought. The earliest leadership "theories"—such as Plato's "philosopher-king" idea that is reflected in historical events of early Greek and Roman civilization—are at most implicit theories which must be abstracted using historical research methods to meaningfully identify the leadership implications of events. Later prescientific conceptualizations of leadership can be used along with the earlier leadership theories to identify variables which should be included in the study of leadership. They also help to understand how basic general morphological concepts may be expressed in particular historical contexts. The transition to modern social science theories of leadership is evident in the systematic sociological theories of such people as Weber (1947), the empirical studies of elites, and the early studies of leadership as an aspect of group dynamics (e.g., Lewin, Lippitt, and White 1939). This historical background of theory and social thought provides the context in which the general morphology of the Performance-Maintenance (PM) theory of leadership has been developed.

Differences between PM Theory and Other Concepts

Although the PM leadership morphology has many basic conceptual similarities to other leadership concepts, important differences are also found. These differences rest in the methodological progression of the PM research program, the basic view taken of survey measures of leadership, and the interactive way in which the P and M concepts are understood.

Methodological Progression of the PM Research Program

The Japanese research program designed to identify forms of behavior found in all leadership situations has been successful in identifying performance-oriented (P) and maintenance-oriented (M) leadership functions and in establishing the general validity of an interactive approach to their study. The performance and maintenance concepts were first developed on the basis of a theoretical consideration of leadership research and theory prior to the end of World War II when the research program began. Other leadership research programs were being pursued simultaneously, notably in the United States. Because these other programs either consciously or tacitly relied on the same heritage of traditional leadership concepts, and because leadership phenomena may well be described according to similar basic concepts in different cultures, ideas very similar to the PM concepts are commonly found throughout the leadership literature. The PM research program in Japan was actually stimulated by the personal interest of Kurt Lewin and has consciously taken advantage of work by leadership researchers abroad whose ideas about social behavior are rooted in the Lewinian tradition. Thus, there is considerable conceptual convergence between the PM leadership morphology and other modern leadership concepts because of the common heritage of traditional leadership concepts, the basic similarity in the phenomena studied, and the common basis of a perspective on social behavior rooted in Lewinian social psychology.

A key characteristic of the PM leadership research program which has contributed to its unique four-part PM typology is its methodological progression. The PM theory began as a conceptual attempt to understand leadership in terms of two basic group functions. The continuing work to design a variety of studies and interpret their results in terms of these concepts lends the research program its distinctive character. Rather than becoming locked in to specific laboratory or field methods, the basic leadership concepts instead of a particular method have served as a unifying theme. Methodological adjustments to particular research topics or field populations have been made like musical variations on a central theme. Thus, the research to establish a behavioral morphology has been devoted to validating basic leadership concepts using a variety of methods rather than validating a single laboratory method for creating leadership conditions or a single field measure for assessing leadership dimensions. Although many other leadership research programs have begun with a good conceptual foundation, some have become unnecessarily sidetracked into a focus on a single methodology.

Not only has the PM research program repeatedly returned to the theme of two basic group concepts, it has also progressed from theory to laboratory tests to field tests whereas many other research programs have tended to skip laboratory tests. The early PM studies of general behavioral morphology were laboratory experiments. Laboratory experiments lend themselves to establishing discrete behavioral conditions as independent variables and to conceptualizing these variables according to discrete types rather than continuous dimensions. The development of the four-part PM typology has been shaped to some degree by the initial choice of experimental settings for testing the PM concepts. Since field studies were only subsequently designed to verify and test the generalizability of the experimental results, the decision to split the P and M dimensions into two parts each for forming the four leadership types was a natural progression. In research programs which have their origin in field research, studying leadership dimensions separately in their continuous forms has seemed most natural to the researchers. The laboratory origins of the study of PM leadership have certainly contributed to identifying interactive effects of the two leadership dimensions.

The priority placed on experimental research in the PM leadership program has also helped to begin with a firm causal inference about leadership behavior. Although much work remained after the initial studies (and much still remains) to determine the causal dynamics of the relationships among leadership, its antecedents, and its consequences, the PM types were shown to be useful in predicting leadership consequences under experimental conditions designed to simulate the real world. Associations found among the four PM types and various outcomes in field settings further support the validity of the PM concepts and indicate the need for further work to clarify the causal dynamics of the relationships found. In summary, the studies designed to test the general PM morphology have been successful in (1) indicating the validity of the PM concepts, (2) showing experimentally that further study is justified to clarify the consequences of these types, and (3) showing that these four types can be measured in field settings in ways that allow comparisons to be made among settings despite particular differences among them.

Questionnaire Measures

Another aspect of the PM leadership research program which distinguishes it from many others is the perspective taken on questionnaire measures of leadership. Leadership research has tended to hold as an ideal the precise description of particular behaviors abstracted from and thus not contaminated by the situations in which they are expressed. Questionnaire measures are often considered invalid to the extent that they depart from this ideal. Questionnaire measures in the PM research program, however, are assumed to reflect behavioral responses to social settings (as elaborated in the following discussion of specific behavior morphology) and both certain commonalities and certain differences in behavioral responses to particular subordinates. Although an attempt has been made to develop questionnaire measures that are generalizable across a broad range of formal organizational settings, this generalizability is not understood to be of singular ultimate value. Equally important is the development of measures which will show different factor structures in different settings. Although some survey measures ceased to be included in the "core" measures of P and M behavior (e.g., questions about obtaining physical equipment in sports teams) they may be accepted as measures of important setting-specific behaviors.

Individual and Group-level Validation

Both unique superior-subordinate relationships and common characteristics of leadership toward a subordinate group are accepted as important in PM theory. In this respect, the PM theory is consistent with the "multiplexed" view of leadership (Dansereau et al. 1982). Leaders interact with individual subordinates at some times and with subordinate groups at other times. Leaders can communicate through memos and meetings involving everyone or through conversations with individuals. Thus, field survey measures were validated at both the individual and group levels of analysis rather than selecting one or the other. Data analysis at both levels involves certain methodological limitations, but neither is considered inherently more appropriate than the other.

The general morphology of PM leadership has been tested using a complementary sequence of studies. This programmatic orientation implies that converging results are emphasized over the abstract methodological perfection of single studies. Seeking methodological purity in an individual study could have led to missing important findings in a research program.

Interactive versus Additive Effects

Most leadership research programs do not study interactions among different dimensions of leadership. The tendency to abstract behavioral dimensions sometimes results from the assumption that all concrete leadership behaviors are oriented toward fulfilling either maintenance or performance functions but not both. If this assumption were correct, conceptual precision and scientific parsimony would argue for giving precedence to studying the separate effects of these two dimensions over their interactive effects (Larson, Hunt, and Osborn 1976). Due to the interest in abstracting the performance and maintenance functions, studies based on the Ohio State and early Michigan measures typically sought direct associations between the separate leadership dimensions and various criteria.

A few of the early studies in the Ohio State research program represented the "consideration" and "initiating structure" variables as each having two levels to form a four-cell matrix (Halpin 1957; Hemphill 1957). However, the two variables remained to be interpreted as having additive effects in promoting subordinate satisfaction and performance. Rarely were interactive hypotheses considered such as the possibility that low levels of both variables might correspond to higher levels of criteria than a high level on one variable and a low level on the other.

Most later contingency models of leadership like the path-goal theory (House 1971) have focused on interactions between each of several leadership dimensions considered separately and task- or personality-related contingencies. Still, little attention is given to the interaction among the leadership dimensions themselves. Fiedler's (1967) Contingency Theory leaves open the possibility that leader personality (as measured by the Least Preferred Coworker or LPC score) and contextual contingencies may interact to determine leadership behavior. However, this possibility is not adequately documented (Rice 1978). Even recent tests of the implications of LPC for leadership behavior have considered leadership behavior dimensions separately rather than in combination (e.g., Bons and Fiedler 1976). The only model which emphasizes an interactive combination of leadership dimensions is the model of Blake and Mouton (1964), an almost strictly normative model which, although based on much previous social science theory, has generated little subsequent supporting research.

Several controversies and new leadership models have arisen about the morphology of leadership since the time of the studies designed to test the validity of the four PM leadership types. One controversy has developed between people working with the Ohio State "consideration" and "initiating structure" survey measures of leadership (Larson, Hunt, and Osborn 1976; Nystrom 1978) and Blake and Mouton (1982). Blake and Mouton have consistently suggested that placing a high emphasis on "concern for people" and "concern for production" is optimal for managerial policy, leader attitudes, and leader behavior (Blake and Mouton 1964). Critics working from the Ohio State measures suggest that the general value of a "high-high" emphasis on two dimensions of leadership behavior has not been empirically demonstrated.

Specifically, Larson et al. argue that the few published empirical studies that hypothesize interactions among consideration and initiating structure or related dimensions are methodologically flawed. These studies are criticized as often not providing statistical tests for interaction effects in addition to the main effects of the separate dimensions. Those studies which have tested for interactions, including Larson's own study and a subsequent study by Nystrom (1978), show little evidence of them. The conclusion is that a morphology of leadership based on separate dimensions is sufficient without adding an interaction component as a complicating factor. These researchers argue further that models emphasizing the value of a "high-high" combination of leadership types reflects a widely held, but erroneous, myth.

The criticism of the leadership morphology implied by the studies reviewed by Larson et al. has some validity. In particular, the early studies the authors note by Misumi and Tasaki (1965) and Misumi and Shirakashi (1966) did not use "fully crossed" experimental designs. The pm type was excluded from these studies, thus not permitting the increment of interactive over additive effects to be completely tested. The field studies discussed in the preceding chapters would also not satisfy Larson's analysis requirements because they use neither analysis of variance nor a multiple regression model to test for unique interaction effects beyond the main effects of P and M treated as dimensions. The inadequacies which may be perceived in the analyses used with the PM field data are due to our hesitance to apply statistical models that imply causality to data which do not allow clear causal inference. However, other experimental studies described in subsequent chapters do allow causal models of interactions between P and M emphases to be adequately tested.

The studies of the four-type PM morphology clearly demonstrated the validity of the P and M concepts and provided substantial evidence that they should be understood to interact in affecting group performance and attitudes. Even among the studies of the basic PM morphology, its potential to provide a better basis for understanding leadership than two-dimensional views is suggested. The coal mining study in particular indicated that a high P emphasis was associated with very low performance in the absence of an M emphasis, but with very high performance in the presence of an M emphasis. The postal trainee experiment indicated that a high M emphasis, when accompanied by a minimal amount of P leadership, is associated with poor performance. However, a high M emphasis is associated with high performance in the presence of a high P emphasis. Later laboratory studies have tested for interactions more fully.

The many organizational studies using attitudinal criteria are, in general, equally consistent with the two-dimensional views as well as with the PM morphology. Subsequent research, however, supports the contention that a four-type morphology more effectively represents leadership, at least in Japan, than would a model suggesting that two dimensions should be considered sometimes and interactions between the dimensions at other times.

There are several possible explanations for the differences between the PM leadership morphology and the morphology developed by the Ohio State researchers. One is that the field methods on which the Ohio State studies have relied are less appropriate than are experimental methods for identifying interactions. A second is that the P and M functions are more conceptually different from the consideration and initiating structure dimensions than they appear to be. Perhaps the deemphasis on pressure for performance in the Ohio State studies has resulted in a conceptualization of initiating structure that approximates the "planning" factor of some PM studies rather than the "pressure" factor emphasized in most field measures of the P component. A third possibility is that the culture of Japan is sufficiently distinct from that of the United States to produce differences in basic forms of leadership. Which alternative among these is most reasonable will require further comparative research.

Blake and Mouton's (1982) response to criticisms leveled against the "high-high" emphasis (Larson, Hunt, and Osborn 1976; Nystrom 1978) and noncontingency orientation (Hersey and Blanchard 1969; House 1971; Vroom and Yetton 1973) of their model is helpful for understanding the similarities and differences between their leadership morphology and the PM morphology. In addition to the criticisms discussed above of "high-high" models, Blake and Mouton's (1964) model has been criticized on the grounds that empirical research has shown different aspects of leadership to require special emphasis under different circumstances. Blake and Mouton's response to both criticisms is that the leadership morphology on which alternative models are based, including that of PM theory, is fundamentally inadequate. Blake and Mouton argue that leadership reflecting very high "concern for people" and "concern for production" involves qualitatively distinct behavior, behavior not reflected in surveys or experimental manipulations that additively combine behaviors placing separate emphasis on each leadership component.

The PM morphology shares the idea that some concrete behaviors reflecting a high emphasis on both the P and M dimensions may be qualitatively distinct in the way that Blake and Mouton suggest. For example, conferring with subordinates about methods to improve group performance would involve making statements that simultaneously reflect a high P and M emphasis. However, supervisors who show such behaviors are also likely to be described by subordinates as placing a high rather than low emphasis on the "P" function and a high rather than low emphasis on the "M" function. Many leadership behaviors judged to be important by practitioners and academics both in developing PM survey measures and in measures for the Ohio State studies (Halpin and Winer 1957) were found to be highly associated with two behavior dimensions. Although these are distinctively "high-high" behaviors, they are represented very well by additive and interactive combinations of more distinctly P-oriented or M-oriented behaviors which provide a sound basis for empirical study.

The interactive or multiplicative perspective on the combination of P and M leadership functions can also be viewed as an elaboration of the "substitutes for leadership" model of Kerr and Jermier (1978) or the "modes of problem solving" model suggested by Peterson (1982). The leadership substitutes model postulates that various characteristics of a social setting besides leadership—such as subordinate acceptance of organization goals or absence of knowledge about how to structure their work activities—affect the contribution leadership can make toward promoting such criteria as good performance and motivation. In a similar way, the extent to which a leader emphasizes the maintenance function is predicted in the PM leadership theory to affect the extent to which subordinates will be responsive to performance-oriented leadership. In other words, the PM leadership theory extends the "substitutes" model by treating each component of leadership as part of the "task situation" which affects subordinates' responses to the other leadership dimension.

In the "modes of problem solving" model, subordinate expectations and felt needs for leadership are postulated to be particularly important in affecting responsiveness to leadership actually provided. From the perspective of this model, maintenance-oriented leadership may contribute to subordinates' belief that direction for task accomplishment should come through the leader rather than through some other source (e.g., senior peers, impersonal rules) or that task direction should not be provided at all.

Two Basic Dimensions of Leadership

Many leadership research programs have sought to identify more than two basic leadership dimension. Yukl (1971) indicates that the degree of participative leadership is a third dimension conceptually distinct from consideration and initiating structure which has also received considerable research attention. In the early studies in Japan which eventually resulted in the development of the PM leadership theory, the degree of leader participation or "democratic" behavior was also studied as an important leadership dimension. Other studies identifying additional leadership dimensions include even the early studies conducted by the Ohio State group. These studies identified the secondary factors of production emphasis and social sensitivity (Stogdill and Coons 1957). Subsequently, Stogdill (1963) identified twelve distinguishable dimensions of leadership while multiple dimensions have also been identified in more recent factor analytic studies of different versions of the Ohio State scales (Schriesheim and Stogdill 1975). Recently, Yukl (1981; Yukl and Nemeroff 1979) has deliberately worked toward identifying many discrete leadership dimensions as well. As will become evident in the Japanese studies reported in Part III of this book, more than two dimensions are often identifiable in studies based on the PM leadership theory.

Why then has the PM research program focused on leadership types reflected in only two basic functions? The answer lies in the belief that all other empirically identifiable dimensions are most important as situationally specific expressions of the basic performance and maintenance functions. Participative or democratic leadership, for example, can be primarily important as an expression of the maintenance leadership function for particular decisions and situations in which participation promotes social integration and group stability. Sometimes, as participation theorists have argued (Vroom and Yetton 1973), participation reflects both a performance-oriented function and a maintenance-oriented function. In some situations, however, participation may be an irrelevant leadership dimension, the more basic performance and maintenance functions being expressed by concrete behaviors of other kinds.

From General to Specific

The next portion of the research program, "specific behavioral morphology of leadership," includes the conceptual and empirical study of characteristics of particular leaders and settings which affect how P and M leadership are expressed and the particular meaning of specific behaviors in specific settings. It is useful in reading this material to develop a perspective on how the same basic leadership functions can be fulfilled through behaviors that appear to be different from each other.

PART III

Specific Behavioral Morphology of Leadership

CHAPTER 5

Leadership in Industrial Organizations

The task of a specific morphology of leadership is to determine the implications that particular individual characteristics and settings have for the way in which basic functions of leadership are expressed. The basic forms of leadership identified in general morphology can appear in quite different ways under different conditions. From a more dynamic perspective, the task of a specific morphology of leadership is to systematically describe differences in leadership phenomena that are associated with differences in personal characteristics and environmental variables.

Every research program designed to identify general patterns of behavior begins by dealing with particular personalities facing specific conditions. This universal characteristic of behavioral research occurs because behavior does not emerge in the abstract, but comes about in response to specific, particular conditions. General patterns of behavior can only be abstracted after observing many individuals in many settings. Complex behavioral responses to specific settings may be described as variations of general behavior principles. The following passage quoted from *The Science of the Artificial* by Simon (1969, 23–24) illustrates the relationship between relatively simple forms of general behavior and relatively complex forms of specific behavior.

> We watch an ant make his laborious way across a wind- and wave-molded beach. He moves ahead, angles to the right to ease his climb up a steep dunelet, detours around a pebble, stops for a moment to exchange information with a compatriot. Thus he makes his weaving, halting way back to his home. So as not to anthropomorphize about his purposes, I sketch the path on a piece of paper. It is a sequence of irregular, angular segments—not quite a random walk, for it has an underlying sense of direction, of aiming toward a goal.

The behavior of the ant described in the passage raises an interesting question. Why does the ant not proceed directly from its starting point to its goal? According to Simon, the answer is obvious. The ant knew the direction of the goal, but it encountered obstructions on the way and had to make a detour at every obstruction.

The point Simon made was that the complexity of the ant's behavior was not due to the inherent complexity of the ant itself but to the complexity of the beach on which the ant moved toward its goal. Basically, an ant's system of behavior is very simple. The complexity in its sequence of actions is nothing but a reflection of the complexity of the environment in which it moves.

The basic form of leadership behavior is relatively simple. The complexity in leader behaviors reflects the complexity of the environment in which leadership is observed. Although complex patterns of leadership behavior are not as explicit as an ant's behavior, they can be systematically observed. Leadership appears in varied forms in many varied social situations. For example, the performance-oriented leadership of top managers, middle managers, and foremen can differ considerably even within the same business enterprise. Details in the expression of performance-oriented leadership in different organizations and groups are likely to vary even more. The results of PM leadership studies have shown that governmental organizations, industrial organizations, classrooms, and families have different kinds of leadership. Part III of the present volume is designed to systematically describe different social and environment variables which are likely to have implications for the way in which leadership is expressed.

Although specific morphology describes behavioral responses to different settings, in essence it is a systematic description of how general forms of behavior appear in specific environments. This description is developed by showing the effects that the particular characteristics of specific environmental settings have on the forms of general behavior which have already been described. Our environmental study of leadership dealt with political, business, and educational organizations, athletic groups, and family groups. In these studies, the ecology of leadership has been investigated under specific environmental conditions.

The study of leadership is being carried out independently in many fields of social science. The study of leadership, however, should not be merely a systematic description and classification of various patterns of leadership behavior in various specific situations. It should also attempt to abstract universal leadership behavior patterns from the particular behavior patterns observed in specific situations. Such conceptual abstraction is necessary to make the science of leadership comprehensible and parsimonious.

The PM Leadership Type and Productivity

Since the initial validation studies, a series of studies has been conducted covering many different industries. Some of the results of a study in the banking industry are presented in tables 19 and 20. The banks in which the data were obtained—"Bank S" and "Bank F"—both have branches in all the prefectures of Kyushu and Chugoko (Misumi, Takeda, and Seki 1967). The employees of the branches of these banks are divided into inside service and public relations personnel. The inside service personnel are engaged in window service, handling things like deposits and loans, accounting, and general affairs. The public relations personnel handle canvassing for fixed deposit, current deposit, and ordinary deposit and similar matters. Each branch is headed by a branch manager who has one or more assistant managers or senior officers as subordinates. The rank and file personnel rated the leadership behavior of both their first-line supervisor (an assistant manager or senior officer) and their second-line supervisor (the branch manager).

The measures of the four PM types were designed using the method described in chapter 3. Productivity was measured according to the net capital growth rate in each branch of the two banks. Bank S was surveyed in 1965, covering 256 employees from twenty-five branches. Bank F was surveyed in 1966, covering 645 employees from fifty-four branches. Pairs of high-producing and low-producing branches located in areas with similar socioeconomic characteristics were selected for each bank. Table 19 and table 20 show the PM leadership types of the second-line and first-line supervisors. The results indicate that many PM-type supervisors were found in high-producing branches and that many pm-type supervisors worked in low-producing branches. However, there are a number of exceptions to this pattern.

Supervisory behavior was also studied in manufacturing companies. Table 21 shows the results of a survey of 1,300 rank and file employees

TABLE 19. Pairs of Second- and First-line Supervisors' PM Leadership Types (Bank S)

High-producing	Low-producing
PM–PM	P–pm
pm–PM	pm–pm
P–M	PM–PM
pm–PM	pm–pm
PM–PM	pm–pm
M–PM	P–pm
PM–PM	P–pm
PM–P	PM–PM

Note: The pairs of high- and low-producing branches on each line come from socio-economically similar geographic areas.

TABLE 20. Pairs of Second- and First-line Supervisors' PM Leadership Types (Bank F)

High-producing	Low-producing
PM–PM	PM–pm
PM–PM	PM–M
P–PM	M–pm
P–PM	PM–PM
P–pm	PM–PM
pm–PM	pm–pm
P–PM	pm–pm
PM–M	
PM–PM	

Note: The pairs of high- and low-producing branches on each line come from socio-economically similar geographic areas.

TABLE 21. Supervisors' PM Leadership Types and Rated Squad Performance in a Bearing Manufacturing Company

PM Leadership Type	Performance		
	High	Medium	Low
PM	16	8	3
P	11	5	4
M	10	8	5
pm	3	13	6
Total	40	34	18

working at a ball bearing manufacturing company. The employees rated the supervisory behavior of their foremen and squad leaders. Based on available objective measures of performance, overall employee performance was rated by the subsection chiefs, section chiefs, and department chiefs as being "high," "medium," or "low." Of the ninety-two squads which were analyzed, twenty-seven were under PM-type leaders, twenty were under P-type leaders, twenty-three were under M-type leaders, and twenty-two were under pm-type leaders. As table 21 suggests, PM leadership ranked first and pm fourth with P and M in between. No significant differences were found using a chi-square test between P and M leadership. Table 22 shows the results of a similar study done in a tire manufacturing company. The results were very much the same as those shown in table 21. Surveys in other industrial companies (coal mining, shipbuilding, tire manufacturing, automobile manufacturing) also indicated that PM leadership ranked first in terms of productivity while pm leadership ranked last regardless of industry. In each study, P ranked second and M third.

TABLE 22. Supervisors' PM Leadership Types and Productivity in a Tire Manufacturing Company

PM Leadership Type	Productivity	
	High	Low
PM	11	6
P	6	7
M	8	8
pm	6	10

Field Experiments to Reduce Accident Rates

Most previous studies of accidents in Europe and America, as well as in Japan, focused on the personalities of people who caused accidents. Many studies were conducted to determine accident proneness and to statistically examine the relationship of accidents to the age, years of experience, intelligence, and personality of people who caused accidents. Consequently, many personality and adaptability tests were developed for studying accident proneness. Especially important among these are studies using the Uchida-Kraepelin Psychodiagnostic Test (Uchida 1951) and the Yatabe-Guilford Personality Test (Jsujioka, Shinohara, and Yatabe 1957; Yatabe 1954).

Since the 1950s, many studies have analyzed the relationship of workplace atmosphere to accident rates. Kerr (1957), in his thesis entited "Contemporary Theories of Safety Psychology," pointed out that accidents caused by accident-prone individuals constituted only 15 percent of all accidents. He also pointed out that a workplace atmosphere in which workers are free to set their own goals is closely related to a low incidence of accidents.

Kerr also notes that psychological and physiological stresses on workers are a cause of accidents. Some stresses come from the physical and environmental conditions in the workplace and poor worker physical condition due to a long period of service or advancing age. Stresses also stem from workers' relations with their colleagues and superiors as well as from characteristics of their own tasks. Kerr concluded that 45 to 60 percent of industrial accidents are attributable to these stresses, while 30 to 40 percent can be blamed on workplacc atmosphere.

Study of the Bus Drivers' Accident Rates

In order to determine the relationship of PM leadership types to accident rates, the rate of accidents attributable to drivers was studied in the Nishinippon Railroad Company (hereafter referred to as Nishitetsu) in relation to bus dispatchers' leadership types. Nishitetsu operates the buses, subways, and railroad in and around Fukuoka. The same questionnaire was distributed twice to bus drivers of the Nishitetsu, once in 1964 and again in 1967 (Misumi and Shinohara 1967).

First Questionnaire Distribution: 1964

The questionnaire was distributed to 949 bus drivers who worked in the nine branches of the Nishitetsu. Their ages ranged from twenty-five to fifty-five with an average of thirty-two years.

The questionnaire included forty-eight items which can be grouped into six categories: (1) the situation of the working group, (2) leadership of the bus dispatcher (the first-line supervisor), (3) a sense of belonging to the company and labor union, (4) matters pertaining to management and administration within the company, (5) job satisfaction (morale), and (6) family affairs. Each item was rated using a five-point scale with higher numbers reflecting more positive perceptions and attitudes.

Data Analysis

Spearman rank-order correlations were calculated between the accident rates in the nine branches and questionnaire item scores using data aggregated within branches. Accident rates were based on the number of accidents blamed on the drivers during a three-year period from April, 1961, to March, 1964. The overall average accident rate for the nine branches was 54.2 accidents over the three-year period per hundred drivers. Accidents attributable to a driver are those accidents which a company committee consisting of union and company representatives judge to be more than 50 percent the driver's responsibility. The punishment for accidents ranges from a warning to a reduction of pay to suspension from work.

Results

Table 23 shows the rank-order correlations between the accident rate per hundred drivers over a three-year period and the questionnaire measures. Significant rank-order correlations ($p < .05$) were found for items 7 (Appropriate procedures for handling accidents), 9 (Willingness of employees to work), 10 (Unity within the work group), 14 (Sense of belonging to the union), and 16 (Supervisor's M leadership). Due to the small sample size ($N = 9$) rank-order correlations of marginal statistical significance ($p < .10$) are also noted in table 23. If measures having marginally significant correlations are also considered, workplace characteristics can be concluded to be associated with accidents attributable to drivers.

The leadership type of the bus drivers' supervisors was also expected to have implications for accident rates. When P and M leadership measures are analyzed separately, only M leadership is found to have a significant relationship to accident rate. However, when the four PM types are identified, other results are obtained.

Leadership of Direct Supervisors and Subordinate-Caused Accidents

Dispatchers directly supervise bus drivers. Each day, the dispatcher gives the drivers their daily route instructions. In the Nishitetsu study, the leadership of

TABLE 23. Rank Correlations between Accident Rate over Three-year Period per Hundred Bus Drivers and Questionnaire Items

Questionnaire Item	Rank Correlation
1. Participation in company recreational activities	−.10
2. Satisfaction with the work environment	−.15
3. Satisfaction with job	−.67*
4. Satisfaction with wages	−.55
5. Fairness of promotion practices	−.65*
6. Discrimination against people who caused accidents	.62*
7. Appropriate procedures for handling accidents	−.72**
8. Coordination between bus maintenance and bus driving activities	−.27
9. Willingness of employees to work	−.74**
10. Unity within the work group	−.62*
Opportunities to talk with others who drive the same bus route	−.27
Maintain good interpersonal relations with others who drive the same bus route	−.70**
Others who drive the same bus route are better than any other drivers	−.26
Have mutual understanding with others who drive the same bus route	−.33
I do not want to be separated from others who drive the same bus route	−.48
11. Personal relationship with conductors	−.18
12. Poor cooperation from conductors	.43
13. Sense of belonging to the company	−.62*
Company acts favorably on employee grievances	−.37
Company conveys information about its overall situation	−.48
Company adopts employees' opinions and desires	−.44
Approval of company policies	−.66*
I am glad that I joined this company	−.57
14. Sense of belonging to the labor union	−.75**
Union conveys its policies to members	−.58
Union is useful	−.70**
Union is run properly	−.68**
Union adopts members' opinions and desires	−.67*
Approve union policies	−.85***
15. Labor-management relations	−.65*
16. Supervisor's leadership: M function	−.73**
17. Supervisor's leadership: P function	−.37
18. Satisfaction with supervisor	−.65*
19. Family members' concern about avoiding accidents	−.20
20. Family members' satisfaction with the company	−.57
21. Size of branch office of bus service (number of drivers)	.04
22. Frequency of absence from work	.03

Note: The significance of correlation coefficients were tested using a two tailed test.

*$p < .10$

**$p < .05$

***$p < .01$

each dispatcher was evaluated by the drivers. Four questionnaire items were used to measure P leadership and four were used to measure M leadership. Items measuring the P leadership dimension were

1. "Is Dispatcher A always fussy about the rules and regulations?"
2. "Does Dispatcher A demand that you run the bus punctually according to the schedule?"
3. "Does Dispatcher A always make you work to your maximum capacity?"
4. "When an accident occurs, is Dispatcher A very apprehensive about its effects on your subsequent bus driving and the damages it has incurred, no matter how inconsequential it may be?"

Items measuring the M leadership dimension were

1. "Does Dispatcher A not bother to listen to you whenever you take your opinions, desires, or suggestions up to him?"
2. "Does Dispatcher A not insist on his own opinion when you disagree with him?"
3. "Can you easily talk with Dispatcher A about your work?"
4. "Does Dispatcher A not change your assignments without first consulting with you?"

The response alternatives for each item were measured using scales ranging from 1 to 5 with higher values reflecting more positive perceptions of leadership. The total scores for each dimension could range from 4 to 20. The dispatchers were classified into one of the four PM patterns according to whether they were above or below the overall averages on the P and M dimensions. Table 24 shows the relationship of the dispatchers' leadership types to the accident rates per hundred drivers during the three-year period prior to the time the survey was conducted in 1964.

The data shown in table 24 indicate that the highest accident rate occurred under pm-type dispatchers and the second highest rate under P-type dispatchers. The results of a Mann-Whitney U test show no significant differences in accident rates between PM and M leadership.

When rank-order correlations were calculated separately for the P and M dimensions, only M leadership was found to be significantly related to accident rates. The correlation between the P and M dimensions was $r = -.10$. However, when partial rank-order correlations were calculated, P is significantly related to accident rate ($r = -.67$, $p < .05$) when M is statistically controlled. M leadership is even more highly associated with accident rate ($r = -.83$, $p < .01$) when P leadership is statistically controlled.

When both table 23 and table 24 are considered, the dispatchers' M behavior is seen to be inversely correlated to accident rate. From the point of view of the PM leadership patterns, however, even P leadership is associated with low accident levels when combined with M leadership. This finding was further confirmed in a follow-up study conducted in 1967.

Second Questionnaire Distribution: 1967

Method

The same drivers were used as subjects as in 1964 and the same questionnaire was used. In 1967, however, the questionnaire was distributed to the drivers at a meeting held specifically for administering the survey.

Results

The rate of accidents attributable to Nishitetsu bus drivers dropped dramatically between 1964 and 1967. Table 25 shows the change in the rate of accidents attributable to bus drivers per 100,000 kilometers of driving distance during the 1964–67 period following a leadership change program (Misumi 1978). The accident rate of 0.816 in 1964 dropped drastically to 0.512 in 1965, 0.219 in 1966, and 0.173 in 1967. The Nishitetsu's accident rate in 1967 was the lowest of all companies in Japan. The hypothesis of the 1967 study was that such a drastic decrease in accident rate was brought about by changes in workplace leadership and in drivers' sense of belonging, interpersonal relations, and degree of satisfaction with assignments (morale).

TABLE 24. Dispatchers' PM Types and Drivers' Accident Rates (1961–64)

PM Type	Accident Rate per Hundred Drivers
PM	44.0
M	42.3
P	52.0
pm	79.1

TABLE 25. Rate of Accidents Attributable to Nishitetsu Bus Drivers

Year	Accident Rate
1962	0.952
1963	1.059
1964	0.816
1965	0.512
1966	0.219
1967	0.173

Note: Accident rates are calculated according to the average number of accidents attributable to drivers per 100,000 kilometers.

Comparison of 1964 and 1967 Results

Table 26 summarizes the results of both the 1964 study and the 1967 study. No significant changes were found in any of the survey measures except in the dispatchers' P and M leadership scores. This finding implies that reduced accident rates were probably due more to changes in leadership than to changes in attitudes. Figure 6 shows the relationship of the four PM leadership types to the rates of driver-caused accidents in 1964 and 1967. The four PM leadership types in the 1967 study were identified based on the mean P and M scores found in the 1964 study.

Accident rates were lowest under M and PM leaders in the 1964 study; the difference in accident rate under these two types of leadership was not statistically significant at that time. However, differences in the drop in accident rate between these two leadership types indicates that PM leadership is more effective than M leadership in reducing accident rates. Although M leadership was also consistent with a reduced accident rate, the PM combination in which P and M complement and supplement each other was particularly useful for reducing accidents. In 1964, the highest accident rates were shown in pm, but this was replaced by P as the most accident-prone leadership type in 1967. Based on the average levels of P and M leadership in 1964, there were no pm leaders in 1967. In summary, the most effective form of

TABLE 26. Change in Nishitetsu Bus Drivers' Work Attitudes and Leadership Scores between 1964 and 1967

Factor	1964	1967	Difference	t-test
Satisfaction with work environment	3.13	3.14	0.01	
Satisfaction with job	3.16	3.07	−0.09	
Satisfaction with wages	1.90	1.78	−0.12	
Fairness of promotion practices	2.10	2.18	0.08	
Opportunities to talk with co-workers	3.43	3.50	0.07	
Mutual understanding among co-workers	3.13	3.16	0.03	
Personal relationship with conductors	3.47	3.64	0.17	
Satisfaction with family life	3.49	3.46	0.03	
Sense of belonging to the company (average score of 5 questions)	2.42	2.35	−0.07	
Sense of belonging to the labor union (average score of 5 questions)	2.89	2.79	−0.10	
Supervisor's P scores (average score of 4 questions)	3.22	3.76	0.54	$p < .01$
Supervisor's M scores (average score of 4 questions)	3.39	3.13	−0.26	$p < .05$
Satisfaction with supervisors	2.97	3.06	0.03	

leadership for reducing accident rates is PM leadership followed by M, P, and pm in that order. This is exactly the same order that is found in the relationship between leadership types and productivity.

Leadership of Engineering Project Managers

Characteristics of Engineering Project Systems

Another study considered the special leadership characteristics of engineering project managers who work in a very different kind of organizational setting from the settings of previous PM leadership studies. The organizational structure in which these project managers worked is a "flatter," problem-solving structure compared to the traditional pyramid-shaped, functional structure of many industrial organizations. Scales had previously been developed to measure the leadership behaviors of foremen (first-line supervisors) and their superiors (second-line supervisors) in various industries and the validity and reliability of these scales had been assessed. However, because the organization structures in these industries tend to be functional, the first-line super-

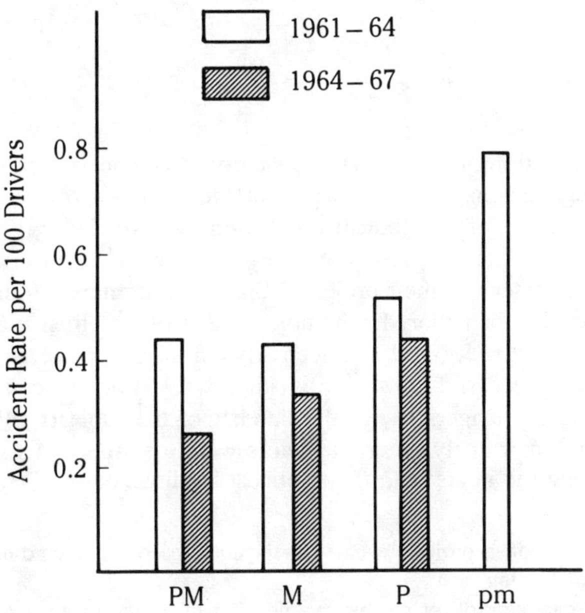

Fig. 6. Leadership types and accident rates per 100 drivers during three years between 1961 and 1964, and 1964 and 1967 respectively. The number of miles per driver was approximately equal each year.

visors' leadership tends to be oriented toward completing specialized organizational functions. By contrast, first-line leaders in engineering organizations as exemplified by plant project managers must have a broad understanding of all phases of a given project including predesigning conditions, design, procurement, construction, and operation. They must also know about various conditions of the project site and be specialists in various aspects of project control including cost control, process control, and delivery-data control. A project manager's responsibilities are often not as clearly defined as are the tasks of managers in functional organizations. Few and far between are the times when a project progresses as originally scheduled. As a project grows larger and increases in complexity, it often must be revised because of some unexpected change in external factors. In other words, the responsibilities involved in the project are oriented more toward complex problem solving than toward the completion of specific tasks because the contingencies surrounding the responsibilities are so uncertain and uncontrollable. Project managers must make prompt assessments of changes in any one of many variables, make quick decisions, and proceed to solve the problems. A project manager's P and M leadership are likely to be expressed in different ways from that of a manager or supervisor in a functionally designed industrial organization.

Rating Project Managers' Leadership Behavior

A scale for measuring the leadership behavior of engineering project managers was developed in 1977–78 as part of the activities of the Human Resources Committee of the Industrial Machinery Association. The subjects used were 490 people who had previous experience in engineering projects. These subjects described their project managers using ninety-four items concerning leadership behavior. Each subject rated two of their managers, the one who was most successful in effectively completing projects and the one who was least successful. In this way, data were collected concerning 980 different project managers, twice the number of the subjects. When the responses were factor analyzed, four factors were identified.

Among the items with the strongest loadings on the first factors are:

"Takes action on a project when work is not proceeding according to schedule." (factor loading .66)
"Delivery-date control for machinery and equipment on order." (.64)
"Man-hour control based on processing plan." (.64)
"Keeps abreast of overall progress in work." (.63)
"Sets policy concerning estimate of project budget." (.62)
"Establishes cost controls based on the project budget." (.59)

"Sets policy concerning processing plan." (.59)
"Demands that time limits for completing work be observed." (.58)
"Sets policy concerning quality control." (.58)
"Checks to see that work is done according to the contract with the customer." (.58)

These and other items loading on this factor concern scheduling, budget estimation, purchasing and contracting, planning work processes, controlling quality and performance, assigning tasks to construction workers and organizing the construction site, controlling costs, estimating man-hour needs and delivery dates, managing relations with subcontractors and clients, and relating to other administrative departments and the home office. This first factor is related to many aspects of project administration. It was named "the factor of planning, control, and coordination."

Among the items that showed the highest loadings on the second factor are:

"Once the supervisor has delegated his authority to his subordinates, he fully entrusts them with it." (.70)
"The supervisor adopts members' opinions and suggestions." (.67)
"The supervisor places the blame for errors on members." (−.65)
"The supervisor serves as a liaison for coordinating work with assistant managers." (.63)
"Delegates authority to his members when circumstances require it." (.62)
"Justly evaluates his subordinates' job." (.61)
"Treats his subordinates fairly." (.60)
"Talks to his subordinates in a friendly way." (.60)

These and other items indicated that the second factor concerns delegation of authority, respect for members' opinions, organizing and managing projects through liaison and coordination within the group, and personal consideration toward individual members. Thus, the second factor is named "the factor of supporting members."

Among the major items showing high loadings on the third factor are:

"Is a capable person." (.59)
"Understands the local geography and weather conditions." (.57)
"Knows about legal problems." (.53)
"Documents the contents of work in writing." (.52)

Thus, the third factor was named "the factor of technical ability."

The items which showed high loadings on the fourth factor are:

"Consideration of the local health, sanitary, and recreational conditions in the area concerned." (.61)

"Concern for improving conditions to avoid any interpersonal tension in the area concerned." (.61)
"Concern for improving the physical work environment in the area concerned." (.59)
"Consideration of team members' health." (.55)
"Concern to create a work environment that facilitates mutual understanding among team members." (.54)
"Concern about solving various problems arising among team members of different ethnic backgrounds." (.50)

Since these items concern improving the work environment and consideration for people working there, the fourth factor was named "the factor of consideration for people working in the area concerned."

In summary, the factor analysis indicated that the leadership of engineering project managers consists of four factors: planning, control, and coordination; supporting members; technical ability; and consideration for people living in the area concerned.

PM Patterns of Successful and Unsuccessful Project Managers

The four PM leadership types were also constructed and used to predict success in project management. The factors of planning, control, and coordination and the factor of technical ability are conceptually similar to the P leadership function. Although "technical ability" per se does not involve any behavior, P behaviors of planning, control, and coordination can be brought into play only when supported by technical knowledge about a particular specialty. The factor of supporting members and the factor of consideration for those persons working in the area concerned are conceptually related to the M leadership function. The P scores were obtained by adding the scores on the planning, control, and coordination factor to the scores on the technical ability factor. The M scores were obtained by adding the scores on the factor of supporting members to the scores on the factor of considering those persons living in the area concerned. Since factor scores are standardized, the averages of P and M scores are 0 and their standard deviation is 1. Data with missing values exceeding one third of the ninety-four items were excluded from the analysis. Project managers whose P and M scores both exceeded the average were classified as PM-type leaders, those whose P scores exceeded the average as P-type leaders, those whose M scores exceeded the average as M-type leaders, and those whose P and M scores both fell short of the average as pm-type leaders. There were 271 PM-type project managers (30.7 percent of the managers), 192 P-type project managers (21.7 percent), 200 M-type project managers (22.7 percent), and 220 pm-type project managers (24.9 percent).

Table 27 shows the relationship between the four PM types and the reported success or failure of the project manager. Of the successful project managers, 52.1 percent were PM-type leaders, 25.5 percent were P-type leaders, 16.2 percent were M-type leaders and 6.2 percent were pm-type leaders. For the PM types of unsuccessful project managers, the pm type came out on top with 47.4 percent, followed by M with 30.4 percent, P with 17.2 percent and PM with 5.0 percent, just the reverse of the order in which the four types were ranked for the projects that succeeded.

In industrial organizations other than engineering project organizations and local government organizations, PM was also the most effective and pm the least effective. However, the relative effectiveness of P and M leadership differed between engineering organizations and organizations in other industries. While M leadership was found to be more effective than P leadership for managers and supervisors in most industrial organizations, local government offices, and in schools, P was found more effective than M for engineering project managers. The difference in the order of P and M effectiveness may be due to specific characteristics of project organizations. Project organizations are involved in complex problem-solving processes while functional organizations are oriented toward the efficient disposition of routine business. Project organization typically involves a sequence of relatively short-term projects involving a changing set of group members. Thus, project managers are required to use a great deal of P-oriented leadership in order to contribute to problem solving. In laboratory situations as well, P-type leadership tends to produce higher performance than M-type leadership. Although a project organization situation and a laboratory situation are very different in many ways, they are relatively similar in the sense that they both are of short duration.

However, the two factors that constitute a project manager's P behavior cannot be interpreted as the same as the experimenter's pressure factor. Likewise, the two factors that constitute M behavior are different from the factor of consideration reflected in M behavior in the laboratory situation. Although the P and M leadership functions are expressed differently in these two set-

TABLE 27. PM Leadership Types (Using Factor Scores) and Engineering Project Managers' Success or Failure

	PM	P	M	pm	Total
Success	251	123	78	30	482
	52.1%	25.5%	16.2%	6.2%	100%
Failure	20	69	122	190	401
	5.0%	17.2%	30.4%	47.4%	100%
Total	271	192	200	220	883
	30.7%	21.7%	22.7%	24.9%	100%

tings, they rank similarly in terms of effectiveness in both. Just as the clouds hanging over Mt. Fuji are entirely different from water running through the Colorado River, yet both the clouds and the water are composed of H_2O. By the same token, the similar ranking may indicate something in common between leadership behavior in project organizations and leadership in a laboratory situation like the H_2O shared by both clouds and river. If so, the PM concept serves to link leadership in project organizations and leadership in laboratory situations.

CHAPTER 6

Governmental Administrative Leadership

Typical examples of administrative leadership can be found in the behavior of administrators and supervisors of local and national government offices. The single most outstanding characteristic of both central and local government bodies in Japan today is their bureaucratic organization. Administrative leadership of Japan is a modern form of bureaucratic leadership.

Bureaucratic characteristics can be found in many kinds of organizations including private corporations, universities, and hospitals. However, the administrative leadership of government and municipal offices differs from that found in other basically bureaucratic organizations. In the present chapter, the characteristics of these government bodies are first analyzed by comparing and contrasting them with the private enterprises that have been examined in previous chapters. Then, the behavior of administrators and supervisors in local government offices is closely examined and scales are described which have been used to measure administrative leadership and study its effectiveness.

A leadership seminar was held in the summer of 1974 at the Hyogo Prefectural Local Government Training Center under the auspices of the Local Government Training Council. Leadership in government and public offices was compared with that in private enterprises at a symposium held as part of the seminar. A basic point made in the symposium was that the goals of private enterprises are becoming somewhat like local government offices in that in Japanese private enterprises, social responsibilities are receiving increasing emphasis. The classic profit goal of private enterprise is being replaced by a multidimensional goal orientation.

Compared to the goals of local government organizations, however, the goals of private enterprises are more limited and simplistic. The goals of local government lie in pursuing the public interest by promoting citizens' welfare. Citizens' welfare runs the whole gamut of life and covers the entire period from cradle to grave. It covers everything from the problems of kindergartners, day nurseries, adult education, aged people, garbage disposal, water supply, sewage, traffic-related problems, and social services, to promoting the welfare of the greatest number of citizens by controlling people's activities through zoning regulations, building codes, and pollution controls. These specific goals may be divided into (1) the goals of providing social services and (2) the goals of providing control by official power. While the former are often found in private enterprises, the latter are especially characteristic of government organizations. The goals involving "control by official power" are supported by laws and regulations.

Leadership by governmental department chiefs and section chiefs involves facilitating the achievement of these two types of goals by using the formal administrative channels of government bureaucracies. While administrative actions designed to provide social services may be similar to managerial actions in private enterprises, those designed to provide social control are likely to differ from the efficiency-oriented principles of providing services. Problems of maintaining social control are less related to efficiency than to ensuring that fair judgments will be reached within a time frame which does not unnecessarily obstruct action. In summary, three characteristics make governmental organizations, particularly local governments, different from private enterprises: (1) management practices are authority-oriented, (2) organizational goals cover a wide range of problems, and (3) government is required to adjust interest claims among citizens and pursue social values (Kato 1975).

Administrative bodies in the age of vigilantes tried to maintain social order on a reactive basis; they would use force to eliminate persons who disturbed the social order. The essential nature of vigilante administration was authoritarian. Although the centralized, regulatory approach to social control has been handed down to modern Japan, the relative importance of providing services to regional communities has increased within the domain of administrative activities. As Japanese society has become industrialized and more sophisticated, the economic situation of the citizens has been improved, their leisure has increased, and their educational level has been raised. Along with these changes, the relative importance of providing services to regional communities has increased within the domain of administrative services. Because a service-oriented administration is basically nonregulatory, Japanese government administration now has a primarily supportive role in providing cradle-to-grave social services. At the same time, a new type of authority-based administration has also grown up in which administrative guidance has partially replaced regulatory control in preventing pollution, preserving the environment, and stabilizing commodity prices. Still, regulatory control has been kept as the government's "trump card" to be played as a last resort. The primary difference between the administrative management of government organizations and the management of private enterprises lies in the orientation of government administration to goals designed to promote the public welfare of citizens by trying to satisfy a varied set of political and administrative needs. The methods used to measure administrative leadership in government organizations and to assess the validity of the measures have taken into account the particular characteristics of government administration.

Development of Items for Measuring Leadership Behavior in Government Organizations

The basic material used to develop scales for measuring leadership behavior in government organizations was unstructured descriptions which local government managers wrote about their leadership roles and behaviors. Department heads, section chiefs, deputy section chiefs, and subsection chiefs in prefectural and municipal government offices in Tochigi Prefecture, Greater Metropolitan Tokyo, Hyogo Prefecture, and Fukouka City were asked to freely describe their activities, their leadership behavior, and their decision making. They were asked to describe their daily activities as well as their activities which require one week, three to six months, or even longer periods of time. A leadership behavior inventory was then developed by analyzing the above data and a questionnaire was developed based on the inventory. Another questionnaire concerning morale-related variables was used to examine the validity of the leadership measures. Each item included in the questionnaire was examined by holding several meetings of specialists before the questionnaires were printed. These consultants included top managers in the personnel section of local government offices, people involved in the training and education of local government workers, university professors studying administrative organizations, and experts in psychometrics and survey methods.

The leadership behavior inventory was prepared by transcribing each freely written description of a leadership behavior onto a separate card. A total of 636 cards were produced in this manner. After those cards were deleted which described basically similar behaviors, 63 cards remained. Questionnaire items were then prepared to measure these 63 different behaviors. Only 58 were considered appropriate for measuring the leadership of subsection chiefs while all 63 could meaningfully be used to describe the behavior of government chiefs.

The questionnaire forms were designed so that subordinates could be asked to describe the leadership behavior of their superiors. Subordinates' descriptions of behavior were used because previous research indicated that they were more highly associated with group outcomes and group member attitudes than were self-descriptions or descriptions by superordinates. The questionnaire was designed so that lower echelon employees first described the leadership behavior of their immediate supervisors (subsection chiefs) and then the leadership of their immediate supervisor's bosses (section chiefs). In addition to questions concerning leadership behavior, the questionnaire contained forty questions concerning job satisfaction, mental health, and performance norms. The specific questionnaire items will be described as the results are presented. The job satisfaction items are understood to have implications for intrinsic work motivation as well as for satisfaction per se.

Method

The questionnaire was distributed to employees of local government offices. The leadership data obtained from the questionnaire responses was factor analyzed. The validity of the PM concepts was assessed through their correlations with the work attitudes noted above. The questionnaire was distributed to a total of 967 employees of eight different prefectural and city government organizations. (Japan consists of forty-seven prefectures. In each prefecture there are more than twenty or thirty cities. A prefecture corresponds roughly to a state in the United States from the administrative point of view.) In the sample, men outnumbered women by 84.2 percent to 13.3 percent. (The percentages for some of the demographic and personal data do not add up to 100 percent due to missing data.) In age, those in their thirties were predominant with 36 percent, followed by age twenty-five to twenty-nine with 21.8 percent, twenty-four or younger with 19.8 percent, and forty or older with 19.6 percent. In terms of the length of continuous service, 34.5 percent had worked for the government five years or less, 14.7 percent had worked five to ten years, 25.3 percent had worked ten to fifteen years, 10.2 percent had worked fifteen to twenty years, and 12.8 percent had worked for their employer longer than twenty years.

The survey was carried out during November and December, 1974. The collective survey method was used (i.e., the surveyors read off all the items in the questionnaire and had the subjects answer the questions). The subjects were asked not to sign their names on the questionnaire.

Factor Analysis Procedure

Factor analysis was applied separately to (1) forty-nine items describing the subsection chiefs' leadership, (2) fifty-four items describing the section chiefs' and deputy section chiefs' leadership, and (3) forty items belonging to the seven categories used as dependent variables (morale-related variables). The data of respondents who did not answer all questions were excluded. As a result, data from 915 respondents were analyzed for subsection chiefs' leadership, from 905 respondents for section chiefs' and deputy section chiefs' leadership, and from 946 respondents for morale-related variables.

Results of the Factor Analysis Concerning Subsection Chiefs' Leadership

Principal components factor analysis with communalities set at 1.0 was used to extract factors which were then rotated using the normal varimax method. A four-factor solution was selected as being the most interpretable after two-factor through eight-factor solutions were considered. The factor loading matrix for the four-factor solution is shown in table 28. Factor I accounts for

TABLE 28. Factor Analysis on Subsection Chiefs' Leadership

	Factor Loading				
Item	I	II	III	IV	Communality
72. He shows special consideration when subordinates make mistakes so that they will not be discouraged.	.716	.258	.092	.179	.620
73. He listens to subordinates' personal problems and offers advice.	.708	.193	.192	−.001	.576
74. He shows appreciation for the services of his subordinates.	.698	.269	.229	.082	.618
70. He seriously considers opinions expressed by his subordinates.	.695	.190	−.025	.207	.563
78. He pays special attention to his subordinates' health.	.694	.188	.265	.180	.619
77. He trusts his subordinates.	.688	.184	−.036	.270	.581
82. He gives careful thought to his subordinates' advancement and security.	.674	.238	.301	.048	.604
80. He treats subordinates fairly.	.667	.262	−.098	.261	.592
71. He pays special attention to ways of improving the work environment to make the work of subordinates easier.	.657	.291	.283	.117	.610
75. His personal likes and dislikes do not affect his work.	.609	.259	−.191	.293	.560
89. Overall, I respect my superior officer from both a professional standpoint and a personal standpoint.	.608	.469	.090	.206	.640

Continued

TABLE 28—*Continued*

Item	Factor Loading I	II	III	IV	Communality
69. He speaks freely to his subordinates.	.606	.164	.048	.057	.400
81. He participates in subordinates' recreational and social activities as much as possible.	.575	.161	.027	.070	.363
84. He uses good judgment in recommending promotions and wage increases for his subordinates.	.575	.252	.319	.004	.496
64. He provides the information that is necessary for subordinates to do their work.	.551	.380	.179	.096	.489
65. He even gives information about organizational matters that is not really essential for subordinates to do their work.	.546	.197	.282	−.013	.417
79. He assists subordinates who are behind in their work.	.518	.404	.058	.128	.451
76. He does not become emotional when reprimanding subordinates.	.516	.234	−.347	.277	.518
83. He uses good judgment in deciding what work to assign to particular subordinates.	.505	.420	.269	.054	.506
60. He tries to train someone else to temporarily fill in for him when he is absent.	.479	.443	.281	.061	.514
43. He has a good grasp of how work is progressing.	.201	.767	.170	.088	.666
44. I have had no problems resulting from a lack of information from my superior.	.154	.745	.020	.085	.586
51. He understands the details of his subordinates' work responsibilities.	.232	.706	.068	.127	.574
45. He is trying to fill in gaps in his knowledge.	.278	.681	.136	.161	.585
46. When necessary, he clearly specifies deadlines for work.	.215	.625	.221	−.003	.486
47. He tells you about his work plans and schedules.	.372	.589	.314	.089	.591
67. He reads the contents of all documents which require his approval.	.193	.570	.126	.309	.474

TABLE 28—*Continued*

Item	Factor Loading I	II	III	IV	Communality
52. He instructs subordinates about how to improve their work methods.	.231	.559	.418	−.018	.540
63. He is flexible in coping with situations that cannot be anticipated.	.424	.557	.114	.070	.508
48. He coordinates work with other departments.	.439	.524	.290	−.009	.552
59. He has never made the mistake of refusing to change plans when changes are needed.	.243	.506	−.043	.235	.372
58. He uses the work completed in one project to plan and conduct similar projects at a later time.	.445	.494	.348	.107	.574
56. He points out to his subordinates issues that are currently pending.	.378	.480	.383	.143	.541
50. He maintains communication with his superior officer.	.400	.472	.254	.019	.447
57. He makes specific work assignments.	.302	.461	.258	.128	.387
61. He leaves precise instructions about work to be done when he is not in the office during working hours.	.393	.460	.381	.151	.534
68. He guides subordinates in a way which increases their level of professional knowledge.	.447	.452	.425	.103	.595
62. He has never made a mistake due to lack of communication with outside organizations.	.392	.447	−.038	.271	.429
49. He calls meetings when they are necessary.	.354	.441	.329	−.007	.429
42. He cautions subordinates to follow the work regulations.	−.087	.022	.682	.055	.476
53. He encourages subordinates to maintain a mental attitude appropriate for civil servants.	.300	.323	.588	.151	.563
85. When necessary, he reprimands his subordinates without hesitation.	.095	.254	.565	−.095	.402
55. He carefully plans his own work each day.	.300	.421	.459	.187	.513

Continued

TABLE 28—*Continued*

Item	Factor Loading				Communality
	I	II	III	IV	
87. He never uses an official car for personal purposes.	.136	.026	.086	.708	.528
86. He does not ask for even small personal favors from his subordinates.	.128	.119	−.123	.642	.459
88. He does not ask his subordinates for help in house moving or work at his home.	.034	−.040	.031	.639	.412
41. My superior obeys the work regulations.	.170	.290	.138	.521	.404
54. He lets people know where he has gone whenever he is not in the office during working hours.	.230	.345	.277	.447	.448
66. He takes prompt action on documents which require his approval.	.139	.381	.032	.404	.329
Factor variance	10.123	8.421	3.676	2.920	25.139
Contribution (%)	20.7	17.2	7.5	6.0	51.3

20.7 percent of the total variance in the forty-nine items, Factor II accounts for 17.2 percent, Factor III for 7.5 percent, and Factor IV for 6.0 percent. These four factors explained 51.4 percent of the total variance and each was conceptually interpretable. The interpretation of each factor was based on items which had a high loading (above .500) on one factor and low loadings (below .400) on the other factors. Based on these items, the factors for subsection chief leadership were labeled Group Maintenance (Factor I), Planning and Plan Executive (Factor II), Pressure to Achieve Goals (Factor III), and Personal Rule Observance (Factor IV).

Results of the Factor Analysis Concerning Section Chiefs' and Deputy Section Chiefs' Leadership

The questionnaire concerning the section chiefs' and deputy section chiefs' leadership included the forty-nine items from the subsection chief form plus five additional items. Four factors were identified and varimax rotation was applied as before. Table 29 shows the factor matrix after the rotation. Factor I accounted for 18.1 percent of the total variance, Factor III for 13.7 percent,

TABLE 29. Factor Analysis on Section Chiefs' Leadership

Item	Factor Loading I	II	III	IV	Communality
72. He shows special consideration when subordinates make mistakes so that they will not be discouraged.	−.686	.229	.296	.140	.630
73. He listens to subordinates' personal problems and offers advice.	−.683	.206	.343	.044	.629
77. He trusts his subordinates.	−.682	.271	.057	.268	.614
82. He gives careful thought to his subordinates' advancement and security.	−.666	.249	.328	.091	.621
78. He pays special attention to his subordinates' health.	−.662	.111	.369	.181	.620
70. He seriously considers opinions expressed by his subordinates.	−.658	.257	.180	.247	.592
69. He speaks freely to his subordinates.	−.657	.124	.175	.039	.480
80. He treats subordinates fairly.	−.632	.306	.048	.318	.597
71. He pays special attention to ways of improving the work environment to make the work of subordinates easier.	−.622	.282	.411	.132	.652
74. He shows appreciation for the services of his subordinates.	−.614	.305	.408	.123	.652
75. His personal likes and dislikes do not affect his work.	−.600	.356	−.081	.407	.658
89. Overall, I respect my superior officer from both a professional standpoint and a personal standpoint.	−.576	.465	.235	.248	.665
84. He uses good judgment in recommending promotions and wage increases for his subordinates.	−.566	.304	.365	.049	.549
76. He does not become emotional when reprimanding subordinates.	−.545	.209	−.125	.422	.534
83. He uses good judgment in deciding what work to assign to particular subordinates.	−.509	.268	.481	.176	.593
81. He participates in subordinates' recreational and social activities as possible.	−.503	.264	.204	.160	.391

Continued

TABLE 29—*Continued*

Item	Factor Loading I	II	III	IV	Communality
64. He provides the information that is necessary for subordinates to do their work.	−.484	.305	.382	.163	.450
79. He assists subordinates who are behind in their work.	−.479	.190	.441	.057	.463
60. He tries to train someone else to temporarily fill in for him when he is absent.	−.465	.407	.428	.088	.573
65. He even gives information about organizational matters that is not really essential for subordinates to do their work.	−.454	.175	.410	.090	.413
92. He is good in negotiating with outside organizations.	−.420	.670	.164	.088	.657
93. He gathers information from many different sources both within and outside the government office.	−.362	.614	.278	.026	.586
63. He is flexible in coping with situations that cannot be anticipated.	−.356	.612	.245	.204	.602
91. He is skillful in acquiring budget allocations.	−.323	.585	.302	−.028	.539
44. I have had no problems resulting from a lack of information by my superior officers.	−.143	.579	.275	.334	.543
62. He has never made a mistake due to lack of communication with outside organizations.	−.240	.572	.043	.368	.522
45. He tries to overcome any deficiencies in his professional expertise.	−.198	.554	.316	.258	.512
59. He has never made the mistake of refusing to change plans when changes are needed.	−.237	.530	.136	.364	.488
90. He aggressively proposes new projects for inclusion in the budget for the next fiscal year.	−.330	.525	.413	.019	.555
50. He maintains communication with his superior officer.	−.348	.520	.288	.190	.511
94. He endeavors to be in full command of the work situation in the field when necessary.	−.437	.512	.334	.137	.584

TABLE 29—*Continued*

Item	Factor Loading I	II	III	IV	Communality
53. He encourages subordinates to maintain a mental attitude appropriate for civil servants.	−.260	.245	.643	.109	.552
42. He cautions subordinates to follow the work regulations.	.054	−.089	.592	.027	.362
47. He makes his work plans and schedules known.	−.363	.266	.587	.218	.594
52. He instructs subordinates about how to improve their work methods.	−.166	.326	.578	.053	.471
56. He points out to his subordinates issues that are currently pending.	−.380	.284	.565	.150	.567
61. He leaves precise instructions about work to be done when he is not in the office during working hours.	−.365	.298	.545	.121	.536
43. He has a good grasp of how work is progressing.	−.238	.455	.534	.198	.588
58. He uses the work completed in one project to plan and conduct similar projects at a later time.	−.341	.446	.498	.132	.581
57. He makes specific work assignments.	−.349	.243	.496	.179	.457
51. He understands the details of his subordinates' work responsibilities.	−.339	.365	.492	.212	.536
55. He carefully plans his own work each day.	−.312	.275	.492	.205	.459
68. He guides subordinates in a way which increases their level of professional knowledge.	−.407	.420	.492	.030	.535
48. He coordinates work with other departments.	−.319	.467	.483	.181	.586
54. He lets people know where he has gone whenever he is not in the office during working hours.	−.238	.233	.474	.390	.488
46. When deadlines are necessary, he clearly specifies what they are.	−.186	.414	.446	.159	.431
85. When necessary, he reprimands his subordinates without hesitation.	−.065	.400	.439	−.114	.370

Continued

TABLE 29—*Continued*

Item	Factor Loading I	II	III	IV	Communality
49. He calls meetings when they are necessary.	−.258	.393	.429	.125	.420
67. He reads the contents of all documents which require his approval.	−.214	.378	.403	.326	.457
87. He never uses an official car for personal purposes.	−.141	.117	.133	.741	.601
86. He does not ask for even small personal favors from his subordinates.	−.084	.094	.076	.729	.553
88. He does not ask his subordinates for help in house moving or work at his home.	−.115	.030	.092	.678	.482
41. My superior obeys the work regulations.	−.160	.170	.430	.460	.451
66. He takes prompt action on documents which require his approval.	−.288	.205	.207	.417	.342
Factor variance	9.792	7.395	7.865	3.940	28.991
Contribution (%)	18.1	13.7	14.6	7.3	53.7

Factor III for 14.6 percent, and Factor IV for 7.3 percent. The accumulated variance accounted for by these four factors reached 53.7 percent of the total variance. As before, each factor was interpreted according to the items which had a high loading (above .500) on only one factor and low loadings (below .400) on the other factors. The four leadership factors for section chiefs and deputy section chiefs were labeled Group Maintenance (Factor I), Planning and Coordination (Factor II), Discipline and Plan Executive (Factor III), and Personal Rule Observance (Factor IV).

Discussion of Leadership Behavior Measures

Comparing the factor structures of the leadership data for subsection chiefs and section chiefs show both similarities and differences in factor structure. In table 30, asterisks have been placed in the column corresponding to those factors on which various items had high loadings in the subsection chief and section chief data. Factor I can be seen to reflect group maintenance–oriented leadership (M behavior) for both groups of leaders. In the data for subsection chiefs, Factor II pertains to the execution of plans while Factor III is a discipline-guidance factor. Both of these factors pertain to group goal achievement–oriented leadership behavior or P leadership. Factor II of section chiefs is a planning and coordination factor, and Factor III is the factor of discipline-guidance and execution of plans. Both of these involve goal achievement. In subsequent analyses, items from both Factor II and Factor III of subsection chiefs were combined to measure P leadership oriented to goal achievement. Factor IV, concerning observance of professional norms, is leadership behavior in setting a good example for subordinates. Although it may have some bearing on goal achievement, few of the items had particularly high loadings on this factor.

In the data presented in table 30, ten of the sixteen group maintenance items which showed high loadings for subsection chiefs also showed high factor loadings for section chiefs. The items with high factor loadings fall into three conceptual categories: (1) personal consideration for subordinates' private problems, complaints, health, and future lives, and willingness to speak to them readily (Q73, 78, 82, 69); (2) consideration for subordinates who failed in something, consideration for subordinates' promotions and pay raises, and consideration for subordinates concerning professional matters, such as trusting them, treating them fairly, and responding to their opinions (Q72, 84, 77, 70, 80); and (3) joining with subordinates in their recreational and social activities (Q81). Six items show high factor loadings only for subsection chiefs. These items concern consideration about professional matters (Q64, 65, 71, 74, 75, 76). It follows that group maintenance–oriented leadership by subsection chiefs dovetails with that of section chiefs in the area of professional matters. However, subsection chiefs are more involved than section chiefs in providing lower-level employees with information, thanking them for their work, and providing them with personal support.

Six of the ten group maintenance items identified for both subsection chiefs and section chiefs also showed high factor loadings on the maintenance factor in industrial organizations (chap. 3). These items were:

73. "He listens to subordinates' personal problems and offers advice."
69. "He speaks freely to his subordinates."
84. "He uses good judgment in recommending promotions and wage increases for his subordinates."
77. "He trusts his subordinates."
70. "He seriously considers opinions expressed by his subordinates."
80. "He treats his subordinates fairly."

Goal achievement factors were also found in the local government study. Subsection chiefs' Factor II was identified as the factor of plan execution. Included in this factor are items concerning subsection chiefs' professional

TABLE 30. Summary of the Factor Analysis of Subsection Chiefs' and Section Chiefs' Leadership

	Subsection Chief Factor No.				Section Chief Factor No.			
Item	I	II	III	IV	I	II	III	IV
A. Group Maintenance								
73. He listens to subordinates' personal problems and offers advice.	*				*			
78. He pays special attention to his subordinates' health.	*				*			
82. He gives careful thought to his subordinates' advancement and security.	*				*			
69. He speaks freely to his subordinates.	*				*			
72. He shows special consideration when subordinates make mistakes so that they will not be discouraged.	*				*			
84. He uses good judgment in recommending promotions and wage increases for his subordinates.	*				*			
77. He trusts his subordinates.	*				*			
70. He seriously considers opinions expressed by his subordinates.	*				*			
80. He treats subordinates fairly.	*				*			
81. He participates in subordinates' recreational and social activities as much as possible.	*				*			
71. He pays special attention to ways of improving the work environment to make the work of subordinates easier.	*							
64. He provides the information that is necessary for subordinates to do their work.	*							
65. He even gives information about organizational matters that is not really essential for subordinates to do their work.	*							
74. He shows appreciation for the services of his subordinates.	*							
75. His personal likes and dislikes do not affect his work.	*							
76. He does not become emotional when reprimanding subordinates.	*							
B. Goal-Attainment								
62. He has never made a mistake due to lack of communication with outside organizations.						*		
50. He maintains communication with his superior.						*		
93. He gathers information from many different sources both within and outside the government office.						*		

TABLE 30—*Continued*

Item	Subsection Chief Factor No.				Section Chief Factor No.			
	I	II	III	IV	I	II	III	IV
63. He is flexible in coping with situations that cannot be anticipated.						*		
91. He is skillful in acquiring budget allocations.						*		
45. He tries to overcome any deficiencies in his professional expertise.		*				*		
44. I have had no problems resulting from a lack of information by my superior.		*				*		
59. He has never made the mistake of refusing to change plans when changes are needed.		*				*		
51. He understands the details of his subordinates' work responsibilities.		*						
67. He reads the contents of all documents which require his approval.		*						
43. He has a good grasp of how work is progressing.		*						
46. When deadlines are necessary, he clearly specifies what they are.		*						
47. He makes his work plans and schedules known.		*					*	
52. He instructs subordinates about how to improve their work methods.							*	
56. He points out to his subordinates issues that are currently pending.							*	
61. He leaves precise instructions about work to be done when he is not in the office during working hours.							*	
53. He encourages subordinates to maintain a mental attitude appropriate for civil servants.			*				*	
42. He cautions subordinates to follow work regulations.			*				*	
85. When necessary, he reprimands his subordinates without hesitation.			*					
C. Observance								
86. He does not ask for even small personal favors from his subordinates.				*				*
87. He never uses an official car for personal purposes.				*				*
88. He does not ask his subordinates for help in house moving or work at his home.				*				*
41. My superior obeys the work regulations.				*				

knowledge, acquisition of new professional knowledge, knowledge of papers submitted to them for approval, and knowledge of the contents of subordinates' work and work progress, help in clarifying work, setting their work schedule and setting time limits. These items concern the basic professional knowledge of subsection chiefs and their use of this knowledge to guide subordinates in doing their work. The items in this factor encompass two stages of work to be done—planning and execution—but do not include the stage of evaluating results. Section chiefs' Factor II involves planning and coordination. This factor primarily concerns communicating with outside organizations and with the section chiefs' superiors, gathering information from various sources, and making appropriate adjustments in original plans that are necessitated by changing external events and conditions.

The factor of planning and plan execution for subsection chiefs corresponds to the factor of planning which had been found in the previous survey of first-line supervisors in industrial organizations. However, the factor of planning and coordination which emphasizes external dealings with other sections was found for the first time in the local government study. This form of leadership may only be characteristic of the role played by such intermediate managers as section chiefs.

Section chiefs' Factor III involves plan execution combined with discipline and guidance. The items pertaining to executing plans in the subsection chief data are included in Factor II. These items concern communicating work policy, scheduling work for subordinates, instructing subordinates about how work should be done during subsection chiefs' absence, and how to improve the work methods. How should the differences between the factor loadings of those items for section chiefs and subsection chiefs be interpreted? The difference may occur in part because subsection chiefs engage in the direct execution of plans, while section chiefs are concerned with executing plans in a more indirect manner. Therefore, section chiefs' behavior in executing plans takes the form of discipline and guidance. While subsection chiefs provide leadership behavior in planning and executing work on a routine, day-to-day basis, section chiefs are concerned with such nonroutine matters as coordinating work activities with other departments and communicating policy decisions to subordinates.

Validation of Items Measuring Leadership Behavior

Questionnaire measures of subordinates' cognitive-affective responses to their work situation were used as criterion variables in order to assess the validity of the various leadership conditions. Although performance outcome measures would have been desirable for assessing validity, it was not practical to measure performance outcomes which would have been sensitive to subordinate work motivation in government offices. Therefore subordinates' cognitive-affective responses to their work situation ("morale-related variables") were studied as intervening variables in local government offices, while the implications of leadership for more ultimate outcomes must be extrapolated from the results of industrial organization surveys and laboratory experiments.

The forty morale-related items used as dependent variables were conceptually divided into seven categories: (1) job satisfaction (Q1–5), (2) satisfaction with compensation (Q6–10), (3) teamwork (Q11–15), (4) meeting quality (Q16–20), (5) communication adequacy (Q21–24), mental health (Q25–29), and (6) performance norms (Q30–34). The seventh category consisted of six items, Q35–40, included as single-item measures of other variables.

The procedure used to factor analyze the forty morale-related items was the same as the procedure used in the leadership factor analysis. Eight factors accounted for 57.4 percent of the total variance. Eight factors were selected for rotation to determine whether the seven a priori categories of items could be identified. The factor matrix after rotation is shown in table 31. Factor I accounted for 10.6 percent of the total variance, Factor III for 8.6 percent, Factor IV for 8.5 percent, Factor II for 8.5 percent, Factor V for 8.3 percent, Factor VI for 4.6 percent, Factor VIII for 4.2 percent and Factor VII for 4.1 percent.

Each conceptual category corresponded fairly closely to one or another of the factors. The five categories of job satisfaction, satisfaction with compensation, teamwork, meeting quality, and communication adequacy clearly corresponded to the first five factors. However, the homogeneity of items in the mental health and performance norms categories was not supported by the factor analysis. Mental health items were associated with both a separate factor and with the communication adequacy factor. Likewise, the performance norms items were associated with two separate individual factors as well as the teamwork factor.

The validity of the criterion variables was also assessed by checking to determine if the intervals between each of the five response alternatives is equivalent. The response scales were analyzed separately for each item using Hayashi's Quantification of Pattern Classification (see Appendix). In this analysis, the correlation ratio is large if respondents tend to answer each question using the same response alternative and if the intervals between response alternatives are equal. If so, then the use of a one-dimensional scale is possible and valid, according to Guttman's (1950) theory. Thus, scores by using the response scales of 1, 2, 3, 4, and 5 are valid. The results suggest that unidimensional analysis using a 1 to 5 response scale is generally valid for the cognitive-affective criterion variables.

The four PM leadership types were derived from subsection chiefs and

TABLE 31. Factor Analysis of Morale-related Items

Item	Factor Loading								Communality
	I	II	III	IV	V	VI	VII	VIII	
1. Are you interested in your present work?	−.823	.124	.157	.065	.120	−.035	.080	−.031	.744
2. Do you find your day-to-day work worthwhile?	−.796	.134	.162	.129	.153	−.082	.143	−.039	.747
3. Do you feel that you have mastered your present job?	−.363	.013	.087	.180	−.186	−.554	−.005	−.147	.534
4. Are you proud of the job you are responsible for?	−.750	.151	.196	.111	.040	−.086	.081	−.067	.656
5. Do you want to gain greater knowledge and skill in the job you are responsible for?	−.615	−.001	.136	−.069	.114	.320	−.000	−.274	.593
6. Are you satisfied with your most recent salary increase?	−.107	.815	−.004	.087	.025	−.033	.051	.024	.688
7. Are you satisfied with your present salary considering the nature of your job and the effort required of you?	−.064	.847	.023	.060	.105	−.013	−.060	−.005	.740
8. What do you think of the bonus system in your company?	−.035	.841	−.001	.083	.072	−.048	.006	−.006	.723
9. Do you think promotions in your company are given on a fair and equitable basis?	−.081	.492	.039	.255	.120	−.051	−.001	−.068	.337
10. How do you feel about your company's fringe benefits by and large?	−.053	.396	.105	.109	.159	−.036	.084	−.081	.223
11. Do your co-workers have a good sense of teamwork?	−.116	.085	.731	.215	.225	−.067	.002	.037	.661
12. Do you get along well with your co-workers?	−.186	.007	.730	.124	.158	−.223	−.055	−.020	.661
13. Do you want to remain a member of the work group?	−.355	.098	.638	.141	.196	−.062	−.002	.086	.613
14. Do your co-workers encourage one another to give their best effort in doing a job?	−.178	.067	.668	.224	.059	−.040	.191	−.065	.578
15. Do your co-workers help you when you need help with your work?	−.095	.082	.711	.078	.241	.073	−.025	−.133	.610
16. Do you think the discussions during these meetings are practically useful?	−.194	.174	.187	.713	.145	−.023	.166	−.116	.675
17. How satisfied are you with these meetings?	−.138	.253	.181	.711	.235	−.056	.145	−.047	.702

18. By and large, do you think these meetings are well run?	−.075	.203	.197	.721	.204	−.082	.108	.003	.666
19. Is there an atmosphere in which you can freely discuss things at these meetings?	−.114	.109	.242	.606	.203	−.166	−.094	−.146	.550
20. Does your superior seriously consider the suggestions and opinions you bring up at those meetings?	−.147	.076	.174	.612	.313	−.018	.063	−.171	.601
21. Does your superior keep in close touch with other workplaces?	−.103	.124	.188	.487	.544	.000	.068	.041	.601
22. Does the company management sometimes fail to let you know things that you should know about?	−.114	.122	.035	.240	.625	.023	.170	.078	.513
23. Are your immediate superior and his superior in close contact with one another?	−.093	.074	.131	.363	.614	−.037	.111	−.039	.555
24. Are there times when the suggestions and opinions that you had submitted seem to have evaporated somewhere along the line and never reached the top management?	−.115	.083	.101	.258	.641	−.032	.010	−.065	.513
25. Do you usually feel under unreasonably strong pressure from your superior?	−.084	.111	.097	.114	.574	−.278	−.220	−.187	.532
26. Do you feel that your area of responsibility is clearly defined?	−.133	.076	.204	.098	.423	−.335	.073	.016	.371
27. Do you feel that you are given more responsibility and authority than is appropriate for the position you now hold?	.196	.247	.142	−.146	.402	−.077	−.126	−.233	.379
28. Do you feel somewhat uneasy when you consider what the future holds in store for you?	−.148	.250	.150	.078	.267	−.477	.129	−.028	.430
29. Are there times when you feel restless?	−.129	.144	.071	.064	.263	−.645	.084	.063	.543
30. Are there times when your co-workers criticize the way things are done in your workplace?	.006	−.027	.576	.151	−.034	−.076	.262	−.121	.445
31. Is there an atmosphere among your co-workers of placing strong pressure on one another to work hard?	−.069	.060	.026	.053	.005	−.063	.778	.026	.621
32. To what extent do your co-workers hate to be outperformed by any other work group?	−.162	.088	.208	.086	.096	−.006	.657	−.268	.598

Continued

TABLE 31—*Continued*

Item	Factor Loading								Communality
	I	II	III	IV	V	VI	VII	VIII	
33. How high is the level of goal attainment that is entertained by the majority of co-workers?	−.087	.082	.249	.172	.149	−.001	.400	−.578	.622
34. How much importance do you yourself place on achieving work goals?	−.261	.078	−.006	.166	.048	−.094	.108	−.740	.672
35. When the set goal is too large, it sometimes becomes a burden.	.088	.111	.054	−.138	.281	−.476	−.235	−.374	.542
36. The present job suits my nature.	−.735	.081	.080	.121	.112	−.310	−.052	.001	.679
37. I feel a sense of responsibility in regard to accomplishing my job.	−.460	.037	.033	.281	−.057	.017	−.025	−.460	.509
38. I can display my ability through this work.	−.691	.054	.100	.208	.056	−.250	.100	−.101	.620
39. I am eager to do work but there is something that hampers me.	−.064	.132	.231	.110	.597	−.153	.012	−.034	.468
40. Sufficient economic compensation is promised for the future.	−.124	.617	.078	.097	.086	−.207	.101	−.066	.477
Factor variance	4.231	3.377	3.430	3.394	3.359	1.847	1.654	1.657	22.949
Contribution (%)	10.6	8.5	8.6	8.5	8.3	4.6	4.1	4.2	57.4

deputy section and section chiefs based on subordinates' descriptions. Seven categories of criterion variables were used for assessing the validity of the leadership types.

Selection of Items to Measure Leadership Types

Eight P items and eight M items were selected based on three criteria:

1. Each P (M) item should have high, primary factor loading on one of the P or M factors.
2. The selected items should cover as broad a range of supervisory behaviors as possible.
3. The number of P items should be the same as the number of M items so that both P scores and M scores can have the same range of values.

The selected items are shown in table 32. Eight items were selected to measure subsection chiefs' P leadership from the three factors involving execution of plans, discipline-guidance, and personal rule observance. Eight items were also selected from the one factor involving M leadership for subsection chiefs. Eight P leadership items were selected from the three section chiefs' factors of (1) planning and coordination, (2) discipline, guidance, and plan execution, and (3) personal rule observance. Eight M leadership items were selected from the one M leadership factor found in the section chief data. The common meaning of P and M leadership for the two kinds of formal leaders is reflected in the partial overlap in items used to measure these dimensions. The setting-specific meaning of P and M leadership is reflected in the nonoverlapping items for the two groups. Section chiefs were classified into one or another of the four PM types depending on whether their P and M scores were above or below the average for their category of leader.

Relationships between Subsection Chiefs' PM Leadership Types and Morale-Related Variables

Respondents provided complete data to the eight items concerning P leadership, eight items concerning M leadership, and thirty-four morale-related items so that 920 subsection chiefs could be studied. Of these 920 subsection chiefs, 354 were rated as PM-type leaders, 143 as P-type, 134 as M-type, and 289 as pm-type leaders. Associations were then assessed between these four leadership types and the scores on morale-related items.

Table 33 shows the means of the seven morale-related variables for each of the four PM types. Analysis of variance (ANOVA) was used to assess the extent to which the morale-related variable scores differed according to the four PM leadership types. The total variance explained (η^2) in each morale-

TABLE 32. Items Selected for Final Measure of PM Leadership Types

Items Measuring Subsection Chiefs' Leadership

P Leadership:

1. The superior officer obeys the work regulations. (Q41)
2. He cautions subordinates to follow the work regulations. (Q42)
3. He has good grasp of how work is progressing. (Q43)
4. When deadlines are necessary, he clearly specifies what they are. (Q46)
5. He understands the details of his subordinates' work responsibilities. (Q51)
6. He encourages subordinates to maintain a mental attitude appropriate for civil servants. (Q53)
7. He reads the contents of all documents which require his approval. (Q67)
8. When necessary, he reprimands his subordinates without hesitation. (Q85)

M Leadership:

1. He speaks freely to his subordinates. (Q69)
2. He seriously considers opinions expressed by his subordinates. (Q70)
3. He shows special consideration when subordinates make mistakes so that they will not be discouraged. (Q72)
4. He listens to subordinates' personal problems and offers advice. (Q73)
5. He trusts his subordinates. (Q77)
6. He treats subordinates fairly. (Q80)
7. He participates in subordinates' recreational and social activities as possible. (Q81)
8. He uses good judgment in recommending promotions and wage increases for his subordinates. (Q84)

Items Measuring Section Chiefs' Leadership

P Leadership:

1. The superior officer obeys the work regulations. (Q41)
2. He cautions subordinates to follow the work regulations. (Q42)
3. He instructs subordinates about how to improve their work methods. (Q52)
4. He points out to his subordinates issues that are currently pending. (Q56)
5. He aggressively proposes new projects for inclusion in the budget for the next fiscal year. (Q90)
6. He encourages subordinates to maintain a mental attitude appropriate for civil servants. (Q53)
7. He gathers information from many different sources both within and outside the government office. (Q93)
8. When necessary, he reprimands his subordinates without hesitation. (Q85)

M Leadership:

1. He speaks freely to his subordinates. (Q69)
2. He seriously considers opinions expressed by his subordinates. (Q70)
3. He shows special consideration when subordinates make mistakes so that they will not be discouraged. (Q72)
4. He listens to subordinates' personal problems and offers advice. (Q73)
5. He trusts his subordinates. (Q77)
6. He treats subordinates fairly. (Q80)
7. He participates in subordinates' recreational and social activities as possible. (Q81)
8. He uses good judgment in recommending promotions and wage increases for his subordinates. (Q84)

related variable by the four PM types is also indicated at the end of each row. The differences among the four PM leadership types in the morale-related variables were statistically significant ($p < .01$). For each morale-related variable, except performance norms, the ranking of PM types was PM, M, P, and pm. The rank order of P and M leadership was reversed for performance norms. These results coincide with those from previous studies of PM leadership types among first-line supervisors in industrial organizations.

The analysis of variance results (η^2) indicate that the leadership types are associated with communication adequacy and meeting quality to an especially large extent. No such conspicuous differences among PM types for these variables were found in the survey previously conducted with first-line supervisors in industrial organizations. Although the rank-order of the PM types is similar between government subsection chiefs and first-line industrial supervisors, the importance of leadership with respect to the seven kinds of morale-related variables differs for these two kinds of organizational leaders. First-line supervisor leadership may be particularly important for communication in governmental settings. Characteristics of leadership by first-line supervisors thus may differ between governmental and industrial organizations.

Relationships between Section Chiefs' PM Leadership Types and Morale-Related Variables

Complete data for the leadership of section chiefs and the morale-related variables was provided by 909 government employees. Based on these data, 363 respondents described their second-line supervisors as PM-type leaders, 113 as M-type leaders, 138 as P-type leaders, and 295 as pm-type leaders. The relationship of these four leadership types to the morale-related variables was assessed for these section chiefs as it was for the subsection chiefs.

TABLE 33. Mean Scores on Morale-related Variables for Subsection Chiefs and Section Chiefs

Morale-related Criterion	Subsection Chiefs' Leadership Types					Section Chiefs' Leadership Types				
	PM	M	P	pm	η^2	PM	M	P	pm	η^2
Job satisfaction	19.0	17.8	17.5	16.8	.065	19.0	17.9	17.9	16.5	.050
Satisfaction with compensation	12.4	11.3	11.2	10.7	.074	12.6	11.2	11.3	10.2	.045
Teamwork	19.9	18.0	17.5	16.0	.109	19.4	18.5	17.2	16.2	.176
Meeting quality	17.9	15.2	14.4	13.8	.218	17.8	15.6	14.9	13.5	.208
Communication adequacy	13.8	11.6	11.5	9.6	.234	13.6	11.9	11.1	10.0	.293
Mental health	16.7	14.7	14.1	13.9	.079	16.3	15.1	14.3	14.1	.117
Performance norms	17.7	16.0	16.4	15.7	.107	18.0	16.3	16.5	15.5	.084

Table 33 also shows the mean of each morale-related variable for each of the section chief PM leadership types as well as the variance explained (η^2) in each variable by the four PM types. Statistically significant differences ($p < .01$) are again found in each morale-related variable according to the types of PM leadership. As for the subsection chiefs, PM leadership typically corresponded to the highest level of the morale-related variables followed by M, P, and finally pm leadership. However, the differences between the M and P leadership types were negligible for job satisfaction and satisfaction with compensation. Also as for subsection chiefs, the P leadership type corresponded to higher levels on performance norms than did the M leadership type.

The variance explained in the morale-related variables by the leadership types of section chiefs was the greatest for communication adequacy followed by meeting quality. As for subsection chiefs, the importance of leadership for communication-related issues appears to be greater for second-level supervisors in governmental organizations than for middle managers in private organizations. Otherwise, the association between PM types and morale-related variables is strikingly similar between the two organization types.

Summary of Governmental Leadership Studies

Field studies have now been described which were designed to compare the characteristics of managerial and supervisory leadership in governmental and private organizations. Items to measure leadership in private enterprises were first selected and empirically evaluated. In the government study, leadership inventories were first developed from open-ended descriptions of leadership, then separate, but largely overlapping, questionnaires were designed to measure the leadership of section chiefs and subsection chiefs. The validity of the government leadership questionnaires was evaluated by calculating the association between the four PM leadership types and seven aspects of employee morale. Although independently measured dependent variables were not available to evaluate the validity of the leadership measures in governmental settings, a limited amount of independent data (concerning achievement and driver accident rates) was available for certain industrial settings.

The study of governmental leadership was begun with the assumption that striking qualitative differences would be found between leadership in government organizations and in private enterprises. Several differences did appear. For example, no P-oriented factor pertaining to direct pressure for work performance and achievement was found in the government study. In government organizations, a clear "bottom-line" indication of organizational success equivalent to profit in private enterprises is not present. Government's responsibilities are oriented around somewhat vague goals such as promoting public welfare through laws and regulations while keeping within a fixed budget. Therefore, the emphasis of managerial and supervisory leadership in Japanese government is to maintain positive employee attitudes toward work by using such forms of leadership as "discipline-guidance" and "rule observance," rather than to achieve a readily quantified performance goal. The government leaders also emphasize maintaining adequate coordination and smooth communication with other sections in the same organization.

In general, the differences between private and governmental leadership primarily involve the work performance function. Leadership oriented toward group maintenance appears to be very similar between these two organization types. The lack of differences in the M function is consistent with the tentative conclusion that basic human relations between superiors and subordinates do not vary with the types of work being done in specific kinds of organizations.

The studies were also designed so that the associations of the four PM leadership types, assessed in ways most suited to each kind of organization, can be compared. No differences were found between governmental and private organizations in the ranking of the four PM types in terms of their association with other variables. For all of the criterion variables in both settings, PM-type leadership ranked first and pm-type leadership ranked last. For all criterion variables except performance norms, M-type leadership ranked second and P-type leadership ranked third. The reverse order of P-type and M-type leadership was found for performance norms in both settings. Such a high degree of similarity was not expected at the outset of the studies. The common conceptual basis of a general morphology of leadership behavior allowed similar basic leadership concepts to be studied in both settings. However, the specific, particular characteristics of government and industry had been expected to produce more substantial differences in the specific expression of the basic types than were actually found.

Although no differences were found between government and private organizations in the order of the associations of the four PM leadership types with criteria, some differences were found in the strength of association between the leadership types and various criteria besides the qualitative differences found in the P leadership dimension. The greatest associations between the four leadership types and the criterion variables were found for communication adequacy, teamwork, and job satisfaction. Differences among the four PM types were especially clear in communication adequacy for the first-line and second-line supervisors in government organizations. Greater differences among the PM types were found in teamwork and job satisfaction in private enterprises than in government organizations.

What may be called the "behavioral ecology" of leadership is the study of particular leadership phenomena which arise from specific work conditions in such settings as private enterprise and government organizations. However, the distinction between studies of specific behavior morphology and general behavior morphology is relative. Even as a single study is being designed, conducted, and interpreted, the emphasis can move back and forth like a ping-pong ball. During the course of an interdisciplinary research program encompassing the fields of public administration and business administration, traditional disciplinary boundaries can tend to suppress commonalities. If commonalities are not clarified, it becomes difficult to distinguish real differences in such phenomena as leadership from merely apparent differences. In the interest of effectively developing an interdisciplinary approach to the behavioral sciences, both similarities and differences in phenomena should be considered simultaneously.

CHAPTER 7

Leadership Provided for Children and Students

One way in which the interdisciplinary orientation of the PM leadership theory is expressed is in the treatment of leadership processes in field settings other than formal work organizations. In the PM leadership studies of schools, family groups, and sports groups, research methods have been designed which allow leadership directed toward basic group dynamics functions to be identified without assuming that the expressions of these basic functions are the same in these settings as they are in work organizations. The similarities and differences between leadership in work organizations and in other social settings is particularly useful for illustrating the necessity of both a general morphology and a specific morphology of leadership.

Leadership in Education

Leadership is at the center of any educational activity. While an unintentional action can be educational, educational excellence can only be brought about through the intentional guiding behavior which constitutes excellent educational leadership. Although education and leadership are indivisibly related, the study of leadership in education has a shorter history than does education itself. What are the essential requirements for educational leadership, then? Basically, educational leadership consists of a relationship between the leader and a group of the led. Educational leadership is a group phenomenon because it involves relations among more than two persons. A good school teacher known as an expert in a particular subject is often also known as an expert in creating a favorable class atmosphere. Lewin, in his paper entitled ''Experiments in Social Space,'' expressed the belief that classroom atmosphere can be a subject for experimental study. This paper was published in the 1939 issue of the *Harvard Educational Review,* a professional journal for school teachers. Lewin stated that the three leadership types being studied at that time—democratic, autocratic, and laissez-faire—created different ''social climates." In this article, he identified classroom education as a new field for the study of group dynamics.

Japan's primary education was influenced by Dewey's pupil-centered education during the period of the so-called Taisho democracy. This influence ceased during the military government period (1940–45). After World War II, American education gave a tremendous impetus to Japan's education again. Against this background, Nagasawa (1958), using fifty-one sixth graders as subjects, compared pupil-centered group learning with curriculum-centered learning, with the result that the pupil-centered guidance proved more effective.

Other studies showed that child-centered or pupil-centered education was inferior, including one by Asch (1951) comparing student-centered discussion and teacher-centered discussion, and one by Guetzkow (1951) that made comparisons between group discussion and recitation and between drill and individual guidance. Wispe (1951) compared instruction-oriented teaching and non-instruction-oriented teaching and reported that students preferred the former because it was more helpful in preparing for examinations. In Japan, Ishiguro (1955), using eighth graders as subjects, found no significant difference in overall scholastic achievement between unit learning and the traditional teaching method. Komuro (1955, 1956) found no significant differences between child-centered guidance utilizing discussion groups and teacher-centered guidance in the knowledge, understanding, and skill that fourth graders developed. However, they found that child-centered guidance excelled in developing spontaneous activity, independence, and cooperativeness. Similarly, Eglash (1954) found no significant difference in scholastic attainments between the two types of guidance. Although this finding does not necessarily imply that they have exactly the same effects, it is noteworthy that democratic guidance has been found more effective than autocratic guidance in some studies while the reverse has been found in others. When Misumi and his colleagues (Misumi and Haraoka 1958, 1960; Misumi and Nakano 1960*a*, 1960*b*) did experimental research similar to the Lewin, Lippitt, and White study (1939), they found that democratic guidance was more effective when the task given was easy for children to carry out and autocratic guidance was more effective when the task was difficult. These results may indicate that the effectiveness of leadership behavior in education varies according to the tasks given to students as has been found in studies of behavior in other fields.

It is not easy to assess the educational advantages of different types of leadership because the effects of educational leadership must be judged according to complex criteria measured over an extended period of time. However, assuming that something universal and basic must apply to leadership behavior in school settings, hospitals, government offices, and private firms, work was begun to measure school teachers' leadership using the concepts and methods that have been described in the preceding discussions of industrial organizations and government offices.

Factor Analytic Studies of Teachers' Leadership Behavior

A number of factor analysis studies of teacher behavior have been conducted in Japan and other countries. Kishida (1958, 1959) identified three types of teachers according to the attitudes which male and female children had toward them. The first type do not endear themselves to children, the second type endear themselves to girls but alienate boys, and the third type endear themselves to both boys and girls.

Takeuchi and Yabuki (1961), using Stephenson's (1953) Q-technique, identified three factors in elementary school teachers' educational attitudes. The first was a factor of compulsion-freedom, the second a factor of leniency-strictness, and the third a factor of unity-alienation.

Tokuda (1962) used Kerlinger's (1956) Q-technique to study the attitudes toward education of college psychology and education professors as well as teachers of elementary, junior high, and senior high schools. Using the centroid method, he found three factors: progressivism, traditionalism, and psychology. Akune (1973) measured teachers' leadership using pupils' ratings and came up with "consideration for learning" as a first factor, "teachers' tolerance, friendliness and confidence toward their pupils" as a second factor, and "discipline and pressure for training and instruction" as a third factor. Haraoka and Shinohara (1975) identified factors in teachers' leadership behavior in a study of junior high school students. The five factors they identified were: (1) considerate instruction, (2) communication concerning matters other than the task assigned, (3) pressure for task achievement, (4) friendliness and motivation, and (5) training concerning the task assigned.

In the United States, Anderson and Brewer (1945) pioneered in the study of school teachers' leadership patterns. They reported that teachers' "accommodating" behavior tended to promote pupils' spontaneity. Further, in schools where teachers behaved in a dominant manner pupils showed uncooperative attitudes toward their teachers, thus giving rise to friction. Withall (1949, 1952) classified teachers' behavior into "student-centered" and "teacher-centered," the former involving more social-emotional support than the latter. Flanders (1951) trained teachers so that they could behave in both teacher-centered and student-centered ways. Flanders (1960) was also able to use behavior observation methods to classify teachers' behavior into "indirect influence" and "direct influence." Amidon and Flanders (1961) further pursued the study to determine whether or not there was any relationship between these two approaches to influence and pupils' sense of dependence.

Reviewing these studies, three important points are evident.

1. The studies were primarily limited to classifying teachers' leadership types and failed to fully examine their relationships to external criteria.
2. In many cases, dimensions of teachers' leadership behavior were identified solely on the basis of factor analytic results without reference to any systematic, integrating conceptual scheme.
3. Others of these prior studies which did not use factor analysis to identify leadership dimensions were conceptually ambiguous and operationally equivocal.

The studies of teacher leadership based on the PM theory were designed to overcome some of these limitations.

A PM Study of Teachers' Leadership Behavior

A measure of teachers' leadership behavior focusing on classroom leadership was designed on the basis of the PM leadership theory. Before the studies of educational leadership were begun, the PM concept already had been applied to several leadership situations outside education. It was hoped that successfully applying the PM concepts to educational situations would allow hypotheses about teacher leadership to be developed based on this prior research.

Questionnaire Preparation

Preparation of a questionnaire to measure teachers' leadership behavior was carried out in several steps. First, it was necessary to gather concrete information about the kinds of leadership behavior teachers show in schools. In order to obtain this information, elementary school teachers from all over Fukuoka City were asked to describe their behavior in an unstructured way. Also, one of Misumi's collaborators, Yoshizaki, joined a fifth grade class in order to share school life with the pupils for two weeks and observe their teacher's behavior. Subsequently, a forty-six-item questionnaire was drafted in collaboration with an ad hoc committee of elementary school teachers each having over ten years' teaching experience. This group met more than ten times over a one-year period to help draw up the questionnaire using all of the material being collected. Since the respondents to be studied were fifth and sixth graders, particular care was exercised to make the questionnaire easily comprehensible to children in this age bracket. The same committee designed another questionnaire concerning school morale for use as an external criterion variable.

A twenty-item "morale" questionnaire was developed to serve as a criterion for evaluating school teachers' leadership behavior. Each item was designed to be rated on a five-point scale. Each teacher's students were used as respondents. The results were then factor analyzed. As a result of the factor analysis, sixteen items were finally selected for further analysis: four items concerning the cohesiveness of the class, three items concerning the class's observance of discipline, three items concerning willingness to study, and six items concerning dissatisfaction with school.

Method

Elementary school teachers in the public school system of Fukuoka City were studied using pupils' ratings to assess their leadership. Out of one hundred elementary schools run by Fukuoka City, twenty schools were selected to represent the various geographic areas of the city. Two fifth grade and two sixth grade classes were selected at each school from among the teachers who volunteered to participate. The data from 3,007 pupils were actually used for analysis. The breakdown of the pupils used as subjects was as follows: boys 50.6 percent, girls 49.1 percent, fifth graders 48.1 percent, sixth graders 51.2 percent. During the first few weeks of February, 1976, the survey was administered on a group basis in each classroom. The questionnaire was passed out to each pupil and the interviewer read it aloud item by item with each pupil checking the response they selected on a five-point scale.

Results

The results of the data were analyzed in four steps: (1) Factor analysis of the forty-six items concerning leadership; (2) Selection of items to measure PM behavior on the basis of the group principal axis factor analysis method; (3) Factor analysis of the twenty items about school morale; (4) Analyses to assess the relationship between teachers' leadership types and pupils' school morale.

Factor Analyses Concerning Teachers' Leadership Behavior

The principal axis method (with communalities set at 1.0) was used to extract factors which were then rotated using the usual varimax method. A five-factor solution was selected as being the most interpretable after two-factor through nine-factor solutions were considered. The factor loading matrix for the five-factor solution is shown in table 34.

The factors can be interpreted by considering those items which showed over .500 factor loadings on one factor and less than .400 factor loadings on all the other factors. The items which showed high loadings on the first factor included ten items such as "Q1: Does your teacher understand your feelings?" (.721). This first factor was labeled "teachers' consideration for pupils.'' The six items which showed high loadings on the second factor covered such topics as ''Q13: Does your teacher scold you when you forget to bring your school things?'' (.695). This factor was called ''discipline and training concerning life and learning.'' The items which showed high loadings on the third factor were four items including ''Q23: Does your teacher play with you all?'' (.671). This factor was called ''teachers' friendliness toward pupils.'' Three items showed high loadings on the fourth factor including ''Q29: Does your teacher sometimes talk about things besides school subjects during class?'' (.732). The fourth factor was given the label ''easing tension in the class.'' The eight items which showed high loadings on the fifth factor included ''Q32: Does your teacher tell you to take good care of school supplies?'' (.592). The fifth factor was called ''training and discipline for promoting social and moral values.''

When classified according to the PM leadership theory, the second and fifth factors are closely associated with the concepts of goal achievement or performance behavior (P behavior) while the first, third, and fourth factors pertain to group maintenance behavior (M behavior). In school settings, P leadership involves urging pupils to study hard and to solve the personal problems they encounter in growing up and helping them learn to conduct meetings and discussion sessions. M behavior by teachers involves giving every consideration to pupils, treating them equally and fairly, avoiding unnecessary tension, and trying to ease any tensions that do occur.

Selection of Items to Measure PM Behavior, Using the Group Principal Axis Method

The items that showed high factor loadings on one of the five factors were divided into five groups corresponding to the five factors. The group principal axis method was then used to produce composite variables that formed the principal axes. Each of the five composite variables are formed using the items which showed the highest loadings on each of the five varimax rotated factors previously identified. Correlations between each item and the resulting composite variables are shown in table 34. The five columns on the far left indicate the composite variable to which each item was assigned. The next five columns indicate the correlation between each item and each composite variable.

The first composite variable corresponds to the factor of ''consideration.'' The items in this group generally show correlations between .604 and .807 with the composite variable (the only exception being Q6 and Q10). The items comprising the second through fifth composite variables all show correlations exceeding .500 with the respective composite variable. In all five cases, the correlations indicate that each composite variable is reasonably homogenous.

TABLE 34. Factor Analysis of Teachers' Leadership Behavior

Item	*[a]					**[b]					*		**	
	I	II	III	IV	V	I	II	III	IV	V	I	II	I	II
1. Understands pupils' feelings	1	0	0	0	0	.807	.034	.293	−.046	.357	0	1	.211	.791
2. Finds out about pupils' feelings by talking things over with them	1	0	0	0	0	.789	.081	.360	−.015	.449	0	1	.290	.792
3. Does not show favoritism and treats all pupils equally	1	0	0	0	0	.709	−.019	.279	−.083	.318	0	1	.150	.694
4. Listens carefully to what pupils say	1	0	0	0	0	.742	.127	.353	−.093	.396	0	1	.283	.751
5. Teaches in a way which makes it easy for pupils to learn	1	0	0	0	0	.658	.194	.290	−.025	.396	0	1	.330	.675
6. Gets angry easily	1	0	0	0	0	−.435	.270	−.006	.120	.034	0	0	.196	−.299
7. Does not scold pupils immediately when they make mistakes, but tries to find out why the mistakes were made	1	0	0	0	0	.655	.036	.260	−.023	.328	0	1	.205	.639
8. Ready to give advice when pupils have problems	1	0	0	0	0	.708	.131	.330	−.070	.388	0	1	.277	.728
9. Explains things clearly so that pupils understand their lessons well	1	0	0	0	0	.604	.163	.246	.006	.342	0	1	.274	.613
10. Scolds endlessly	1	0	0	0	0	−.409	.213	−.079	−.015	.024	0	0	.135	−.285
11. Dismisses class immediately when the school day is over	0	0	0	0	0	.347	−.013	.179	−.055	.094	0	0	.044	.325
12. Praises pupils	0	0	0	0	0	.521	.227	.324	−.091	.416	0	0	.359	.542
13. Scolds pupils when they forget to bring school things	0	1	0	0	0	−.012	.719	.021	.067	.187	1	0	.567	.023
14. Cautions pupils not to forget their school things	0	1	0	0	0	.114	.771	.108	.011	.355	1	0	.706	.156
15. Is strict in telling students to do their homework	0	1	0	0	0	.088	.688	.191	.003	.269	1	0	.591	.141
16. Strict about details such as wearing name tags and bringing handkerchiefs	0	1	0	0	0	.115	.673	.140	.059	.312	1	0	.608	.145

Continued

TABLE 34—*Continued*

Item	*[a]					**[b]					*		**	
	I	II	III	IV	V	I	II	III	IV	V	I	II	I	II
17. Is always telling pupils to "work harder, work harder"	0	1	0	0	0	−.163	.563	.009	.006	.141	0	0	.348	−.109
18. Urges pupils to keep their desks and school bags in order and to hang their caps in the proper place	0	1	0	0	0	.109	.580	.213	.021	.303	1	0	.541	.147
19. Urges pupils to show their report cards to their parents	0	0	0	0	0	.065	.360	.159	.049	.205	0	0	.327	.105
20. Tells pupils not to watch television too much	0	0	0	0	0	.078	.414	.088	.018	.334	0	0	.413	.106
21. Scolds pupils when they forget to perform their group task to clean up after school	0	0	0	0	0	.023	.418	.138	.022	.338	0	0	.462	.067
22. Gives homework assignments	0	0	0	0	0	−.103	.344	.083	−.080	.076	0	0	.259	−.062
23. Plays with pupils	0	0	1	0	0	.306	.025	.721	.103	.177	0	1	.116	.421
24. Checks pupils' notebooks	0	0	1	0	0	.182	.236	.618	−.055	.232	0	0	.270	.237
25. Moves around the class to work with pupils individually	0	0	1	0	0	.288	.121	.693	−.069	.210	0	1	.187	.410
26. Talks with pupils over lunch during the lunch periods	0	0	1	0	0	.293	.089	.666	−.071	.281	0	0	.198	.337
27. Checks homework assignments	0	0	0	0	0	.143	.324	.388	−.054	.103	0	0	.264	.195
28. Is available to teach during breaks or after school if pupils do not understand something	0	0	0	0	0	.437	.188	.391	.001	.304	0	0	.276	.478
29. Sometimes talks about things besides school subjects during class	0	0	0	1	0	−.097	.064	−.085	.846	.033	0	0	.064	−.085
30. Makes pupils laugh by saying funny things	0	0	0	1	0	.214	.138	.154	.725	.234	0	0	.220	.226
31. Sees that pupils keep their desktops neat	0	0	0	1	0	.337	.173	.164	−.525	.224	0	0	.222	.333
32. Tells pupils to take good care of school supplies	0	0	0	0	1	.216	.254	.135	.056	.608	1	0	.518	.247
33. Tells pupils to be friendly with one another	0	0	0	0	1	.339	.231	.240	.079	.702	1	0	.547	.369

34. Tells pupils to state their opinions clearly	0	0	0	0	1	.278	.268	.221	.071	.669	1	0	.573	.313
35. Strict about observing regulations	0	0	0	0	1	.185	.372	.177	−.015	.624	1	0	.612	.232
36. Encourages pupils to help one another in their studies and in physical exercises	0	0	0	0	1	.386	.185	.287	.011	.675	0	0	.408	.404
37. Tells pupils not to discriminate against anyone	0	0	0	0	1	.360	.174	.126	.073	.583	0	0	.364	.375
38. Is careful to make sure that air is circulating in and out in the classroom	0	0	0	0	1	.316	.209	.257	−.061	.544	0	0	.350	.337
39. Tells pupils not to hesitate to ask other pupils about something they do not understand or to try to find out themselves	0	0	0	0	1	.307	.285	.212	.035	.607	1	0	.550	.326
40. Tells pupils to eat the lunch served at school no matter whether they like or dislike the food being served	0	0	0	0	0	.202	.266	.147	−.025	.353	0	0	.350	.234
41. Tells pupils not to laugh when someone gives a wrong answer	0	0	0	0	0	.394	.117	.241	.008	.414	0	0	.295	.411
42. Teaches table manners when they have a meal	0	0	0	0	0	.169	.362	.172	.044	.391	0	0	.435	.211
43. Teaches pupils how to give reports in class	0	0	0	0	0	.314	.249	.249	.064	.446	0	0	.389	.336
44. Tells pupils to watch television programs related to school subjects and to read newspapers and books	0	0	0	0	0	.229	.320	.131	.035	.398	0	0	.389	.246
45. Says ''Good morning'' and ''Goodbye''	0	0	0	0	0	.472	.102	.357	−.108	.367	0	0	.261	.494
46. Scolds pupils for whispering or playing with toys while at school	0	0	0	0	0	−.012	.343	.114	.009	.263	0	0	.383	.028
Eigen value						4.412	2.693	1.826	1.516	3.158			3.402	4.412
Contribution (in group items) %						44.12	44.88	45.65	50.53	39.48			34.02	44.12

[a] * = Grouping of items in group principal axis method

[b] ** = Correlations between composite variables and items in group principal axis method

Table 35 shows the correlations among the five composite variables. The fourth composite variable which includes items concerning easing tension showed uniformly low correlations with the other composite variables. The second composite variable, including items concerning discipline and training for life and learning, showed low correlations with the first composite variable representing consideration (.070) and the third composite variable representing friendliness (.168), but showed a moderate correlation of .393 with the fifth composite variable concerning promoting social and moral values. The first composite variable showed correlations of .399 with the third composite variable and .474 with the fifth composite variable. These results imply that the factor concerning promoting social and moral values which conceptually fits with P leadership was perceived as partially reflecting "consideration."

As stated above, the second and fifth factors are conceptually related to P behavior while the first, third, and fourth factors pertain to M behavior. In order to measure P and M leadership, those items which showed high factor loadings on either the second or fifth factors were included in the group of P behavior items. By the same token, the items which showed high factor loadings on either the first, third, or fourth factors were included in the group of M behavior items. These two groups were then used to form the composite variables for the group principal axes of P and M leadership. These were analyzed by means of the group principal axes method keeping in mind the need to maintain low correlations between the P and M composite variables because of the conceptual distinction between these behavior dimensions. The results of this analysis are shown in the last four columns of table 34.

A fairly low correlation coefficient of .354 was found between the two composite variables when Q13, 14, 15, 16, 18, 32, 33, 34, 35, and 39 were included in the P behavior group and Q1, 2, 3, 4, 5, 7, 8, 9, 23, and 25 were included in the M behavior group. The correlation coefficients between the composite variables and their component items are shown in the right column of table 34. The correlations of Q33 and Q25 with their composite variables is rather low, but all the other items showed high correlations with the composite variables to which they belonged. Based on the above analyses, ten

TABLE 35. Correlations among Composite Variables

Composite	I	II	III	IV	V
I	1.000				
II	.070	1.000			
III	.399	.168	1.000		
IV	−.068	.042	−.030	1.000	
V	.474	.393	.331	.053	1.000

items were selected to measure P behavior (Q13, 14, 15, 16, 18, 32, 33, 34, 35, and 39) and another ten items (Q1, 2, 3, 4, 5, 7, 8, 9, 23, and 25) were chosen to represent M behavior.

Factor Analysis of School Morale Items

Factors were extracted for the school morale variables using the same procedure as the one applied to the leadership items. A four-factor solution was used to determine if the four variables intended as the external criterion variables could be identified. The four-factor solution was considered adequate since it represents 49.6 percent of the variance in the items being analyzed. The factor loading matrix is shown in table 36. The factors were interpreted and named on the basis of those items which showed factor loadings exceeding .500 on one factor and loadings less than .400 on all the other factors.

The four items that showed high loadings on the first factor included "Q1: Is there a pleasant atmosphere in your class?" (.845). This factor was named "cohesiveness in the class." Six items had high loadings on the second factor. These included "Q5: Do you ever feel like being absent from school?" (.785). The second factor was labeled "dissatisfaction with school." The three items which showed high loadings on the third factor included "Q11: Do you like to study hard?" (.698). This factor was called "willingness to study." Three items showed high loadings on the fourth factor. These included "Q14: Does your class stick to the goals that class members have set for themselves?" (−.724). The fourth factor was named "observing discipline."

TABLE 36. Factor Analysis of School Morale Items

	Factor Loading				
Item	I	II	III	IV	h^2
1. Is there a pleasant atmosphere in your class?	.845	−.172	.007	−.052	.746
2. Is there an exciting atmosphere in your class?	.837	−.112	−.003	−.062	.717
3. Is your class a tightly knit group, and better than other classes?	.612	−.075	.057	−.334	.495
4. Are you glad when someone praises your class?	.493	−.089	.220	−.227	.351
5. Do you ever feel like being absent from school?	−.116	.785	.016	.117	.643
6. Are there any times when you hate going to school?	−.199	.784	.037	.147	.678

Continued

TABLE 36—*Continued*

Item	Factor Loading I	II	III	IV	h^2
7. Are there any times when you cannot understand the subject you are studying and lose all interest in studying at all?	.008	.647	−.297	.062	.511
8. Do you find it more interesting to play than to go to school?	−.156	.581	−.128	.191	.415
9. Do you feel that you cannot keep up with other pupils no matter how hard you study?	−.077	.580	−.242	−.047	.397
10. Do you enjoy going to school?	.441	−.545	.166	−.104	.530
11. Do you like to study hard?	.110	.004	.698	−.092	.508
12. Do you find it interesting to study, because you can understand the subject you are studying very well?	.229	−.297	.669	−.037	.590
13. Do you study at home because you want to study?	−.022	−.166	.630	−.102	.436
14. Does your class stick to the goals that class members have set for themselves?	.120	−.109	.111	−.724	.563
15. Do your class members work hard when cleaning your classroom?	.121	−.097	.033	−.717	.540
16. Does everyone in your class carry out the group task of cleaning up after school?	.111	−.099	.098	−.671	.481
17. Are there many pupils who are so selfish that there is no unity in your class?	−.321	.292	.198	.459	.438
18. Do you feel like transferring to some other school?	−.372	.420	.223	.106	.376
19. Do you enjoy your school lunch hour?	.402	−.101	.138	−.122	.206
20. Are your class meetings very active?	.296	.023	.258	−.392	.308
Factor variance	2.901	3.094	1.774	2.157	9.926
Contribution (%)	14.51	15.47	8.87	10.79	49.63

Relationship between Teachers' Leadership Types and Pupils' Morale

The classification of teachers' leadership types. Ratings by 3,007 pupils were used to classify teachers' leadership types. Teachers who received scores exceeding the average P and M scores (P = 37.70, M = 34.08) were classified as PM-type teachers; those who received P and M scores below the average were classified as pm-type teachers; those who received P scores above the average P scores and M scores below the average M scores were classified as P-type teachers; those who received lower P scores than the average P scores and higher M scores than the average M scores were classified as M-type teachers. Each teacher's leadership scores were represented by the average of the scores given by his or her pupils (36.2 pupils on the average). The 83 teachers rated were classified into four types as follows: 23 as PM, 18 as P, 16 as M, and 26 as pm. Of the 3,007 pupils, 830 were under the guidance of PM-type teachers, 658 pupils under P, 559 under M, and 960 under pm teachers.

Pupils' morale variables as external criteria. Four factors were used as the basis for forming external criterion variables. These factors were represented by sixteen items: class solidarity (Q1–4), dissatisfaction with school (Q5–10), willingness to study (Q11–13), and observance of discipline (Q14–16). The indices used to measure these variables were formed by summing the items in each set.

The relationship between teachers' leadership types and morale variables. Table 37 shows the averages for each of the morale variables separately for each type of teacher leadership. Statistically significant differences were found among the four leadership types for all of the factors. The PM type showed the highest scores of any type for the factors of class cohesiveness, willingness to study, and observance of discipline and the lowest scores for the factor of dissatisfaction with school. The pm type showed the second highest scores after P on the factor of dissatisfaction with school and the lowest scores for all the other three factors. The M type showed the second lowest scores after PM on the factor of dissatisfaction with school and the second highest scores after PM on all the other three factors. The P leadership type showed the highest scores on the factor of dissatisfaction with school and the third highest score on all the other three factors. Generally speaking, pupils' school morale is highest under PM-type teachers followed by M, P, and pm teachers in that order. This order is consistent with that found in businesses and government offices. Judging from the squared correlations (representing variance explained) and Cramer's coefficients (data not shown), the effects of leadership manifest themselves most conspicuously in the factors of class solidarity and discipline observance.

General Discussion

In the study of educational leadership, PM was found to be the most effective leadership type, followed by M, P, and pm in that order. In order to evaluate the validity of these leadership types for promoting learning, however, it will be necessary to consider their relationship to scholastic attainments while taking into account intelligence and other important variables. These topics will be left for future study. Also remaining for future research is a method for measuring the leadership behavior of instructors who teach children other than fifth and sixth graders. Consequently, it is premature to draw any general conclusion about all educational leadership based on this particular study. Still, it is important to notice that the order of the four PM leadership types for these school teachers is the same as it is for managers and supervisors in private industry and government offices.

The items used to measure P and M leadership obviously had to differ among the questionnaires designed for private industries, government offices, and schools. The leadership types were classified and their validity assessed on the basis of these differing questionnaires. Still, the leadership types were ranked in the same order according to the different criterion variables used in the studies of private organizations, government offices, and schools. If these findings continue to prove replicable, then each of these specific and limited settings do not need to be considered unrelated. Instead, a broadly applicable PM theory of leadership in Japan can be developed which cuts across professional lines.

Parental Leadership in Family Groups

The second major source of adult leadership experienced by children besides teacher leadership is the leadership provided by their parents. Parental leadership differs from educational leadership in the biological basis, enduring

TABLE 37. Mean School Morale Scores under Teachers Showing Each Leadership Type

Morale Variable	Leadership Types: PM	P	M	pm	Total Mean	F-ratio	Squared Correlation Ratio (r^2)
Cohesiveness in the class	16.63 (2.80)	15.07 (3.72)	16.15 (3.08)	14.17 (3.44)	15.41 (3.43)	96.18*	.088
Dissatisfaction with school[a]	14.58 (4.54)	16.52 (5.06)	14.79 (4.33)	16.13 (4.60)	15.54 (4.71)	31.56*	.031
Willingness to study	10.29 (2.25)	9.86 (2.45)	9.99 (2.41)	9.36 (2.55)	9.83 (2.45)	22.44*	.022
Observing discipline	9.91 (2.27)	8.93 (2.34)	9.03 (2.02)	8.59 (2.27)	9.11 (2.30)	53.72*	.051

Note: Values in parentheses are standard deviations.
[a]Smaller scores indicate greater satisfaction.
*$p < .01$

character, intimacy, and broad overall responsibility which parental leadership involves. The study of parental leadership from the perspective of PM theory is an important component of an interdisciplinary perspective which attempts to deal meaningfully with leadership in all kinds of human groups.

Unlike schools, hospitals, and other work organizations, the family is not an instrumental group which is organized to perform tasks or solve problems. The family is a human group whose members consist of parents, their children, and/or close relatives, and whose "purpose" includes all the complexities of living together as a group. However, in maintaining its viability, the family cannot avoid adapting to changes in its surrounding environment. The family takes on an instrumental role in this process of adaptation by promoting problem solving and goal attainment by individual members.

In the adaptation process of the family, leadership is a necessary group function. Parental leadership is typically the primary form of leadership. Leadership in the family is also manifested in personal relationships between wife and husband or among siblings, and in grandparents' leadership of children. However, the most explicit leadership relationship in the family is between parents (or parental substitutes) and children. Since childrearing roles and expectations are culturally established in Japan, parental leadership is clarified by recognized duties and responsibilities.

The relationship between parents and children ordinarily involves two interrelated roles. The biologically based role developed through childrearing and nursing is the role which reflects the basic purpose of the family relationship. At the same time, the relation between parent and child includes a value-expressive function which involves the child's training and discipline. Thus parental leadership can potentially be evaluated according to normative value-related criteria. Good instrumental parental leadership may not, however, correspond to parental behavior which is conscious, systematic, or purposely directed toward the child.

Sometimes the nonpurposeful, unconscious, and nonsystematic expression of natural love can be evaluated as positive leadership, while overprotection of a child can be evaluated as negative leadership. Further, parental behavior toward children which might be evaluated as negative by an observer sometimes may be considered positive according to the child's standards for evaluating parental acceptance. Thus research must carefully consider the viewpoint being taken on parental leadership in order to establish appropriate criteria for evaluating its effectiveness.

Research on Parent-Child Interaction

Many factor analytic studies of parental leadership behavior or childrearing attitudes have been published. In a review of factor analytic studies of children's descriptions of their parents' behavior, Goldin (1969) mentioned Schaefer's (1965) and Seigelman's (1965) research as representative.

Schaefer extracted three orthogonal factors from the CR-PBI (Children's Report of Parental Behavior Inventory). These factors were Acceptance-Rejection (A-R), Psychological Autonomy–Psychological Control (PA-PC), and Firm Control–Lax Control (FC-LC). Similarly, Seigelman derived three orthogonal factors labeled "Loving," "Demanding," and "Punishment." The corresponding factors in both studies are almost identical. Seigelman's "Loving" factor refers to parental support, participation, praise, and affection for the child, while Schaefer's A-R factor involves expressions of affective support, positive evaluation, and equalitarian treatment at one pole and detached hostile reactions at the other pole. A close correspondence also appears between PA-PC and "Demanding." PA-PC refers to behavior which facilitates or impairs a child's ability to develop independently from the parents, while "Demanding" refers to controlling, demanding, protective, and intrusive parental behaviors. One difference between "Demanding" and PA-PC is that "Demanding" incorporates strictness to a greater extent than does PA-PC. The "Punishment" factor is somewhat different from FC-LC. While the FC-LC factor refers to establishing and enforcing rules and regulations, "Punishment" refers to arbitrarily using physical and nonphysical punishment with little concern for the feelings and needs of the child.

But Goldin, in his review of factor analytic studies and other studies examining children's reports of parental behavior, found that a large portion of earlier research included variables which could be classified into the Schaefer-Seigelman category of A-R (Loving). Over 60 percent of the articles dealt with some variation of "acceptance" such as democratic family relations and affective family adjustment. In addition, a number of other studies have dealt with a global evaluation of the negative or positive quality of family relations. More than 50 percent of the studies reported in the literature investigated variables such as dominance, intrusive parental direction, demand for achievement, and indulgence, restriction, and power. These variables are related to the "Demanding" and PA-PC factors. Over 40 percent of past studies included variables concerning parental punishment. These studies dealt exclusively with punitive treatment, aggression, and hostility primarily of a physical character. However, this hostility also involves destructive psychological influences.

Two researchers followed similar methods in research outside of the United States. In Japan, Kojima (1968, 1970, 1973) found three factors using the CR-PBI: Acceptance-Rejection, Psychological Autonomy–Psychological Control, and Firm Control–Lax Control. Similarly, Renson, Schaefer, and Levy (1968) found three factors in the CR-PBI administered in Belgium:

Acceptance-Rejection, Psychological Autonomy–Psychological Control, and Lax Control–Firm Control. These findings provide evidence that the three factors of the CR-PBI have a certain degree of cross-cultural validity.

The studies briefly described are representative of factor analytic parental leadership studies. An "experimental" approach has also been taken to parental leadership through the use of a typological conceptual scheme. Symonds (1939) proposed to use the graph shown in figure 7 to represent different types of parental leadership. The two dimensions of Rejection-Acceptance and Dominant-Submissive were used to define the X axis and Y axis respectively to represent parent-child relations. He argued that the point of intersection (0,0) is the ideal parent-child relation type.

Ishiguro and Fujiwara (1954) studied authoritarian, overprotective (dotage), laissez-faire, and democratic patterns of parental childrearing attitudes. A factor analysis of their data revealed the two factors of "Love" and "Compulsion." According to Ishiguro and Fujiwara, the laissez-faire pattern does not contain either love or compulsion, the democratic pattern contains love but not compulsion, and the overprotective and authoritarian types include both love and compulsion. Though obvious phenomenological differences are evident between the dotage and authoritarian types (the doting parent tends to

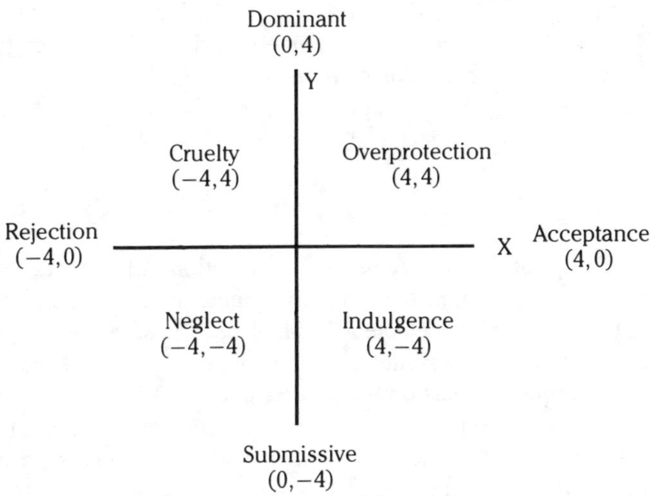

Fig. 7. Types of relationships between parents and children

use love as an outlet) there is no fundamental difference between these two forms. Furthermore, the researchers write, "it is estimated that the dotage parent type is substantively similar to the authoritarian type, because the child, either consciously or unconsciously, equates the parents' blind love with external compulsion" (p. 38). Summarizing the literature, Furukawa (1970) suggested that a combination of two kinds of parental leadership is preferred for the development of a child. One is emotional interaction which is necessary for the child's well-being and for maintaining and reinforcing the parent-child relationship. The other is socialization, or discipline and training for adaptation to society and for facilitating independent learning on the part of the child. The first of these can be identified with the maintenance function (M) while the second can be equated with the performance function (P) in PM leadership theory.

Study of Parental Leadership for Elementary School Children

Furukawa, Misumi, and Shinohara (1969) studied 211 elementary school children (age ten to eleven) living in Fukuoka. They used a questionnaire to study the parental leadership of the children's fathers and mothers. Two main factors were revealed. One factor includes items of parental guidance and strictness while the second includes items of parental loving and emotional support. The researchers called Factor I "performance" and Factor II "maintenance." Factor I accounted for 33.6 percent of the total variance for fathers and 30.2 percent for mothers. Factor II accounted for 44.4 percent of the total variance for fathers and 36.5 percent for mothers. Furukawa prepared parental leadership measures based on the PM factors.

Method

Children's perceptions and parents' self-perceptions of parental leadership were first measured. Similarities and differences in perceptions were then assessed. Sixty items were selected that had been used earlier in studies of parent-child relationships. Parallel questions were asked of children and their parents. For example, a question for parents asks, "Do you tell your child to study harder?" while the item for children is, "Does your mother (or father) tell you to study harder?" The five-point response alternatives for each kind of item are similar. Furukawa found two factors (P and M factors) in the questions asked of children.

Another questionnaire was designed to measure criterion variables which could be used to evaluate the validity of these two factors. The questionnaire contained several aspects of children's general attitude toward their parents.

These attitude items concerned (1) understanding, (2) compliance, (3) pride, and (4) intimacy. Each item was responded to using a five-point scale. The validity of the four PM types was evaluated against these external criteria.

The respondents were sixth grade children in elementary schools in Fukuoka (N = 135), their fathers (N = 108), and their mothers (N = 132). The fathers' mean age was 43, and the mothers' mean age was 39.

Results

Items were selected with factor scores over 0.5 on either of two parental leadership factors to use in classifying parents into the PM leadership types. Since the number of items with loadings over 0.5 was very small for mothers' self-descriptions, items with loadings of over 0.4 were selected for this group. Ten P-function items and ten M-function items were selected (table 38).

Table 39 shows the means and standard deviations for the P and M scores. P and M scores which parents give themselves are higher than those which children give their parents. This tendency is similar to the difference found in business (Misumi 1972) between superiors' self-reports and subordinates' reports. There are no significant differences between children's and mothers' descriptions of mothers' M leadership, however.

The correlations between the P and M scores which parents give themselves and those which are given to them by their children are reported in table 40. None of the correlations between parents' self-reports and children's reports of parental leadership is particularly high. Although the correlations between mothers' self-reports and children's reports are significant and higher than those between the reports of fathers and children, they are not very high. These low correlations are consistent with the low correlations between self- and subordinate ratings found in other settings such as government offices and industry. Even though the same basic questionnaire is being used, the differences between parents' descriptions and children's descriptions of parental leadership is quite substantial.

The correlations between self-reports of fathers and mothers are significant. High correlations also appear between children's description of the leadership provided by their father and mother (.703 for P, .637 for M). These correlations are higher than the correlations between fathers' and mothers' self-reports. It may be that since the leadership behavior of fathers and mothers is similar the correlation between the two scores is high.

Tables 41 and 42 show the associations between the parental leadership types measured through parents' self-reports and through children's reports. Descriptions were classified as either high or low on the P and M dimensions depending on whether they were above or below the mean scores based on the children's descriptions of their parents. Although a small degree of correspon-

TABLE 38. Questionnaire Items Used to Measure Parental Leadership

Describe your father and mother.

M Items:

1. Does your father praise you for your good behavior and work?
   How about your mother?
2. Does your father stand by you?
   How about your mother?
3. Does your father try to make your home cheerful?
   How about your mother?
4. Do you help your father?
   How about your mother?
5. Do you obey your father's orders?
   How about your mother's?
6. When you face a problem that you cannot solve by yourself, is your father eager to help you?
   How about your mother?
7. When you get in trouble or are worried about something can you ask your father for advice?
   How about your mother?
8. Is your father careful not to let you get sick or hurt?
   How about your mother?
9. When you are studying, does your father turn down the TV and radio?
   How about your mother?
10. Does your father play with you and help you study?
    How about your mother?

P Items:

11. Does your father tell you not to whine or make noise in the house?
    How about your mother?
12. Does your father tell you to behave politely and follow the rules?
    How about your mother?
13. Does your father give you strict rules about using your allowance?
    How about your mother?
14. Does your father tell you to put away your toys and study materials?
    How about your mother?
15. Does your father tell you to be punctual about things like going to bed on time and not being late for school?
    How about your mother?
16. When you need to do something difficult, does your father tell you to do it by yourself?
    How about your mother?
17. Does your father tell you to play with good friends?
    How about your mother?
18. Does your father scold you severely when you do something wrong?
    How about your mother?
19. Does your father force his orders on you?
    How about your mother?
20. Does your father tell you to become a respectable person?
    How about your mother?

Note: The response alternatives were: (1) Always, (2) Sometimes, (3) Not at all.

TABLE 39. Means and Standard Deviations for Measures of P and M Leadership

Parent	Rater	P Function		M Function	
Father (N = 108)	Self	31.94 (5.87)	τ = 5.50*	36.44 (5.39)	τ = 3.57*
	Child	27.49 (5.91)		33.52 (6.79)	
Mother (N = 132)	Self	34.38 (4.50)	τ = 3.47*	37.57 (4.16)	τ = 1.47
	Child	32.09 (4.89)		36.54 (5.89)	

Note: Standard deviations are shown in parentheses following mean scores.
*$p < .001$

dence is found between children's reports and fathers' reports that the father provides a PM type of leadership, no substantial correspondence between children's reports and parents' reports appears in the table as a whole. In parental self-reports, the PM type appears most frequently followed by the P, M, and finally pm types.

Relationships were also assessed between the four parental leadership types based on both parental self-reports and children's descriptions and children's attitude scores. The results for PM types based on parents' self-reports are presented in table 43 while those based on children's reports are presented in table 44. Children generally express the most positive attitudes (understanding, compliance, show more positive understanding, reliance, famil-

TABLE 40. Correlations among P and M Scores

Fathers' self-reports	P	.481*	M		Mothers' self-reports	P	.337*	M
	.154		.248			.272*		.308*
Children's reports for fathers	P	.408*	M		Children's reports for mothers	P	.147	M
Fathers' self-reports	P		M		Children's reports for fathers	P		M
	.437		.514*			.703*		.637*
Mothers' self-reports	P		M		Children's reports for mothers	P		M

*$p < .05$

iarity, intimacy, respect, and pride) for parents who rate themselves as being PM and P types, and for parents whom the children rate as being PM and M types. PM-type parents have children who tend to express positive attitudes, regardless of whether the leadership rating is done by the parents or the children. However, the apparent appropriateness of the P and M leadership types differs depending on whether parents or children are describing parental leadership.

How can this difference be interpreted? Perhaps parental self-reports are a defensive response. But the relationship that a child experiences with a parent is formed through conscious as well as unconscious actions by the parent. Thus when children describe parental leadership, they may respond to the parent's unconscious behavior which parents do not include in their self-reports, because it is not intentional. Children's standard for evaluating parental leadership may emphasize a strong M component. That does not mean that children prefer low P leadership. However, they may never want a strong P component in the absence of a strong M component. Parental self-reports of strong P leadership may be a socially conditioned expression of generally strong concern about the parental role. In Japan, such parents' high consciousness of social expectations may take precedence in their answers over their naturally loving interaction with their child. Such an explanation is consistent with the greater emphasis on self-reported P leadership by fathers than by mothers in tables 42 and 43.

Leadership in Collegiate Sports Groups

Many people would be interested in finding out what kind of leadership helps a sports team win games. Despite the popularity of sports, however, few scientific studies have been conducted to shed light on this question. Without

TABLE 41. Fathers' PM Leadership Pattern

Fathers' Self-report	Child's Description				
	PM	P	M	pm	Total
PM	26	9	9	12	56
P	7	12	6	6	31
M	3	1	4	4	12
pm	2	2	2	3	9
Total	38	24	21	25	108

Note: Figures in the table are the number of instances in which a particular leadership type based on parents' self-reports coincides with a leadership type based on their child's descriptions.

TABLE 42. Mothers' PM Leadership Pattern

Mothers' Self-report	Child's Description				
	PM	P	M	pm	Total
PM	15	13	13	13	54
P	9	9	8	10	36
M	13	6	4	5	28
pm	1	4	2	7	14
Total	38	32	27	35	132

Note: Figures in the table are the number of instances in which a particular leadership type based on parents' self-reports coincides with a leadership type based on their child's description.

TABLE 43. Child's Evaluation of Parental Attitude and Parents' Self-report of Leadership

Parental Self-report	Parental Attitude as Seen by Child									
	Understanding		Compliance		Pride		Intimacy		Respect	
	F[a]	M	F	M	F	M	F	M	F	M
PM	62	67	74	82	72	53	76	84	84	72
P	70	65	69	71	54	39	75	84	54	62
M	45	47	63	83	42	35	62	75	70	57
pm	33	46	66	62	33	30	44	69	66	54

[a]F = father, M = mother

Note: Figures represent the percentage of children describing their parent as showing each leadership type who answered "yes" when asked if their parent expressed each kind of attitude.

the advantage of prior research in sports settings, a new instrument was designed to measure leadership behavior in intramural college sports teams.

Collegiate athletics in Japan differ from collegiate sports in the United States in ways which affect the way in which participant leadership is expressed. Collegiate sports rely on student initiative and direction to a considerably greater degree than they do for major sports in the United States. Universities in Japan typically have one major team in each sport which represents the university in intercollegiate matches, and other more strictly recreational teams which resemble intramural sports in the United States. Unlike the major intercollegiate university teams in the United States, Japanese students who participate in intercollegiate sports do not receive any

TABLE 44. Child's Evaluation of Parental Attitude and Childs' Report of Parental Leadership

Child's Report of Parental Leadership	Parental Attitude as Seen by Child									
	Understanding		Compliance		Pride		Intimacy		Respect	
	F[a]	M	F	M	F	M	F	M	F	M
PM	69	85	87	82	68	58	69	95	79	83
P	42	41	50	65	50	31	71	81	68	48
M	80	74	80	89	75	71	85	93	90	82
pm	28	46	44	63	32	28	36	67	24	40

[a]F = father, M = mother

Note: Figures represent the percentage of children describing their parent as showing each leadership type who answered "yes" when asked if their parent expressed each kind of attitude.

special consideration in admission to the university or any financial support through tuition waivers or scholarships. Also unlike intercollegiate athletics in the United States, the faculty sponsor typically takes a less active role in establishing practice schedules or securing athletic equipment than do coaches in the United States. Student team captains have a generally greater role in determining the activities of their team than is the case for intercollegiate sports in the United States.

College sports groups in Japan are organized to engage in sports and other recreational activities. These are primarily recreational groups and are not required to undergo the kind of rigorous training followed by more formalized groups. The typically high turnover rate in these groups has the consequence that their social structure tends to be rather unstable. This instability is a major problem that sports group leaders face. Students making up the groups always face some conflict within themselves, because they feel obligated to pursue the goals of their sports groups while they also feel under pressure to pursue their academic work. Therefore, sports group leaders must give the members sufficient training to win victories over other teams, and at the same time maintain their group's cohesiveness. Unlike student sports groups, work groups in major Japanese businesses are oriented toward lifetime employment and thus their survival is usually not in jeopardy. However, while employees' motivation to work is an important leadership problem in employment settings, it is less of an issue in college student sports groups because people join the groups voluntarily.

Measuring Leadership Behavior in College Students' Sports Groups

An instrument was developed to measure leadership in college sports clubs. It was then administered to athletes participating in the Kyushu Regional Intercollegiate Athletic Meeting. The study consisted of two surveys. The purpose of the first survey was to factor analyze items designed to measure leadership behavior in sports clubs, while the second survey was aimed at examining the validity of the PM leadership types in sports groups. Prior to the first survey, data was collected from all the sports clubs of Kyushu University about their leaders' behavior during the preceding week, the preceding month, the preceding three to six months, and the period of time preceding the last six months. The data served as the basis for the questionnaire which was designed to measure leadership behavior. A questionnaire consisting of fifty-seven items was drafted on the basis of the above data. The draft was carefully examined by more than twenty people who had once been members of sports clubs, including some who had once been leaders. The fifty-seven items that make up the questionnaire are shown in table 45.

TABLE 45. Factor Analysis of Leadership Behavior in Sports Groups

Item	Factor Loading I	II	III	IV
39. Thinks about things from the standpoint of group members	.648	.173	.022	.217
42. Trusts group members	.626	.242	.145	.045
28. Tries to bring about unity in the club as a whole	.616	.314	.094	.157
30. Tries to make it easier for newly recruited members to fit in	.606	.217	.064	.318
46. Tries to solve troubles or problems within the club	.595	.247	.269	.135
19. Shows consideration when group members make mistakes in practice or in matches with other teams	.590	.081	−.114	.272
25. Tries to reflect club members' opinions in running the club	.573	.094	.051	.281
36. Pays due attention to maintaining teamwork within the club	.570	.268	.203	.072
43. Tries to develop club members' individual abilities	.558	.283	.210	.156
44. Maintains club members' willingness to practice	.554	.324	.199	.121
29. Takes care that club members do not get injured	.549	.191	.121	.232
32. Creates an atmosphere in which club members can express their opinions freely	.532	.161	.144	.120
23. Treats all club members fairly and equally	.532	.348	.015	.168
48. Draws up practice schedules that the club members can keep up with	.520	.187	.180	.080
52. Advises club members about how to handle their personal problems	.505	.090	.073	.171
11. Tries to heighten the teamwork among club members when participating in matches with other teams	.438	.329	.249	.225
38. Is willing to listen to club members who wish to quit the club	.385	.012	.175	.181
21. Tries to interact with club members outside of club activities by having drinks together, etc.	.369	.039	.241	−.026
49. Learns club members' names accurately	.326	.165	.120	.045
57. Places importance on keeping in touch with other colleges' teams	.282	.115	.260	.167
51. Doesn't use the club's equipment or rooms for personal purposes	.209	.195	.056	.037
26. Helps club members feel that he can be relied upon during matches	.214	.692	.096	.149

Continued

TABLE 45—*Continued*

Item	Factor Loading I	II	III	IV
3. Acts with complete self-confidence	.130	.657	.160	.101
27. Excells in the techniques of the sport	.208	.654	.116	.067
40. Enjoys the confidence of club members	.405	.653	.065	.077
45. Has a record of performance befitting a club leader	.148	.629	.214	.075
5. Has the entire club under his complete command	.375	.605	.137	.106
6. Behaves with a sense of responsibility as the leader	.220	.593	−.198	.219
7. Provides each club member with guidance when practicing	.147	.485	.147	.345
4. Considers the well-being of the entire club	.368	.462	.167	.180
2. Remains under control without being carried away by emotion	.322	.456	.063	.251
54. Behaves in a consistent way	.369	.456	.148	.157
8. Practices according to plans at all times	.190	.437	.311	.309
35. Knows the abilities of all the club members	.316	.411	.256	.037
55. Abides by the club's rules	.217	.380	.319	.194
41. Has the final say in running the club	.186	.352	.328	−.005
56. Places personal affairs above matters concerning the club's practice and other activities	−.054	−.348	.013	−.031
9. Is creative and imaginative in planning the club's practice	.136	.343	.272	.323
31. Is deeply devoted to the club	.311	.311	.301	.022
1. Participates intensely in the club's practice	.061	.299	.246	.052
34. Harshly reprimands members for coming late	.115	.052	.637	.080
33. Harshly reprimands members for being absent from practice	.101	.103	.609	.063
50. Provides a place for discussion among club members	.272	−.001	.493	.022
47. Places importance on improving techniques at all times	.261	.367	.451	.038
20. Arranges special practice sessions prior to matches with other teams	.008	.138	.449	.089
10. Vigorously engages in practice	.021	.421	.443	.194
17. In matches, he always aims at winning the championship (specific goal)	.077	.206	.440	.084
37. Keeps in touch with former club members	.269	.163	.430	.099
22. Tries to build and maintain the traditions of the club	.332	.345	.397	.187
24. Keeps club members informed about plans and dates for practice	.291	.190	.382	.186
53. Asks personal favors of club members	−.089	−.204	.239	−.066
13. Pays attention to maintaining the club's tools and equipment	.194	.188	.117	.678

TABLE 45—*Continued*

Item	Factor Loading I	II	III	IV
14. Always willing to coach newly recruited members on techniques	.311	.229	.007	.590
12. Is enthusiastic about recruiting new members	.275	.037	.063	.547
18. Tries to supply and replenish tools and equipment needed for practice and for matches with other teams	.355	.117	.190	.521
15. Carefully works out annual plans for practice, matches, and other club activities	.226	.290	.350	.418
16. Pays attention to keeping club members healthy	.345	.211	.187	.382
Variance explained (%)	13.7	11.6	6.4	5.3

First Survey

The first survey was conducted in May and June, 1977, by distributing the fifty-seven-item questionnaire to 761 persons who belonged to the sports clubs of Kyushu University and Seinan Gakuin University. Males comprised 76.6 percent of the respondents, while 11.7 percent were female; the sex of the remaining 11.7 percent was unknown. Twenty-seven different kinds of sports including almost all the sports played by college sports clubs were represented. The fifty-seven leadership items were factor analyzed and sixteen were selected for later use to measure PM leadership behavior.

Second Survey

To verify the validity of the PM leadership types in sports groups, a second survey was carried out using these sixteen items, plus eight items designed to measure teamwork, morale, communication adequacy, and meeting quality (two items each) as external criteria to validate the leadership types. The questionnaire was distributed in July, 1977, to members of the athletic clubs at universities and junior colleges in Kyushu. There were 5,251 respondents, 66.5 percent of whom were male and 27.8 percent of whom were female (the sex of the others was not recorded). Twenty different kinds of sports were represented, including almost all the sports played by college sports clubs.

Factor Analysis of Leadership Behavior

The fifty-seven items which were designed to measure leadership behavior in the first survey were factor analyzed. Initial communalities were estimated using squared multiple correlations. Factors were extracted using the principal axis method and applying the varimax rotation procedure. A four-factor solution was selected for interpretation. The respondents studied were the 574 people who answered every question on the survey.

Table 45 shows the factor matrix obtained as a result of the factor analysis. The variance explained by each factor were as follows: Factor I, 13.7 percent, Factor II, 11.6 percent, Factor III, 6.4 percent, and Factor IV, 5.3 percent. These four factors account for 37.0 percent of the overall variance. They can be interpreted based on those items which showed a loading of .500 or greater on one factor and .400 or less on the other factors.

The items that showed high loadings on Factor I were Q39, 42, 28, 30, 46, 19, 25, 36, 43, 44, 29, 32, 23, 48, and 52. Since these items concern the leader's consideration for either the entire club or individual club members, Factor I was designated "Consideration." The items that showed high loadings on Factor II were Q26, 3, 27, 40, 45, 5, and 6. Since these items concern the leader's capability and his ability to control and lead the club, Factor II was labeled "Control." The items that showed high loadings on Factor III were Q34 and 33. Since these items concern the rigor with which club members are trained and disciplined, Factor III was called "Rigor of Training." The items that showed high loadings on Factor IV were Q13, 14, 12, and 18. Since these items concern the supply and maintenance of equipment needed for practice and competition as well as for recruiting and training new members, Factor IV was designated "Club Maintenance."

These four factors can be understood from the point of view of the PM leadership theory. The goals of sports clubs are to enhance individual members' abilities and techniques through everyday practice and to promote the abilities of the clubs as a whole, thus enabling them to win matches with other teams. Of course, some college students join sports clubs for the purpose of developing interpersonal relationships that they could not develop in the course of their ordinary campus lives. Even so, interpersonal relationships in sports clubs are developed as club members work hard together to upgrade their skills in specific sports. Therefore, the primary goal of sports clubs lies in trying to upgrade their members' skills. Of the four factors found in the factor analysis, the factors of "Control" and "Rigor of Training" involve leadership oriented toward achieving the goals of the sports clubs; these are the P factors. The factors of "Consideration" and "Club Maintenance" involve leadership oriented toward maintaining a group; these are M factors.

Validity of the PM Leadership Type Classifications

Based on the factor analysis results, eight items were selected from those which showed high loadings on either "Control" or "Rigor of Training" to measure P behavior. Eight other items were selected to measure M behavior from among those items showing high loadings on "Consideration" or "Club Maintenance." Table 46 shows the items which were selected to measure P and M leadership behavior.

The second survey was carried out using these sixteen items, plus eight additional items concerning teamwork, morale, communication adequacy, and group meeting quality as criterion variables.

The average of the P scores obtained by adding up the scores of the eight items used to measure P behavior was 31.1. The average of the M scores obtained by summing the scores of the eight M behavior items was 31.3. The four leadership types—PM, P, M, and pm—were classified according to whether a leader's behavior was above or below the average P and M scores. Measures of teamwork, morale, communication adequacy, and group meeting quality were derived by summing the pairs of items used to measure each of these variables.

Table 47 shows the scores for the criterion variables grouped according to the four PM leadership types. The application of one-way analysis of variance indicated significant differences among the leadership types for all of the criterion variables ($p < .01$). For all criteria, scores were highest under PM-type leaders followed by M, P, and pm in that order.

TABLE 46. Items to Measure PM Leadership Behavior

Items to Measure P Behavior

1. Do you think that the captain behaves with self-confidence? (Q3)
2. Does the captain control and lead the club as a whole very well? (Q5)
3. Does the captain act with a sufficient sense of responsibility? (Q6)
4. Do club members feel that the captain is reliable during matches with outside teams? (Q26)
5. Does the captain excel in techniques? (Q27)
6. Does the captain have record of performance befitting a captain? (Q45)
7. Does the captain reprimand club members for being absent from practice? (Q33)
8. Does the captain reprimand club members for coming late for practice? (Q34)

Items to Measure M Behavior

1. Does the captain try to maintain the unity of the club? (Q28)
2. Does the captain try to help new members fit in? (Q30)
3. Does the captain think about things from the standpoint of club members? (Q39)
4. Does the captain trust club members? (Q42)
5. Does the captain try to solve trouble or problems among club members? (Q46)
6. Is the captain enthusiastic about recruitment of new club members? (Q12)
7. Does the captain pay attention to the maintenance of tools and equipment of the club? (Q13)
8. Does the captain coach new members on techniques? (Q14)

TABLE 47. Scores of Criterion Variables under Each Leadership Type

	Leadership Type			
Criterion Variable	PM	M	P	pm
Team work	8.3	7.7	7.6	6.8
Morale	7.5	6.9	6.7	6.4
Communication adequacy	7.7	7.2	6.8	6.3
Group meeting quality	7.8	7.3	6.7	6.5

Discussion

The results of the factor analysis concerning leadership behavior in sports clubs has interesting relationships to the results of the factor analysis concerning leadership behavior of first-line supervisors in industrial organizations, leadership behavior of subsection chiefs and section chiefs in local government offices, leadership behavior of school teachers, and leadership behavior of parents in families.

In the study of sports groups the factors of ''Control'' and ''Rigor of Training'' were identified pertaining to P leadership. The factor of ''Control'' has to do with the leader's control or command over his group members and is based on the leader's own skill and expertise. It reflects the characteristics of a leader who must control and lead members who volunteered to join a sports club for the purpose of improving their skills in specific sports. By contrast, the factor of ''Rigor of Training'' is similar to the factor of ''Pressure'' in industrial organizations and the factor of ''Discipline and Guidance'' in local government offices.

Two factors concerning M behavior, the factor of ''Consideration'' and the factor of ''Club Maintenance,'' were found. The factor of ''Consideration'' corresponds to the factor of ''Group Maintenance'' in industrial organizations and local government offices. The factor of ''Group Maintenance'' which was the only factor pertaining to M behavior found in industrial organizations and local government offices, is primarily the consideration the leader shows toward individual members and toward the group as a whole. In the study of college sports clubs, another factor pertaining to M behavior was found, namely the factor of ''Club Maintenance.'' The factor of ''Club Maintenance'' is substantially different from the factor of ''Consideration''. College sports clubs are groups made up of volunteers. The clubs are held together by club members and by those tools and equipment which are supplied and maintained by them. If club members neglect to recruit and replenish new human and material resources, the clubs can deteriorate to the point of extinction. In industrial organizations and local government offices, the recruitment and replenishment of human and material resources is incorporated into formal systems of the organizations. Consequently, the factor of "Club Maintenance" found in this study is a particular characteristic of leadership in groups of volunteers. Despite some differences between the specific morphology of leadership in sports groups and in the other groups studied, criterion variables were associated with leadership types in the same order as in industrial organizations and local government offices.

Summary

The studies described in this chapter have used the PM leadership theory to investigate educational, parental, and sports group leadership. These studies are useful for understanding some of the specific ways in which leadership for children and students differs from leadership for adults. In each study, leadership questionnaires were constructed using questions which reflect the particular behaviors of leaders in each kind of group. In the studies of educational and sports group leadership, the questionnaires were developed in consultation with people experienced in each area through a careful analysis of the specific behaviors which leadership in each situation involves.

Some of the specific leadership behaviors and associated factors which were identified in these studies differ from those found in studies of leadership for adults. In educational settings, for example, the P factors involving training and discipline concerning "life and learning" and "social and moral values" clearly involve different tasks and require different behaviors than do the work performance factors found in other settings. Although many of the specific categories of behavior reflected in P and M items and factors in each setting differ from those found in studies of leadership provided for adults, the general P and M functions are still clearly identifiable.

The order of PM types with respect to attitudinal effectiveness criteria is also generally consistent with that found in field studies of adults. The order of PM, M, P, and pm which is characteristic of industrial, governmental, and political leadership was also found for children's attitudes in studies of educational leadership and for participants' attitudes in studies of athletic groups. The order of PM types in parental leadership of children is somewhat more complex. Some of the data indicate that children express equally positive or more positive attitudes toward parents whom they experience as providing M-type behavior as they do to PM-type parents. Overall, the studies support the approach to identifying specific behaviors to describe leadership in particular settings and classifying them on the basis of the general PM concepts in order to predict their relative effectiveness.

CHAPTER 8

Issues in the Specific Morphology of Leadership

The studies based on the PM leadership theory have been designed to describe the specific morphology of leadership in many different field settings. They were conducted during a period in which social scientists outside Japan were conducting similar field studies designed to demonstrate the convergence between survey measures of leadership and various criteria. The Ohio State researchers developed the Leadership Behavior Description Questionnaire (LBDQ) for general use (Halpin and Winer 1957) and also developed a special form for use in industrial settings with lower-level employees (Fleishmann 1953). Somewhat later, a form of the LBDQ with ten leadership subscales in addition to revised versions of the initial consideration and initiating structure dimensions was developed and incorporated into the LBDQ—Form XII. The tradition of the early Michigan studies focusing on the closeness of supervision (Katz, Maccoby, and Morse 1950) was continued and modified in the four-factor theory of leadership (Bowers and Seashore 1966) which later became a central part of the research instrument (the "Survey of Organizations") used by Bowers at the Institute for Social Research and by the consulting firm of Rensis Likert Associates (Taylor and Bowers 1972). The attempt to identify additional dimensions of perceived leadership using survey methods has continued in developing leadership dimensions for the Michigan Assessment of Organizations (Cammann et al. 1983). However, survey forms following either the Ohio State or Michigan traditions which have attempted to develop more than two basic dimensions have received relatively little research attention.

Two Basic Leadership Functions

Similarly, in the PM research program, the two basic functions of performance and maintenance have been consistently emphasized. They have provided an organizing framework for understanding additional particular dimensions specific to some settings. While these two basic functional concepts point to general categories of behavior, they do not identify highly specific behaviors which individual leaders can be instructed to display toward a particular group of subordinates in a particular situation. Instead, they suggest that a formal leader might be wise (1) to consider what tasks his subordinate group is seeking to accomplish and what behaviors might be useful to direct subordinates and facilitate task accomplishment, and (2) to simultaneously consider how to express concern for subordinates taking into account the personal problems and frustrations their task situation might place on them as well as the leader's own personal and situationally provided resources which can be used on behalf of subordinates.

However, the purpose of field studies in the PM research program has not been to test basic causal propositions to the same extent that it appears to have been in the early Ohio State studies as well as in more recent studies such as those designed to test path-goal theory. Causal reasoning in the PM studies is based on experimental research while specific field studies have been undertaken to help estimate generalizability. Thus less attention in the PM research program has been given to developing a survey instrument for use in all settings than has been done in some survey-based leadership programs. The greatest attention to developing a single relatively generalizable instrument has been given in the series of studies conducted in industrial settings. Thus while the content validity of many of the leadership measures in studies of specific morphology with respect to particular settings is clear, and concurrent validity involving convergence with attitudinal criteria has been demonstrated, other aspects of validity such as predictive validity still need to be determined in some settings. In those particular studies which could be designed to assess the equal interval scaling of response alternatives and the predictive validity of specific measures, the results have tended to support their adequacy.

Although leadership research in the United States has not emphasized specific morphology and the setting-specific meaning of leadership questionnaires, the study of specific morphology is not completely unfamiliar in the leadership field. Other research programs being pursued outside Japan at the same time the PM leadership theory was being developed involved studies of different social systems. Even in the early compilation of studies in the Ohio State research program (Stodgill and Coons 1957), separate forms of the leadership instrument are noted for bomber crews (with 20 of the 150 LBDQ items eliminated because they were "inappropriate"), school superintendents (Seeman's [1957] four "specific scales") and industrial supervisors (Fleishmann's Supervisory Behavior Description Questionnaire [SBDQ]) in addition to the basic 150-item form initially used to measure consideration and initiating structure. Further recognition of the specific nature of leadership is evident in descriptions of factor analyses conducted separately in different settings to identify the particular items which best represented what were emerging as two basic conceptual dimensions of leadership.

While an emphasis on the two basic performance and maintenance concepts is quite useful and constructive—studies of PM leadership have demonstrated that many leaders have yet to learn the ordinarily constructive results of a combined emphasis on both functions—the study of specific morphology is useful for giving additional substance to the meaning and expression of P and M leadership in particular settings. Research in the United States to develop the additional indices of the LBDQ—Form XII (Stogdill 1963) and the Michigan Organizational Assessment Questionnaire (Cammann et al. 1983) are useful for identifying specific situational expressions of the basic leadership functions.

In the specific studies of PM morphology, however, analysis has consistently returned to a grouping of specific concepts and measures according to the two basic leadership functions. Rather than treating specific expressions of leadership as concepts on equal footing with the P and M concepts, they are treated as theoretically linked expressions of leadership on a separate level of abstraction from the P and M concepts. Further, they are understood to have their associations with objective and cognitive criteria primarily because of their link to the basic P and M functions.

Recent research in the United States indicates that many partially differentiable aspects of leadership may be identifiable in some work settings if they are specifically sought. Yukl and Nemeroff (1979), for example, identify a total of thirteen dimensions. Their description of these dimensions appears in table 48. Eight of these (positive reinforcement, production emphasis, work facilitation, planning, coordination, role clarification, goal setting, training) are specific expressions of performance-oriented behavior, many of which are reflected in one or another of the performance dimensions identified in Japan. Consideration and conflict management are aspects of some of the field measures of M-oriented behavior. Others, including the decision-making dimensions (i.e., decision participation and autonomy-delegation) and interaction facilitation have both P-oriented and M-oriented components. As is characteristic of survey-based concepts, it is more difficult to unequivocally equate naive constructs partially reflecting respondents "implicit theories" of leadership (Eden and Leviatan 1975) with deductively derived concepts. It is interesting that greater empirical differentiation in field research appears possible among primarily P-oriented constructs than among M-oriented constructs in the United States just as in Japan.

Other field research approaches being followed outside Japan show promise for developing a specific morphology of leadership. Particularly noteworthy among them are the observational approaches initiated by the

TABLE 48. Yukl and Nemeroff's Leader Behavior Dimensions

Consideration: the extent to which a leader is friendly, supportive, considerate, open, and honest in his or her behavior toward subordinates and tries to be fair and objective.

Positive Reinforcement: the extent to which a leader provides praise and recognition to subordinates who perform effectively, bases recommendations for pay increases and promotions on subordinate performance, and tries to provide supplementary rewards or benefits for subordinates with superior performance.

Decision Participation: the extent to which a leader consults with subordinates and otherwise allows them to participate in making decisions, and the amount of subordinate influence over the leader's decisions that results from this participation.

Production Emphasis: the extent to which a leader emphasizes the importance of subordinate performance, tries to improve productivity and efficiency, tries to keep subordinates working up to their capacity, checks on their performance, and lets them know when it is not up to expectations.

Work Facilitation: the extent to which a leader obtains for subordinates any necessary supplies, equipment, support services, or other resources, eliminates any problems in the work environment, and removes other obstacles that interfere with the work.

Autonomy-Delegation: the extent to which a leader delegates responsibility and authority to subordinates and allows them to determine how to do their work.

Interaction Facilitation: the extent to which a leader tries to get subordinates to be friendly with each other, cooperate, share information and ideas, and help each other.

Conflict Management: the extent to which a leader helps subordinates settle conflicts and disagreements, restrains them from insulting each other, and encourages them to resolve conflicts in a constructive manner.

Planning: the extent to which a leader plans and schedules the work in advance, plans how to efficiently organize the work, plans for future manpower and resource needs, and makes contingency plans for potential problems.

Coordination: the extent to which a leader coordinates the work of subordinates, emphasizes the importance of coordination, and encourages subordinates to coordinate their activities.

Role Clarification: the extent to which a leader informs subordinates about their duties and responsibilities, specifies the rules and policies subordinates must observe, and lets subordinates know what is expected of them.

Goal Setting: the extent to which a leader sets specific performance goals for each important aspect of a subordinate's job, measures progress toward the goals, and provides feedback to subordinates.

Training: the extent to which a leader determines training needs and provides adequate skill training to subordinates.

Source: Yukl and Nemeroff 1979, p. 180.

innovative study of senior managers by Mintzberg (1973) and subsequently being followed in educational organizations by Martinko (Martinko and Gardner 1982). One of the purposes of some of these studies, particularly Mintzberg's study, has been to develop the idea that managers are engaged in many other tasks besides providing leadership. This is a particularly useful emphasis in understanding the specific expressions of leadership in work organizations. Actions which a supervisor or manager may intend to be part of roles other than leadership may be seen and interpreted from a leadership perspective by subordinates. Similarly, the model of multiple roles suggested by Mintzberg provides a possible basis for understanding why some managers may provide pm-type leadership—their attention is being drawn by problems not directly associated with those of their subordinates. The idea of multiple roles may have similar implications for educational leadership, parental leadership, and leadership in other settings when viewed from the interdisciplinary perspective of the PM leadership theory.

Research Methods

Several issues for the study of specific morphology are raised by observational studies of leadership and by a comparison of the strengths and weaknesses of survey research and observational research. Especially important are the differences in the kinds of reliability and validity problems associated with each. The purpose in studies of specific morphology is to identify particular expressions of P and M leadership in particular settings and to assess their importance by determining their association with behavioral and cognitive criteria. The usefulness of research methods designed to study specific behavioral morphology needs to be evaluated against the criterion of how well the methods fulfill this purpose.

A basic problem in evaluating questionnaire measures for identifying the specific expression of P and M leadership is the issue of the meaning and importance of associations between leadership measures based on subordinates' perceptions and cognitive or attitudinal variables also based on subordinates' reports. Two questions are raised by this research approach. First, do respondents' attitudes about their work distort their perceptions of leadership? Second, are associations between experienced leadership (as distinguished from actual behaviors) and other attitudes and perceptions important? The answer to the first of these questions is a qualified yes—the experienced work situation may well affect how leadership behaviors are perceived and interpreted. The answer to the second question, however, is also yes—associations between experienced leadership and work-related attitudes are important as well.

The qualified affirmation that work experiences affect leadership perceptions is consistent with the ''implicit leadership theory'' idea (Rush, Thomas, and Lord 1977) and the attributional approach to leadership (Calder 1977) being advociated by many researchers in the United States. These perspectives suggest that when individuals experience one event or situation—for example, a cohesive group of co-workers—they may come to attribute the cause of that phenomenon to some other event or condition—good leadership, for example—which may or may not have caused it. Further, a consistent picture of leadership may be developed by filling in gaps about how a supervisor would probably have behaved in the absence of information about how the leader actually behaves. Even worse from a survey measure point of view, specific actions by a leader which are inconsistent with overall impressions may be ignored or otherwise distorted in order to maintain a consistent picture of the leader's behavior. Such arguments are consistent with a large quantity of social psychological research and theory concerning social information processing (Salancik and Pfeffer 1978) and person perception (Markus 1977).

Leadership research, however, has shown that questionnaire responses can reflect a considerable amount of real information about leadership. Stogdill (1969) showed a convergence between the leadership behaviors shown by actors and the LBDQ descriptions of naive observers. Bales and Isenberg (1982) have found that the descriptions of leadership by naive observers converge very well with observers' records. Even studies designed to show the effects of extraneous information on leadership descriptions have indicated that actual behavior is significantly and substantially reflected in questionnaire responses (Rush and Beauvais 1981).

Experimental studies in the PM research program including the study by Misumi and Shirakashi (1966) have shown that subjects' questionnaire descriptions of the PM leadership types are generally consistent with the intended PM conditions. Exceptions, however, are found which may indicate that the backgrounds of some respondents distort their perceptions of the leadership with which they are provided. In some studies, the leadership types were found to be more highly related to nonattitudinal criteria than were other work attitudes. This finding further suggests that perceptions of leadership differ from general work attitudes.

One series of studies designed to test the specific dynamics of leadership (see chap. 14) provides additional evidence supporting the validity of the industrial measures of PM leadership types. These studies provide test-retest reliability coefficients for leaders over one- and two-year periods. For leaders who stay in the same position and are described by the same group of subordinates, the correlations between leadership descriptions at one-year intervals range from .35 to .88 (median = .65) for P scores and from .51 to .80 (median = .55) for M scores. Further, for those supervisors who were transferred but to similar kinds of departments in a different geographic location, their P scores based on their new subordinate group's descriptions were still significantly correlated with their prior P scores. For those supervisors transferred to departments doing different work in the same geographic location, significant correlations were found between their M scores before and after the transfer.

These results are discussed in chapter 14 with respect to their implications for forces promoting leadership stability and change. However, they also support the validity of the leadership survey measures used to test the PM theory.

Context of the Research

Perceived leadership and its associated correlates are also conceptually and pragmatically important. The study of leadership is necessarily tied to the study of leadership in a context because leadership never occurs in the abstract. Any research approach which attempts to completely abstract leadership from a context is likely to face considerable difficulties. Thus, in the experimental studies described thus far and in Part IV, leadership perceptions of subordinates are always assessed as a check on the experimental leadership conditions implemented. Performance-oriented behavior which involves giving directions, for example, may have a different meaning for different subordinates if directions are given with a degree of complexity which is interpretable by some subordinates but not others. Maintenance-oriented behavior which involves expressing personal concern about a subordinates' private life may have a different meaning for subordinates who try to integrate their private life and work life than for subordinates who try to divorce the one from the other.

In laboratory studies the experience of experimental leadership behavior by different subjects is likely to be reasonably similar. All subjects are ordinarily dealing with an identical task, all begin their work at the same time, all have had the same basic relationship with the supervisor. However, any given leadership behavior may not be experienced similarly by all subordinates in a field setting such as, for example, a coal mining operation. Different miners will be performing somewhat distinct work activities that are likely to change in difficulty or complexity over the course of days and weeks. Each person may have seen the supervisor at different times dealing with different problems in different ways. Making a suggestion about how to work more effectively may be intended as (and experienced as) supportive help in learning by a new miner, as harassment or unwanted pressure by an unmotivated miner who has a generally negative affective relationship with the supervisor, or as personal support and encouragement by an experienced miner having a basically friendly relationship with the supervisor. Much of the meaning of a behavior would be lost if it were measured in the field without regard to the details of the situations to which it is a response. Observational studies of specific morphology are likely to face extremely great problems in field settings if objective, average levels of behavior are measured across all the diverse subordinates and changing work situations being faced. Attempting to use observational methods to identify specific responses to specific situations may introduce an unmanageable degree of complexity in many field settings. Questionnaire methods, on the other hand, are uniquely suited to handling these difficulties as long as their meaning—perceived leadership in context—is understood and they are included in a research program which emphasizes laboratory experiments as well.

Based on a consideration of the meaning of questionnaire measures of leadership as measures of behavior in context, the usefulness of seeking associations between questionnaire measures of leadership and cognitive criteria can be evaluated from the perspective of the specific morphology of leadership. Basically, such correlational studies help to identify settings in which the results of experimental studies are most reasonably and least reasonably applied. If no association is found, for example, between perceived supervisor leadership type and experienced stress in some industrial settings, then one might expect that the experimental studies which show such associations in the laboratory may not be applicable.

The PM studies of specific morphology conducted thus far have emphasized the differences in the expression of the P and M functions among several major categories of employing organizations—industrial, governmental, and educational—and between employing organizations and other social systems—political, family, sports, and educational. Typically, the measures used in these studies have been developed by asking people active in each kind of social system to identify the particular leadership behaviors which are especially consequential in the social settings with which they are familiar. In this way, leadership behaviors have been identified and questionnaire items have been designed to measure leadership in a way uniquely appropriate for each major category of leadership situation. In the laboratory studies described thus far and those to be presented in the section that follows, some of the specific characteristics of leadership in the laboratory will be discussed as possible limitations in the applicability of these studies to field settings.

However, basic leadership functions may also be specifically expressed in different ways within each of these major categories of social settings. For example, the analysis of leadership by section and subsection chiefs within governmental organizations has shown that an important component of the leadership that section chiefs provide for their subordinates is to keep their section informed about changes in other sections, in part by maintaining personal contacts with other sections. This expression of performance-oriented leadership is less important for subsection chiefs. The difference between the expressions of leadership between the two groups is reflected in differences in factor structure for the questionnaires designed for each group. Factor structure differences among particular organizations, cultures, hierarchical levels, and departments are one way in which specific expressions of leadership are indicated in field studies. The PM leadership surveys conducted in many different types of organizations have typically shown similar but not identical factor structures. Research is currently being conducted in the United States, China, and Europe that will help determine the extent to which the morphology of PM leadership is specific to particular countries.

The two basic leadership functions may even need to be expressed in ways that take into account more specific variables than the tasks and norms of particular work groups. The personal situation and task situation of individual subordinates may even require that different actions be taken to promote the social integration or work coordination of different subordinates. All possible P-oriented and M-oriented behaviors are never provided at one time for the same subordinate. An important part of leadership in any social context is understanding unique personal and work needs and recognizing how these needs fluctuate, even within a single day, and evolve over time. Effective leadership requires an understanding not only of the specific leadership morphology associated with a major kind of social context, but also the highly specific morphology of behaviors as they will be experienced and accepted by individual subordinates.

Two aspects of the specific morphology findings also have implications for the general morphology of PM leadership types. The specific morphology studies consistently show (1) that the P and M components can be assessed relatively independently by field survey measures, and (2) that the PM types consistently converge with criteria such that the PM type is associated with the most positive criterion levels and the pm type with the most negative. Both of the results are very different from those found using the Ohio State "consideration" and "initiating structure" measures within work organizations (Kerr and Schriesheim 1974; Korman 1966).

In summary, the PM research program thus far has addressed a number of the specific expressions of the four basic leadership types in different kinds of social settings. Differences in the expression of leadership functions have also been shown to be present at different levels within a single type of organization—local government bureaucracies. Conceptually, these studies serve to demonstrate the validity of the basic PM concept by showing that it is recognizable in many social contexts although it is expressed somewhat differently in each. Pragmatically, the studies encourage leaders to assess the task and personal situations which they face and creatively select behaviors supporting both the P and the M functions in ways which are appropriate to their specific settings.

Considerably more research is needed to understand important variations in the expression of basic leadership functions in different departments of the same organization and perhaps even for different kinds of subordinates in the same department. The cultural differences of countries may even require that somewhat distinct specific morphologies are needed for similar social settings in different countries. The experimental studies of the general dynamics of leadership which are presented in Part IV are based on the belief that the causal significance of the PM types for criteria lies primarily in the basic, general morphology of leadership rather than in its specific mode of expression.

PART IV

General Behavioral Dynamics of Leadership

CHAPTER 9

Leadership Dynamics and the Learning Process

Generally speaking, if one type of leadership is typically found to be associated with higher performance and more positive attitudes than a second type, the question remains of what causal dynamics account for the difference. The search for integrated principles to explain the typical differences in effectiveness associated with leadership types—the search for scientific laws—is the task of the general behavioral dynamics of leadership. Since a law in science reflects a tested causal hypothesis, behavioral dynamics can be studied using those field and laboratory research methods that test causal hypotheses.

Since leadership phenomena are conspicuously group phenomena, the behavioral dynamics of leadership is one aspect of group dynamics. In his 1939 study entitled "Experiments in Social Space," Kurt Lewin, the founder of the study of group dynamics, advocated the legitimacy of experimental reserach in the social sciences in discussing his experimental studies of leadership. He writes,

> I am persuaded that it is possible to undertake experiments in sociology which have as much right to be called scientific experiments as those in physics and chemistry. I am persuaded that there exists a social space which has all the essential properties of a real empirical space and deserves as much attention by students of geometry and mathematics as the physical space, although it is not a physical one. (P. 71)

In this work, Lewin used the conceptual framework of field theory to describe the leadership experiments conducted with Lippitt and White in 1939 that initiated the study of group dynamics. Even compared to the history of experimental psychology, the history of social psychology and group dynamics is very short. The history of experimental psychology is the history of scientific research to identify the general behavioral dynamics or basic causal processes (i.e., laws) of psychological behavior. Studies in animal psychology and experimental studies concerning perception, learning, and motivation principally involve the search for laws from the perspective of general behavioral dynamics. Like research in experimental psychology, research into the behavioral dynamics of leadership is part of the investigation into the laws of behavior.

Experimenter's Effects on Reminiscence

The effects of one person's leadership on another's learning process is probably one of the most neglected areas in both the experimental study of learning and in the study of leadership. Hypotheses about the probable effects of leadership on learning can be based to some extent on studies of the mere presence of one person on another's learning ("social facilitation," Zajonc 1965), on studies of the learning effects of a competitive learning atmosphere, and on studies of the effects that an experimenter's behavior have on the learning process. Experimental conditions reflecting the four PM types were induced in a series of studies designed to ascertain the effects of leadership on perceptual-motor learning tasks, word association tasks, and false equation tasks.

Studies of Reminiscence

Ebbinghaus (1885) was the first psychologist to demonstrate that learning retention generally decreases with the passage of time. However, Ballard (1913) showed that memory could better be reproduced after the lapse of a short period of time than immediately after the memorizing was done. He called this phenomenon reminiscence. Ballard had twelve-year-old children memorize various kinds of poems and reproduce their memories after a lapse of one, two, three, four, five, six, and seven days. He found that the children could recite the poems after the lapse of one or two days even better than immediately after they memorized the poems. This long-term reminiscence phenomenon was subsequently confirmed by Williams (1926) and came to be known as the Ballard-Williams phenomenon. As experimental methods improved and learning theories developed further during the 1930s, some psychologists argued that there were close relationships between reminiscence and distributed learning effects. "Distributed learning effects" refers to the finding that spreading or "distributing" short learning periods over a long period of time produces better recall than concentrating or "massing" the learning process within a short period of time. Apparent differences between distributed learning effects and reminiscence effects were argued to be merely particular phenomena caused by the operation of different experimental conditions, and that they were fundamentally linked together by the same psychological mechanism.

Ward (1937) had subjects memorize twelve nonsense syllables (using the serial anticipation method) and asked them to reproduce their memories after lapses of six seconds, thirty seconds, two minutes, five minutes, ten minutes, and twenty minutes. Ward found that the subjects reproduced their memories most accurately after a rest of thirty seconds to two minutes rather than immediately after they memorized the items. This kind of short-term reminiscence was confirmed by Hovland (1938) and is referred to as the Ward-Hovland phenomenon.

In perceptual-motor learning, as shown in the experiments by Kimble (1949*a*) and others, performance improves when a rest period is given after a concentrated or "massed" learning period. The increase in performance after a short rest is so similar to the long-term reminiscence effect identified by Ballard and others that it has also come to be referred to as reminiscence. The similarity between reminiscence and distributed learning effects led to attempts to develop a unified theoretical explanation for both. Representative of these integrative theories is the inhibition theory advanced by Hull (1943) and Kimble (1949*a*).

The inhibition theory, centering on Hull's Postulate 8, is explained as follows:

> Postulate 8: Whenever a reaction (R) is evoked in an organism, a primary negative drive (D) is created as a result; (1) this has an innate capacity (IR) to inhibit the reaction potentiality (sER) to that response; (2) the amount of net inhibition (IR) generated by a sequence of reaction evocation is a simple linear increasing function of the number of evocations (n); (3) it is a positively accelerated increasing function of the work (W) involved in the execution of the response; (4) reactive inhibition (IR) spontaneously dissipates as a simple negative growth function of time (t).

Based on this postulate, Hull said that IR (reaction inhibition) reduced the effective reaction potential (sER or expressed recall) brought about by reaction evocation (repeated learning practice). However, since IR, as described in Postulate 8(4), spontaneously dissipates as a function of time, the lapse of a certain amount of time creates some degree of spontaneous recovery from inhibitory potential (IR). As a result, a lapse of time increases the "strength of effective potentiality" (sER) or the extent to which learning is evident. Hull equated the increase in sER with reminiscence.

Kimble (1949*a*) advanced a "two-factor theory" regarding inhibition based on the basic inhibition theory. Two factors, reactive inhibition (IR) and conditioned inhibition (sIR), were used to explain distributed learning effects and reminiscence in perceptual-motor learning. sIR derives from Hull's Postulate 9. A stimulus (S) closely associated with the cessation of a response (R) (*a*) becomes conditioned to the inhibition (IR) associated with the evocation of that response, thereby generating conditioned inhibition; (*b*) conditioned inhibition (sI_R) adds up physiologically to reactive inhibition (I_R) against reaction potential with respect to a given response.

The process by which I_R is developed through repeated learning trials also was hypothesized to be associated with motivation. Specifically, the hypothesis was suggested that the total amount of I_R which will accumulate is a proportionate function of motivation and the amount of effort exerted. The more motivated a learner is, the higher the level of I_R the learner will tolerate and still continue at the learning task. I_R does not accumulate infinitely; it increases only to the point where it matches the strength of motivation. Therefore, reminiscence is postulated to increase to a higher point under the condition of high motivation than under the condition of low motivation. Since learning continues to occur after I_R has developed, inhibition theory implies that learning performance will be higher under conditions of high motivation than under conditions of low motivation.

Kimble (1950), in a study of man-to-man competition using a pursuit rotor task, found that performance and reminiscence were both higher in high-motivation groups than in low-motivation groups. Wasserman (1951) conducted an experiment in which motivation was manipulated by verbal instructions (ego-oriented and task-oriented instructions). Using an inverted alphabet printing task, he obtained results that coincided with the findings of Kimble (1950). These studies showed that both prerest preformance and postrest reminiscence were significantly higher in high-motivation groups than in low-motivation groups. The results of these studies supported the inhibition theory.

However, the studies of Eysenck and his collaborators (Eysenck and Maxwell 1961; Eysenck and Willett 1961; Willett and Eysenck 1962) produced findings contradicting the inhibition hypothesis. Their studies compared groups with high motivation and low motivation by giving a pursuit rotor task as part of the selection process for new mechanics. The results indicated that although the prerest performance of highly motivated groups was not higher than that of less motivated groups, reminiscence effects were relatively stronger in more highly motivated groups than in less motivated groups. Furthermore, Eysenck (1964), in an experiment in which a pursuit rotor task was given to highly motivated subjects, found that prerest performance and ability to perform the task were not directly related to reminiscence.

Eysenck argued that it was difficult to unequivocally explain the lack of correspondence between reminiscence and prerest performance in terms of the inhibition hypothesis. Instead, he maintained that the reminiscence effects in his experiments resulted from the consolidation of learning during the rest period. He stated that reminiscence in tasks which require new learning, such as pursuit rotor and memory learning tasks, could be explained by the consolidation hypothesis. However, in the case of tasks which required no special learning, such as tapping and vigilance, reminiscence could be explained by the inhibition hypothesis.

In connection with the studies of reminiscence, a series of experimental studies concerning the effects of an experimenter's leadership on performance and reminiscence in perceptual-motor learning were studied from the perspective of the PM leadership theory.

PM Leadership Types and Reminiscence

First Study

Sato (1968) and Misumi and Sato (1968) conducted experiments which involved giving an inverted Chinese alphabet printing task to eighty female high school students. Sensorimotor learning was assessed as the increase in speed with which the inverted alphabet symbols were copied. The experiments were carried out under the condition of massed learning in which thirty prerest trials and five postrest trials (a trial lasted for thirty seconds and the rest periods lasted ten minutes) were given. In these experiments, an experimenter's behavior toward different groups was used to reflect the four PM types. The experimenters' behavioral styles were similar to those used in the studies by Misumi and Shirakashi (1966).

P-type Leadership
A P-type leader urges his subordinates to perform their task by saying, "work more quickly," "work more efficiently," "work accurately," "don't talk and work more quickly," and "don't be outperformed by anyone else."

M-type Leadership
An M-type leader is careful to relax the feelings of his subordinates and break the tension among them by saying such things as, "please try to have a pleasant time while working," "I am sorry that I have to make you work hard," "I know your work is hard, but please cooperate," "please be relaxed, don't hurry," "take it easy," and "don't work so hard that you get tired."

PM-type Leadership
A PM-type leader combines the qualities of both P and M leadership types. He tries to make the best of both worlds. He tries to expedite the performance of the task while at the same time paying careful attention to his subordinates' feelings by saying the kinds of things which are said by leaders of both the P and M types.

pm-type Leadership
A pm-type leader combines a low emphasis on the qualities of both the P and M leadership types. An experimenter providing pm-type leadership does not say a word once he has explained the procedure for performing the task even though he remains in the experimental situation.

The experimental procedure involved an initial period to establish a baseline for performance and a subsequent test period. During the first through the third trials, no supervisor was present and no PM leadership conditions were introduced. These trials permitted an assessment of the amount of learning which would occur without a supervisor. Neither were the supervisory conditions used during the two trials when reminiscence was being measured—the last trial before the rest and the first trial after the rest. Otherwise, the supervisory conditions were introduced once or twice per trial during the fourth through twenty-ninth trials. Four male students majoring in psychology served in the experimenter-supervisor role.

Table 49 shows observers' reports of P and M supervisory behavior in the four PM conditions. The table shows that the pm-type supervisor provided neither P nor M behavior. Overall, the four conditions were successfully achieved.

The results showed the greatest increase in learning performance in the prerest trials (trials 4 through 29) under PM-type supervision followed by P, M, and pm supervision in that order. No significant differences among the four PM types were found in learning performance at the end of the thirty prerest trials. Although learning performance was slightly higher under P supervision, no difference at all was found between PM and M supervision and learning was lowest under pm supervision. Reminiscence, the difference

TABLE 49. Frequencies of P and M Behaviors by Supervisors Representing Four Leadership Conditions

Leadership Type	All Trials		Prerest Trials	
	P	M	P	M
PM	11 (42%)	15 (58%)	9 (43%)	12 (57%)
P	33 (94)	2 (6)	28 (97)	1 (3)
M	0 (0)	22 (100)	0 (0)	19 (100)
pm	0 (0)	0 (0)	0 (0)	0 (0)

Note: Figures not in parentheses indicate the frequencies of P and M behaviors. Figures in parentheses indicate the percentage of P and M behaviors relative to the total number of behaviors by leaders in each condition during each set of trials (i.e., either "all trials" or "prerest trials").

in learning between the final prerest trial (trial 29) and the postrest trial (trial 30), was significantly greater in the PM condition than in the other conditions, but no significant differences were found among the other conditions.

In order to further test the propositions of reminiscence theories, subjects under the PM leadership conditions were divided into a high-performance group and a low-performance group based on their prerest performance. When their degree of reminiscence was compared, no significant difference was found (Misumi, Yoshida, and Sato 1969). Thus, no direct correspondence appears between performance in the prerest trials and reminiscence. This finding contradicts the hypothesis of Hull and Kimble who tried to interpret the reminiscence phenomenon on the basis of reactive inhibition theory. A second study was conducted in order to confirm this conclusion and to reexamine the effects of the four PM types on learning and reminiscence (Sato 1972).

Second Study

The same PM supervisory types were induced in the second study as in the first study. Table 50 shows the observers' records of the experimenter's supervisory behavior beginning in the fourth session. Again, the PM types were effectively demonstrated by the supervisors.

The task involved copying an inverted "hiragana" alphabet character. The subjects were 834 female high school students. A male graduate student played the role of the experimenter-supervisor for each of the four PM leadership conditions. Different groups of subjects performed ten, twenty, thirty, or forty massed practice trials with each trial lasting thirty seconds. A rest period following the last massed practice trial lasted ten minutes. Five trials were carried out after the rest period.

The effects of the leadership conditions were found to vary somewhat according to the number of prerest trials. No significant differences were found among the leadership conditions in prerest performance in the ten-trial condition. The PM leadership type resulted in the highest performance under the twenty-trial condition, while the P leadership type showed the highest performance under the thirty- and forty-trial conditions. However, none of the differences were statistically significant. Greater differences among the experimental conditions were found in reminiscence.

The PM type of leadership (table 51) showed the highest reminiscence under all of the trial conditions (ten, twenty, thirty, and forty trials) followed by P, M, and pm in that order. A significant amount of reminiscence was found under P-type leadership in the twenty and forty prerest trial conditions. A significant amount of reminiscence was found under M-type leadership only in the twenty prerest trial condition. No significant reminiscence effects

TABLE 50. Frequencies of P and M Behaviors by Supervisors

Condition	P	M
PM_{10}	5 (0.71)	4 (0.57)
PM_{20}	7 (0.41)	12 (0.71)
PM_{30}	19 (0.70)	22 (0.81)
PM_{40}	24 (0.65)	29 (0.78)
P_{10}	9 (1.29)	0 (0.00)
P_{20}	22 (1.29)	0 (0.00)
P_{30}	34 (1.26)	0 (0.00)
P_{40}	39 (1.05)	1 (0.03)
M_{10}	0 (0.00)	8 (1.14)
M_{20}	0 (0.00)	24 (1.41)
M_{30}	0 (0.00)	32 (1.19)
M_{40}	1 (0.03)	39 (1.05)
pm_{20}	0 (0.00)	0 (0.00)
pm_{30}	0 (0.00)	0 (0.00)
pm_{40}	0 (0.00)	0 (0.00)

Note: Figures not in parentheses indicate the cumulative frequencies of P and M behavior beginning in the session when the leadership conditions were first introduced (i.e., the fourth session). Figures in parentheses indicate the average frequency of P and M behavior (i.e., the cumulative frequency since the fourth session divided by the number of sessions beginning in the fourth session).

were found under any of the other prerest trial conditions and pm-type leadership showed no significant reminiscence effects. Reminiscence under PM-type leadership tended to increase as a function of the number of prerest trials, while reminiscence under P, M, and pm leadership tended to level off or decline.

These results verify those of the first study. They indicate that reminiscence is not best accounted for by reactive inhibition theory alone. A better interpretation of the results is that reminiscence effects are not unequivocally determined by performance levels in prerest trials, but are due instead to the learner's motivation levels affected by the PM leadership conditions. Consequently, the results of these two studies are compatible with the hypothesis of Eysenck and his co-workers which postulates that reminiscence effects are an objective index of motivation.

Although Kimble and Wasserman regarded the reminiscence phenomenon as an objective, observable index of motivation, their motivation hypothesis was only understood within the theoretical framework of reactive inhibition (IR). Eysenck, however, accepted the IR theory in the case of a simple task, but moved away from IR theory to explain reminiscence in learning tasks by positing a separate motivation hypothesis. He suggested that reminiscence in learning tasks can be due to motivated cognitive activity to consolidate learning during rest periods. Thus leadership may affect reminiscence by affecting motivation during both learning trials and rest periods.

Third Study

A third study was designed to test the motivation hypothesis about reminiscence under the condition of distributed learning. Misumi, Yoshida, and Sato (1969) used experimental tasks similar to those used in the second study except that a distributed practice approach to learning was used in place of a massed practice approach. A distributed practice approach to learning involves alternating periods of work and rest. No conspicuous reminiscence effects are found in distributed learning because accumulated IR dissipates every time a rest period is given between trials. Because IR does not accumulate throughout the prerest trials, a specific period of rest after the full set of distributed practice trials does not produce a reminiscence effect (Ammons 1950; Archer 1954; Hayashi 1963; Kimble 1950). Consequently, if reminiscence is found in distributed learning of a perceptual-motor task, it is not due to the dissipation of IR but rather to the learner's internal motivation as evoked

TABLE 51. Reminiscence in Each Experimental Condition

Condition	Prerest (a)	Postrest (b)	Reminiscence (b − a)	t	Difference in Reminiscence among PM Types
PM_{10}	14.2	16.3	2.1	2.56***	F = 2.21
P_{10}	13.3	14.3	1.0	1.32	df:2/48
M_{10}	13.8	15.1	1.3	1.92*	n.s.
PM_{20}	14.9	17.2	2.3	3.81****	F = 4.32
P_{20}	14.3	16.5	2.2	2.50***	df:3/103
M_{20}	14.4	15.9	1.5	2.60***	$p < .01$
pm_{20}	14.1	14.4	0.3	0.34	PM = P = M > pm
PM_{30}	14.5	17.4	2.9	4.55****	F = 6.93
P_{30}	16.0	17.1	1.1	1.53	df:3/119
M_{30}	15.3	16.1	0.8	1.16	$p < .01$
pm_{30}	15.4	15.4	0.0	0.00	PM > P = M = pm
PM_{40}	17.2	20.8	3.6	4.77****	F = 19.55
P_{40}	17.9	19.7	1.8	2.13**	df:3/83
M_{40}	16.5	15.9	−0.6	0.51	$p < .01$
pm_{40}	16.7	17.8	1.1	1.27	PM > P = pm > M

a = performance in the last trial of the prerest trials; b = performance in the first trial of the postrest trials
*$p < .10$
**$p < .05$
***$p < .02$
****$p < .001$

by the PM leadership conditions. This is the main hypothesis of the third experiment.

The 357 subjects in the third experiment were male students in seven high school classes with each class consisting of forty-five to fifty-five students. The task was the same as in the second study—printing inverted "hiragana" alphabet characters. Seven behavioral patterns were introduced as the experimenters' supervisory types—PM–I, PM–II, P–I, P–II, M–I, M–II, and pm (since the pm condition was represented by leaders who did not speak, no distinction was made between I and II).

Type I leaders (PM–I, P–I, and M–I) differ from Type II leaders (PM–II, P–II, and M–II) according to when they make their performance-related comments. Type I leaders make their performance-related comments (if any, depending on leadership type) while the task is being carried out and the maintenance-related comments (if any) during the rest period. Type II leaders make both their performance- and maintenance-related comments while learners are resting. Type I leadership permits more adaptability and responsiveness to task-related problems that arise than does Type II.

The results showed no significant differences in prerest performance among the four main supervisory conditions. However, significant interactions were found between the four supervisory conditions and the two supervisory types. No significant reminiscence effects were found in most of the supervisory conditions. Significant reminiscence effects were found only under the PM–I supervisory condition, where the P function is introduced during the working (learning) periods and the M function is introduced during the rest periods. In this condition, the working (learning) conditions and supervisory functions appear to fit together in an optimum way.

In summary, the results of the three studies show significant reminiscence effects most consistently under PM-type supervision in both massed and distributed learning. Significant reminiscence effects were not always found under the P, M, or pm supervisory conditions even in massed learning. The results also indicate that performance levels in prerest trials do not always correspond to the amount of reminiscence shown in postrest trials. Because of these results, it is inappropriate to interpret reminiscence effects within the theoretical framework of the reactive inhibition theory. This conclusion leads to the hypothesis that experimenter behavior representing the PM leadership types affects subjects' motivation and consequently the end results of performance and reminiscence in perceptual-motor learning. The results of the studies indicated that the effects of the leadership conditions on subjects' motivation are reflected more when performance is resumed just after a rest period following the completion of the learning trials than it is in the last of the learning trials.

Performance and Experimenter's Effects

Purpose and Method of the Study

The three preceding studies of perceptual-motor learning showed no significant differences among the four leadership types in the total amount of prerest performance. However, the studies were also designed to determine whether or not differences among the leadership types would be found if changes in both prerest and postrest performance were traced by dividing the trials into three different stages—initial, intermediate, and final. Accordingly, the data from the experiments were reanalyzed to test the following hypotheses:

Hypothesis I. If the learning trials are divided into three distinct stages—initial, intermediate, and final—the performance curves for the inverted "hiragana" printing will show:

a) the highest scores in the initial stage under P-type leadership;
b) no significant differences among the four types of leadership in the intermediate stage;
c) the highest scores in the final stage under PM-type leadership.

Hypothesis II. If subjects' performance is divided into the two categories of "above average" and "below average" based on the profiles of scores during the above three stages:

a) the number of subjects whose performance for all trials is below average will be larger under the M and pm types than under the PM and P types of leadership;
b) among the subjects showing above average performance for all trials, those whose scores become higher in the final stage than they are in the initial stage will be found mostly under PM-type leadership, while the subjects under P-type leadership will tend to score less in the final stage than in the initial stage.

In order to test these hypotheses, the data for those 87 of the 834 subjects in the second study who carried out forty prerest and five postrest trials (lasting thirty seconds each) with a ten-minute rest between the fortieth and the forty-first trials were reanalyzed. The success in implementing the experimental conditions can be considered for these subjects before results are presented.

At the end of the experimental procedure, the subjects in each test group were asked to answer a questionnaire covering the following variables: "Leader's P and M behavior," "Willingness to work," "Tiredness felt," "Interest in work," and "Degree of work effort." The items used to measure these variables were rated on seven-point scales ranging from 1 ("not at all") to 7 ("very much"). The questions used to measure P behavior were:

1. How concerned was your leader with enhancing the efficiency of your work?
2. How concerned was your leader with the accuracy of your work?
3. How hard was your leader trying to make you print as many letters as possible?

M behavior was measured by the following questions.

1. How much understanding did your leader show of your feelings?
2. How concerned was your leader to create a congenial atmosphere in your group?
3. Did your leader show concern or give suggestions to make the work easier to perform?

Results

Assessment of Leadership Behavior by the Observer and by Subjects

Table 52 presents the results of the assessment of the experimenter's behavior by the observer. The data clearly show that the experimental conditions were successfully induced.

Figure 8 shows the subjects' assessment of the experimenter's P and M behavior. The figure shows each intended leadership type as falling into one or another of four quadrants. The lines dividing the figure into quadrants are based on the average P and M scores that subjects assigned to the leaders. The quadrants thus represent four perceived PM types. The number of subjects in each experimental condition who accurately placed their leader in each PM type is shown in parentheses for each condition. The data indicate that twenty-eight subjects appropriately identified their leader as falling into the PM type, seventeen as falling into the P type, twenty in the M type, and twenty-two in the pm type. The total number of subjects who actually participated in the experiment (eighty-nine) was larger than the total of the above figures (eighty-seven). The two subjects who either made errors in performing the task or

TABLE 52. Leader's Behavior as Described by the Observer

Experimental Condition	Frequency of P-type Remarks	Frequency of M-type Remarks
PM	24 (0.65)	29 (0.78)
P	39 (1.05)	1 (0.03)
M	1 (0.03)	39 (1.05)
pm	0 (0.00)	0 (0.00)

Note: Numbers in parentheses represent the average frequency per trial, obtained by dividing the total number of remarks made by the experimenter during the fourth through fortieth trial by the number of trials (thirty-seven).

inappropriately classified their leader were omitted from the results shown here.

Table 53 gives the results of t-tests comparing the subjects' assessment of the experimenter's leadership behavior in the different conditions. Two significant differences appear which ideally would not be found. Ideally, subjects would report similarly low levels of M-oriented behavior under both the P and the pm conditions. Also, they would report equally low P-oriented behavior under both the M and the pm conditions. However, the P level in the M condition and the M level in the P condition are both slightly higher than the P and M levels, respectively, in the pm condition. Still, subjects evaluations show that the conditions designed for the experiment were successfully created.

Number of Trials and Performance

Figure 9 shows the performance results for all trials before and after the rest period. The letter "B" (base) indicates the mean values of performance for the first through the third trials where no PM leadership conditions were introduced. The values given at B, which would identify any differences in the subjects' inherent ability to perform the task, indicate that there were no significant differences in ability among the groups under the different PM leadership conditions (F = 0.28, df = 3/83, n.s.).

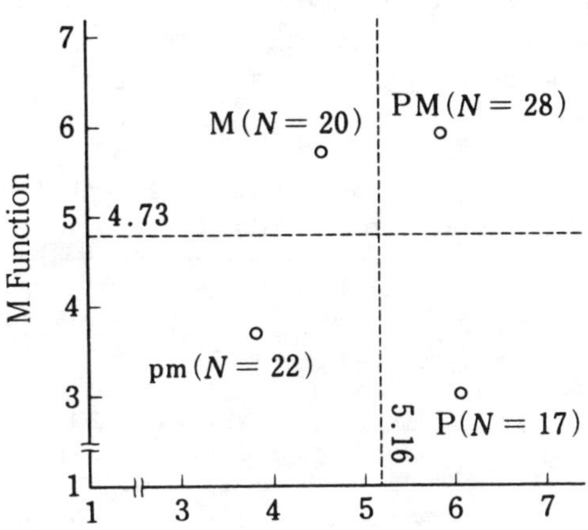

Fig. 8. Experimenter's behavioral pattern as assessed by subjects

TABLE 53. Comparison of P and M Leadership as Perceived by Subjects for Pairs of Leadership Conditions

Leadership Types Compared	Levels of Significance: P Function	Levels of Significance: M Function
PM—P	n.s.[a]	.001
PM—M	.001	n.s.[a]
PM—pm	.001	.001
P—M	.001	.001
P—pm	.001	.01[a]
M—pm	.01[a]	.001

[a]No significant differences were intended for these particular pairs of conditions on this particular behavior dimension noted.

Significance levels are for two-tailed T-tests.

Table 54 shows the results of a two-way analysis of variance using data from the fourth through the forty-fifth trials (Winer 1962). The main effect of the leadership conditions is not significant (F = 1.784, df = 3/83, n.s.), indicating that there are no differences due to leadership conditions in average performance for the whole range of trials. However, both the main effect of the three sets of trials (F = 65.928, df = 41/3403, $p < .01$) and the interaction of leadership type and trial (F = 2.275, df = 123/3403, $p < .01$) are significant. This result is consistent with the results shown in figure 9. The levels of performance gradually increase as the number of trials increases and the profiles of performance show divergent curves for different leadership conditions. Next, two-way analyses of variance on the prerest trials (table 55)

TABLE 54. Analysis of Variance on the Learning Results of the Fourth through Forty-fifth Trials

Source	df	*M S*	F
Between all subjects	86		
Leadership type (A)	3	391.052	1.784
Differences between subjects (C)	83	219.218	
Within subjects	261		
Trials (B)	41	163.879	65.928*
A × B	123	5.656	2.275*
B × C	3,403	2.486	

Source: Based on data shown in figure 17.

*$p < .01$

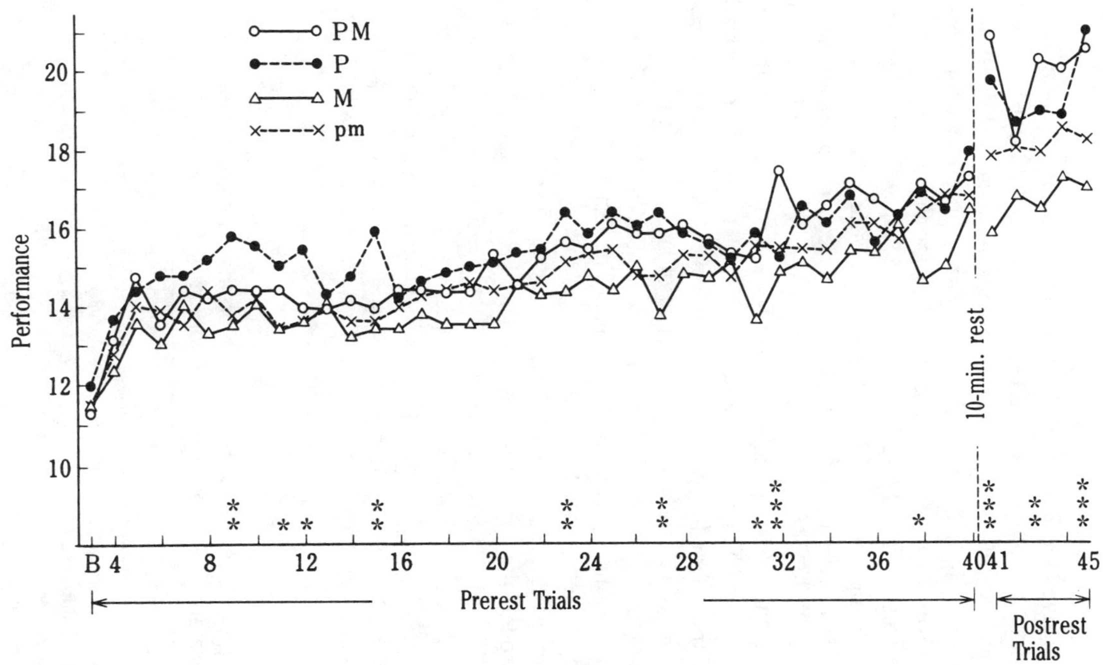

Fig. 9. Levels of performance under different PM leadership conditions. The trials for which significant differences among leadership types were found using one-way analysis of variance are marked with: $*p < .10$; $**p < .05$; $***p < .01$.

and postrest trials (table 56) as well as a one-way analysis of variance on individual trials (table 57) were conducted to determine which particular trials were responsible for the significant interaction between trial and leadership type revealed by table 54.

Table 55 gives the results of the two-way analysis of variance on the fourth to fortieth (prerest) trials. The results show, as did table 54, that there are no significant differences in the total performance among the leadership conditions (F = 1.443, df = 3/83, n.s.). The main effect of the trials is significant, however, implying that levels of performance tend to increase as the trials progress (F = 27.227, df = 36/2988, $p < .01$). Further, the significant interaction of trial and leadership type means that the performance profiles take on different patterns depending on leadership conditions (F = 1.736, df = 108/2988, $p < .01$). Performance under P-type leadership increased sharply in the comparatively early stage up to the ninth trial, while performance under PM-type leadership rose most rapidly from around the thirty-second trial in the late prerest stage. However, since it was not yet clear which particular trials marked the emergence of such statistically significant differences among the leadership types, it was necessary to conduct a one-way analysis of variance on individual trials. (The results are shown in table 57 and are discussed below.)

Table 56 gives the results of the two-way analysis of variance on the forty-first through the forty-fifth (postrest) trials. The main effect of leadership types (F = 4.141, df = 3/83, $p < .01$), the main effect of trials (F = 3.444, df = 4/332, $p < .01$), and the interaction of leadership type and trial (F = 3.798, df = 12/332, $p < .01$) are all significant. Since the main effect of leadership type is found to be significant, average levels of performance were compared using the Tukey test between each pair of leadership types.

TABLE 55. Analysis of Variance on the Learning Results of Prerest Trials (fourth through fortieth)

Source	df	*M S*	F
Between all subjects	86		
Leadership type (A)	3	267.726	1.443
Differences between subjects (C)	83	185.518	
Within subjects	261		
Trials (B)	36	63.788	27.227*
A × B	108	4.068	1.736*
B × C	2,988	2.343	

Source: Based on data shown in figure 17.
*$p < .01$

The results indicated that performance under the PM and P types was greater than that under the M type and that performance under the PM type was greater than that under the pm type ($p < .05$). The finding that the main effect of the trial is significant may reflect the trend shown in figure 9 that after the second postrest trial, performance levels under all leadership types increased as the trials progressed. The significant interaction between leadership type and trial can be ascribed to performance in the first postrest trial under PM- and P-type leaders being markedly higher than under M- and pm-type leaders.

Factor Analysis of Performance in Individual Trials

The first seven columns of table 57 show the results of a series of one-way analysis of variance computations assessing the effects of leadership types on performance in each individual trial. The last four columns show the results of a factor analysis of performance curves using geomax rotation. Both analyses are designed to determine which particular trials were responsible for the significant interaction between the leadership types and trials.

In the factor analysis, the initial factor loading matrix was obtained by applying the principal axis method to the 42 × 42 correlation matrix for the fourth through the forty-fifth trial. Axis rotation was then conducted using the geomax method (Kashiwagi 1965) for the three principal factors having eigenvalues larger than 1.0. The factor variance accounted for by the three factors was very high—74.0 percent of the total variance. The contributions by the separate factors were: 21.5 percent for Factor I, 26.2 percent for Factor II, and 26.3 percent for Factor III. For the sake of convenience, only those trials whose factor loadings are larger than .550 will be considered in interpreting each factor.

TABLE 56. Analysis of Variance on the Learning Results of the Postrest Trials (forty-first through forty-fifth)

Source	df	*M S*	F
Between all subjects	86		
Leadership type (A)	3	174.239	4.141*
Differences between subjects (C)	83	42.081	
Within subjects	261		
Trials (B)	4	7.874	3.444*
A × B	12	8.683	3.798*
B × C	332	2.286	

Source: Based on data shown in figure 17.

Note: The differences between leadership types found using Tukey's post hoc comparison test showed the following: PM > M and pm, and P > M.

$^*p < .01$

The three factors correspond to three stages in the experimental trials. The high loadings on Factor I in the initial stage (the fourth through the seventeenth trials) indicate that Factor I is a factor of "initial-stage effort." Loadings on this factor suggest that there were some subjects whose performance was particularly high in the initial stage. Because the trials showing high loadings for Factor II are found from the fourteenth through the fortieth trials, it may be called the factor of "intermediate-stage effort." This factor implies that there are other subjects whose performance rose after the initial stage during an intermediate stage. The trials having factor loadings above .550 for Factor III are found during the last stage of the prerest trials and throughout the postrest trials. This factor is the factor of "final-stage effort." This factor reflects the rise in performance for some subjects following the plateau of the intermediate stage extending to the postrest period where the favorable effect of the rest becomes evident.

The interaction between leadership type and trial stage that has been shown in tables 54, 55, and 56 can be clarified by noting how many significant differences among leadership types are found for trials associated with each factor. Significant differences among leadership types ($p < .01$) were identified using one-way analysis of variance for twelve trials. These significant differences were distributed among trials as follows: four out of eleven trials associated with Factor I (36.4 percent), two out of seventeen for Factor II (8.5 percent), and six out of thirteen for Factor III (46.2 percent). These ratios show that the interaction of leadership type and trial appears most frequently in the trials representing Factor III (the factor of final-stage effort) followed in frequency by those representing Factor I (the factor of initial-stage effort). Significant differences among leadership types are less apt to appear in the trials related to Factor II (the factor of intermediate-stage effort).

TABLE 57. Results of ANOVA on the Trial-by-trial Effects of Leadership Types and Geomax-rotated Factor Loadings between Trials

	Mean Values under Total F-ratio							Geomax-rotated Factor Loadings			
Trial	PM	P	M	pm	$\bar{X}$	*SD*	*F*-ratio	I	II	III	h^2
4	13.2	13.8	12.4	12.8	13.0	3.2	0.70	*.601*	.493	.387	.754
5	14.7	14.4	13.6	14.0	14.2	3.0	0.52	*.586*	.426	.496	.771
6	13.6	14.8	13.1	13.9	13.8	2.5	1.51	*.586*	.427	.286	.608
7	14.4	14.8	14.1	13.5	14.2	2.7	0.76	*.706*	.073	.489	.743
8	14.2	15.2	13.4	14.4	14.3	2.8	1.38	*.619*	.493	.385	.775
9	14.4	15.8	13.6	13.7	14.3	2.5	2.98*	*.557*	.385	.435	.647
10	14.4	14.5	14.1	14.3	14.3	2.1	0.18	.410	*.635*	.241	.630

TABLE 57—*Continued*

Trial	Mean Values under Total F-ratio PM	P	M	pm	$\bar{X}$	*SD*	*F*-ratio	Geomax-rotated Factor Loadings I	II	III	h^2
11	14.4	15.0	13.5	13.5	14.1	2.1	2.36†	*.638*	.406	.423	.750
12	13.8	15.4	13.6	13.6	14.0	2.3	2.63†	*.692*	.150	.476	.727
13	14.1	14.3	14.0	13.9	14.0	2.6	0.09	*.566*	.472	.410	.711
14	14.1	14.7	13.3	13.6	13.9	2.4	1.24	.421	*.555*	.497	.732
15	13.9	15.9	13.5	14.6	14.4	2.8	2.98*	*.649*	.365	.432	.740
16	14.3	14.2	13.5	14.0	14.0	2.4	0.46	.443	*.585*	.450	.741
17	14.4	14.6	13.9	14.4	14.3	2.4	0.36	*556*	*.605*	.227	.726
18	14.3	14.8	13.6	14.5	14.3	2.4	0.82	.463	*.579*	.371	.687
19	14.4	15.0	13.6	14.6	14.4	2.5	1.15	.363	*.551*	.476	.661
20	15.3	15.1	13.6	14.4	14.6	2.6	2.10	.549	.466	.472	.741
21	14.5	15.3	14.5	14.5	14.7	2.5	0.45	.526	*.658*	.250	.772
22	15.2	15.4	13.8	14.6	14.8	2.6	1.59	.456	.438	*.607*	.769
23	15.5	16.4	13.9	15.1	15.2	2.7	2.74*	.406	.537	*.635*	.856
24	14.9	15.8	14.2	15.4	15.0	2.7	1.29	.442	.495	.515	.705
25	15.6	16.4	13.9	15.4	15.3	2.8	2.81	.500	.397	*.571*	.734
26	15.8	16.0	15.0	14.8	15.4	2.8	0.92	.336	*.753*	.298	.768
27	15.8	16.2	13.8	14.7	15.1	2.8	3.27	.462	.434	*.597*	.759
28	16.0	15.8	14.4	15.3	15.4	2.7	1.52	.380	*.550*	.543	.742
29	15.6	15.6	14.3	15.3	15.2	2.9	1.02	.246	*.692*	.350	.662
30	15.3	16.2	15.1	14.8	15.3	2.7	0.88	.515	.416	.480	.677
31	15.2	15.8	13.7	15.6	15.0	2.8	2.43†	.491	.505	.445	.694
32	17.4	15.2	14.9	15.5	15.9	2.8	4.11**	.305	*.586*	.436	.626
33	16.1	16.5	15.1	15.4	15.8	2.9	0.94	.516	.505	.498	.769
34	16.5	16.0	14.7	15.3	15.7	2.8	1.78	.342	*.610*	*.576*	.820
35	17.1	16.8	15.4	16.0	16.4	2.9	1.49	.456	.450	*.591*	.760
36	16.7	15.6	15.4	16.1	16.0	2.9	0.92	.414	*.564*	.476	.717
37	16.3	16.3	16.1	15.9	16.1	3.0	0.10	.261	*.644*	.460	.695
38	17.0	16.8	14.7	16.3	16.3	3.0	2.67†	.277	*.566*	*.662*	.836
39	16.6	16.4	15.1	16.7	16.2	3.0	1.34	.385	.517	*.591*	.764
40	17.2	17.9	16.5	16.7	17.0	2.8	0.86	.339	*.635*	.487	.756
41	20.8	19.7	15.9	17.8	18.7	3.7	9.91**	.151	.374	*.797*	.798
42	18.6	18.6	16.8	18.0	18.0	3.3	1.54	.270	.538	*.649*	.783
43	19.2	18.9	16.5	17.9	18.2	3.2	3.59*	.286	.357	*.798*	.847
44	19.0	18.8	17.3	18.5	18.4	3.2	1.28	.193	*.591*	*.630*	.784
45	19.5	20.4	17.0	18.2	18.8	3.4	4.18**	.246	.343	*.817*	.846
Factor variance								9.035	11.020	11.028	31.083
Contribution (%)								21.5	26.2	26.3	74.0

Note: Degrees of freedom for F-ratio are 3 and 83 for all trials: †$p < .10$, *$p < .05$, **$p < .01$. Values of factor loadings of .550 or larger are printed in italics.

Analyzed in this way, the results shown in figure 9 and table 57 indicate that the highest performance in the initial-stage trials was achieved under P-type leadership, while that in the final-stage trials occurred under PM-type leadership.

Table 58 presents the results of three one-way analysis of variance calculations predicting factor scores for individual subjects (derived using the above factor analysis procedure) on the basis of the four leadership types. This table reveals significant differences among leadership types both for initial-stage effort (F = 2.753, df = 3/83, $p < .05$) and final-stage effort (F = 7.528, df = 3/83, $p < .01$). No such differences are found for scores on the intermediate-stage effort factor. Further, the Tukey test for differences between pairs of leadership types in the initial- and final-stage effort factors indicates that performance under P-type leadership was significantly higher than that under PM-type leadership for initial-stage effort and that performance under PM-type leadership was significantly higher than under M-type leadership for final-stage effort.

In summary, the results shown in tables 57 and 58 explain the significant interaction between leadership type and trial shown by the ANOVAS in tables 54, 55, and 56. This interaction can be attributed to the fact that the highest performance in the initial stage occurred under P-type leadership while the highest performance in the final stage was attained under PM-type leadership.

Classification of Subjects by Factor Score Pattern

In addition to analyzing the interactive effects of leadership type and trial, profiles of the three-factor scores for individual subjects were studied in order to find out how frequently specific patterns appear under each leadership type.

TABLE 58. Means of the Scores of the Three Factors under Different Leadership Conditions

	Leadership Type				
Score	PM (*N* = 28)	P (*N* = 17)	M (*N* = 20)	pm (*N* = 22)	F
Initial-stage factor	−0.334	0.449	0.139	−0.085	2.753*
	(0.94)	(1.04)	(1.01)	(0.86)	PM < P[a]
Intermediate-stage factor	0.073	−0.262	−0.025	0.132	0.567
	(0.86)	(0.88)	(1.24)	(0.93)	
Final-stage factor	0.471	0.287	−0.720	−0.171	7.528**
	(1.03)	(0.96)	(0.78)	(0.70)	M < PM[a]

Note: Figures in parentheses are standard deviations.
[a]results of Tukey test
$*p < .05$, $**p < .01$

The initial factor loading matrix was obtained by applying the centroid method to the matrix of Cattell's coefficients (Cattell 1949) between every two subjects and was submitted to geomax rotation. The result showed that 81.5 percent of the trace of the coefficient matrix was accounted for by six factors. Table 59 shows the number of subjects falling under each of the six factor axes subdivided according to whether the factor loadings are positive or negative. Eight or more subjects were found in seven patterns (in order of frequency): II^+, I^+, III^+, V^+, IV^+, IV^-, and VI^+.

The charts shown in figure 10 trace the average standardized trial-by-trial performance for subjects showing each of those nine patterns which are represented by three or more subjects. In table 60, the pattern groups in figure 10 are reclassified into three performance profiles—horizontal (I^+, I^-, II^+, III^+, and V^+), descending (III^-, IV^+, and VI^+), and ascending (IV^-). The correspondence between the leadership types and the three performance patterns is statistically significant ($\chi^2 = 14.592$, df $= 6$, $p < .025$). A large proportion of the subjects show a horizontal pattern under all four leadership types. The percentage of subjects with a horizontal performance pattern is reasonably similar for all four leadership types. It ranges from a low of 58.8 percent in the P type to 75.0 percent in the PM and M types. Additional analyses not shown in table 60 compared above-average and below-average performance groups within the horizontal pattern group. The results indicate that under M-type leadership, 55.0 percent of the horizontal performance group showed below-average performance, while under PM-, P-, and pm-type leadership 41.2 to 46.4 percent showed above-average performance.

Table 60 also shows that the descending performance pattern is found more frequently under P-, M-, and pm-type leadership than under PM-type leadership, but that the ascending performance pattern is found most fre-

TABLE 59. Number of Subjects with Positive and Negative Loadings on Patterns According to Cattell's Coefficients under Different Leadership Types

Leadership Type	Axis I +	I −	II +	II −	III +	III −	IV +	IV −	V +	V −	VI +	VI −	Total
PM	6	1	7	0	3	0	0	6	4	0	1	0	28
P	5	0	2	0	2	3	2	1	1	0	1	0	17
M	2	2	2	0	5	0	4	0	4	0	1	0	20
pm	2	0	7	1	2	0	2	1	2	0	5	0	22
Total	15	3	18	1	12	3	8	8	11	0	8	0	87

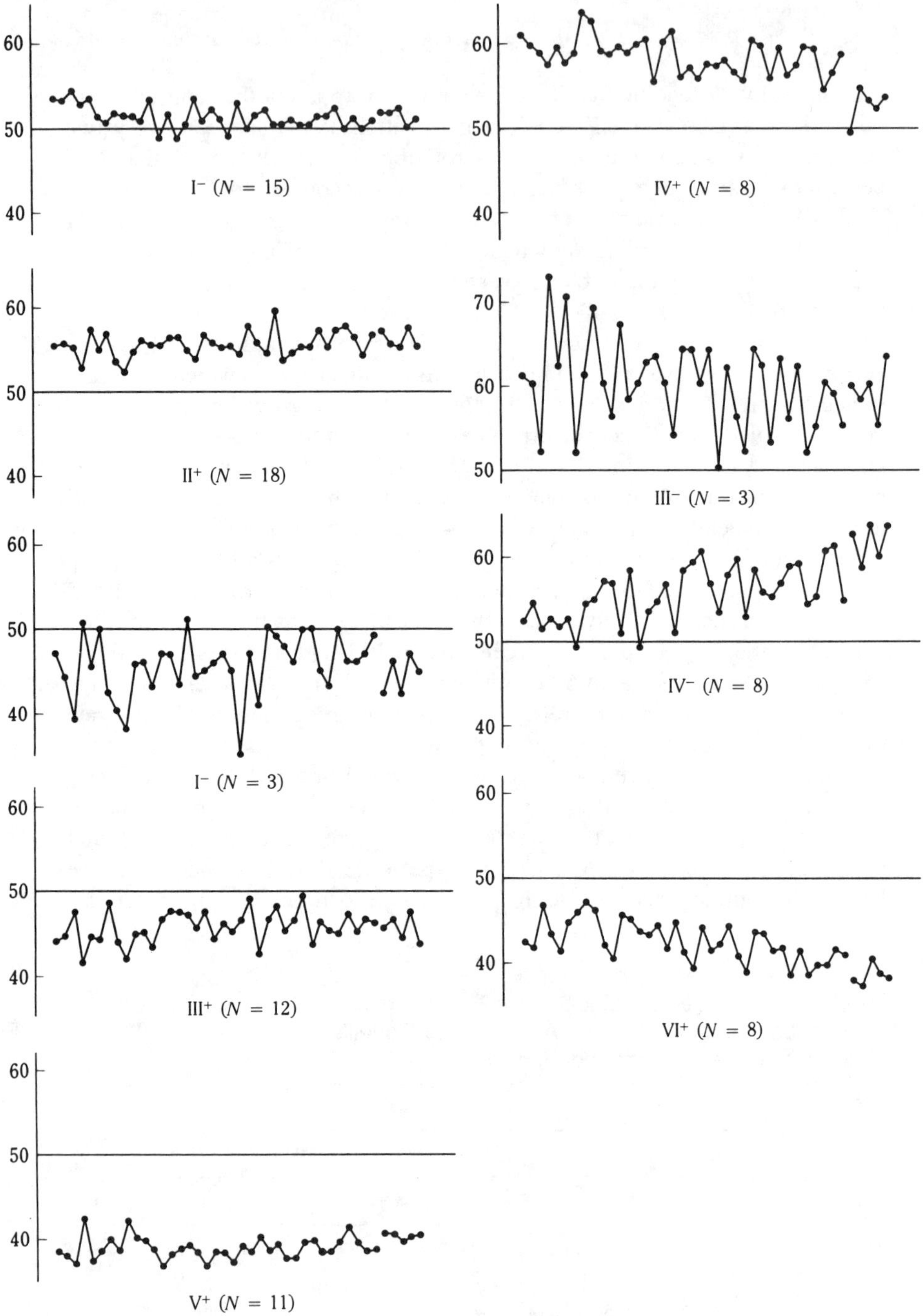

Fig. 10. Average performance of nine pattern groups classified by coefficients. X-axis is the trials (4 through 45), y-axis is the scores in each trial.

quently under PM-type leadership. By applying a chi-square test to the data for pairs of leadership types, the distribution of performance patterns under the PM type was confirmed to be significantly different from that under the three other leadership types. (In the comparison of PM and P, PM and M, and PM and pm, χ^2 scores were 8.88, 8.57, and 9.14, respectively, df = 2, $p < .02$). The differences between pairs of the P-, M-, and pm-type leadership conditions did not reach statistically significant levels.

Moderately high ratios of descending performance were found under the P, pm, and M types of supervision (35.3, 33.3, and 25.0 percent, respectively). Among these three leadership conditions, 23.8 percent of the subjects under pm-type leadership showed below-average performance, while under the P and M types the rates of above-average performance were higher.

The highest ratio of subjects showing an ascending performance pattern occurred under PM-type leadership (21.4 percent), while the ratios under the other three leadership conditions were as low as 0 to 5.9 percent. All subjects belonging to the ascending pattern group also showed above-average overall performance.

Discussion

Results have been presented which indicate that the experimental leadership conditions were successfully induced as reflected in both observer's reports (table 52) and subjects' perceptions (fig. 8). No significant differences were found among the leadership types in overall performance across all trials. The lack of differences may have occurred in part because the task of inverted "hiragana" printing was too easy for senior high school students to produce any differences due to the effects of leadership on motivation. Another expla-

TABLE 60. Leadership Types and Three Patterns of Performance

Leadership Type	Pattern of Performance			Total
	Horizontal[a]	Descending[b]	Ascending[c]	
PM	21 (75.0%)	1 (3.6%)	6 (21.4%)	28
P	10 (58.8)	6 (35.3)	1 (5.9)	17
M	15 (75.0)	5 (25.0)	0 (0.0)	20
pm	13 (61.9)	7 (33.3)	1 (4.8)	21
Total	59	19	8	86

Note: $p < .02$ significant differences exist between PM and the other three leadership types. Three patterns deduced from the nine groups in fig. 18 (omitted: II^-type, $N = 1$, in table 59)

[a] I^+, I^-, II^+, III^+, V^+

[b] III^-, IV^+, VI^+

[c] IV^-

nation might be that the number of trials (forty-five) was not large enough to induce any significant differences. This latter explanation is more likely. Although the PM type was better than the M and pm types in postrest performance, and the P type was better than the M type, another difference also appeared. Subjects' answers to other questionnaire items showed that subjects under PM-type leadership scored the highest ($F = 2.56$, $df = 3/83$, $p < .10$) in "willingness to work" during the postrest period. This suggests that significant differences in motivation due to leadership type occur although they are not reflected in overall task performance across all trials. Moreover, since the interaction between leadership type and trial is significant (fig. 9 and 10), it is evident that differences among leadership types can be expressed in various ways during the progress of trials. In particular (fig. 9 and table 57), performance in the first stage (up to the sixteenth trial) was the highest under P-type leadership. But after the thirty-second trial, and particularly during the postrest period, performance under PM-type leadership became distinctly superior to performance under the P, M, and pm types of leadership. Factor analysis on trials (table 57) showed that three phases in the learning trials could be identified: initial, intermediate, and final. The effects of leadership type can be properly determined only by distinguishing among such stages.

Hypothesis I-a was supported by the finding that performance scores in the initial-stage factor were the highest under P-type leadership. Since P-type leadership is oriented toward task performance, subjects under P-type leadership felt compelled to aim at high-level performance in the initial stage.

Hypothesis I-b was also supported because no significant differences were found among the four leadership types for performance scores on the intermediate-stage factor (table 58). Most subjects registered a plateau-shaped profile in performance during the intermediate stage.

Hypothesis I-c was also supported. The performance scores on the final-stage factor were the highest under PM-type leadership with the scores under M-type leadership being significantly lower than those under PM-type leadership. The scores of the final-stage factor were above average under the PM and P types of leadership while scores under the M and pm types of leadership were below average. The high performance scores for PM-type leadership are consistent with the finding that the "willingness to work" of subjects under this type of leadership during the postrest period was distinctly higher than the willingness to work of other subjects. Moreover, the finding that subjects under the PM and M types of leadership answered the questionnaire item concerning "interest in the work" more positively than did others seems to confirm the interpretation that "the optimum situation for stimulating an increase in productivity and morale is the one in which the M-type function of leadership exerts catalytic effects on the P-type function" (Misumi and Shirakashi 1964, 126).

Hypothesis II suggests that below-average performance will be seen most often under M- and pm-type leaders, and that increasing performance will be found for PM-type leaders and declining performance under P-type leadership. When performance curves are classified according to typical profiles (table 60), the pattern of ascending performance is found most frequently under PM-type leadership, while descending performance appears frequently under the three leadership types of P, M, and pm but rarely under PM leadership. This finding leads to the conclusion that the effects of the leadership conditions can be more distinctly detected during the final-stage trials than during the earlier trials.

Both figure 9 and table 60 show that the level of performance was lowest under the M-type leadership conditions. What does this mean? In the massed learning of such a simple task as the inverted "hiragana" printing, a subject may experience high tension because he would consider the work a test of his personal ability. M-type behavior on the part of the leader during massed learning would certainly have the effect of reducing the subject's tension with the result that performance under M-type leadership would be lower than that under pm-type leadership. If the M-type leadership condition is analogous to the "inadaptable type of leadership" defined as M_{II} in the study by Misumi, Yoshida, and Sato (1969), it may be quite understandable that the trials under M-type leadership should register the lowest performance. The degree of "inadaptability" of M-oriented behavior in the PM-type leadership conditions, however, will be reduced because M behavior is complemented by P-oriented behavior. M and P leadership behavior tend to strengthen one another with the result that subjects' interest in the task and willingness to work will be enhanced during the final stage at which time the level of performance will markedly increase.

Recall and Leadership Dynamics

Yamauchi and Yamaguchi (1973) examined the effects of leadership behavior on paired-associates learning as part of a series of studies concerning the relationship between PM leadership types and anxiety. A number of studies concerning the effects of anxiety on the learning of tasks with different degrees of difficulty have been conducted by Spence, Taylor, and Ketchel (1956) using the Manifest Anxiety Scale (MAS). Their results showed that the level of performance and speed of work of a high-anxiety group was inferior to that of a low-anxiety group in learning difficult tasks. However, in learning easy tasks, the high-anxiety group scored better than the low-anxiety group. Similar results were obtained in studies by Spence, Farber, and McFann (1956) of paired-associates learning. However, researchers like Alper (1948), Heyer and O'Kelly (1949), and Ishiguro (1963) have studied the effects of experimenter-induced motivation on learning retention. Their studies showed that highly motivated subjects scored better in retention than low-motivated groups. Sarason (1957) found both significant main effects and significant interaction effects in his study of the consequences that anxiety and the experimenter's instructions for motivation (using "subject-oriented," "experimenter-oriented," and "neutral" instructions) had for language learning (which is not, however, paired-associates learning).

Misumi, Ikeda, and Yamaguchi (1971) designed their experiment on the premise that the experimenter-subject relationship was analogous to the leadership relationship of a superior to his subordinates in a workshop. The styles of giving instructions were classified into four types according to the PM leadership behavior hypothesis. Differences in the subjects' performance in paired-associates learning under the four leadership types were examined. The results showed that the highest performance occurred under PM-type leadership followed by the P, M, and pm types in order of effectiveness. In conjunction with these studies, Yamauchi and Yamaguchi designed a method to institute the PM, P, and M types of leadership by manipulating the experimenter's instructions to subjects. By dividing the subjects into high-anxiety and low-anxiety groups based on the MAS, they examined the effects of anxiety and the three leadership types on the performance of two kinds of paired-associates learning with different levels of difficulty.

Method

The 311 subjects were students of a girls' senior high school in Fukuoka City, divided into six classes. The difficult learning task involved a set of sixteen false equations ($1 \times 16 = 45$, for example) including four addition, four subtraction, four multiplication, and four division equations. The easy task was a list of sixteen nonsense word pairs in "kana" script. Each pair (*ike-kuya,* for example) was made up of a cue (stimulant) of a "hiragana" dyad whose association value was 0 to 4 according to Umemoto's scale (Umemoto, Morikawa, and Ibuki 1955), and its response to a "katakana" dyad with the association value of 30 to 34. In preparation for the experiment, these two sets of tasks were pretested with a group of fifteen junior high school students. The number of correct responses for the nonsense word task was larger than that for the false equation task, indicating that the former was clearly easier than the latter.

The subjects were divided into six groups according to the three leadership conditions and the two paired-associates learning tasks. For the nonsense word pair learning task, three groups were composed under PM-, P-, and M-type leadership consisting of 52, 53, and 52 subjects. For the false-equation learning task, another three groups were set up for PM-, P-, and M-type leadership made up of 51, 52, and 51 subjects. One week before the experiment, the anxiety of subjects in the six groups was rated using the MAS. Fifteen subjects in each group whose scores ranged from 6 to 18 were selected as low-anxiety subjects, while another fifteen whose scores were 25 to 36 were identified as high-anxiety subjects.

After a preliminary explanation by his assistant, the experimenter showed the subjects a sample pair to be learned and had them practice learning it. Then he showed each pair of the sixteen-item series one by one for three seconds with an interval of half a second. Having presented all sixteen pairs, he then showed the list of cues for the sixteen items assigned to the group (''IKE'' or ''1 × 6,'' for example) and made the subjects write the responses for the cues (''KUYA'' or ''45,'' for example) on the answer sheets which had been given to them in advance. In each trial, which lasted ninety seconds, the subject started writing at the experimenter's order, ''Start!'', trying to recall as many correct responses as possible until the order to stop was given. The order of the cues was changed at random in each trial. There were eight trials for subjects carrying out the paired word task and eight for those doing the false equation task.

The roles for all three types of PM behavior were performed by the same experimenter. The experimenter gave verbal instructions only during the thirty-second interval between trials. The experimenter had an assistant who gave the preliminary explanation at the start of the experiment, operated the slide projector during it, and later assessed the subjects' perceptions of the experimenter's behavioral type using a questionnaire.

The preliminary explanation given by the assistant to the subjects was to the following effect: ''The work we are about to ask you to do has nothing to do with your school grades. First, you are to memorize all the paired ''kana'' words (or equations) which will be projected one by one on that screen. Then you are to fill in the blanks on the answer sheet with the answers to the cues projected on the screen.''

The remarks the experimenter made in order to express the three different types of PM leadership behavior were as follows.

For the P type. ''Please try to give as many right answers as possible,'' ''Now, this time try to remember more accurately and memorize as many answers to the cues as you can,'' ''It's no good if you forget what you have memorized and give wrong answers. So try hard to keep the answers firmly in your memory,'' and other remarks placing pressure on subjects toward speedier and more accurate learning and placing emphasis on the performance of the task.

For the M type. ''Take it easy! Do your work in a relaxed way. We are in no hurry,'' ''Sorry to have asked you to do such a troublesome thing during your free study period,'' and other remarks aimed at easing the tension of the subjects and creating a congenial atmosphere between the experimenter and the subjects.

For the PM type. "Please be relaxed, but I hope you will do your best. Try to memorize as accurately as possible," "Can you do your work a little more quickly? But don't get too worked up. Take it easy!" and similar remarks combining the characteristics of both the P and M types.

The differences that subjects perceived among the three types of leadership behavior was evaluated using the following questionnaire items related to P behavior:

1. How much did your experimenter urge you to work as hard as you can?
2. How much did your experimenter stress the need for memorizing correctly?
3. How much did your experimenter urge you to do your work quickly?
4. How much did your experimenter urge you to memorize as many answers as possible?

Questions related to M behavior were as follows:

1. How much did your experimenter try to lessen your tension?
2. How much sympathy did your experimenter show to you?
3. How much did your experimenter try to make you work without considering your feelings?
4. How much did your experimenter try to create a congenial atmosphere in your group?

Results

Analysis Based on the Originally Designed Experimental Conditions

Figure 11 shows the average number of correct responses in the twelve experimental groups divided according to the three leadership types, the two tasks assigned, and the two levels of subjects' anxiety. The word "block" refers to the combined score of two trials, so that 1 represents the sum of correct responses in the first and second trials, 2 represents that of the third and fourth trials, and so on. Table 61 gives the results of an analysis of variance conducted using the values shown in figure 11. The results of an F-test on subjects' scores in the first trial, which was conducted before combining the trials into blocks, showed no significant differences among the twelve groups indicating that the subjects' ability for recalling could be considered equal.

The ANOVA results show no significant differences in the average number of correct responses among groups in different PM leadership conditions. Among low-anxiety groups performing the nonsense word task, however, the score of the PM groups was the highest, followed by the P and M groups in that order. Among the high-anxiety groups, the score of the M

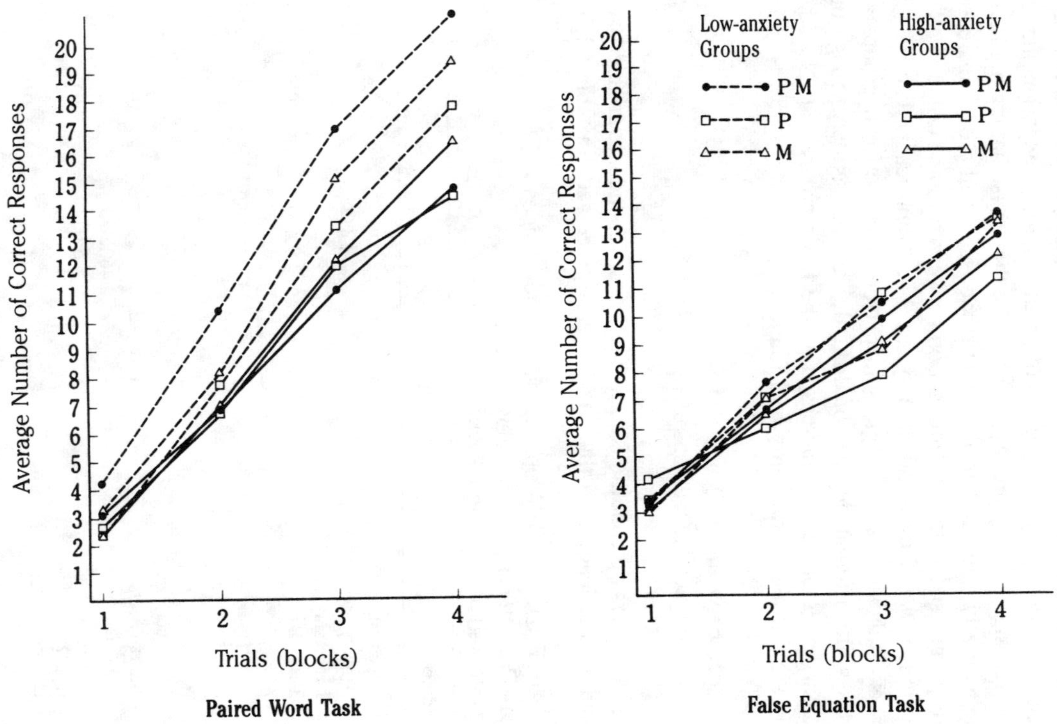

Fig. 11. Learning curves representing the number of correct responses in each experimental condition

group was the highest, followed by the P and PM groups while the scores of the latter two groups were roughly the same.

A comparison among the groups assigned tasks of different degrees of difficulty indicates that the groups given the easier task performed better than those given the harder one. In both kinds of groups, subjects experiencing low anxiety showed significantly higher performance than those having high anxiety. Quite naturally, the number of correct responses by all groups increased as the trials progressed so that the interaction between trial and task as well as the interaction between trial and anxiety are both significant. The data in figure 11 also indicate that differences in performance between groups assigned tasks with different degrees of difficulty as well as between groups with different levels of anxiety increased as the trials progressed. No other statistically significant interactions were found.

Correspondence between the Three PM Leadership Conditions and Subjects' Leadership Descriptions

The three PM leadership conditions introduced as independent variables were checked against the leadership that the subjects perceived. In table 62, the

TABLE 61. ANOVA on Learning Performance as Predicted by Anxiety Level, Trial, Leadership Type, and Task

Source	df	F	*p*
Between subjects	179		
Anxiety (A)	1	5.414	.025
Leadership type (C)	2	—	
Task (D)	1	9.420	.005
A × C	2	—	
A × D	1	1.639	
C × D	2	—	
A × C × D	2	—	
Error (between)	168		
Within subjects	540		
Trial (B)	3	460.015	.01
A × B	3	5.052	.05
B × C	6	—	
B × D	3	24.474	.01
A × B × C	6	—	
A × B × D	3	—	
B × C × D	6	—	
A × B × C × D	6	1.042	
Error (within)	504		
Total	719		

Source: Based on data shown in figure 19.

subjects who experienced each of the three leadership conditions are classified into four categories according to whether they identified the experimenter as a PM-, P-, M-, or pm-type leader. The number of subjects placing the experimenter in each category is shown for the two kinds of learning task. Table 62 indicates that subjects tended to place the experimenter into the appropriate category.

Figure 12 illustrates subjects' learning curves reflected in the number of correct responses during different blocks of trials in the learning tasks. The data are presented separately for subjects who performed the easier and the more difficult tasks. Separate learning curves are graphed for those subjects in each leadership condition whose descriptions of the experimenter's behavior were consistent with the intended leadership type. Table 63 gives the results of an ANOVA based on the data shown in figure 12.

The ANOVA shows that the differences in performance among the three PM types were not significant, but that generally speaking the rate of correct responses was the highest for the PM group, followed by the P and M groups in that order. Very clear, significant differences were found between tasks, among trials, and in the interaction between task and trial.

Performance Differences among Perceived PM Leadership Types

In figure 13, the average numbers of correct responses are rearranged under the four PM leadership types based exclusively on subjects' perceptions of

TABLE 62. Learning Performance Associated with Various Combinations of Intended PM Types and PM Types as Assessed by Subjects

Intended PM Types	Subjects' Assessment	Paired Words	False Equations
PM	PM	20	22
	P	11	12
	M	10	2
	pm	11	15
P	PM	4	12
	P	38	37
	M	0	1
	pm	11	2
M	PM	2	10
	P	0	0
	M	43	33
	pm	9	8
Total		159	154

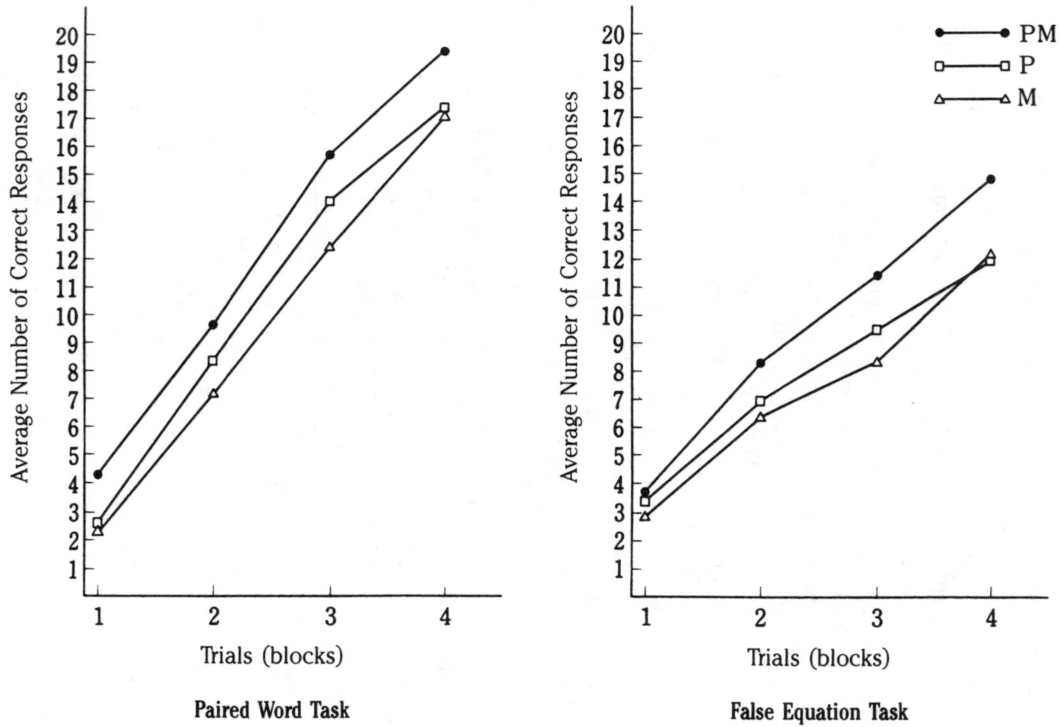

Fig. 12. Learning curves representing the number of correct responses in each experimental condition for those subjects who perceived their supervisor as providing the intended leadership style

TABLE 63. ANOVA on Learning Performance for Subjects Who Perceived the Leadership Received as Consistent with the Leadership Intended

Source	df	F	*p*
Between subjects	190		
Task (A)	1	15.244	.001
Leadership type (B)	2	2.460	
A × B	2	—	
Error (between)	185		
Within subjects	573		
Trial (C)	3	714.719	.001
A × C	3	40.498	.001
B × C	6	1.863	
A × B × C	6	—	
Error (within)	555		

Source: Based on data shown in figure 20.

leadership without regard to the three PM types originally designed as independent variables. (When assessments by subjects are used as the basis of classification, it is possible to identify a pm group in addition to the three originally designed groups.) Table 64 gives the results of an ANOVA based on the data shown in figure 13. This table shows that there are significant differences among the four groups for both learning tasks. The average number of correct responses was the largest in the PM group, followed by the P, M, and pm groups in that order, although no significant difference was

TABLE 64. Learning Performance Using Subjects' Assessment of Leadership Type as a Predictor

Source	df	F	*p*
Between subjects	312		
Task (A)	1	20.088	.001
Leadership type (B)	3	3.075	.05
A × B	3	—	
Error (between)	305		
Within subjects	939		
Trial (C)	3	792.135	.001
A × C	3	52.843	.001
B × C	9	1.613	
A × B × C	9	—	
Error (within)	915		

Source: Based on data shown in figure 21.

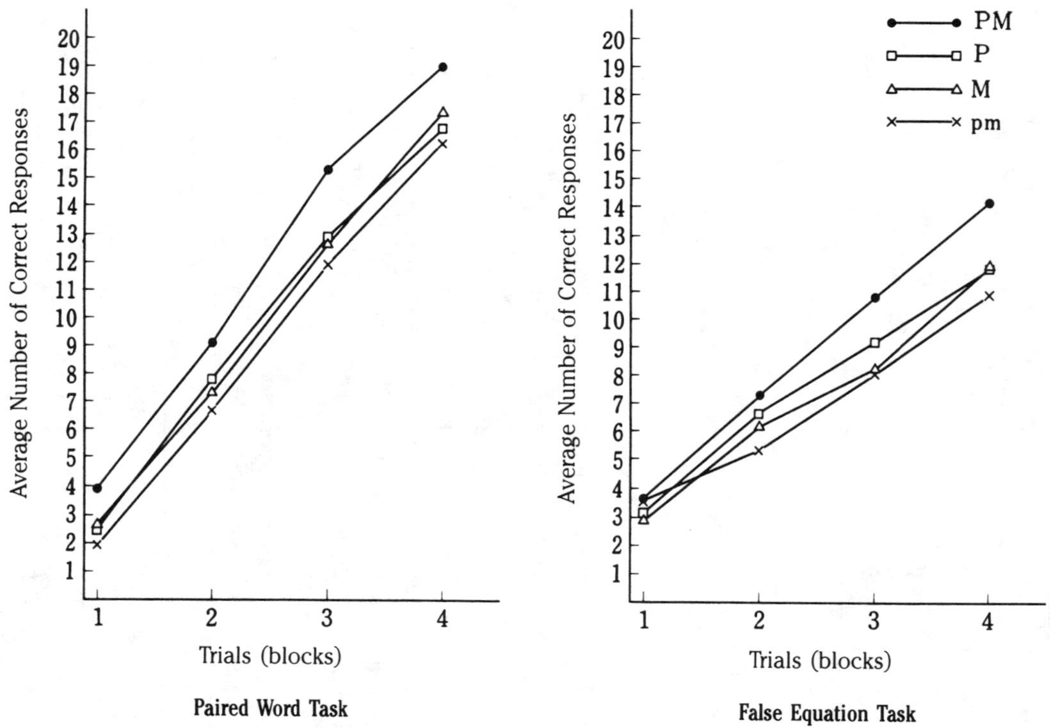

Fig. 13. Learning curves representing the number of correct responses according to the four PM types based exclusively on subjects' assessment

found between the P and M groups. The effects of task and trial on learning performance as well as the interaction between the two are also significant.

Discussion

The learning performance data from this experiment were analyzed using three indicators of leadership as predictors: (1) the behavioral patterns the experimenter set up as independent variables without reference to the subjects' perception of leadership types, (2) the behavioral patterns intended by the experimenter using only subjects who perceived the leadership behavior in the intended way, and (3) the experimenter's behavioral patterns identified exclusively through subjects' perceptions. Significant differences in learning among leadership types were found only when leadership conditions were represented as indicated in (3). However, the results of (1) and (2) showed similar trends as in (3) although the effects were not statistically significant. These findings indicate that the behavioral type an experimenter assumes in guiding subjects through verbal instructions, and particularly the way the subjects perceive the experimenter's behavior, affect learning recall.

Strictly speaking, the word *leadership* as ordinarily used is not a scientific term embodying a clear-cut concept. But the experimenter-subject relationship in the laboratory can certainly be compared to that of a superior and his subordinates in the workshop. Therefore, the PM behavior types can be applied to the behavior of an experimenter toward his subjects. Obviously a teacher's behavior in the classroom, a situation reflected in the study, has unmistakable effects on individual students, as is well recognized. However, it is interesting to speculate about the extent to which social scientists take into account the effects of experimenter leadership behavior when interpreting experimental data on learning.

CHAPTER 10

Leadership Dynamics and Problem Solving

PM Leadership Types and the Einstellung Effect

One of the central tasks of the PM leadership theory is to devise experimental studies which help to interpret the ''multiplicative'' or ''interactive'' effects of combining P and M leadership behavior. Fujita (1975*a*) has substantiated and helped to explain such interactive effects by examining the consequences that the four PM leadership types have for the development of ''Einstellung effects'' in problem-solving processes.

While any process of problem solving may be understood as one of forming an Einstellung (Yatabe 1949), the concept of a strong, rigid, or fixed Einstellung has a particular meaning (English and English 1958). The term ''Einstellung'' was introduced in Gestalt psychology to describe the process by which an individual develops a particular approach to solving a specific category of problems. Experimental research (Luchins 1951, 1961) indicates that under some conditions, subjects become fixated on one particular method of approaching a specific type of problem. Subjects will continue to try to use that method even for similar problems that are better solved in another way. When such a rigid, uncreative approach to problem solving occurs, a ''fixed set'' or Einstellung has developed.

The Einstellung effect brought about by a leader is important because the rigidity or flexibility of cognitive problem-solving processes is one of the determining factors in productive thinking. In studying the effects of PM leadership types on concept learning, Fujita (1970) found that subjects under P-type leadership tended to repeat the same errors. A fixed set or very strong Einstellung which made the subjects repeat the same errors mechanically tended to occur more under P-type leadership than under any of the other three types. Since this initial finding, Fujita (1975*a*) has been conducting experimental studies to understand the effects of the PM leadership types for the development of fixed Einstellung effects following the early Einstellung research conducted by Luchins (1942).

Early Studies of the Einstellung Effect

Luchins (1942) began his experimental studies of the Einstellung effect by using the "water-jar problem" as an experimental task. The water-jar problem is a mathematical task which involves drawing a specified amount of water using three jars holding different volumes. For example, subjects might be asked how to combine three jars with capacities of 21 (A), 127 (B), and 3 (C) to draw a required quantity of 100 units (D) of water. The general strategy in this case is $B - A - 2C = D$.

Luchins's water-jar problem is an exercise consisting of ten experimental tasks. The first five of these ten experimental tasks are designed to familiarize the subjects with the particular problem-solving strategy described above ($B - A - 2C = D$). These first five tasks help to form a fixed problem-solving method which is called the Einstellung method. The other five are test tasks. Four of these second five can be solved using the Einstellung method, but can also be solved using other simpler methods such as $A + B = D$ or $A - C = D$. These simpler methods are called "directive methods." The exception, the third test question in the second half of the exercise, cannot be solved using the Einstellung method but can only be solved using the directive method. This task is called an "extinctive problem" because it makes the previously established Einstellung method extinct. Both the percentage of subjects who solved the four test tasks by the Einstellung method rather than the simpler directive method and the percentage who failed to solve the third test question are used as quantitative measures of the Einstellung effect initially produced. These measures of the Einstellung effect indicate the degree of persistence in holding on to previously established problem-solving methods. English and English (1958) refer to such persistence as fixation or rigidity and Luchins (1942) describes it as mechanization. It corresponds to the "building effect" of mechanical repetition in a sequence of assigned tasks (Wertheimer 1943).

Luchins's original study of the water-jar problem involved an experimental group ($N = 1{,}039$) and a control group ($N = 970$). After being made familiar with the procedure and doing exercise tasks to form an Einstellung, 83 percent of the subjects continued to use the Einstellung method while only 0.6 percent of the control group subjects used that method.

Using similar procedures to study performance on such problem-solving tasks as "complex drawing" (Luchins 1945) and "impression of personality" (Luchins 1961*a*), Luchins found that an initial period of training consistently produced the observed Einstellung effect. He concluded that the Einstellung effect occurred because of past habits developed by drill and by the kind of learning atmosphere typically found in schools (Luchins 1951; Wertheimer 1943). Luchins's research suggests that teaching methods used in school and the style of leadership used by teachers are important factors in the formation of an Einstellung.

Luchins (1944, 1945, 1961*b;* Luchins and Luchins 1955, 1966) also sought to identify conditions which would make problem solving either completely dominated by an Einstellung effect or not affected by the Einstellung effect at all. The most representative and famous of the resulting studies concerns the relationship between Einstellung and conformity. The hypothesis which guided this study was that the conditions which increase conformity would also tend to increase the Einstellung effect. Besides supporting this hypothesis, the study also indicated that the Einstellung effect is increased by factors which add tension to the ego.

Other early studies of the Einstellung effect include a study that analyzed the results of inducing ego anxiety, fear, and stress for Einstellung formation (Luchins and Luchins 1959; Van de Geer 1957) and studies which investigated the correlation between Einstellung and anxiety tendencies and stress (Cowen 1952*a,* 1952*b;* Malzman, Fox, and Marrisett 1953).

Fujita's Hypotheses

Based on these studies of variables which contribute to Einstellung formation, Fujita proposed several hypotheses about the effects of the PM leadership types on a learner's reliance on a fixed Einstellung in problem-solving processes. These hypotheses were developed around ideas about the way that P and M behavior would affect problem solving. P leadership behavior consisting of pressure and planning was understood from prior research to promote tension as reflected in psychophysical indices. Thus, subjects under a P-type leader were expected to experience a stronger Einstellung effect than those under pm-type or M-type leaders whose behavior includes no performance emphasis. On the other hand, since M leadership behavior reduces tension and anxiety, the Einstellung effect experienced by subjects under M- and PM-type leaders would be weaker than that of subjects under the P-type leader. In summary, the first hypothesis was that the Einstellung effect would be strongest under P-type leadership.

Fujita also considered it important to take into account the internal anxiety levels of subjects because leadership conditions were expected to affect the subjects by either increasing or lowering their tension. Since the pm type is the external experimental condition involving the weakest leadership, it is not likely to evoke tension on the part of subjects with low internal anxiety even though it will not contribute to further tension reduction. However, when the internal anxiety of the subjects is high, the pm type would result in a strong Einstellung effect because of the absence of external stimuli needed to reduce tension. On the other hand, since M-type leadership reduces the subjects' anxiety level, subjects with a high level of internal anxiety would experience a stronger Einstellung effect under pm-type leadership than those under M-type leadership. This is Hypothesis 2. Similarly, Hypothesis 3 suggests that subjects with a high anxiety level would experience a stronger Einstellung effect under pm-type leadership than would those with a low level of anxiety.

Method

The subjects ($N = 111$) were students of a women's college in Fukuoka, Japan. The experimental task consisted of a total of forty-five questions. The first five of these were the five drill questions used in the water-jar problem devised by Luchins (1942) for the purpose of inducing an initial Einstellung. Subjects recorded the way that they would use three jars (A, B, and C) with specified volumes to fill a fourth jar (D) with a specified volume of water. The method of solving the five drill questions followed the formula B − A − 2C = D. The remaining forty test questions were used to test the persistence of the Einstellung effect. All questions could be solved by the common method of B − A − 2C = D (i.e., the Einstellung method), but they were also designed so that the even-numbered questions could be solved by the formula A − C = D, and the odd-numbered ones by the formula A + C = D, as shown in table 65. These two alternative formulas represent the directive

TABLE 65. Water-Jar Problem

Problem	Measures Given to Subjects			Amount of Water to Be Drawn (D)
	Jar A	Jar B	Jar C	
1	21	127	3	100
2	14	163	25	99
3	18	43	10	5
4	9	42	6	21
5	20	59	4	31
6	26	55	3	23
7	23	61	5	28
8	21	53	11	10
.	.	.	.	.
.	.	.	.	.
.	.	.	.	.
45	25	92	14	39

method. The formulas which equate the Einstellung and directive methods are B = 2A + C for even-numbered tasks and B = 2A + 3C for odd-numbered ones. In addition to determining the method used to solve each problem, the time taken for solving the problems was also measured. Before being administered the water-jar problem, the subjects were informed that the tests were designed to study the structure of teaching materials in mathematics.

Measuring the Einstellung Effect

The number of test questions (from No. 6 to No. 45) for which the subjects used the Einstellung method (i.e., B − A − 2C = D) was used as the measure of the Einstellung effect. The Einstellung effect score for those who solved question 6 using the directive method (i.e., A − C = D) was zero, while a score of 40 was given to those who continued to solve questions 6 through 45 using the Einstellung method instead of the directive method of A − C = D or A + C = D.

Supervisors and Their Leadership Patterns

Under the supervision of graduate students, the four supervisory leadership types of PM, P, M, and pm were introduced in the same way that they were used by Misumi and Shirakashi (1963, 1966). Under P-type leadership, supervisors spoke a few words such as "Hurry up! hurry up!" "Don't make mistakes!" "Do as much as you can," at approximately one minute intervals. Under M-type leadership, supervisors said such things as "Enjoy the work!" "Take it easy," "Be relaxed," "You must be tired," "Thank you for doing the work." The PM-type supervisors combined the leadership behavior of both P and M types while the pm type lacked the characteristics of the P and M types. The pm supervisors simply explained the procedures to the subjects. (However, it must be remembered that the pm supervisors also uttered such simple words as "hai"—indicating "now" [literally "yes"] as did the supervisors in the other conditions.) Since the four PM leadership types ultimately depend on the experiences of the subjects, subjects' perceptions were assessed by questionnaire. Table 66 shows differences among the four experimental leadership conditions in experienced leadership using three questions each to measure the P and M dimensions.

Anxiety Level Measures

The level of subjects' anxiety was measured with the MAS. Using the average anxiety score of 24.36 as a criterion, subjects were divided into high-anxiety and low-anxiety groups as shown in table 66.

TABLE 66. Means and Standard Deviations of P and M Scores in Different Experimental Conditions

	Leadership Type							
	PM		P		M		pm	
	High Anxiety	Low Anxiety	High Anxiety	Low Anxiety	High Anxiety	Low Anxiety	High Anxiety	Low Anxiety
N	10	15	14	14	17	17	12	12
P score	18.00	17.07	18.43	19.14	4.18	4.41	6.08	3.4
(SD)	(2.54)	(2.91)	(2.56)	(1.92)	(1.42)	(1.73)	(2.19)	(0.66)
M score	14.30	14.13	6.07	5.14	17.00	16.53	6.92	5.33
(SD)	(3.50)	(4.65)	(2.43)	(2.21)	(2.45)	(3.08)	(1.68)	(2.74)

Experimental Procedures

The experimenter first explained to the subjects that the water-jar problem was important for understanding the structure of teaching materials in mathematics and that the test results would not be affected by the subjects' ability or personality. After these preliminary introductions, the experimenter used an example to explain how the water-jar problem could be solved. The subjects were then instructed to put a check mark on the answer sheet to indicate their solution whenever the supervisor said "hai" (meaning "now"). Finally, the experimenter introduced the supervisors to the subjects. The supervisors began the session by saying "start" and indicated when subjects were to complete their answers by saying "hai" every three minutes. The subjects completed the five trials to generate an Einstellung followed by forty test trials. After the experiment was over, the supervisors left the room and the experimenter returned to examine the subjects' solutions.

Results and Discussion

The 111 subjects in the study were assigned to the PM-type leadership condition (25 subjects), the M-type (34), P-type (28), or pm-type condition (24). Two additional experimental conditions representing anxiety level were set up by dividing subjects into high-anxiety and low-anxiety groups based on their score on the MAS. Table 66 shows the P and M scores of supervisors instructed to behave according to the four PM leadership types in high- and low-anxiety groups.

Figure 14 shows the number of subjects who used the Einstellung method to solve different numbers of problems. The data presented include both

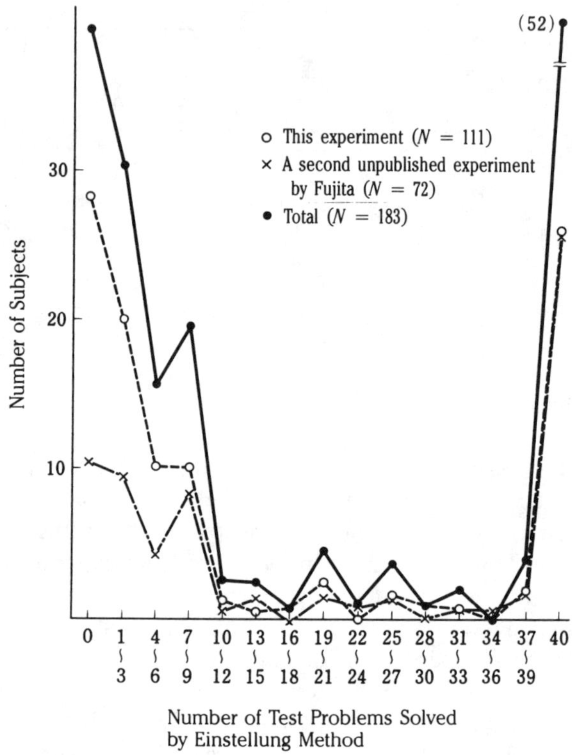

Fig. 14. Frequency distribution of number of subjects using Einstellung method to solve test problems

the results of this study and those of another of Fujita's unpublished studies. The figure indicates that the frequency with which subjects used the Einstellung method does not form a normal curve within its range from 0 to 40, but instead shows a bimodal distribution. Consequently, analysis of variance is an inappropriate statistical technique for analyzing the results. Using the median frequency of 8, subjects were divided into a weak Einstellung group (those using the method on zero to seven problems) and a strong Einstellung group (those using the method to solve eight or more of the problems). The χ^2 test was used to identify the effects of leadership and anxiety level (Snedecor and Cochran 1980, 414ff.).

Influence of Leadership Types and Anxiety Factors on the Einstellung Effect

Table 67 presents results concerning the influence of leadership and anxiety factors on the Einstellung effect. Statistical tests for overall effects of leadership and anxiety level are shown in table 68. The results in table 68 indicate that a significant difference was found among the four leadership types as well as in the interaction between leadership types and anxiety levels. The significant differences are discussed in detail below.

First, the significant overall difference in Einstellung effect among the four leadership types is reflected in the percentage of subjects in each leadership condition showing a strong Einstellung effect (table 68). Under PM-type leaders, 24.0 percent showed a strong Einstellung effect while 64.0 percent of subjects under a P-type leader, 35.3 percent of those under an M-type leader, and 45.8 percent under a pm-type leader showed a strong Einstellung effect. The order of leadership types from greatest to least Einstellung effect is P > pm > M > PM. Significant differences between two pairs of these leadership types, P > PM and P > M, are found as shown in tables 72, 73, and 75. These results partly support Hypothesis 1 which suggests that the Einstellung effect will be stronger under P-type leaders than under leaders of the three other types. The results of differences between the high and low levels of each of the two main leadership factors (i.e., P-type leadership and M-type leadership) as analyzed using the Angular transformation are shown in table 69.

Table 69 indicates that a significant difference in Einstellung effect is found only between the levels of M-type leadership behavior but not in levels

TABLE 67. Effects of Leadership Types and Anxiety Levels on the Einstellung Effect

	Leadership Type							
	PM		P		M		pm	
	High Anxiety	Low Anxiety	High Anxiety	Low Anxiety	High Anxiety	Low Anxiety	High Anxiety	Low Anxiety
Strong Einstellung effect	4	2	7	11	3	9	7	4
(%)	(40.0)	(13.3)	(50.0)	(78.6)	(17.7)	(52.9)	(58.4)	(33.3)
Weak Einstellung effect	6	13	7	3	14	8	5	8
(%)	(60.0)	(86.7)	(50.0)	(21.4)	(82.3)	(47.1)	(41.6)	(66.7)
Total	10	15	14	14	17	17	12	12
χ^2 test	$\chi^2 = 1.11$ n.s		$\chi^2 = 1.40$ n.s.		$\chi^2 = 3.22$ n.s.		$\chi^2 = 0.67$ n.s.	

TABLE 68. Analysis of Variance on Einstellung Effects (Total) Using Leadership Type and Internal Anxiety Levels as Predictors

	SS	df	χ^2	
Leadership type (A)	591.82	3	9.68	$p < .025$
Anxiety (B)	6.29	1	0.10	n.s.
A × B	649.90	3	10.63	$p < .02$
Total				
Between groups	1247.91	7	20.40	$p < .005$
Within groups		$\sigma\omega^2 = 61.16$		

TABLE 69. Analysis of Variance on Einstellung Effects (Total) Using Levels of P and M Behavior as Predictors

	SS	df	χ^2	
P behavior (A)	3.40	1	0.11	n.s.
M behavior (B)	229.55	1	7.61	$p < .001$
A × B	82.25	1	2.73	n.s.
Total				
Between groups	315.22	3	10.45	$p < .05$
Within groups		$\sigma\omega^2 = 10.17$		

TABLE 70. Analysis of Variance on Einstellung Effects (High-anxiety Subjects) Using Levels of P and M Behavior as Predictors

	SS	df	χ^2	
P behavior (A)	32.62	1		n.s.
M behavior (B)	248.76	1	3.87	$p < .05$
A × B	75.81	1	1.18	n.s.
Total				
Between groups	357.19	3	5.56	n.s.
Within groups		$\sigma\omega^2 = 64.24$		

TABLE 71. Analysis of Variance on Einstellung Effects (Low-anxiety Subjects) Using Levels of P and M Behavior as Predictors

	SS	df	χ^2	
P behavior (A)	0.91	1		n.s.
M behavior (B)	217.56	1	3.79	$p < .10$
A × B	678.61	1	11.81	$p < .01$
Total				
Between groups	897.07	3	15.64	$p < .01$
Within groups		$\sigma\omega^2 = 57.47$		

TABLE 72. Analysis of Variance on Einstellung Effects Using Two Leadership Types (PM and P) and Anxiety Levels as Predictors

	SS	df	χ^2	
Leadership type (A)	540.57	1	8.50	$p < .005$
Anxiety (B)	0.00	1	0.00	n.s.
A × B	307.93	1	4.84	$p < .05$
Total				
Between groups	848.50	3	13.33	$p < .005$
Within groups		$\sigma\omega^2 = 63.63$		

TABLE 73. Analysis of Variance on Einstellung Effects Using Two Leadership Types (PM and M) and Anxiety Levels as Predictors

	SS	df	χ^2	
Leadership type (A)	28.09	1	< 1.00	n.s.
Anxiety (B)	4.91	1	< 1.00	n.s.
A × B	392.04	1	6.70	$p < .01$
Total				
Between groups	424.54	3	7.26	n.s.
Within groups		$\sigma\omega^2 = 58.50$		

TABLE 74. Analysis of Variance on Einstellung Effects Using Two Leadership Types (PM and pm) and Anxiety Levels as Predictors

	SS	df	χ^2	
Leadership type (A)	148.84	1	2.17	n.s.
Anxiety (B)	259.21	1	3.78	n.s.
A × B	2.56	1	< 1.00	n.s.
Total				
Between groups	410.6	3	5.99	n.s.
Within groups		$\sigma\omega^2 = 68.55$		

of P-type leadership behavior, nor in the interaction between levels of P and M leadership. Consequently, the results showing differences among the leadership types can be considered to be a reduction of Einstellung effect brought about by levels of M-oriented leadership behavior.

Secondly, analyses were conducted to determine whether or not this reduction in Einstellung effect by high levels of M-oriented leadership behavior can be found in both high- and low-anxiety groups. Analyses were conducted separately for high-anxiety and low-anxiety subjects to determine whether or not differences among the leadership types could be identified for each. The analyses showed significant differences among the leadership types for both the high-anxiety subjects ($\chi^2 = 24.28$, df $= 3$, $p < .01$) and the low anxiety subjects ($\chi^2 = 49.04$, df $= 3$, $p < .01$). Is it possible then that these significant differences simply occurred because M-oriented leadership weakened the Einstellung effect?

Analyses designed to identify specific direct and interactive effects of levels of P and M behavior on Einstellung are presented separately for high- and low-anxiety subjects in tables 70 and 71. Significant differences in the presence of an Einstellung effect depending on levels of M leadership are found in both the high-anxiety group ($p < .05$) and the low-anxiety group ($p < .10$). These results indicate that the tendency of M-oriented leadership behavior to minimize the Einstellung effect (i.e., low Einstellung effects under M-type and PM-type leadership) can be found both in high- and low-anxiety groups. An interesting additional finding in this analysis is that significant differences ($p < .01$) were found in the interaction of P and M behavior in the low-anxiety group (table 71). This result suggests that the Einstellung effect is influenced not only by M-oriented leadership behavior but also by P-oriented behavior for this group.

The nature of the influence exerted by P-oriented leadership on the Einstellung effect is further clarified in figure 15. As illustrated in the figure,

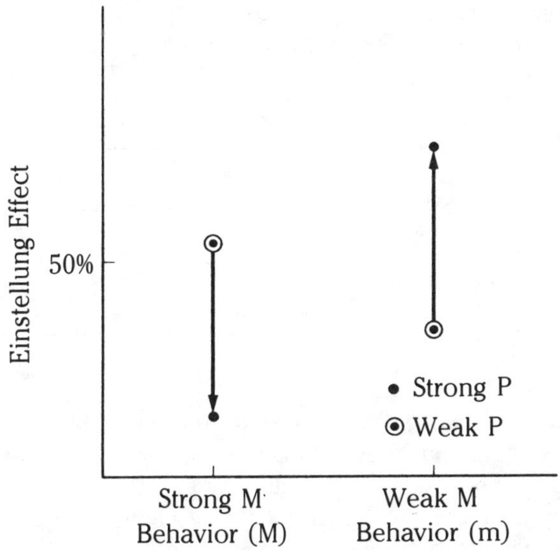

Fig. 15. Effect of P leadership behavior on Einstellung in low-anxiety condition

when M-oriented leadership is weak—in the P- and pm-type leadership conditions—P-oriented leadership increases the Einstellung effect. However, when M-oriented leadership is strong—in the PM- and M-type leadership conditions—P-oriented leadership reduces the Einstellung effect. It is this difference in the influence of P-oriented leadership which is shown in the significant interaction between P-oriented leadership and M-oriented leadership.

Discussion

The validity of the leadership behavior conditions was confirmed again in relation to subjects' perceptions as it had been in previous experimental studies (table 66). Having established the validity of the experimental conditions, Hypothesis 1, which suggests that the Einstellung effect would be the strongest under P-type leadership, was tested. In general, P-type leadership was found to show a stronger Einstellung effect than either the PM or M leadership types as evident in tables 67, 68, and 69. A significant difference in Einstellung effect between P-type and pm-type leadership was found only among low-anxiety subjects, not in the group of high-anxiety subjects (see tables 68 and 76). In the low-anxiety group, the strongest Einstellung effect

TABLE 75. Analysis of Variance on Einstellung Effects Using Two Leadership Types (P and M) and Anxiety Levels as Predictors

	SS	df	χ^2	
Leadership type (A)	322.21	1	6.01	$p < .05$
Anxiety (B)	386.13	1	7.21	$p < .01$
A × B	5.05	1	< 1.00	n.s.
Total				
Between groups	713.39	3	13.32	$p < .005$
Within groups		$\sigma\omega^2 = 53.57$		

was induced by P-type leadership, the second strongest by M-type leadership, the third strongest by the pm type and the least strong by the PM type. Thus, Hypothesis 1 was supported in the low-anxiety group.

Fujita interpreted the finding of little Einstellung effect in the high-anxiety group as being a consequence of their initial level of tension. If the tension of subjects exceeds a given level, further external or internal sources will not increase the tension beyond that level. According to this interpretation, the external influence of P-type leadership behavior will not increase internal tension of those subjects who were initially identified as having a high level of internal anxiety. Fujita explains the lack of a significant difference between pm- and P-type leadership in the high-anxiety group on this basis.

Analyses were also conducted to test Hypothesis 2, which suggests that because M-type leadership behavior promotes tension reduction, the high-anxiety subjects will show a weaker Einstellung effect under M-type leadership than under pm-type leadership. The results indicated that M-type leadership weakened the Einstellung effect for subjects who had a high anxiety level because of their high level of internal tension, and also for subjects

TABLE 76. Analysis of Variance on Einstellung Effects Using Two Leadership Types (P and pm) and Anxiety Levels as Predictors

	SS	df	χ^2	
Leadership type (A)	122.10	1	1.93	n.s.
Anxiety (B)	2.10	1	< 1.00	n.s.
A × B	254.40	1	4.02	$p < .05$
Total				
Between groups	378.61	3	5.98	n.s.
Within groups		$\sigma\omega^2 = 63.31$		

whose high anxiety level was induced externally by P-type leadership. In short, in the high-anxiety group M-type leadership was more effective in minimizing the Einstellung effect than pm-type leadership (tables 67 and 77). By contrast, in the low-anxiety group no significant difference in Einstellung effect was found between M-type and pm-type leadership (see tables 67 and 77). On the contrary, the Einstellung effect in the low-anxiety group was weaker in PM-type leadership than under leadership of other types (see tables 67 and 72).

In summary, analyses designed to test Hypothesis 2 indicated that M-type leadership behavior weakens the Einstellung effect whenever subjects experience tension from either internal or external sources. However, when tension is below a given level as in the situation of low anxiety and weak P leadership, M-oriented leadership behavior does not exert a significant influence on the Einstellung effect. Consequently, Hypothesis 2 is substantiated.

Hypothesis 3 suggests that the subjects with a high level of anxiety would show stronger Einstellung effects under pm-type leadership than those with low anxiety. However, no significant difference was found between the high- and low-anxiety groups under any of the four PM leadership types (table 67). Likewise, no significant main effects of anxiety level were found (table 68). Thus, Hypothesis 3 is not supported.

The significant findings supporting Hypotheses 1 and 2 may be summarized as follows.

1. In the low-anxiety group, P-type leadership increased Einstellung effects, but in the high-anxiety group, there is no significant difference in Einstellung effects between P- and pm-type leadership behavior.
2. When subjects have a high level of either internally or externally induced tension, M-type leadership behavior weakens the Einstellung effect. In the low-anxiety group, no significant difference is evident between M- and pm-type leadership.

TABLE 77. Analysis of Variance on Einstellung Effects Using Two Leadership Types (M and pm) and Anxiety Levels as Predictors

	SS	df	χ^2	
Leadership type (A)	46.24	1	< 1.00	n.s.
Anxiety (B)	12.96	1	< 1.00	n.s.
A × B	327.61	1	5.61	$p < .05$
Total				
Between groups	386.81	3	6.62	n.s.
Within groups		$\sigma\omega^2 = 58.43$		

Some of the results of Fujita's study, however, cannot be explained by these two conclusions. First, in the low-anxiety group, there is no significant difference between M- and PM-type leadership behavior; second, a stronger Einstellung effect is found under M-type leadership than under PM-type leadership. (The interaction of leadership types and anxiety is significant at the 1 percent level as shown in table 73.)

In order to interpret these findings, the influence of leadership behavior on the Einstellung effect shown by subjects with different degrees and levels of anxiety must be reconsidered. Table 69 shows the combined results for high- and low-anxiety subjects. According to this table, no significant difference in Einstellung is found according to levels of P-oriented leadership behavior or the interaction between levels of P and M leadership behavior; the only significant differences found were according to levels of M-oriented leadership. Similarly, in the high-anxiety group the only significant differences found were between levels of M-oriented leadership behavior (table 70). In the low-anxiety group, however, the largest significant difference found was in the interaction of P and M leadership behavior. These findings seem to suggest that the interaction of P-oriented and M-oriented leadership behavior—that is, in the multiplicative effect of P and M leadership behavior (P × M)—influences the Einstellung effect. In other words, in the low-anxiety group, the Einstellung effect was empirically shown to be weakened only when there was a multiplicative combination (i.e., P × M) of P and M leadership behaviors which differs from both P-type and M-type leadership. As explained by Fujita, the reason why the multiplicative effect of P and M leadership (P × M) is not found in the high-anxiety group is probably because the tension-inducing effect of P-oriented leadership behavior is restricted for high-anxiety subjects. In the high-anxiety group, PM- and M-type leadership show relatively weak Einstellung effects and there is no significant difference between PM and M leadership types. Because the tension-increasing effect of P-type leadership is not induced easily in the high-anxiety group, PM-type leadership seems to produce an effect similar to that of M-type leadership.

It is also necessary to further consider why in the low-anxiety group the Einstellung effect is weakest when strong P-oriented and M-oriented leadership behaviors are combined. In the low-anxiety group, the strongest Einstellung effect is found under P-type leadership, the second strongest is under M, the third under pm, and the weakest under the PM type (see table 67). Taking the low-anxiety group under pm-type leadership as a control group, each low- and high-anxiety group under three leadership types may be compared.

The "low-anxiety–P leadership" group and "low anxiety–M leadership" group show stronger Einstellung effects than the "low anxiety–pm leadership" group. But the "low anxiety–PM leadership" group produces weaker Einstellung effects than the "low anxiety–pm leadership" group. In short, for the same low-anxiety subjects, Einstellung effects will be considerably weaker when P- and M-oriented leadership behaviors are both present. The effect of P-type leadership or some multiplicative effect of P and M leadership have emerged which are qualitatively different from the Einstellung-reducing effect of M-type leadership behavior.

PM-type leadership has been found to be remarkably effective in reducing habitual sets (i.e., Einstellung effect) which may produce barriers in the problem-solving process. Its effectiveness is not due to the independent, additive effects of P and M leadership, but to the multiplicative effect of their combination. The Einstellung effect in the low-anxiety group is weaker under PM-type leadership than under any of the other three leadership types. This finding using the water-jar problem as an experimental task may indicate that the weakest fixed, habitual sets affecting problem solving in other kinds of tasks may be found under PM-type leadership. In terms suggested by previous Einstellung theorists, since the lowest amount of "overdependence" on "habitual problem-solving" methods (Hilgard 1962) is found under PM-type leadership, problem solving is best promoted by the multiplicative effect of P × M leadership in contrast to the three other leadership types.

PM Types, Anxiety Levels, and Escape from a Maze

Another study following a similar fixation theme involved using a three-dimensional maze created with a microcomputer graphic display to examine the interactive effects of P-oriented and M-oriented leadership on escape behavior under fear and nonfear conditions. The interactive effect hypothesis (Hypothesis 1) postulates that pressure-oriented P behavior, when combined with M-oriented leadership behavior, decreases the tendency for followers' behavior to become fixated in escaping from the maze. Hypothesis 2 postulates that followers' experience of pressure-oriented P behavior, when combined with M behavior, undergoes a qualitative transformation to become similar to the planning-oriented P factor found in many field survey studies.

Previous experimental studies of escape behavior from emergency situations (Kugihara et al. 1982; Kugihara, Misumi, and Sato 1980; Kugihara and Misumi 1984; Misumi and Sako 1982) indicate that leadership has a striking effect on escape behavior and the rate of successful escape. These studies also suggest that an anxiety-producing situation amplifies the effect of leadership. Therefore, it is postulated that the P × M interactive effect will appear more strikingly in a threatening situation than in a nonthreatening situation. If so, then followers' fixation should be lower under a PM-type leader than under a leader of any other type, especially in a threatening situation. In terms of the task used here, low fixation should be reflected in reducing the distance of movement through the maze actually taken to escape.

The second purpose of this study was to examine Hypothesis 2 concerning the behavioral meaning of "Pressure P" (Misumi 1982). Misumi suggests that as the M behavior provided in conjunction with P behavior increases, perceived P behavior involving pressure changes into something approaching planning-oriented P. (See Misumi et al. 1970, and chap. 3 of this book).

A previous experimental study (Misumi and Sato 1968) suggested that pressure-oriented P arouses psychological resistance among followers and for that reason results in a gradual deterioration in their performance. Under PM-type leadership, performance does not go down, but goes up. This finding can be explained by postulating that M serves to abate the negative psychological resistance that pressure-oriented P gives to followers. The pressure factor can only be said to be present in cases where it arouses some psychological resistance or tension. Consequently, followers' perceptions of planning-oriented P are likely to be higher under PM-type leadership than under any other condition. The above experimental hypotheses can be summarized as follows.

1. The fixation of followers' behavior within a maze will be significantly smaller under the PM-type leadership condition than under the P-type or M-type conditions. The difference in the effects of leadership conditions on fixation will be greater under the fear condition than under the nonfear condition.
2. Followers' planning-oriented P perception scores vis-à-vis a PM-type leader will be greater than under a leader of the P or M types.
3. Followers' perceptions of unreasonable pressure from a P-type leader will be larger than those under a PM-type or M-type leader.

Method

The subjects were sixty-six male college students. A fear condition was induced by telling subjects that they would receive an electric shock at the end of the experiment that would be greater the poorer their performance; a nonfear condition contained no such instruction. Three leadership conditions (P, PM, M) were used for eight trials providing a 2 × 3 × 8 design with repeated measures.

Two booths were set up in the room where the experiment was conducted, one for the leader and the other for the subject. A TV monitor, headphone, and electric shock system were placed on the desk in each booth. A box with four switches was also placed on the desk of the booth for subjects.

The maze built for this experiment consisted of 127 blocks, with fourteen T-shaped turning points. The maze was laid out so that when one came to a dead end (e.g., point E in fig. 16), backtracking and then going straight toward a wall at the end of a path would place the subject in a passage leading to the exit. The TV monitor seen by the subjects was not a "bird's eye" view of the maze, but a view representing what they would see if they were actually inside the maze

Fig. 16. Maze layout. The numbers represent divergent points in the maze.

(i.e., stereographical line drawings). Figure 17 shows an example of what a subject could see when he looked toward point D from point C in figure 16. As a follower proceeded through the maze or changed direction, the scene shown on the TV changed.

Movements within the maze could be made by using four switches (proceed forward, turn right, turn left, and turn around). When the subject pressed the "proceed forward" switch six times in succession, he would proceed forward by one block. If he pressed each of the other switches three times, he would change his direction. To proceed in a new direction, he has to change his direction first. It takes considerable physical strength to press these switches, so subjects get tired from pressing them.

Both leader and follower saw the same pictures on the TV monitor. However, on the leader's TV, the kinds of words he was supposed to say were shown in the lower part of the screen. The symbols seen by the leader were P, M, and arrows. Arrows were used to show the direction toward the exit (right and left) and to indicate that a follower was moving in the wrong direction. The places in the maze where an arrow was supposed to point to the right or left had been determined beforehand. An arrow, used for only six of the fourteen turning points, was located two blocks before each of these turning points. The places where arrows were placed changed from session to session. Thus, over the course of the eight sessions, the subjects had to learn the route to the exit from all the turning points. An arrow indicating that a follower was moving in the wrong direction appeared on the leader's screen one block before the follower reached the first turning point after he started moving in the wrong direction. For instance, if a follower starts moving in the wrong direction after having proceeded to point B in figure 16, the arrow indicating his movement in the wrong direction would appear at point A. Whenever an arrow appeared on the screen, the leader told the follower which direction the arrow pointed, i.e., right, left, or backward.

The places where P or M appeared on the leader's screen were programmed in advance. When P appeared on the screen, the leader said something to put pressure on the follower to escape quickly. Likewise, when M appeared on the screen, the leader said something to the follower to encourage the follower to become emotionally stable and relaxed. P appeared one or two blocks after the follower passed a turning point and M appeared two blocks before he reached a turning point. The points at which P and M appeared in the maze remained constant throughout all sessions.

The synthesizer's sound coming through the subjects' headphone became increasingly loud as each session progressed. When the follower failed to escape within fifteen minutes after a session started, the session was discontinued and the sound coming from the synthesizer stopped.

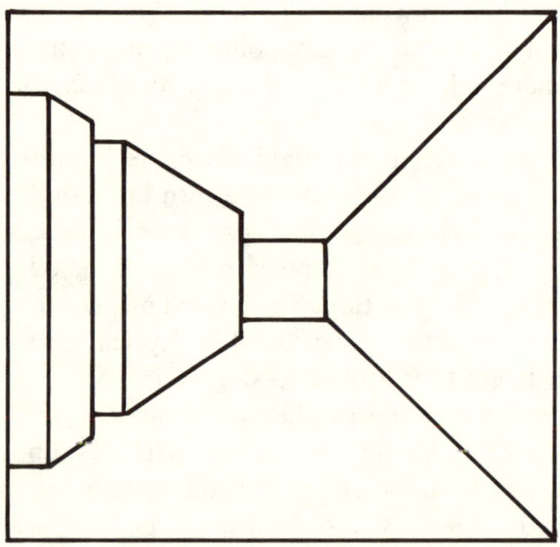

Fig. 17. TV monitor display as seen from point C looking toward point D in the maze shown in figure 16

The confederate "leader" and the follower first entered the room and sat in front of the two booths. The screen which would later be extended to separate the booths was drawn back. The purpose of doing this was to make the subject understand that the same pictures were shown on the confederate's TV monitor and the follower's TV monitor.

After the follower took his seat, an experimenter explained to him how to operate the switches and how to interpret what was to appear on the screen of the TV monitor. After having confirmed that the follower understood the system, the experimenter gave him an exercise session using a different maze than the one prepared for the experiment. The experimenter explained in detail the kinds of scenes that appear on the TV monitor during the process of the follower's movement to the exit, e.g., impasse, corner, exit, and wall. The experimenter also instructed the follower to use the hand with which he could handle things more efficiently to press the switch controlling his movements in the maze. Upon the completion of the practice session, the experimenter gave the following instructions to the confederate (seated on the left) and the follower (seated on the right).

1. "You two will cooperate in escaping the maze eight times in succession."
2. "The person seated on the left will play the role of the leader and give information and instructions to the person seated on the right. The same pictures will appear both on the TV monitor on the left and the TV monitor on the right."
3. "Although the leader has participated in this kind of experiment before, he will find many parts of the maze unfamiliar because the maze prepared for this experiment differs substantially from those used for previous experiments. Consequently, in many instances, it is important for the follower to proceed on his own judgment."

The following instructions were also given in addition to the above.

1. "The last session will be carried out with no information or instructions given by the leader. The follower should move through the maze independently."
2. "The follower's performance in escaping the maze in the last session will be rated on the basis of the time it takes him to escape."

The follower was also told that the overall performance score for the eight sessions would be disproportionately weighted. That is, 10 percent of the score would depend on performance in each of the first seven sessions (70 percent in all) and 30 percent would depend on the time it took to escape in the eighth session. These instructions were given to prevent the follower from depending too much on the leader, thus neglecting to try to learn the layout of and escape route from the maze.

The fear condition was induced by giving the following instructions.

"This experiment is designed to simulate escaping in an emergency situation. For that purpose, an electric shock will be given which will be stronger the more time it takes the follower to escape the emergency situation." The follower was told that the electric shock would be given to simulate a situation where someone was killed or injured because of a disaster such as a fire. A "sample shock" was given once by attaching electrodes to the second and third fingers of his left hand if he was a right-hander, or his right hand if he was left-handed. After the sample shock was given, subjects were told that "the electric shock we will give you in the real experiment will be over ten times greater than this, causing a considerably stronger and more unpleasant shock to you." Subjects were told that the shock would be given upon completion of all eight sessions.

Under the nonfear condition, however, no such instructions concerning shock were given. After the explanation in the fear condition was done, the follower and the leader entered their respective booths and put on their headphones. At this point, the experimenter extended the partition between the two booths, thus completely separating the booths. The leader then placed a list of the remarks reflecting the PM types on his own desk. This list could be read by the light from the TV monitor. Otherwise, the room was dark while the sessions were conducted. Questionnaires were passed out and completed after the first and seventh sessions. The leader's remarks under PM, P, and M conditions are as follows.

1. PM condition: With the exception of the eighth session, the leader made the M-oriented remarks shown in table 78 immediately before and after each session. Also, during the course of the sessions, a randomly ordered list of M-oriented and P-oriented remarks, (B) and (C) in table 78, were placed on the desk. The leader read aloud P-oriented remarks when "P" appeared on the TV screen and M-oriented remarks when "M" appeared on the screen.
2. M condition: As in the PM condition, the remarks labeled (A) in table 78 were read aloud immediately before and after each session. During the course of the sessions, the leader made the remarks labeled (B) in table 78 every time either "P" or "M" appeared on the screen.
3. P condition: The leader made remarks neither before nor after any sessions. When P and M appeared on the screen during the course of the sessions, the leader made the P-oriented remarks (C) shown in table 78.

Results

Experimental Manipulation Checks

The effect of the electric shock manipulation was measured by the degree of tension the follower reported during the course of the experiment using one

TABLE 78. Leader's Remarks

(A) Leader's M-type remarks before and after the trials

Trial 1: As we are sure to get out, let's not work ourselves up but take it nice and easy.
You must be worn out.
Trial 2: Don't get tensed up like that, let's take it calmly.
It's tiring, isn't it? Swing your hands up and down and you'll feel much better.
Trial 3: Don't get too tired. Let's try to do it leisurely together.
Your shoulders are stiff, aren't they? Take it easy and relax.
Trial 4: As we have to do it anyhow, let's plan it as pleasant as we can.
Thank you for your trouble. Have a good rest.
Trial 5: Though it's a really hard job, let's work in a relaxed manner.
I think your hands must be getting tired but bear with me for a little more.
Trial 6: Let your shoulders relax a bit and then we'll start again.
We are out! We are out!
Trial 7: Just a little more now, so let's make one final effort.
I appreciate your labor.

(B) Leader's M-type remarks during the trials

Take it easy.
Be calm.
Be leisurely.
Relax yourself.
Don't be nervous.
Take a comfortable position.
Take it nice and easy.
Don't be tense.
Make yourself comfortable.
Take it slow and easy.

(C) Leader's P-type remarks during the trials

Hurry up.
Get on with it.
Be faster! faster!
Decide quickly.
There's no time left.
Don't dawdle!
Don't slow your pace!
Too slow!
Don't stop work.

item on a scale of 1 to 7. Significant differences ($F = 7.28$, $df = 1/60$, $p < .01$) were found between the nonfear condition ($\overline{X} = 2.28$) and the fear condition ($\overline{X} = 3.30$).

The validity of the leadership behavior conditions was assessed by asking the followers four questions.

1. "How much did the leader try to hurry you?"
2. "Was the leader strict about your work progress and quickness?"
3. "Did the leader help you make yourself comfortable?"
4. "Was the leader considerate of you?"

Questions 1 and 2 have to do with P-oriented behavior and 3 and 4 have to do with M-oriented behavior. The results showed that the intended differences among leadership conditions were found for all these questions. The means for each question in each leadership condition are as follows:

1: PM-3.98, P-5.14, M-1.20 ($F = 157.54$, $df = 2/60$, $p < .01$);
2: PM-3.80, P-4.55, M-1.95 ($F = 35.04$, $df = 2/60$, $p < .01$);
3: PM-4.27, P-1.86, M-5.25 ($F = 37.86$, $df = 2/60$, $p < .01$);
4: PM-4.15, P-2.16, M-4.84 ($F = 34.56$, $df = 2/60$, $p < .01$).

From the above results, it appears that the leader had high scores for both P-oriented behavior and M-oriented behavior under the PM condition, whereas under the P condition, only P-oriented behavior scores were high and under the M condition, only M-oriented behavior scores were high.

Analysis of Movement Distance

The number of block movements is the distance the follower had "walked" by the time he reached the exit. The smaller the number of block movements was, the less frequently he entered an impasse and thus the less frequently he repeatedly walked back and forth over the same place and the more smoothly he reached the exit.

Table 79 shows the results of the experiment. When the follower failed to reach the exit within the time limit of fifteen minutes, his number of block movements was calculated according to the following formula:

A = the number of blocks the follower actually walked in fifteen minutes,
B = the point of arrival, that is, the shortest distance (the smallest number of blocks) from the starting point to the place where the follower is fifteen minutes after the beginning of the experiment, and
C = the shortest distance from the place where the follower is fifteen minutes after the beginning of the experiment to the exit ($C = 127 - B$).

$A/B \times C$ is used to estimate the number of block movements necessary to reach the exit from the point of arrival by going through the maze at the regular pace. Suppose, for example, that the time limit runs out when the follower is one block short of the exit (126 blocks away from the starting point) after having moved through 200 blocks. The estimated number of block movements would be $200 + 200/126 \times 1$.

TABLE 79. Number of Block Movements

Trial	Fear Condition PM	Fear Condition M	Fear Condition P	Nonfear Condition PM	Nonfear Condition M	Nonfear Condition P
1	200.9	254.5	350.7	225.6	261.8	249.7
	M–P: *; PM–P: **					
2	182.7	256.8	245.5	243.8	204.3	248.3
	PM–M: *; PM–P: †					
3	162.3	230.3	245.4	170.8	198.7	199.7
	PM–M: *; PM–P: **					
4	154.6	179.9	232.3	158.7	178.9	179.6
	PM–P: *					
5	155.5	192.8	206.3	157.0	185.4	200.5
	PM–P: †					
6	153.4	184.5	155.5	155.2	163.2	155.1
	PM–M: †					
7	156.0	167.6	191.2	147.8	164.3	153.9
8	167.3	162.1	240.7	153.5	168.9	192.8
	M–P: †			PM–P: *		
Sum of trials 1–7	1,165.4	1,466.4	1,626.9	1,258.9	1,356.6	1,386.8
	PM–M: *; PM–P: **					

Note: The number of block movements is 127 when subjects take the shortest route.
Significance levels for Ryan test of post hoc comparisons:
†$p < .10$
*$p < .05$
**$p < .01$

Analysis of variance showed significant main effects for leadership (F = 3.92, df = 2/60, $p < .05$) and for sessions (F = 22.55, df = 7/420, $p < .01$).

A Ryan test (for post-hoc comparisons) conducted separately under the fear condition and the nonfear condition only showed an effect of leadership under the fear condition. In other words, under the fear condition the number of block movements was always less under the PM condition than under the other two conditions.

Analysis of Fixation Tendencies

The tendency to become fixated was calculated by subtracting from the total number of block movements the number of block movements in which the follower made just one round trip in the direction of a dead end and the shortest distance (127 blocks) from the starting point to the exit. In this way, it is possible to calculate the number of block movements in which the follower went back and forth over the same place two or more times (table 80). For instance, in cases where at some point the follower made three round trips into a dead end, the number of block movements exceeding that which he needed to make to find out that he had reached a dead end becomes an index of fixation. Therefore, if the follower proceeded toward a dead end once, the fixation index is zero if he then immediately returned to the right route.

An analysis of variance showed a significant effect of leadership (F = 4.06, df = 2/60, $p < .05$) and a main effect of the sessions (F = 19.85, df = 7/420, $p < .01$). Here again, a Ryan test conducted separately for each block under the fear condition and the nonfear condition indicated that, in many instances, significant differences were found between leadership conditions only under the fear condition. The fixation tendency was almost always less apparent under the PM condition than under any other leadership condition.

Analysis of the Follower's Perception of Planning-Oriented P Behavior

In the present context, planning-oriented P behavior involves leadership behavior in explaining of the means of escape from the maze. Planning-oriented behavior was measured on a scale of 1 to 7 using a question asking the extent to which the follower was instructed about how to escape. These data were analyzed only for those cases where the follower succeeded in escaping in all eight sessions. This analysis strategy was taken to avoid any differences due to initial success or failure on perceptions of planning-oriented P leadership.

Analysis of variance showed a significant main effect of leadership (F = 9.35, df = 2/44, $p < .01$) and a significant interaction between fear and

TABLE 80. Fixation Tendency

Trial	Fear Condition			Nonfear Condition		
	PM	M	P	PM	M	P
1	33.9	96.4	191.0	65.6	103.7	87.1
			*			
		**				
2	24.1	98.1	84.9	88.3	45.8	90.3
	*					
		†				
3	3.2	66.7	85.8	18.7	41.4	40.8
	*					
		**				
4	5.8	18.7	74.2	0.0	27.5	24.0
		**		*		
		**				
5	3.5	34.1	46.9	0.0	27.9	42.9
		†				
6	2.0	37.4	11.4	0.0	11.1	5.2
7	2.5	14.9	40.0	0.9	14.6	7.0
8	7.8	6.7	75.9	0.0	11.3	27.1
Sum of trials 1–7	75.0	366.3	534.2	173.5	272.0	297.3
	*					
		**				

Significance levels for Ryan test of post hoc comparisons:
†$p < .10$
*$p < .05$
**$p < .01$

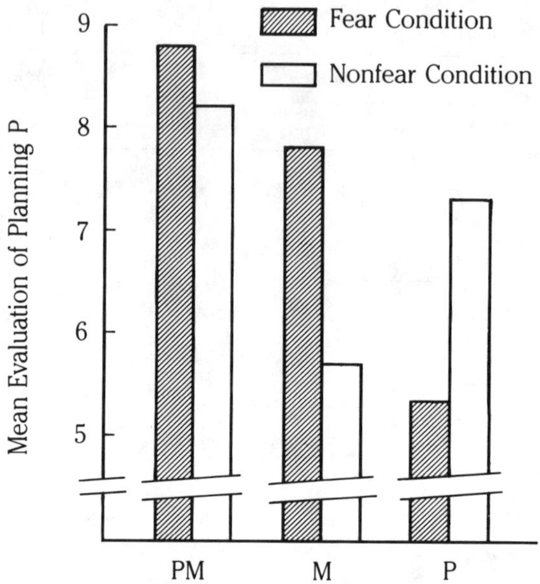

Fig. 18. Followers' perception of planning P under different leadership types

leadership (F = 5.32, df = 2/44, $p < .01$). A main effect of sessions (that is, a difference in perception between the first and the second surveys) was not found. Figure 18 shows the results based on the data combined across the two surveys. The results indicate that, regardless of the presence or absence of fear, perceptions of planning-oriented P are the greatest under the PM condition. Under the fear condition, perceptions of planning-oriented P is also greater under M-type than under P-type leadership. Under the nonfear condition, however, the perception of planning-oriented P is greater under the P-type condition than under the M-type condition. This result supports the hypothesized interaction between fear and leadership.

Analysis of Perceptions of Unreasonable Pressure from the Leader

The perception of unreasonable pressure was measured using a question rated on a 1 to 7 scale. An analysis of variance showed a significant main effect of leadership (F = 20.97, df = 2/60, $p < .01$). Figure 19 diagrams the results for the two surveys with the fear and nonfear conditions combined. Figure 19 shows that the perception of unreasonable pressure is the greatest under the P condition. Multiple comparisons (Ryan test) showed significant differences between the PM and P conditions (t = 4.72, df = 63, $p < .001$) and between the M and P conditions (t = 6.42, df = 63, $p < .001$). However, no significant difference was found between the PM and M conditions (t = 1.72, df = 63, n.s.). These results indicate that perceptions of unreasonable pressure lessened because of the presence of M regardless of the presence of P.

Discussion

Hypothesis 1 suggests that the trend of fixation would be smaller in the PM condition than in the M and P conditions. As shown in table 79, the hypothesis is supported by the results of this experiment. It is also clear that followers reached the exit more smoothly and walked a shorter distance under a leader of the PM type than under a leader of the P or M type. When data were analyzed separately for the fear and nonfear conditions, no clear difference was found among the three leadership types under the nonfear condition. However, significant differences were found among the PM, P, and M types under the fear condition. One of the reasons why leadership conditions make a difference under the fear condition seems to be the extent to which the follower relies on the leader. In this experiment, the extent to which the follower relies on the leader was measured using a questionnaire item rated on a scale of 1 to 7. The results indicated that the follower relies on the leader more under the fear condition than under the nonfear condition (F = 2.99,

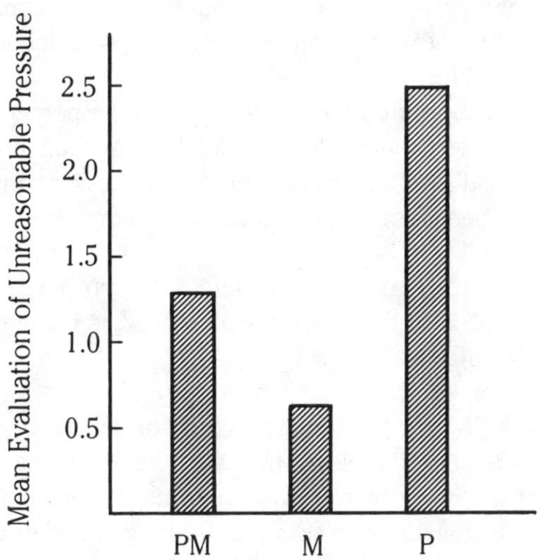

Fig. 19. Followers' perception of unreasonable pressure under different leadership types

df = 1/60, $p < .10$). It also has been pointed out by a number of researchers (Abe 1978; Bass 1974; Mintzberg 1979; Smelser 1963; Strauss 1944) that leadership behavior takes on particular importance in a crisis situation.

Hypothesis 2 suggested that perceptions of planning-oriented P by the follower would be greater under the PM condition than under the P and M conditions. As shown in figure 18, this hypothesis was supported. However, success or failure in escape could affect the perceptions of planning-oriented P shown in figure 18. Some studies indicate that subordinate performance affects the perceptions of leadership (Furukawa 1972; Sakamaki 1974; Farris and Lim 1969). In order to control for the effect of success or failure in escape which might affect perceived leadership, data were analyzed only for those followers who succeeded in escaping in all eight experimental sessions. Even so, the possibility that perceptions of planning-oriented P were affected by the time it takes to escape is not eliminated. However, the time it took to escape in the first session (perceptions of planning-oriented P were measured immediately after the first session and the seventh session) was the longest in the M condition and very similar in the PM- and P-type leadership conditions under both fear and nonfear conditions. Thus, it is unlikely that the perceptions of planning-oriented P, rated immediately after the first session at least, were affected by the time it took to escape. Judging by the fact that the results of the second session for perceptions of planning-oriented P completely coincided with those of the first session, it is reasonable to believe that perceptions of planning-oriented P were not affected by the time it took to escape. In any event, it is clear that leadership conditions affected the perception of planning-oriented P such that it was greater under PM-type leadership than under P- or M-type leadership.

Hypothesis 3 is supported by the finding that the perception of unreasonable pressure is smaller under PM-type leadership than under P-type leadership. It follows that part of the perception of pressure under P-type leadership is abated when P-oriented behavior is combined with M-oriented behavior.

From the findings for Hypotheses 2 and 3, the proposition that part of P's pressure is abated through the catalysis of M and is changed into planning-oriented P was supported.

As stated above, the hypothesis about the presence of a multiplicative effect between P and M and the transformation of perceived pressure-oriented P into planning-oriented P was verified and the PM type was found to be superior to any of the other types. However, this experiment did not indicate that follower's performance increases regardless of the follower's situation if only the leader displays both P-oriented behavior and M-oriented behavior at the same time. In this experiment, the leader gave instructions to the follower as to which direction to proceed at six of the fourteen turning points in the PM, P, and M conditions. In a preliminary experiment conducted prior to the one reported here, the leader gave no instructions whatsoever as to which way to proceed, but instead provided P behavior and M behavior at random at predetermined intervals that did not correspond to where the follower was within the maze. The results were that the follower soon began to ignore the leader's remarks. It became clear in this preliminary experiment that what the follower expected the most while going through the maze was the leader's instructions as to which way to go. It was found that any P- or M-oriented remarks by the leader without instructions about which way to go had no direct effect on the follower.

In the maze escape experiment, the PM-type leader always acted with M behavior before a turning point and with P behavior after passing it. Had he acted the other way around, i.e., had he acted with P behavior before a turning point and with M behavior after passing it, the follower would not have been able to escape the maze as smoothly. The leader's P behavior before a turning point would lessen the follower's calmness, and M behavior after passing a turning point would lessen the follower's motivation to escape.

Viewed in this light, the multiplicative effect of P and M seems to be produced under the following conditions; first, a specific amount of planning-oriented P must be present, and second, P and M must be brought into full play at the time and in the place that fits the follower's immediate situation. The results indicated that the multiplicative effect becomes particularly salient in the crisis situation studied.

CHAPTER 11

Physiological Responses to Leadership

Psychophysiological Studies of the PM Leadership Theory

In previous laboratory studies and field surveys, various indices of performance and cognition were used to examine the validity of four PM leadership types and to understand the reasons for their effects. In order to continue the process of determining the causal dynamics of leadership, a series of studies were conducted to examine the effects of the P, M, and PM leadership types on psychophysiological processes. Psychophysiological processes were considered a particularly important class of dependent variables because other research such as the Einstellung studies had indicated that leadership had important implications for cognitive expressions of stress in problem solving. The first of the studies concerning psychophysiological processes focused on the expression of P-type and M-type leadership while other studies also considered PM-type leadership. Six of the studies in this series are described below.

Experiment I

Misumi and Kawazu (1970) created P-type and M-type leadership conditions in the laboratory, and examined their effects on subjects' plethysmogram. A plethysmogram is obtained using a machine that records cardiac function based on readings taken continuously from a subject's fingertip. Heart rate and blood flow (pulse volume amplitude) readings can be obtained. The subjects were four female students. A male graduate student played the role of their supervisor. The task assigned to the subjects was to count as quickly and accurately as possible the number of holes in IBM punch cards with the graduate student role-playing supervisory behavior reflecting the P and M leadership types. When providing P-type supervisory behavior, the supervisor gave instructions designed to apply pressure on the subjects to increase their productivity such as "Work more quickly," "Work accurately," "You could do more," "Hurry up, we haven't much time left," and so on. Instructions for the M type were as follows: "Let's do the job pleasantly without overworking," "It is quite a big job, isn't it?" "Let's be relaxed," and so on. This role-playing procedure was the same as that used by Misumi and Shirakashi (1963). A total of six work sessions were conducted, each session lasting thirty-five minutes with a five-minute break.

A transducer of the plethysmograph was attached to each subject on the left middle fingertip, and the plethysmogram was recorded continuously throughout each session. Data were analyzed using the mean readings during three sessions for the three subjects. Figure 20 shows the results of the plethysmogram readings. The data show consistent differences in the change

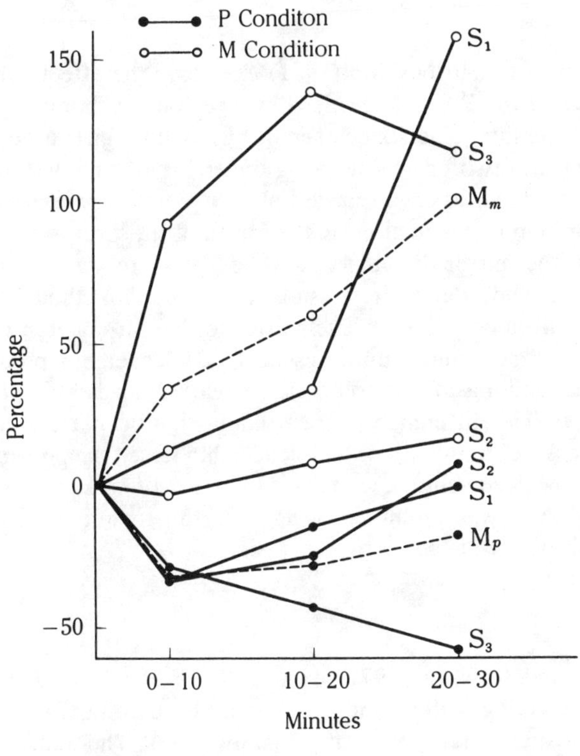

Fig. 20. Rate of change compared with initial pulse-volume amplitude in each subject. M_m and M_p are the mean values for the three subjects.

in plethysmogram readings of pulse-volume amplitude between P-type and M-type leadership during the course of the trials. The pulse-volume amplitude decreased under P leadership and increased under M leadership. The differences in change were statistically significant. In other words, the P condition had the effect of raising physiological arousal levels while the M condition had the effect of reducing them.

In terms of performance, the total amount of work done in the P condition was more than that in the M condition. However, the rate of accurate work was higher in the M condition than in the P condition. These results are consistent with those of previous laboratory studies using cognitive indices such as feelings of hostility against the leader and anxiety over the experimental situation as criteria. These cognitive studies also indicated that P conditions were found to be more unpleasant, to create more hostility against the leader, and to cause a higher degree of anxiety than were the M conditions.

Experiment II

Osato, Ogawa, Misumi, and Nishino (1971) examined the effects of verbal instructions reflecting the P and M leadership types on psychomotor performance and blood pressure. The sixteen senior high school girls used as subjects were divided into two groups working under P-type and M-type leadership. A mirror drawing task was carried out ten times. The experimenter gave the P-type or M-type instructions in the fourth, fifth, sixth, seventh, and eighth sessions of the mirror drawing test. Blood pressure was measured at rest, during the test, and after the test using Riva-Rocci's method.

Compared with blood pressure levels prior to the introduction of the P and M conditions (first through third sessions), M leadership produced a decrease in systolic and diastolic blood pressure while P leadership produced an increase in both. The difference was especially significant statistically in diastolic blood pressure. In other words, P leadership raised the physiological arousal level and M leadership lowered it. In terms of task performance, speed but not accuracy was promoted by P leadership, while M leadership promoted accurate performance.

Experiment III

Misumi, Ogawa, and Kawazu (1971) examined the effects of P and PM leadership types by taking plethysmogram readings on the fingertip and head (the left temporal artery branches in the shallow side). The subjects were nineteen male students in a special psychology course. The students were divided into two groups. Ten subjects were placed under an experimenter showing supervisory behavior of the P type, while nine subjects were placed in the PM condition. The task assigned to groups with three to four subjects each was to count the number of holes in IBM punch cards as was done in Experiment I.

The plethysmogram on the fingertip and head was recorded for five minutes at rest and thirty minutes during task performance for subjects working under each of the leadership conditions. Pulse-volume amplitude was found to decrease in the fingertip and increase in the head under both P and PM conditions. There was no difference between the two conditions in the decrease in the fingertip pulse-volume amplitude, but the increase in the pulse-volume amplitude in the head was significantly larger under the PM condition than under the P condition. Changes in heart rate under both conditions were also small, but showed a slight decrease under the P condition. The differences in heart rate change between the two conditions were not great enough to be significant. Overall, both the P and PM conditions acted to raise subjects' physiological arousal level, but the increase under the PM condition was somewhat higher than under the P condition.

Several task performance and attitudinal criteria were also studied. The total amount of work under the P condition was significantly larger than under the PM condition, but the accuracy of the work was significantly higher under the PM condition. Levels of anxiety for the experimental situation and task motivation did not differ significantly between the two conditions. However, hostility toward the leader was higher under P than under PM leadership.

Experiment IV

Kawazu, Misumi, and Ogawa (1972) experimentally studied the effects of three leadership types—P, M, and PM—on galvanic skin response (GSR) and heart rate (HR). Fifty-eight junior high school boys were divided into three groups—nineteen in P conditions, twenty-two in M conditions, and seventeen in PM conditions. The subjects carried out the task of counting the number of holes in IBM punch cards. The leadership types in this experiment were implemented by having experimenters administer supervisory instructions written on paper (refer to Experiment I for information on their contents). Each subject rested for five minutes and then performed the task for twenty minutes. A total of twelve instructions were administered at specific periods of time while the task was being performed.

The records of physiological processes indicated that both HR and GSR increased significantly under P conditions. HR decreased under M conditions, while GSR increased and HR did not change under PM conditions. Based on the heart rate data, P conditions raised physiological arousal levels and M conditions reduced them. Under the PM conditions, arousal rose in some subjects and declined in others, but no overall change was found.

As for task performance, the total amount of work was somewhat higher under P conditions than under other conditions. No significant difference was found among the conditions in either total amount of work or the accuracy of work done. The results for the cognitive indices showed that the degree of interest in the task of counting cards and in the experiment as a whole was highest under the PM conditions followed by the M conditions and the P conditions in that order. The "comfortableness" that subjects showed regarding the supervisory instructions indicated that M came first, followed by PM and P. Subjects' degree of anxiety and uncomfortableness concerning the experimental situation was highest under the P conditions, followed by the PM and M conditions. Although no significant differences were found in the index of performance, results for the physiological indices indicated the validity of PM leadership theory.

Psychophysiological Placebo Studies of PM Leadership Theory

In the experimental studies testing the PM theory which have been conducted from the psychophysiological point of view, the validity of the PM leadership behavior types was examined using physiological indices as dependent variables. The study of behavioral dynamics continued by using the results of some of the psychophysiological studies of the P and M leadership types as clues. The psychophysiological studies to identify mechanisms through which the effects of P-oriented behavior and M-oriented behavior interact were conducted from the standpoint of the general behavioral dynamics of leadership. The basic hypothesis was as follows:

> Multiplicative effects (P × M) are induced when the effects of P and M leadership behavior are combined with one another.

In order to verify this hypothesis, an alteration in the experimental procedure used earlier was made. This alteration involved establishing "precipitating conditions" for leadership. A favorable precipitating condition may be prepared for M leadership behavior (or P behavior) when it is preceded by P behavior (or M behavior). Under such precipitating conditions, the multiplicative PM effects may occur when the complementary M behavior (or P behavior) follows.

Placebo administration was used to prepare a precipitating condition for the P-type (or the M-type) leadership that followed. The multiplicative interactions between the two conditions were then assessed. This experiment was based on the findings of experiments reported in the previous section which indicated that P leadership behavior may increase the arousal level of the follower while M leadership behavior may decrease it.

Experiment V

Kawazu et al. (1973) studied the effects of the interaction between the stimulant (or depressant) suggestion of a placebo and the P-type (or M-type) leadership conditions on the performance of a mirror drawing task and concomitant physiological responses. Employed as subjects were forty college students (both male and female) enrolled in a psychology class. The subjects were divided into four groups of ten each. The groups were given: (1) stimulant placebo instruction under P-type leadership (S-P), (2) depressant instruction under P-type leadership (D-P), (3) stimulant instruction under M-type leadership (S-M), and (4) depressant instruction under M-type leadership (D-M). A placebo capsule containing lactose was administered to subjects in each group. In the "depressant instruction" condition, subjects were told that the drug would decrease both emotional and somatic functions. In the "stimulant instruction" condition, subjects were told that the capsule would activate these functions. The mirror drawing task was performed once before placebo administration and three times beginning thirty minutes after placebo administration. Upon completion of the second session (the first placebo session), either P-type or M-type instructions were given. Heart rate was analyzed as an indicator of physiological response. However, no clear differences were found among the four conditions.

Task performance was calculated as the number of blocks traced correctly divided by the frequency of errors in tracing blocks (K). The K-values were used to identify multiplicative interaction effects between the effects of the placebo instructions and those of the leadership conditions (fig. 21). The pair of bars on the left in figure 21 depicts the effects of the P conditions and the M conditions regardless of placebo instruction. The graph on the right presents the results for the leadership conditions separately for the two placebo instructions.

The overall results showed that the depressant instruction was associated with higher performance than was the stimulant instruction. Moreover, the depressant instruction when combined with P-type leadership promoted high task performance. Conversely, the depressant instruction when combined with M-type leadership impaired work performance. No interactive effects were found between stimulant instruction and PM leadership type.

Experiment VI

Kawazu, Ogawa, and Misumi (1974) carried out another experiment to confirm the results of the study described above. Seventy-four female university students were divided into four groups: nineteen in the S-P condition, nineteen for D-P, seventeen for S-M, and nineteen for D-M. Thirty minutes after

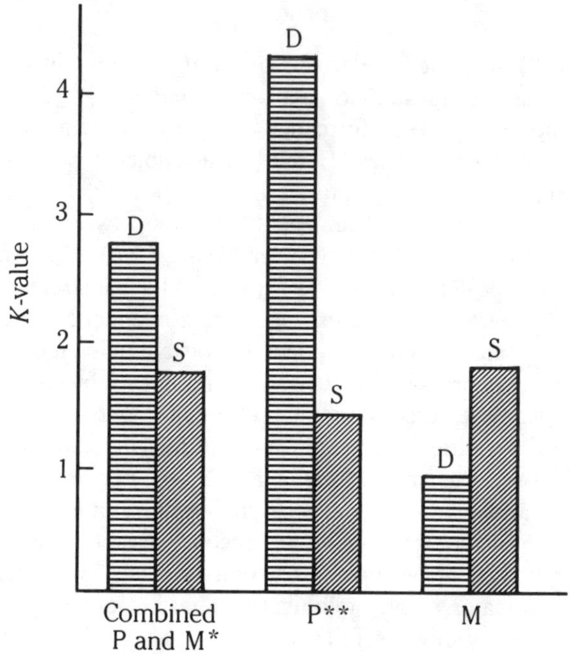

Fig. 21. Effects of placebo and PM leadership on performance (*K*-value). Significance levels for difference in performance between stimulant and depressant placebo instructions: $*p < .05$; $**p < .01$.

placebo administration, ten trials of the mirror drawing task were performed. At the end of the first, fourth, and seventh trials, either P-type or M-type leadership instructions were given by an instructor who was a student majoring in psychology.

Heart rates in the S-M group remained at the pretrial level, those in the S-P group and the D-P group showed a slight increase, while those in the D-M group showed a remarkable increase. An analysis of variance showed significant differences in heart rate change between the S-P and S-M, D-M and D-P, and D-M and S-M conditions.

As in figure 21, data are presented both for the overall leadership conditions and for the four combinations of leadership condition and placebo instruction. In task performance, the error time under the stimulant placebo instruction was less than under the depressant instruction. Thus, the stimulant instruction produced more favorable effects on work performance than did the depressant instruction (fig. 22). Task performance in the four conditions showed the following order: S-M > S-P = D-P > D-M; the task performance of the S-M group was significantly superior to that of the D-M group.

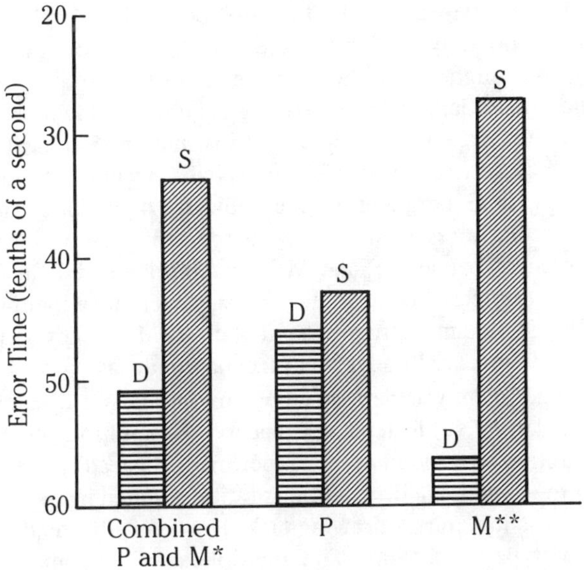

Fig. 22. Effects of placebo and PM leadership on performance (error time). Significance levels for difference between stimulant and depressant placebo instructions: $*p < .05$; $**p < .01$.

Summary of Psychophysiological Placebo Studies

The results of Experiment V showed that the hypothesized multiplicative interaction effects of P and M leadership are evident in task performance in the depressant placebo instruction conditions. However, the anticipated effects in the stimulant placebo conditions were not found. In Experiment VI, the interactive effects of P and M leadership was demonstrated in the S-M conditions but not in the D-P conditions.

These findings, however, do not conflict with the basic interaction hypothesis. In order to understand the differences in the results of the two experiments, characteristics of the experimental conditions including the subjects used and instructions given to them should be considered.

The subjects in Experiment V were freshmen and the instructor was their professor in a psychology course. The experiment was also performed in a laboratory of the psychology department. Thus, the subjects may well have experienced high tension-inducing conditions. However, the subjects in Experiment VI were senior students and the instructor was a student in a psychology course. The degree of tension associated with the experimental situation for these subjects was likely to have been considerably less. This assumption is supported by the fact that the initial heart rates of the subjects in Experiment V were higher than those of the subjects in Experiment VI.

The higher the initial level of physiological arousal, the more responsive the subject is likely to be to the depressant instruction. Similarly, the lower the initial arousal level, the greater is the probable response to the stimulant instruction. Thus, in Experiment V, the subjects' high initial arousal level made them particularly responsive to the depressant placebo instructions so that clear differences between P and M leadership appeared. In Experiment VI, however, the subjects' lower initial arousal level made them particularly responsive to the stimulant instruction so that clear differences between P and M leadership only appeared under this placebo condition.

Another experiment was performed by employing an anti-anxiety drug (a benzodiazepine derivative) instead of a placebo. No multiplicative interaction in the D-P condition was found in this experiment. Instead, P-type leadership provided after the depressant drug administration resulted in an increase in the frequency of errors in a mirror drawing task. However, this tendency was not found under M-type leadership. The multiplicative PM interaction effect hinges on the motivation level of the subject. The motive level may be related to the defensive process of the central nervous system. Further study is needed to shed light on the question of the relationship between drug effects and the motivation level of subjects.

CHAPTER 12

Leadership Dynamics and Group Structure and Performance

The experimental study of democratic and autocratic leadership by Lewin, Lippitt, and White (1939) was not intended as an experiment to guide the future use of democracy or autocracy, but rather as a quest to learn how different types of leadership behavior give rise to disparate group dynamics. However, in order to develop a complete scientific understanding of leadership, it is not sufficient to study only the general behavioral dynamics at which Lewin aimed.

At about the same time that the early studies of the behavioral dynamics of leadership were being carried out in the United States, similar research was being conducted in Japan by Toki (1935). Toki's research involved setting up groups of children and studying the effects of changes involving informal emergent leaders and senior formal leaders (adult experimenters and teachers). The subjects were seventy elementary and nursery school children. One of the purposes of the research was to determine the effects that the physical distance separating leaders and followers had on group processes. Another purpose was to determine the consequences of the time at which the separation occurred relative to the beginning of group activities.

Two levels of physical distance were established as experimental conditions: distant separation and near separation. In the distant separation condition, the leader was isolated outside the room where the subjects were located while in the near separation condition the leader was removed to a separate location within the same room. When the experimental conditions were established outdoors, a separation of seventy meters was considered distant separation, while a separation of no more than five meters was considered near separation.

Three experimental conditions were established which varied in the timing of separation—early, late, and prior separation. Early separation involved removing the leader approximately ten minutes after the commencement of the experiment, while late separation involved removing the leader after approximately forty minutes. The condition of prior separation involved delaying the leader's arrival. In each of the three conditions, the leader was returned to the group after five minutes. Thus, by establishing the two levels of distant and near separation for the distance variable, and the three levels of early, late, and prior separation for the timing variable, six experimental conditions were established.

The two kinds of activities which Toki selected for the children were sports activities involving cooperative games and crafts activities which involved joint creative projects. Toki found that the removal and reintroduction of an emergent leader had a substantial effect on group activities in those conditions involving either "near" or "early" separation. In other experiments conducted as part of the same study, Toki compared the consequences of separating emergent leaders versus nonleaders, situations in which children direct themselves versus classroom situations in which they are guided by teachers, and circumstances where a leader is necessary versus those where no leader is needed.

Although the research which Toki conducted may be described as a laboratory experiment, he tried as much as possible to create a group situation which was not artificial or contrived. The results of the experimental conditions were recorded unobtrusively, primarily through observation.

One part of the results involved comparing the effects of early or late separation of the emergent leader on group dynamics. In the "near" and "early" separation condition, the productive activity of the subordinate group became disorganized in both the sports and the crafts activities when the emergent leader was removed. Toki recorded the events in the following way.

Observation 1: The researcher led the children into a playroom and said, "Well now, let's all do something interesting together. Anything is fine, so everybody decide, and I'll just watch, o.k.?" Shortly child A emerged as a leader. He led the group well. The children selected a relay race as an activity and the race progressed smoothly. Once the activity was under way, leader A was roughly separated from the group and set down in a nearby spot in the room. The remaining subordinate group completely collapsed and the game stopped.

Observation 2: The researcher instructed, "Now then, from now on I'd like everyone to paint a picture together. I don't want everybody to paint a different picture, but I want everyone to plan together and help each other paint one picture." Soon after the directions were given child B came forward and began to draw. Following his example, the other children also took a half-standing posture watching him as if asking for his direction. Before long, B began to direct the others and the leader-subordinate role differentiation was born. At first, however, the children were not certain what was going to be drawn as there was only a single line resembling a mountain. Finally it was agreed that the picture was indeed a mountain. At that point approximately ten minutes had elapsed, and the researcher approached B and took him to a different location, saying, "Let's leave this picture up to the others. Won't you come with me and paint a different picture?" At this the other children acted lost and stopped their work. They asked out loud, "What shall we paint now," or "I'd like to draw a boat," but they only stood in front of B who did not answer. When B finally gave them some guidance they suddenly gathered strength and continued their work to the extent of B's directions. But when they had completed his directions they again stopped. Five minutes later the researcher returned B to his previous position and the group structure returned to the way it had been previously.

In summarizing the results of these and other observations, Toki interpreted the complete disintegration of the subordinate group's structure under the conditions of near-early leader separation as being a result of the initial centrality of the leader-subordinate structure to group maintenance. However, in the condition involving distant-late leader separation, the structure of the subordinate group was maintained considerably more adequately. The previous leader-subordinate structure also came to be replaced by a new substitute leader-subordinate structure. The experimental conditions involving distant-early or near-late separation resulted in an incomplete breakup of the subordinate structure, which implies an incomplete leader-subordinate structure, and the development of a state of frustration.

In all conditions where a separated emergent leader was restored to the group, the returning leaders regained their original leadership position and both frustration and the substitute leader-subordinate structure dissolved. However, in those conditions where an adult leader was introduced, the leader-subordinate structure centering on the child leader collapsed. Separating a nonleader from a group had no effect, confirming that only the emergent leaders were critical to maintaining the group's structure. Other results indicated that some group conditions required a leader role to become differentiated from the role of followers while other conditions did not.

In comparing Toki's research to the studies by Lippitt and White, the age difference of the children studied must first be considered. Toki's subjects were children from nursery school and the primary grades of elementary school (ages approximately five to nine years). Research in developmental psychology indicates that children's groups in the lower elementary years give rise easily to a pecking order based on muscular strength. Leadership in these groups is centered on the physically developed child leader. Lippitt's subjects, however, were ten- and eleven-year-olds from the upper elementary school grades and the leaders were adults.

The results of Toki's research resemble those of Lippitt and White's autocratic leader group and laissez-faire leader group. However, Toki's research did not include an equivalent of the democratic leadership condition.

Although Toki did not record observations of the interaction process between a leader and group members as did Lippitt and White, his study is still important as an attempt to explain group dynamics through the experimental study of leadership conditions.

Kamitake (1939*a*, 1939*b*, 1939*c*) also studied the behavioral dynamics of the command process in juvenile groups. From the time of Kamitake's studies until the end of World War II there are no other noteworthy Japanese studies of this type.

Leadership and Group Norms

The norms of any specific group constitute a standard of behavior that is held in common by group members. When a group member transgresses a norm, he or she receives some kind of "negative sanction" from the group; when a member conforms to group norms, negative sanctions are avoided and positive reinforcement and approval is typically experienced. Hollander (1958) indicates that norm conformity is one important way in which a new member initially achieves acceptance and status.

While leadership always involves fulfilling group functions, it can do so in a manner which either supports or attempts to change group norms. In any particular group, the leader's behavior may conform to or deviate from the norms of the group. Leadership in the PM theory is viewed as a normative phenomenon in the sense that it contributes to achieving group goals. Leadership is the behavior of a certain group member that has been instigated to bring about some type of "good result" for the group. For example, leadership in economic enterprises involves efforts intended to promote the achievement of the enterprise's financial goals. But why do group norms that effectively suppress group productivity sometimes develop in enterprises where this type of leadership should be at work?

The Hawthorne research by Roethlisberger and Dickson in 1939 clearly showed the existence of productivity-restraining norms among switchboard wire coiling workers. Coch and French (1948) also report that productivity-restraining norms were strongly influencing the work of women laborers who had undergone personnel reassignment and work procedure changes at a pajama sewing factory. Furthermore, according to the experimental research of Schachter et al. (1951) and the follow-up studies by Berkowitz (1954) and Maeda (Maeda, Kojima, and Noma 1960; Maeda, Kojima, and Nakashima 1962), the relationship between group productivity and cohesion is strongly influenced by group norms.

In groups sharing a norm for high productivity, group cohesion shows a positive relationship to productivity, but where the opposite norm exists, the relationship is negative. Seashore (1954) and Osuga (1959) have documented this tendency among groups of workers in actual business enterprises. Osuga conducted a survey in Japan using a group of keypunchers as subjects. Osuga found that work motivation tended to drop as group cohesion increased and that conformity tendencies were strongest among groups with low productivity and motivation. Stogdill's (1972) review of research concerning group cohesiveness, drive, and productivity supports the view that cohesion is associated with low group drive under conditions experienced as threatening. None of these studies attempted to clarify the relationship between leadership variables and productivity as affected by group norms. However, because a relationship between leadership and group productivity is clearly evident, a close relationship between leadership and group performance norms can be postulated. Such associations have been found in many of the field studies described in this book.

Although leadership behavior can be in conformity with or deviation from the norms of a particular group, it would be an oversimplification to describe actual leadership behavior as generally either conforming to or deviating from group norms. Certain aspects of a particular leadership pattern might conform to a given group's norms while other aspects of the same pattern might deviate from those norms. Moreover, groups are likely to hold norms relevant to both the P and M functions. By conforming with or deviating from norms relevant to either of these dimensions, the relationship of the leader to the group norms changes. Actual relationships between leadership patterns and group norms are complex and dynamic. For purposes of analyzing the dynamic relationship between these variables, several studies have been designed to assess the relationship of PM leadership patterns and group norms.

Laboratory Studies of PM Leadership Patterns and Group Norms

Sasaki and Yamaguchi (1971) have attempted to analyze the relationship between the leadership conditions postulated in the PM model and both productivity and productivity norms through laboratory studies based on Jackson's return potential model of group norms (1960). They hypothesized that "the supervisory leadership of a work group promotes the development of group norms reflecting that leadership type; and, at least in part, influences the productivity of the group through the process of norm formation" (Sasaki and Yamaguchi 1971, 223).

The subjects for Sasaki and Yamaguchi's experiment were 160 second-year junior high school students with equal numbers of boys and girls. The students were divided into sixteen groups of five boys and sixteen groups of five girls. Through the use of previously administered sociometric tests, the groups were formed to be as homogeneous in terms of mutual liking and attraction as possible. The students were told that they were to help make geometrical figures to be used in intelligence tests given at nursery schools. The task was basically one of cutting out figures printed on five different shades of colored paper. The students were asked to assemble as many sets of five figures with one figure of each color as possible. The experiment was divided into work sessions of five minutes each; one practice session and twelve regular sessions were conducted. Questionnaire surveys were given before, during, and after the twelve sessions. Survey 1 was administered before the start of the experiment, Survey 2 at the midpoint between the first and second halves of the experiment, Survey 3 immediately after the tenth work session, and Survey 4 at the end of all twelve sessions.

Each group was guided by a leader (college student) who had been trained to perform the role of the PM-, M-, P-, or pm-type leader. The behavior used to represent each leadership type was basically the same as that described in the laboratory work of Misumi and Shirakashi (1966).

P Type

The P-type leader supervised in such a way as to directly emphasize the achievement of group performance goals. The type of directions that the leader actually used were as follows:

To speed up the work: ''Make them faster,'' ''You're working too slowly,'' ''Hurry up,'' ''We don't have much time,'' ''Don't play, work,'' ''Come on, one after the other,'' ''I think you can do better than this,'' ''You can't make them while you're looking around.''

To encourage careful work: ''Cut more carefully,'' ''Can't you cut a little more carefully?'' ''Kindergarten children are going to use these so cut them nicely,'' ''If you aren't more careful we won't be able to use your work.''

To compare the group with other groups: ''You're behind the other groups,'' ''This is the slowest group of all,'' ''The other groups are making more,'' ''The other groups are doing better.''

While recording production quantity: ''Is this all you've made?'' ''You've got to make more,'' ''There are a lot here that won't count,'' ''You didn't make as many as last time,'' ''Work harder to make more next time,'' ''This is less than I expected, you should be able to make more.''

M Type

The M-type leader tried to maintain and strengthen the group. Actual expressions used were as follows:

To encourage the test subjects: "Let's have a good time," "Let's be a little more friendly," "It's kind of fun, isn't it?" "Have fun together while you work," "You're all doing a real good job," "The boys are pretty good with scissors, too, aren't they?" "You're doing great," "Excellent work," "If everyone did as well as you there would be no complaints."

To sympathize with the test subjects: "Aren't your fingers starting to hurt?" "Just a little longer so hang in there," "You're probably tired but please don't stop," "We will finish in just a minute so hang on."

While recording production quantity: "You're really working together well, aren't you?" "I'm glad that you're having a good time working together," "Sure enough, our group is the best," "You're all veterans, aren't you?" "This isn't a competition, so get along with each other."

Occasionally the leader would joke and make other comments to relieve tension and create a relaxed atmosphere.

PM Type

The PM-type leader sometimes tried to speed up the work by stressing goal achievement and sometimes sympathized with and encouraged the test subjects in order to create a relaxed atmosphere and maintain group integrity and processes. Actual expressions used were similar to those used by both the P and M types.

pm Type

The pm-type leader paid attention to neither group goal achievement nor group maintenance. He restricted communication with test subjects to simple answers to questions and the instructions and feedback necessary as part of general procedures.

Figure 23 shows the productivity results in terms of the number of sets of paper figures produced. The production averages for each leadership type and the results of a U-test for both the first half (sessions 1–5) and the second half (sessions 6–10) of the experiment are given at the bottom of figure 23. The data indicate that although no difference between the groups was evident in the practice session, the groups with the PM- and P-type leaders showed significantly greater productivity during the first half of the experiment than the groups under the M-type leaders, while the PM-, P-, and pm-type groups all showed greater productivity than the M-type groups during the second half. Productivity rankings put the PM-type groups at the top, followed in order by the P-type, pm-type, and M-type groups. According to the graph, the M-type groups fell behind the pm-type groups at the second session and the PM-type groups passed up the P-type groups at the fourth session. These

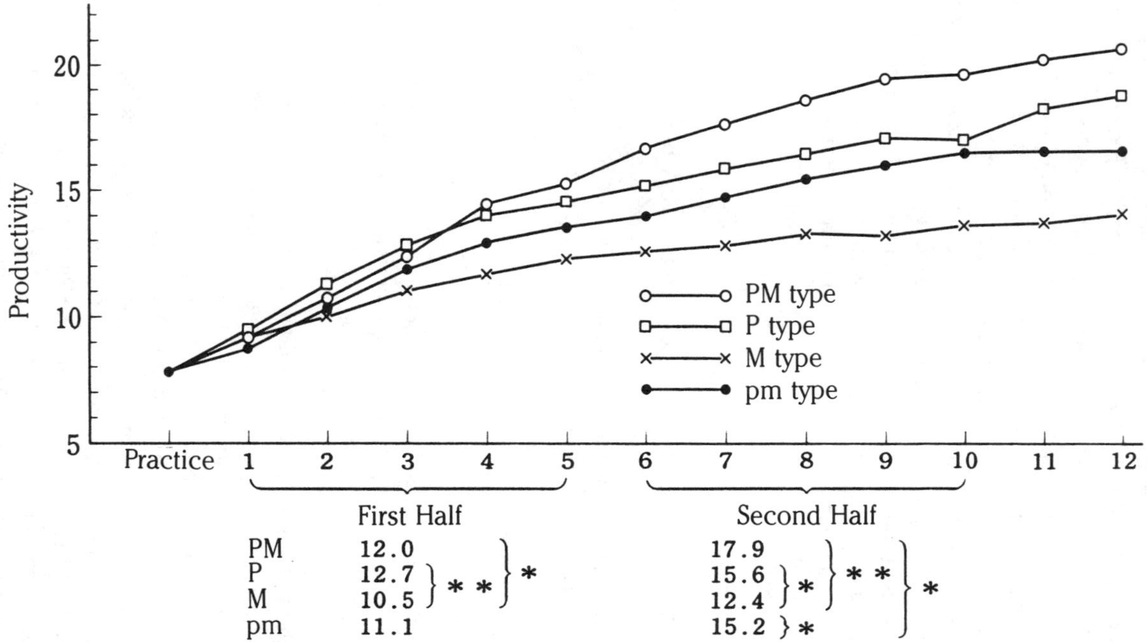

Fig. 23. PM leadership types and productivity of experimental groups. Median of productivity and results of U-test: $*p < .05$; $**p < .01$.

results conform closely with those of previous studies concerning the productivity of the various PM leadership styles.

As mentioned before, Jackson's return potential model was used in measuring group norms concerning productivity. This model utilized the "return potential curve" and the various indices that reveal the curve's peculiar composition. The related indices are:

1. *Point of maximum return:* the point on a behavior dimension that is maximally approved by group members.
2. *Range of tolerable behavior:* the range on a behavior dimension that incorporates allowable behavior.
3. *Crystallization of a norm:* shows the degree of agreement or disagreement among group members about the desirability of behavior at each scale point on a behavior dimension. It is derived by taking the mean of the variances computed for each scale position on the behavior dimension. A small mean—a small average variance—indicates a high degree of crystallization.
4. *Intensity:* the overall intensity of feeling in the group, whether of approval or disapproval, regarding a particular dimension of behavior.
5. *Potential return difference:* the differences in evaluation dimension values at each scale position on the behavior dimension of the two return potential curves of group norms and person viewpoints.

The group productivity norms during each measurement period were evaluated using the chart shown in figure 24 based on the following question: "If you were to say to your fellow group members 'let's make 5 sets in the next 5 minutes,' would they support your proposal, or would they oppose you? If you proposed to make 10, 15, 20, . . . 50 sets, what would they say? Try to imagine their feelings as you answer the question." Group acceptance of supervisor-proposed norms was evaluated in the same manner, using the following question: "If your group leader were to say 'let's make 5 sets in the next 5 minutes,' what would be the reaction of your group members? Would they support him, or oppose him? Try to imagine the feelings of your group members as you answer the question."

Figure 25 shows the productivity norms (in terms of return potential curves) that each group developed in each of the different leadership conditions. No significant differences appeared among the leadership types in Survey I, which was administered before the start of the experiment, or in Survey II, which was administered during the first part of the experiment. However, in Survey III, significant differences can be seen in the curves that correspond to different leadership types. In particular, the curve associated with the PM type is quite different from the P, M, and pm type curves. Table 81 shows the composition characteristics of the various curves.

The above findings bear out the notion that when newly formed work

(a) If you propose making	(b) Group members will Agree very strongly	Agree to some extent	Agree a little	Neither agree nor oppose	Oppose a little	Oppose to some extent	Oppose very strongly
5 sets	7	6	5	4	3	2	1
10 sets	7	6	5	4	3	2	1
15 sets	7	6	5	4	3	2	1
20 sets	7	6	5	4	3	2	1
25 sets	7	6	5	4	3	2	1
30 sets	7	6	5	4	3	2	1
35 sets	7	6	5	4	3	2	1
40 sets	7	6	5	4	3	2	1
45 sets	7	6	5	4	3	2	1
50 sets	7	6	5	4	3	2	1

Fig. 24. Questionnaire used for measuring group productivity norms

TABLE 81. Composition Characteristics of Return Potential Curves for Performance Norms

Leadership Type	Point of Maximum Return I	II	III	Range of Tolerable Behavior I	II	III	Crystallization[a] I	II	III	Intensity I	II	III
PM	10.0	18.8	25.5	10.0	17.5	15.0	2.04	2.62	2.86	12.6	12.0	10.4
P	10.0	12.5	20.0	15.0	15.0	17.5	1.48	1.42	1.90	12.9	14.4	12.7
M	10.0	15.0	20.0	17.5	12.5	15.0	1.20	1.70	1.73	13.9	12.7	13.0
pm	7.5	15.0	16.3	10.0	17.5	20.0	1.61	1.61	1.88	14.2	11.7	10.6
U-test	PM > pm*	n.s.	PM > pm*** PM > M**	n.s.	n.s.	n.s.	n.s.	n.s.	PM > M* PM > pm**	n.s.	n.s.	n.s.

Note: The values in the table represent medians. Roman numerals designate survey administration. Survey I was administered before the experiment began, Survey II between the fifth and sixth trials, and Survey III after the tenth trial.

Source: Sasaki and Yamaguchi 1971, p. 217.

[a]The smaller the values, the greater the crystallization.

*$p < .10$

**$p < .05$

***$p < .01$

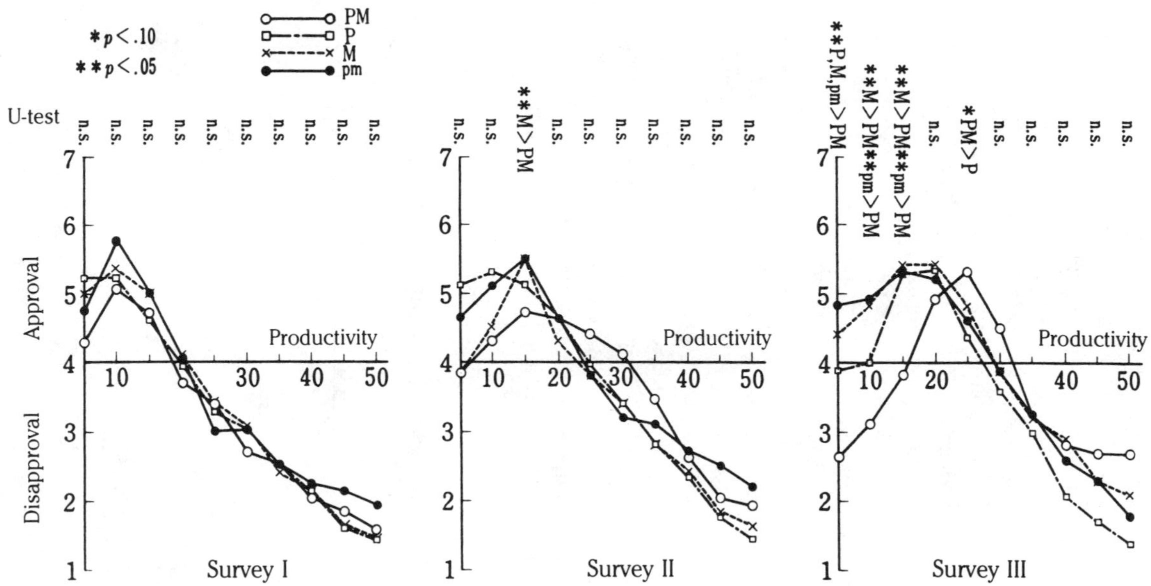

Fig. 25. Return potential curves for group productivity norms developed according to different PM leadership types

groups are placed under the supervision of different types of leaders, the groups will, with the passage of time, develop different production standards. Moreover, when groups are under the direction of a PM-type leader, the highest return score corresponds to a relatively high production standard, with production-promoting norms that are characterized by strong disapproval of low productivity and strong approval (or lack of disapproval) of high productivity. In contrast, the return potential curve in the third measurement period indicates that the group led by the P-type leader developed negative norms toward high production. The groups led by the M- and pm-type leaders developed norms which tolerated low production and to a certain degree which did not tolerate high production. Furthermore, even though the groups led by M-type leaders expressed higher group cohesion, worker motivation, and group member cooperation than the groups led by the P- and pm-type leaders, and although their group norm scores were the same as in the P-type groups, groups led by M-type leaders accepted the lowest production standard from their supervisor and showed the lowest actual production levels. No significant differences were found in the degree of influence that P-, M-, or pm-type leaders had on the formation of group norms.

Sasaki and Yamaguchi also looked at how different leadership patterns influence the extent to which group members accept productivity standards set by the supervisor. Table 82 shows the characteristics of the return potential curves for norms concerning leader suggestions. As is found for group performance norm formation, the significant differences found are between PM-

TABLE 82. Structural Characteristics of the Return Potential Curve for Receptivity to Leader's Productivity Suggestions

Leadership Type	Point of Maximum Return	Range of Tolerable Behavior	Crystallization[a]	Intensity
PM	25.0	28.5	3.02	10.4
P	20.0	26.0	1.71	12.7
M	16.3	22.5	1.63	13.3
pm	18.8	30.5	1.99	9.9
U-test	PM > M** PM > pm**	n.s.	PM > P* PM > M** PM > pm**	M > PM**

Note: All values are medians. The smaller the number is, the greater the correspondence.
Source: Sasaki and Yamaguchi 1971, p. 218.
[a]The smaller the values, the greater the crystallization
*$p < .05$
**$p < .01$

type leaders and leaders of other types. The highest return scores are found in more instances for groups under PM-type leaders than under either M- or pm-type leaders. Actual production amounts under the PM-type leaders were also higher than those under any other type of leader. The degree of cooperation under PM-type leaders was higher than that under the other leadership types. Under PM-type leadership, group members indicated that suggestions from supervisors to reduce production would be disapproved, but suggestions to raise production would meet with more approval than they would under any other type of leadership.

Field Survey Study of PM Leadership Patterns and Group Norms

The above study of Sasaki and Yamaguchi illustrates the effect of leadership conditions on the formation of group work norms and actual work performance. Laboratory research has the limitation that its results are a function of the peculiar social conditions of the laboratory. Compared with everyday life, these conditions are artificial and extremely short-lived. Human psychology in these conditions invariably includes at least a certain amount of experiment-related expectations or "mind-set" on the part of subjects. Accordingly, it is appropriate to verify the results of a laboratory study in actual field conditions to determine their relevance to everyday life.

Patchen (1962) has conducted some interesting field research concerning the relationship of leadership to work norms and group cohesion. In essence, Patchen has shown that when a supervisor promotes efficiency while at the same time showing concern for "subordinate remuneration," high work norms can be achieved. In particular, he has found that "meticulous supervisors" induce their subordinates to adopt high work norms under conditions of "good remuneration" and "high cohesion."

Kidosaki (1973), as well as Tasaki and Misumi (1976), have carried out studies about the relationship between the effectiveness of PM leadership types and work norms through on-the-job surveys in business enterprises. In carrying out his research at a chemical apparatus manufacturing company, Kidosaki had 1,301 employees evaluate their immediate supervisors to obtain the superiors' P and M leadership scores. The number of employees under any supervisor (all foremen) ranged from 3 to 21 with an average of 6. The number of supervisors evaluated was 207. In a similar study, Tasaki and Misumi surveyed 66 first- and second-line supervisors and 681 general employees at a bank. The questions used to measure performance norms in both surveys were as follows.

1. "At your workplace, do you and your fellow workers occasionally take the opportunity to freely discuss and criticize things concerning your work?"

2. "Do you feel that the atmosphere at your workplace is strained, with tension among your fellow workers?"
3. "To what extent do you think there is a feeling of competition toward other work groups among your fellow workers?"
4. "How do you think the majority of your fellow workers feel about achieving your work goals?"
5. "How do you personally feel about achieving your work goals?"

Tables 83 and 84 show the relationship between the PM patterns and performance norms using a five-step evaluation based on each of the above questions. Both charts show a similar trend. Group performance norm scores under the PM-type leader are considerably higher than those under leaders of the other three types. The P, M, and pm type follow in that order, but the differences among them are relatively negligible, particularly those between the P and M types. These on-the-job studies corroborate the results of the laboratory studies previously discussed.

The field data were analyzed further to confirm that the PM type of leadership is associated with higher performance norms than are the other

TABLE 83. PM Leadership Types and Performance Norms

Leadership Type	*N*	Performance Norm	*SD*
PM	400	3.22	3.28
P	219	2.96	3.04
M	168	3.02	3.12
pm	337	2.88	3.11
Total	1,124	3.04	3.20

Source: Kidosaki 1973, p. 109.
F = 0.009, n.s.

TABLE 84. PM Leadership Types and Performance Norms

Leadership Type	*N*	Performance Norm	PM vs. P	PM vs. M	PM vs. pm
PM	17	17.3	**	*	**
P	11	15.7			
M	13	15.5			
pm	25	14.8			

Source: Tasaki and Misumi 1976, p. 2.
$*p < .02$
$**p < .01$

three leadership types. The research of Sasaki and Yamaguchi indicates that under the relatively short-term conditions of laboratory studies, M-type behavior does little to promote high performance norms. In contrast, the type of leadership most likely to directly promote high performance norms in the laboratory is P-type leadership.

Kidosaki sought further to determine whether or not the same result would be borne out under the long-term conditions of a field setting. In Kidosaki's research, P-type behavior is found to be composed of two factors: a pressure P factor and a planning P factor. Kidosaki reports that the correlation between these factors and group performance norms are 0.40 and 0.39 (respectively) when M scores are large, and 0.02 and 0.18 (respectively) when M scores are small. In other words, when M scores are sufficiently large (above the mean), performance norm scores are higher the higher the P scores; when M scores are below the mean, no relationship is found between P scores and performance norm scores.

Analyses were conducted to determine whether or not similar results would be found in the data collected by Tasaki and Misumi. The results of these analyses are shown in table 85. The results indicate that even when M scores are below the mean, a correlation appears between P scores and performance norms. However, when M scores are above the mean, the correlation rises substantially. The difference in correlation of P behavior with performance norms between the two levels of M behavior in Tasaki and Misumi's data supports the results of Kidosaki's research. The differences in the results of the two studies originates in the place that the line is drawn between a large and a small M score. When the M scores are very low, the same trends are found in Tasaki and Misumi's survey that were evident in the Kidosaki study.

In summarizing the results of the two surveys, the deciding factor in determining the effectiveness of the performance norm formation process is not only in the level of P-oriented behavior, but also the level of M-oriented behavior. In situations where sufficient M-oriented behavior is present to catalyze P-oriented behavior, a high degree of correspondence is found between performance norm scores and P scores.

TABLE 85. Correlations between P Scores and Performance Norms for Leaders with High M Scores or Low M Scores

	N	*r*
M score below the average	36	.43*
M score above the average	30	.68*

Source: Tasaki and Misumi 1976, p. 4.
*$p \nless .01$

Leadership Dynamics, Need for Achievement, and Motivation

One of the PM studies published in English (Misumi and Seki 1971) reports an experiment designed to identify the effects of PM leadership type on subordinate motivation considering possible differences among subjects having varying levels of need for achievement (n-Ach). In previous PM leadership studies, effectiveness as reflected in productivity and morale indices was found to be highest in groups led by PM-type leaders and lowest in groups led by pm-type leaders. Groups under M-type leaders were found to be second highest in morale while groups under P-type leaders were the second highest in productivity in laboratory experiments. However, in some of the field studies, M-type leadership produced greater productivity than P-type leadership. Furthermore, subjects under a pm-type supervisor showed the lowest productivity and satisfaction and had the highest hostility score toward their superior (Misumi, Takeda, and Seki 1967). The constructive effects of PM-type supervision were suspected to be due to its effects on the subjects' high motivation. The results seem to indicate that the productivity of subjects with low initial motivation would reach a higher level than expected from their initial motivation if goal achievement or performance was stressed—that is, under P-type supervision—but that this external pressure would arouse hostility in the subjects. The longer and stronger the pressure for goal achievement, the greater the subjects' hostility would become until the productivity resulting from the emphasis on performance would reach a plateau or begin to decline. At this point, an emphasis on the maintenance function would become necessary. When both M and P functions are emphasized, that is under PM-type supervision, the level of productivity should be greater than under P-type supervision. These considerations led to the following hypotheses.

Hypothesis 1. In groups with high achievement motivation, both productivity and satisfaction would be highest under PM-type supervision and lowest under pm-type supervision with productivity and satisfaction under the P and M types ranking in between.

Hypothesis 2. In groups with low achievement motivation, productivity would at first be the highest under P-type supervision, but in later stages, productivity would be higher under supervision of the PM type. Satisfaction under P-type supervision would decline in the later stages, eventually resulting in a decrease in productivity.

Hypothesis 3. In groups under pm supervision, subjects with high achievement motivation would experience strong frustration, but subjects with low achievement motivation would not. Consequently, both the productivity and the degree of satisfaction of the high n-Ach group would gradually decrease, but those of the low n-Ach group would not.

Need for Achievement and PM Leadership Type Effectiveness

Preliminary Experiments

Two preliminary laboratory experiments were conducted based on the same hypotheses as those described above. In the first study, forty junior high school students were divided into ten groups with either four boys or four girls in each. Groups with high, medium, and low motivation were each placed under a PM-type and M-type supervisor, groups with high and medium motivation were each placed under a P-type supervisor, and groups with high and low motivation were each placed under pm-type supervisors. The results obtained were similar to those of the study described below.

The second experiment was started with seventy-eight subjects divided into ten groups. However, the results were unsatisfactory because a number of the subjects stopped coming in the course of the experiment. In general, however, the results did not contradict the results of the first experiment or the one described below.

Method

The final experiment, conducted for the purpose of verifying the results of the two preliminary ones, used students of a women's college as subjects. These subjects were chosen partly because they were thought less prone to absenteeism than those in the second group, and because the preliminary experiments had shown no significant difference between sexes. Subjects were juniors in a four-year undergraduate program.

Three weeks before the experiment, the achievement motivation of the subjects was measured on the basis of their responses to four Thematic Apperception Test slides in accordance with the scoring method developed by McClelland and his colleagues (1953) using slides which were similar to those used by McClelland. Twelve subjects who ranked high in achievement motivation (mean = 7.8) were divided into four groups of three members each; twelve who ranked low (mean = −1.0) were similarly divided into four groups. The request to attend the experiment was made to the subjects one week before the day of the experiment. Subjects in the low motivation groups participated less readily than those in the high motivation groups; the number of volunteers was smaller, and the number of latecomers greater.

The job assigned to the subjects was to count as quickly and accurately as possible the number of holes in IBM punch cards during a given period of time with the three members of the group working as a team under the supervisor. Four postgraduate students of Kyushu University acted as supervisors, each playing a different behavioral role—PM, M, P, or pm.

To impress the subjects with the importance of their task of counting holes in IBM cards, the following instruction was given to them before starting the experiment: "Your job is to put some of our research materials in order. Very important scientific data is punched on these IBM cards, and it is necessary to add them up and find totals as quickly as possible. Please begin the tabulation under the direction of your supervisors."

The work session proceeded in the following way:

1. The three workers were seated side by side before a long table.
2. Worker A took out one of the punched IBM cards which were stacked up in front of her. She counted the number of holes in the first through the fifth column of the card, wrote the number down on a tabulation sheet, and passed the card and the tabulation sheet to worker B seated next to her.
3. Worker B counted the number of holes in the sixth through the ninth column, wrote it down on the tabulation sheets, and passed the card and the tabulation sheet to worker C.
4. Worker C counted the number of holes in the tenth through the twelfth column, wrote the number down on the tabulation sheet, and added all three tabulations to get the total number of holes in the card, and put the card in the place assigned to it according to the number of holes. The IBM cards, eighty lines by twelve columns, had sixty-eight, sixty-nine, seventy-one, seventy-two, or seventy-three holes punched at random.

One room with one supervisor was allotted to two groups; one group had three subjects with high achievement motivation and the other had three subjects with low achievement motivation. The supervisor did not know the achievement motivation levels of the groups.

The supervisor was seated or moved about in front of the subjects. A total of seven work sessions were conducted, each session lasting fifteen minutes with five-minute intervals between sessions. The subjects were not told when the experiment would end. None of the leadership patterns for the experiment was introduced until the second session.

Measurement of Group Productivity

The productivity of each group was measured by the total number of cards for which the holes had been counted correctly by the three subjects, working as a team, in fifteen minutes. To detect errors in counting the holes, the cards were designed in such a way that the number of holes on each was indicated by the location of a hole on some specific line of the card. For example, a card with seventy-one holes in it was identified by a hole punched in the first column on

TABLE 86. Frequency of Supervisor Behaviors Based on Observers' Reports

Observed Behavior	Supervisory Behavior			
	PM	P	M	pm
P function				
N	32	51	0	0
%	49.1	68.0	0.0	0.0
M function				
N	26	0	53	0
%	40.1	0.0	82.8	0.0
Others				
N	7	24	11	10
%	10.9	32.0	17.2	100.0
Total *N*	65	75	64	10
Significance level	n.s.	$p < .01$	$p < .01$	n.s.

the fiftieth line, a card with seventy-two holes was identified by a hole in the second column on the same line.

Behavior of Group Members

A trained observer recorded the behavior of subjects and the supervisor during the course of their work using an observation sheet prepared beforehand. A questionnaire survey was administered after the experiment to measure attitudes of the subjects. The questionnaire included items such as hostility toward the supervisor and the sense of satisfaction among the subjects.

Validity of Supervisory Behavior Types

The supervisors' behavior types constituted the experimental conditions. Table 86 shows the association between the leadership conditions and observed supervisors' behavior in the six sessions following the initial practice session. The figures in the table indicate the frequency with which P and M behaviors were observed in each condition. The results indicate that the supervisors' behavior was definitely oriented toward the supervisory types specifically assigned to supervisors as experimental conditions.

Perceptions by Subjects

The questionnaire used for obtaining subjects' perceptions of the different behavioral types shown by the supervisors included four questions concerning supervisory behavior. Subjects responded on a 1 (not at all) to 5 (very much) scale. For the P function, the questions were:

TABLE 87. Subjects' Perceptions of Supervisors' Behavior

	P Score		M Score	
Supervisory Condition	High n-Ach	Low n-Ach	High n-Ach	Low n-Ach
PM	7.3	6.0	7.3	8.3
P	7.3	7.0	3.3	2.0
M	2.7	4.0	7.3	8.5
pm	2.3	3.3	3.3	5.0
Kruskal-Wallis H test	H = 15.7, df = 3		H = 16.1, df = 3	
Significance level	$p < .001$		$p < .001$	

1. "How much was the supervisor in your room concerned with increasing the efficiency of production?"
2. "How much was he concerned with the accuracy of your work?"

For the M function, the questions were:

1. "How much was he concerned to create an amicable atmosphere so that the three of you could work comfortably?"
2. "Could you talk freely with your supervisor concerning your work?"

The responses of the subjects to the questions about supervisory behavior are shown in table 87. These results also show that the four types of supervisory behavior were expressed as the experimental conditions required. Although there was some variability in perceptions depending on the strength of achievement motivation, no significant differences were found between groups with high and low achievement motivation under the same type of supervisor while there were significant differences in perceived leadership among the four leadership types.

Productivity of Experimental Groups

The productivity indices for the experimental groups were obtained by using the following formula:

$$Pn = \left(\frac{fn-f1}{f1}\right)\left(\frac{fn}{tn}\right) \times 100$$

where

Pn = productivity index at the nth session;
fn = the number of cards correctly calculated at the nth session;
$f1$ = the number of cards correctly calculated at the first session;
tn = the total number of cards calculated at the nth session.

The productivity results are presented in table 88 and the indices are shown plotted in figures 26 and 27 after smoothing by a method designed to eliminate fluctuations (the moving average method).

An analysis of variance predicting performance in the different experimental conditions indicated that there were significant differences in performance depending on the strength of achievement motivation (F = 12.88, df = 1/47, $p < .01$), supervisory type (F = 2.87, df = 1/47, $p < .05$), and the interaction between the two (F = 24.83, df = 3/47, $p < .01$). A further analysis of the interaction shows that in groups of subjects with high achievement motivation, workers under PM-type leaders scored highest in productivity, followed by P, M, and pm, in that order. In groups of subjects with low achievement motivation, no significant differences were found among groups of workers under P, M, and pm leaders, although P-type leaders proved to promote the highest productivity. In fact scarcely any difference appears between the productivity of groups with high and low achievement motivation under P-type supervision.

Satisfaction in Experimental Groups

Table 88 also shows that satisfaction under pm-type supervision is lowest in groups with high achievement motivation, and second highest, next to the PM type, in groups with low achievement motivation. The degree of satisfaction is represented by the sum of questionnaire responses concerning involvement in the work and the attractiveness of the task.

Group cohesiveness is represented in table 88 by the sum of questionnaire responses concerning group attractiveness, cooperation among group members, and ego involvement in the group. Groups with low achievement motivation showed significant differences in group cohesiveness under different types of leadership with cohesiveness being highest under the P and M types of supervision.

Hostility toward the supervisor was measured using the semantic differential method (Misumi, Takeda, and Seki 1967). Hostility was highest in groups under P-type supervision, and was higher for groups having low achievement motivation than for groups with high achievement motivation. Hostility was comparatively weak in groups with high achievement moti-

TABLE 88. Productivity, Satisfaction, Cohesiveness, and Hostility in Relation to Achievement Motivation and Supervisory Behavior

	Productivity		Satisfaction		Cohesiveness		Hostility	
Supervisory Condition	High n-Ach	Low n-Ach	High n-Ach	Low n-Ach	High n-Ach	Low n-Ach	High n-Ach	Low n-Ach
PM	55.1	20.9	6.3	7.0	12.3	12.3	24.0	19.0
P	38.3	38.0	5.0	2.5	11.0	14.0	34.0	42.0
M	33.3	12.1	5.7	3.5	11.7	15.0	19.3	24.0
pm	19.8	23.0	4.0	5.7	13.0	12.0	24.7	27.3
Significance level	$p < .01$	$p < .01$	$p < .02$	$p < .02$	n.s.	$p < .05$	$p < .05$	$p < .05$

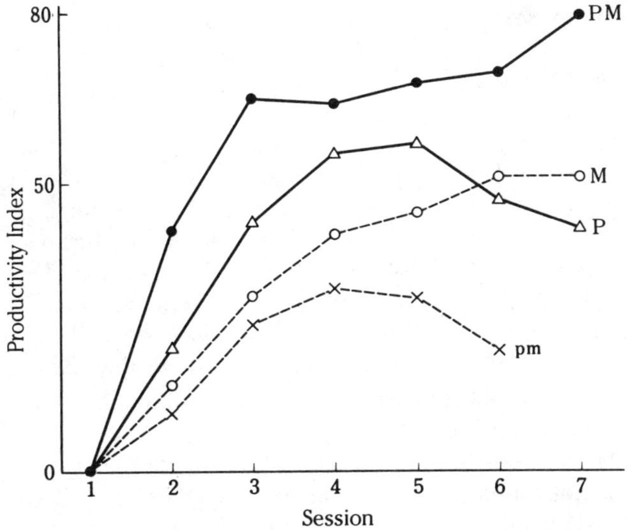

Fig. 26. Productivity of groups with high achievement motivation

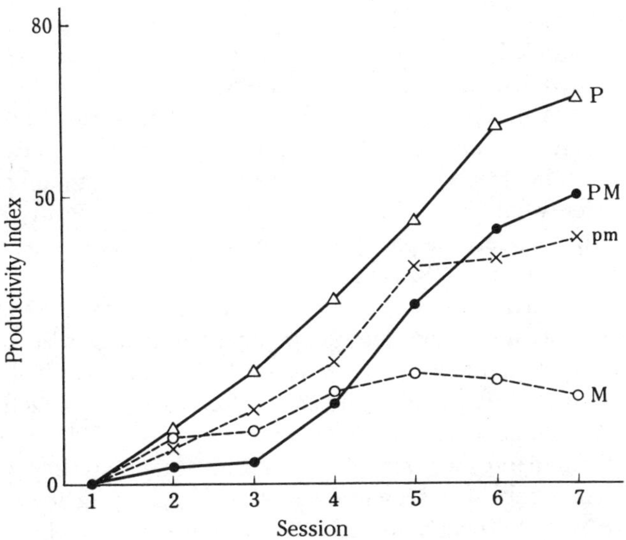

Fig. 27. Productivity of groups with low achievement motivation

vation under M-type supervision and in groups with low achievement motivation under PM-type supervision.

Discussion and Summary

The experiment demonstrated that in general the groups with high achievement motivation performed better than the groups with low achievement motivation (table 88). Hypothesis 1 was supported by the findings. In groups with high achievement motivation, PM-type supervisory behavior proved to be the most effective in terms of productivity, with the P and M types ranking in between, and the pm type the least effective. It was also found that M-type groups tended to outperform P-type groups in the last stage of the experiment. As for satisfaction, the PM type was highest, followed by M, P, and pm, in that order. These results are basically in accord with the findings of previous experiments and field studies.

Hypothesis 2 was also supported by the findings. In groups with low achievement motivation, the P type showed the highest productivity, followed by the PM and pm types in that order, while the M type proved to be the least productive. The degree of satisfaction was the highest and hostility the lowest under PM-type supervision. Under P-type supervision, the hostility scores were much higher than under the other three types, and the degree of satisfaction was the lowest. The finding that group cohesiveness was relatively high under P-type supervision may be attributed to the emergence of solidarity among the subjects due to their shared negative feelings such as dissatisfaction, frustration, and hostility toward this type of supervisor driving them to a position of united resistance against the supervisor (Seashore 1954). Had the experiment continued for a longer period, groups under PM-type supervision could be expected to supersede the other three supervisory types. It seems improbable that, in groups of subjects with low achievement motivation, pm-type supervision would result in greater performance than PM-type supervision in the long run, because pm-type groups scored lower in satisfaction and higher in hostility than the PM-type groups.

Hypothesis 3 was also supported. In previous studies, individuals with high achievement motivation showed better performance than individuals with low achievement motivation (Atkinson 1958; McClelland et al. 1953). In this experiment, however, no significant differences in productivity were found between groups of subjects with high and low achievement motivation under pm-type supervision; rather, groups with low motivation were more productive than groups with high motivation, although the difference was not significant (table 88). This finding is noteworthy. Apparently what determines group productivity is not only the strength of initial achievement motivation, but also the kind of situation-related motivation due to supervisory behavior.

The conclusion of previous achievement motivation studies that the degree of productivity is proportional to the strength of n-Ach should be modified to take into account the effects of supervisory behavior.

The question arises as to why, under pm-type supervision, the productivity of the group of subjects with high achievement motivation was lower than that of groups with low achievement motivation. It is not difficult to understand that the higher a subject's achievement motivation the greater would be the disappointment or frustration felt under pm-type supervision.

The results can be summarized as follows.

1. The validity of P, M, PM, and pm types of supervisory behavior introduced as experimental conditions was supported by both the perception of the subjects and the observers' records.

2. In groups with high achievement motivation, the PM type of supervisory behavior resulted in the highest productivity, followed by P, M, and pm, in that order. In terms of the degree of satisfaction, too, the PM type scored highest, followed by M, P, and pm, in that order. These results are basically in accord with the findings of previous experimental studies.

3. In groups of subjects with low achievement motivation, P-type supervisory behavior resulted in the highest productivity, followed by PM, pm, and M, in that order, although no significant differences were found among the latter three types. The degree of satisfaction was the lowest, the hostility toward the supervisor the strongest, and the group cohesiveness the greatest under P-type supervision. The degree of satisfaction was the highest and the hostility toward the supervisor was the weakest under PM-type supervision.

4. Under pm-type supervisory behavior, no significant differences in productivity were found between groups of subjects with high and low achievement motivation.

Leadership and Group Structure

Kano (1970) has conducted experimental studies in Japan to identify the interactive effects of structural variables and leadership variables on group performance. This work is based on previous research conducted in the United States concerning group structure (Cartwright and Zander 1953; Collins and Raven 1969; Harary 1959; Krech, Crutchfield, and Ballachey 1962) and communication networks (Lyle 1961; Shaw 1955, 1959). The communication structures Kano used included the most highly centralized structure, the wheel form, and the least centralized structure, the completely connected or "com-con" form.

He also considered three of the four PM types: PM, P, and M. Combining these two structural forms and three leadership types, he established six experimental conditions: (1) wheel-PM, (2) wheel-P, (3) wheel-M, (4) com-con-PM, (5) com-con-P, (6) com-con-M.

The problem assigned to each group was to correctly match up the radical and body of Chinese characters which had been separated beforehand. Using an experimental procedure developed by Leavitt, the group members communicated with each other by writing messages on memo paper. However, the leader communicated with the other members orally rather than by using the memo paper. The subjects were 120 female college students who were placed into experimental groups composed of 5 members each, one of whom took the role of leader. Those who played the role of leaders received training in role-playing the PM, P, and M types of leadership. During the experiment, in addition to performing her prescribed role, the leader also participated in problem solving as a member of the problem-solving group. Four separate experimental groups were organized to represent each of the six experimental conditions, for a total of twenty-four groups. The time required for problem solving, the satisfaction of the group members with the assigned task, member motivation, and member satisfaction with leadership and structural conditions were measured as dependent variables.

The data showed several major tendencies. The first concerns the interaction between structural factors and leadership factors. In the wheel structure, the more a leader was described as showing P-type behavior, the quicker was the problem-solving time, while the more a leader was described as showing M-type behavior, the more time problem solving required. In the com-con structure, the more a leader was described as showing P-type behavior, the more time was necessary, while the more M-type leadership provided, the quicker problem solving was accomplished. The PM-type was found to rank first in efficiency in the com-con structure, with the M type second, and P-type leadership lowest; but in the wheel structure, the P type ranked first with PM second and M lowest. No recognizable difference in satisfaction was found according to structural conditions. Therefore, the efficacy of different PM leadership types is contingent on the structural characteristics of problem-solving circumstances.

CHAPTER 13

Research Methods for Leadership Dynamics

The purpose of studying the general dynamics of leadership behavior is to understand the causal processes explaining the associations between leadership and value-related criteria. Unfortunately, leadership cannot ordinarily be fully controlled in field settings. The lack of fully adequate experimental control is evident in the field experiment involving Nishitetsu bus drivers described in chapter 5. Many other variables besides leadership affect any criterion in most social settings and most value-related criteria are too multifaceted to be rigorously studied. Therefore, the contrived laboratory experiments described in the preceding chapters have been conducted in order to identify causal processes which may help explain relationships found among variables in field research.

A few of the guiding laboratory studies and many field surveys have now been described which have contributed to developing the PM morphology of leadership. Questionnaire research uses statistical procedures to document the cognitions of a respondent. Laboratory research involves establishing controlled conditions and manipulating experimental variables to determine their effects on cognitions, behavior, and performance. However, the issue of the validity of any questionnaire research concerning leadership has been questioned as discussed in chapter 8.

An overall model depicting causal processes surrounding leadership is illustrated in figure 28. Although the studies conducted thus far have emphasized selected consequences of leadership, a more comprehensive model is needed to keep these studies in perspective and to guide further research. Five main categories of variables are shown in figure 28 which should be considered when framing a research question concerning leadership.

The figure indicates that behavioral dynamics involve a changing process by which actual social events are faced, cognitively assessed by a leader who behaves in response. Social events are reciprocally affected by leadership behavior and the whole process occurs within the context of more stable,

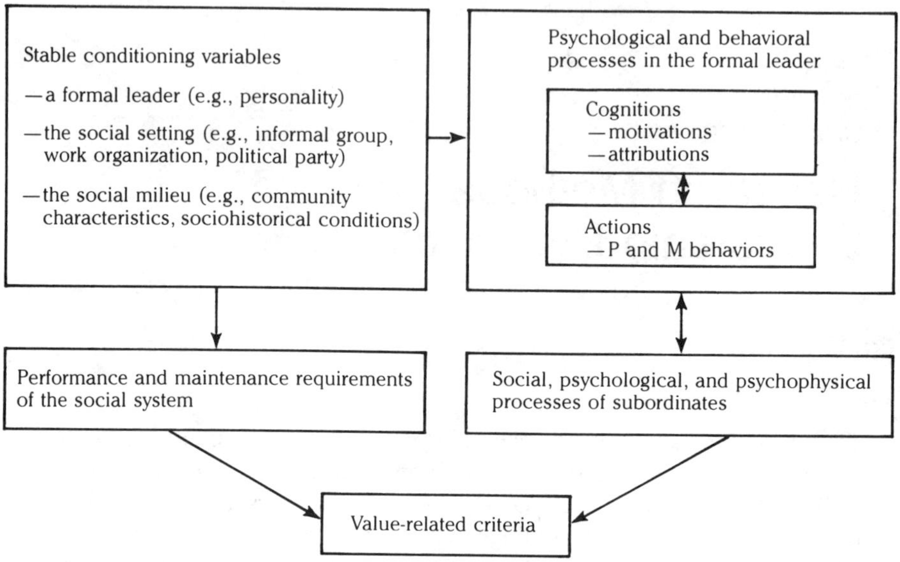

Fig. 28. A summary model of causal processes and conditioning factors surrounding leadership

largely structural variables. Leadership processes are affected by such stable conditioning variables as the background and personal characteristics of a formal leader. These variables affect how a leadership situation is cognitively interpreted and the particular behaviors a leader is most able to provide in response. As indicated in studies of the specific morphology of leadership, the social setting in which a leadership process occurs also determines the particular ways in which performance and maintenance leadership functions are expressed.

These relatively stable conditioning variables primarily reflect the specific conditions affecting, on the one hand, the leadership requirements and, on the other hand, the particular leadership behaviors associated with specific settings. The emphasis in studies of general behavioral dynamics has been on causal relationships between leader behavior and the social, psychological, and psychophysical processes of subordinates. Although studies of the reciprocal effects that such processes have on a leader's cognitions and behavior are an important component of an overall model of general leadership dynamics, only a few studies addressing this component from the PM perspective have been conducted. These studies take the point of view of specific dynamics and are discussed in the chapters that follow.

The first of our laboratory studies paralleled the study of democratic, autocratic, and laissez-faire leadership conducted in the United States by Lewin, Lippitt, and White (1939). Although this study attempted to improve upon the research design used in the Lewin, Lippitt, and White study, a major intent was to determine whether or not "democratic" leadership was as consistently superior to "autocratic" leadership in the traditionally somewhat autocratic culture of Japan as it was found to be in the United States. The results did indicate that groups of boys in Japan working under an autocratic leader showed a certain enthusiasm for work and did accomplish work which was in some respects superior (e.g., quality in difficult tasks) to that of boys working under democratic leaders. However, as the results were being interpreted, it became clear that differences in experimental settings—especially the voluntary nature of the boys' clubs in the United States study compared to the less voluntary school-related tasks in the Japanese study—might have encouraged boys under the latter conditions to respond more positively to autocratic guidance from adults than under the former conditions. Thus, while the Japanese study indicated that there were some conditions under which leadership that might be called "autocratic" could have some desirable consequences, it did not unequivocally indicate the extent to which cultural differences between Japan and the United States accounted for these differences.

The use of the concepts "autocratic," "democratic," and "laissez-faire" leadership were also abandoned after the conclusion of this study, since these concepts were considered to lack necessary precision and to include a large amount of emotive significance. These two characteristics of the terms interact to make it difficult to objectively state and test scientific hypotheses based on them.

Although another early experimental study (Misumi and Shirakashi 1966) has been described from the perspective of general behavioral morphology, it also has implications for the study of general dynamics. The experimental study of postal trainees working under PM leadership conditions provided initial evidence that PM leadership types could be distinguished. This study also indicated that the PM leadership types affected performance, but left the explanation for these effects largely undetermined.

Many of the subsequent studies have used the same basic experimental leadership conditions first developed in the study of postal trainees to determine the consequences of leadership types for learning and reminiscence (chap. 9), stress as expressed in a fixed mind-set (chap. 10) and physiological arousal indicators (chap. 11), and group processes (chap. 12). These intervening processes are especially appropriate to the study of general dynamics because they are relevant to most leadership situations whereas most task-related outcomes are specific to a particular technology.

A major goal of laboratory studies concerning the general dynamics of leadership is to understand why the typical ordering of PM types—PM > M > P > pm—is found with respect to many attitudinal and behavioral criteria in field studies. The studies of general dynamics have provided some useful information for understanding the usual superiority of the PM type in the field. Reminiscence was found in three studies to be promoted by PM-type leadership, especially as the length of the experimental task (number of trials) increased and especially when P-oriented behavior was provided during work periods and M-oriented behavior during rest periods. PM-type leadership was also found to produce less of a rigid mind-set (Einstellung) in problem solving than do other leadership types. This leadership type also resulted in higher group performance norms than did even the P type, which some leaders might intend to enforce a performance orientation on their subordinates.

The order of the P, M, and pm types varied in a complex way in laboratory studies involving different tasks and different dependent variables. Among the more consistent findings were that P-type leadership brought about the highest levels of subject anxiety as expressed in a fixed problem-solving mind-set, low pulse-volume amplitude, and other physiological indications of stress. Although M-type leadership ordinarily resulted in less physiological arousal or stress than did P-type leadership, it did not produce consistently less arousal than PM-type leadership. The pm type of leadership always produced low and often the lowest levels in most performance-related experimental dependent variables (e.g., learning, reminiscence, performance norms). Characteristics of each leadership type will be discussed further from the perspective of behavioral dynamics after the PM studies of specific dynamics are described.

In summary, the studies of general leadership dynamics have shown a number of links between a leader's actions and the social, psychological, and psychophysical responses of subordinates. Although these responses are more "general" than value-related criteria in the sense that they are likely to occur in all social systems, they may have some characteristics which make their expression in laboratory settings somewhat different than their expression in field settings.

General and Specific Causal Processes Shown in Experimental Studies

The challenge can be presented to experimental research of whether or not naturally occurring phenomena can be adequately represented in the "miniature nature" of a laboratory. Perhaps the "bluebird" of truth for which we search can survive only within nature itself. Though the bluebird is sought in the small world of the laboratory because we are unable to search for him in the complex, thick growth of nature, he may not be able to survive in that small world. This is the viewpoint that sociologists often take in refuting experimental studies of social phenomena. However, group dynamics research began with experimental research concerning human relations and small groups. Without knowing whether it is an illusory bluebird, something similar to the leadership phenomenon seems to be producible in the small world of the laboratory. Nevertheless, this phenomenon in the laboratory rarely appears to be identical to the phenomenon as it is found in the field.

The quest for laws of human group behavior using laboratory studies which have people as their objects is more a search for causal relationships between specific limited factors which are difficult to study in nature than an attempt to construct a small-scale "nature." Laboratory conditions are more a specific situation than a miniature. This specific situation attempts to control many diverse variables while altering only certain other carefully limited variables. Thus, a high resemblance between laboratory conditions and the spontaneous conditions of everyday life is not an essential requisite of laboratory research.

Laboratory research is essentially a search for the dynamics of basic factors, i.e., laws. Both laboratory conditions and the conditions of everyday life may be viewed as specific circumstances in which causal social processes occur. The "naturalness" of all social situations is a relative question. Are the contrived conditions of education and employment "natural"? There is often greater similarity between an experimental laboratory situation and an industrial work situation, for example, than there is between an industrial work situation and a political leadership situation. Research based on PM leadership theory has been carried out under several specific conditions including both field and laboratory settings. In both field research and laboratory research the same leadership concepts have been used. However, conceptual similarity does not automatically guarantee empirical similarity between PM leadership conditions established in the laboratory and PM conditions abstracted from the analysis of survey questionnaires. Consistent results must be sought to determine the extent to which PM studies using field methods and laboratory methods are mutually applicable. Generally speaking, it is better to test several different methods under several different circumstances than just one method in one setting. Only then can conditional analysis progress and limitations in generalizability be identified.

An overview of the subjects and tasks used in the studies of general dynamics is important for understanding the extent to which they are useful for developing a truly "general dynamics" rather than for showing certain "specific dynamics" of leadership. The subjects used in most of the studies concerning the effects of PM leadership types have been high school and college students, typically working in same-sex experimental groups. It might be argued that relying primarily on subjects within a relatively narrow age range may make the causal inference process more "specific" than "general.'' This perspective on the studies requires consideration and has some legitimacy. However, most of the dependent variables in the studies were selected and most of the causal processes were proposed because they helped to make field findings involving broader samples interpretable. Thus, the experimental studies are theoretically tied to the field studies and were conducted both conceptually and historically in conjunction with the field studies. Empirical field data shows that experimentally identified causal processes have some analogy in various work organizations as well as in educational, family, and political settings.

However, some subject-specific characteristics of the studies are likely. For example, Misumi and Seki (1971) showed that over the relatively short duration of their experimental tasks, low need for achievement (n-Ach) subjects showed relatively high performance and very low satisfaction under P-type leaders while high n-Ach subjects showed the more typical ordering of PM types with the PM type highest and pm type lowest for both criteria. Other research indicated that high-anxiety subjects performed better in a learning task under M-type than under P- or PM-type leadership.

Unintended specific dynamics may be reflected in the results of other studies. For example, the subjects used might respond more strongly to experimental leadership conditions than would older, more experienced subjects. Uniquenesses in the responsiveness of subjects to experimental leadership conditions, however, is more likely to influence the degree of difference in reactions to leadership types than the basic order of the types.

The experimental tasks used may also imply certain specific as well as general causal processes. Some of the tasks—notably the task of counting holes in IBM cards—are extremely routine and involve subjects working together in a clear assembly-line style. Other tasks—notably the mirror drawing and learning tasks—are somewhat more challenging and are performed individually. Results for the routine tasks might be expected to be the more applicable of the two task types to industrial line employees, while the moderately complex, individual tasks might be seen as more similar to the work done by many line managers, craftsmen, and students. The applicability to creative individual and collaborative work is somewhat more speculative as is the applicability to relatively unstructured social systems such as families and political leadership situations. The learning studies in which an immediate demonstration of learning (prerest learning) was compared with delayed demonstration of learning (postrest reminiscence) typically showed an order of PM > P > M > pm. The learning tasks used included both memory-related tasks (paired associates tasks) and skill development tasks (inverted hiragana alphabet printing). To the extent that learning is important to performance in accomplishing similar moderately challenging tasks in field settings, these results help to explain the typical field result that the PM type tends to be the most effective and the pm type the least effective. Similarly, to the extent that basic performance quantity and high performance norms without excessive physiological stress (and possibly behavioral expressions of it) contribute to overall long-term success for people performing repetitious work in industry, the studies of physiological arousal, work output, and performance norms also suggest that PM-type leadership will be superior to other leadership types. By and large, the studies using different kinds of tasks help explain why the same basic ordering of leadership types with the PM type first and the pm type last is typically found in the field even though the particular causal reasons for the ordering may vary from some settings to others.

A final consideration is the "specific" characteristic of laboratory research itself. In particular, the short-term nature of laboratory studies may account for one discrepancy between the typical ordering of P-type and M-type leadership in laboratory and field studies. In field studies, M-type leadership tends to rank after the PM type as the second most effective, while the P type ranks second in laboratory studies. This possibility will be considered more fully after the studies of specific leadership dynamics are discussed in the chapters that follow.

General Dynamics and Determinants of Leader Behavior

A general dynamics perspective on the determinants of leadership behavior emphasizes basic cognitive processes associated with a leader's response to his or her context and the resulting emphasis placed on the P and M functions. Research concerning causal processes involving the choice of setting-specific behaviors to express the P and M functions is part of the specific dynamics of leadership. Although the general dynamics perspective has not yet been taken in the study of the determinants of PM leadership, a body of theory is beginning to emerge in the United States to guide that study.

The PM leadership program has progressed to the point where change programs to help organization managers, government administrators, teachers, and parents learn to provide PM-type leadership can be justified on the grounds that PM-type behavior is consistent with generally positive outcomes, at least in Japan. The PM leadership theory was thus used to guide the development of a safety program for workers at the Nagasaki Shipyard (Misumi 1975). Although this particular program resulted in a reduction of accidents at work, the questions remain of exactly what brought about supervisor behavior changes, why they occurred, and what might promote or inhibit them. Change studies addressing the causes of PM leader behavior thus far have been conducted in such a narrow range of settings that they should be considered as part of the specific rather than the general dynamics of PM leadership.

Research in the United States, however, has indicated that subordinate performance affects leadership behavior (Farris and Lim 1969; Lowin and Craig 1968) in part through a leader's cognitive attributions about the reasons for the particular level of performance shown by subordinates (Green and Mitchell 1979). The earlier of these studies are presented and appear to have been conducted largely to make the point that the relationship between leader behavior and subordinate performance is embedded within a larger framework of causal relationships not clearly explicated when empirical relationships found at one point in time are reported. Thus, their relevance for understanding why leader behavior occurs or how it may be changed is limited. Reviews of longitudinal and experimental research concerning the antecedents and causes of leadership (Peterson 1981; Yukl 1981) indicate that most studies of leadership antecedents are also difficult to apply to help understand how leadership can be changed. This difficulty occurs because most research which identifies personality or situational variables associated with leadership behavior are difficult to apply to problems of changing leadership even when causal relationships are clearly shown. Rather, they indicate that some personality or situational variables represent constraints on changing leadership. Personality, on the one hand, is typically quite difficult to change and organization design, on the other hand, typically must be established according to other criteria besides promoting constructive guidance of subordinates. Most studies of leadership antecendents appear to support in principle if not in detail Fiedler's (1972*a,* 1972*b*) contention that leadership change programs should be designed to improve personality-situation fit. However, some studies assessing leadership training programs have shown that training can change leadership (Yukl 1981, 279–84).

A conceptual basis for understanding the cognitive processes which causally link situations to leader behavior is provided by Green and Mitchell's (1979) description of attributional processes of leaders. The authors base their model on the broad social psychological literature concerning attribution theory, particularly as developed by Kelley (1967, 1972, 1973). Although Green and Mitchell indicate that Kelley's model is somewhat rationalistic, they concur that attributions which leaders make about subordinate behaviors are based on the leader's observation of ''covariation'' between subordinate behaviors and such events as task characteristics, the behavior of other subordinates, and extraneous personal events affecting the subordinate. The three most important variables entering into the covariation a leader perceives are: (1) distinctiveness (whether or not the subordinate has behaved similarly when given other tasks), (2) consistency (the extent to which a subordinate has behaved similarly in other situations), and (3) consensus (the extent to which the subordinate's behavior is similar to that of other subordinates performing similar tasks).

In applying Kelley's basic attributional model to explaining leader behavior, Green and Mitchell note six examples of "moderators" or characteristics of leader-subordinate relationships in organizational settings which are likely to affect leaders' attributions of their subordinates' behavior. The first, the leader's basis of consensus information, involves the tendency of a leader to make attributions about the causes of subordinate task performance based on what the leader perceives himself as being able to do rather than on information about what other subordinates have been able to do. Second, an important characteristic of a leader acting in the role of observer is that, like other observers, the leader is more apt to attribute subordinate behavior to personal characteristics of a subordinate (e.g., motivation) than is the subordinate as one who is acting based on perceptions of external conditions. Third, commonly identified self-serving attributions when applied to the leadership situation may result in a leader tending to attribute group successes to his or her own actions and group failures to actions by subordinates. Fourth, the psychological closeness between a leader and a subordinate may affect, among other things, the extent to which subordinate behavior is attributed to subordinate personality (in a distant relationship) or to external factors as is the case in self-attributions of behavior (in a close relationship). Fifth, personal characteristics of subordinates (e.g., race and sex) and of the leader (e.g., locus of control, need for achievement) may affect attributions. Finally, prior expectations about the likelihood of a subordinate's success or failure may affect attributions about the causes of behavior which actually turns out to be effective or ineffective.

The basic outline of the Green and Mitchell model has now been briefly reviewed without reference to particular behaviors. The authors apply their model primarily to examples of attributions about whether a subordinate's personal motivation or external forces cause effective and ineffective performance. The leader behaviors which receive most attention are leader rewards and punishment (associated with motivation-based attributions) and leader training and guidance (associated with external and ability-related attributions). However, attributions concerning other variables besides motivation are likely to be relevant to understanding the precursors of PM behaviors.

Attributional models are beginning to be used with some success in PM research to understand how people draw causal inferences about responsibility for task success or failure. Studies of escape from emergency situations have presented subjects with videotaped simulations of emergencies. Questionnaires have been used to determine the extent to which subjects attribute responsibility for their successful or unsuccessful escape to luck, characteristics of the task situation, their ability, their effort, or the leader. Experimental variables used to predict attributions have been the success or failure of escape from the emergency situation, and leadership conditions representing pressure P, planning P, PM, and M leadership types. In one study, subjects attributed about one-third of the responsibility for their performance to the leader, about one-third to their own effort, and one-third to the other factors considered. The results also indicate that subjects under pressure P leaders attribute about 40 percent of the responsibility to their leader if they fail, but only 10 percent to the leader if they succeed. Attributional frameworks appear likely to contribute further to the development of PM theory.

Pending further research into the general dynamics of PM leadership antecedents, the attributional model provides a viable basis for forming hypotheses about the general causes of leadership. The issue of the specific dynamics of both the causes and consequences of leadership as well as other links in the model presented in figure 28 are considered in the following chapters.

PART V

Specific Behavioral Dynamics of Leadership

CHAPTER 14

Field Studies of Causal Processes Surrounding Leadership Stability and Change

The study of the specific dynamics of leadership behavior was carried out to identify causal relationships that occur under specific conditions and to apply general dynamics principles to such particular situations. As in the study of behavior morphology, any single study of leadership dynamics is conducted under specific, individual conditions. However, the laboratory studies described in preceding chapters have been based on general assumptions about leadership. The research to be described in the following chapters includes both laboratory experiments and field studies that allow situation-specific causal processes of leadership to be identified. The importance of research emphasizing the specific character of causal processes has become increasingly evident as modern social science research has progressed. A situationally specific application of basic causal processes is necessary where the relationship between performance criteria and leadership measures varies depending on the level of particular situational variables.

G. H. Mead (1936) distinguishes modern research science from the Renaissance science that prevailed until the nineteenth century. Whitehead (1925) differentiates modern science as an organic science from the prior stable, mechanical science. The perspective taken by modern science which treats any empirical regularity as a "hypothesis" means that behavioral dynamics only remain "general" until "exceptional" findings circumscribe their universality. However, just as specific morphology emphasizes the specific, concrete expression of basic behavioral types, specific dynamics emphasizes the specific expressions of general underlying causal dynamics.

The studies of general leadership dynamics indicate that leadership can have an effect on learning, problem solving, experienced stress, work performance, and physiological processes under laboratory conditions carefully contrived to show these effects. Studies of general and specific morphology have also demonstrated the concurrent validity of the PM leadership types by showing their association with attitudes, performance, accident rate, and other criteria in the "real world." However, the question of causal processes surrounding leadership in the real world remains as a problem for general dynamics research. The topics addressed below fall into two major categories. First, to what extent does a Japanese leader's behavior type tend to remain stable or change over time? Second, what causal relationship over time is there between perceived leader behavior on the one hand and subordinates' attitudes on the other?

Stability and Change in PM Leadership Behavior Descriptions

Several early industrial leadership studies conducted in the United States addressed the first issue—what degree of stability can be expected in leader behavior over time? These studies involved exchanging leaders of groups that had been effective with leaders of groups that had been less effective (e.g., Feldman 1937; Jackson 1953; Wyndham and Cooke 1964). The results of these studies indicated that the quality of group performance tends to be a function of the leader who is present rather than the group with which the leader is associated.

The strategy employed to assess the degree of spontaneous change that can be expected in a Japanese leader's behavior has involved comparing the stability of leadership perceptions by subordinates over time under similar conditions of leader transfer compared to situations where leaders were not transferred. Sakamaki (1974) studied the stability of P-oriented and M-oriented leadership using longitudinal data sets obtained from two banks in Kyushu. "Bank A" has branches throughout Kyushu and "Bank B" has its branches in northern Kyushu. Annual surveys were carried out for four years in Bank A and for three years in Bank B. The questionnaire used in the surveys included the same twenty-four leadership questions and the same or slightly modified work attitude measures as those described in chapter 3. Each rank and file employee rated their immediate supervisor (first-line supervisor) and their supervisor's superordinate (second-line supervisor). Second-line supervisors were branch managers, and first-line supervisors were either acting branch managers or deputy branch managers. Surveys were administered following the usual procedure in which a graduate student visited each branch, gathered the employees into one room, read the questions orally, and asked the respondents to check on an answer sheet the answers they selected.

Data were analyzed by comparing the average score assigned to a leader between a previous year and a following year. Comparisons were made using the first two years for which data were available for each leader. For example, if a person were a branch manager during each of four consecutive years, the data from the first and second years would be used. If data were available for only the third and fourth years, the data from these years would be used. The number of supervisors studied in this way included 254 first-line supervisors and 85 second-line supervisors. The number of respondents providing usable data for first-line supervisors was 1,543 for the prior year and 1,519 for the subsequent year. For second-line supervisors, 1,271 respondents provided usable data for the preceding year and 1,275 for the following.

Data were analyzed separately in those instances where a supervisor transfer had taken place between the two surveys and where no transfer had occurred. Table 89 shows correlations between leadership scores (for both P-oriented and M-oriented behavior) in the preceding year and the following year separately under circumstances where a transfer occurred and where no transfer occurred. Where no transfer occurred, the correlations between scores in the prior year and in the subsequent year are all statistically significant ($p < .05$) for both the M-oriented behavior scores and the P-oriented scores of first-line and second-line supervisors. For the cases of transfer, there are no statistically significant correlations between scores in the prior and subsequent years for either behavior dimension for either first-line or second-line supervisors. These results imply that a leader seems to behave in a stable way under stable conditions, but will also often behave in a different way when faced with a new situation.

Misumi and Mannari (1982) analyzed additional data collected at one-year intervals for five years in a third bank, "Bank C," and for six years at a fourth bank, "Bank D." The same measures, data collection procedures, and data analysis procedures were used as those used in the Sakamaki study. All

TABLE 89. Correlations between Previous and Following Year Leadership Scores in Two Banks

	First-line Supervisors			Second-line Supervisors		
	Not Transferred ($N = 121$)		Transferred ($N = 133$)	Not Transferred ($N = 66$)		Transferred ($N = 19$)
P scores	.354	**	.027	.740	*	.287
M scores	.526	***	−.074	.588	**	−.078

*$p < .05$, **$p < .01$, ***$p < .001$

employees including supervisors described their immediate supervisor. Data were obtained for 565 leaders from Bank C and 1,489 leaders from Bank D. Usable data were obtained from 2,538 respondents in Bank C for the previous year and 2,589 respondents for the subsequent year. In Bank D, 9,209 respondents provided data for the preceding year and 9,043 provided data for the following year.

Tables 90 and 91 show the correlations between leadership scores in previous and subsequent years for Bank C and Bank D, respectively. Data are presented separately for those cases where a supervisor's position changed and those cases where there was no such change. The first pair of columns in each table presents data for all formal leaders combined, while the second, third, and fourth pairs present data, respectively, for upper-level, middle-level, and lower-level managers. For both P and M scores at all managerial levels, correlations are significantly higher for supervisors who stayed in the same position than for supervisors who were transferred.

Table 92 provides data concerning the nature of leadership behavior changes in further detail by identifying the changes in PM types that occurred for those leaders who changed positions. About 50 percent of the PM-type leaders and about 40 percent of the pm-type leaders retained the same leadership type they had previously. A substantial proportion of leaders initially showing P-type or M-type behavior also kept the same behavior type (about 30 percent) after their job change. However, very few M-type leaders switched to P-type supervision or vice versa.

Having established that leadership behavior change often accompanies job change, the next step is to determine the extent to which the behavior change is temporary or permanent. That is, are leaders striving to return to a preferred style and just having trouble doing so immediately, or does situation change induce more enduring behavior change? Table 93 shows the results of analyses assessing behavior change both one and two years after position change. The data for assistant managers in Bank C show low correlations between behavior before a job change and behavior both one and two years after the change. However, the correlations between the scores one and two years after the job change were significantly higher than those obtained in the period from before to twenty-four months after the job change. Similar results were obtained for Bank D. Apparently, changes that took place in leadership behavior following a job transfer continued for at least a year or two.

Tables 94 and 95 present data separately for three kinds of transfers: (a) transfers to similar departments of different branches, (b) transfers to different departments of different branches, and (c) transfers to different departments within the same branch. The results indicate that people transferred to different branches show significantly more stable P-oriented behavior when they were assigned to the kind of department in which they had worked previously

TABLE 90. Correlations between Previous and Following Year Leadership Scores in Bank C

	All Managers Combined		Upper-level Managers		Middle-level Managers		Lower-level Managers	
	Not Transferred ($N = 205$)	Transferred ($N = 257$)	Not Transferred ($N = 27$)	Transferred ($N = 20$)	Not Transferred ($N = 20$)	Transferred ($N = 7$)	Not Transferred ($N = 158$)	Transferred ($N = 202$)
P scores	.702^{+++}	.304^{+++}	.564^{++}	.340	.879^{+++}	−.280	.652^{+++}	.286^{+++}
(difference)	***				**		***	
M scores	.632^{+++}	.350^{+++}	.766^{+++}	.296	.797^{+++}	−.276	.534^{+++}	.351^{+++}
(difference)	***		*		*		*	

Significance levels for correlations (two-tailed) $^{++}p < .01$, $^{+++}p < .001$
Significance levels for differences between correlations (two-tailed) $^{*}p < .05$, $^{**}p < .01$, $^{***}p < .001$

TABLE 91. Correlations between Previous and Following Year Leadership Scores in Bank D

	All Managers Combined		Upper-level Managers		Middle-level Managers		Lower-level Managers	
	Not Transferred (N = 1,095)	Transferred (N = 242)	Not Transferred (N = 124)	Transferred (N = 29)	Not Transferred (N = 525)	Transferred (N = 121)	Not Transferred (N = 446)	Transferred (N = 92)
P scores	$.689^{+++}$	$.550^{+++}$	$.662^{+++}$	.202	$.682^{+++}$	$.478^{+++}$	$.526^{+++}$	$.251^{+}$
M scores	$.637^{+++}$	$.492^{+++}$	$.566^{+++}$	.027	$.543^{+++}$	$.378^{+++}$	$.505^{+++}$	$.244^{+}$

Significance levels for correlations (two-tailed) $^{+}p < .05$, $^{+++}p < .001$
Significance levels for differences between correlations (two-tailed) $^{*}p < .05$, $^{**}p < .01$

TABLE 92. Change in PM Leadership Types before and after Changing Jobs

Before Transfer	Transferred Department Heads in Bank C after Transfer					Transferred Department Heads in Bank D after Transfer				
	PM	M	P	pm	Total	PM	M	P	pm	Total
PM	29	12	7	11	59	27	3	10	7	47
	(49%)	(20%)	(12%)	(19%)	(29.2%)	(57%)	(6%)	(21%)	(15%)	(38.8%)
M	13	12	2	16	43	11	7	1	2	21
	(30)	(28)	(5)	(37)	(21.3)	(52)	(33)	(5)	(10)	(17.9)
P	13	6	11	7	37	4	2	2	4	12
	(35)	(16)	(30)	(19)	(18.3)	(33)	(17)	(17)	(33)	(19.7)
pm	20	10	7	26	63	8	11	6	16	41
	(32)	(16)	(11)	(41)	(31.2)	(20)	(27)	(15)	(39)	(33.9)
Total	75	40	27	60	202	50	23	19	29	121
	(37.1)	(19.8)	(13.4)	(29.7)		(41.3)	(19.0)	(15.7)	(24.0)	

Note: Percentages given in parentheses.

TABLE 93. Correlations between Leadership Scores before and after Transfer and during the Posttransfer Period

		N = 52		N = 55	
Correlations between scores before and one year after transfer	P scores	.299^{+}		.534^{+++}	
	M scores	.351^{+}		.358^{+}	
Correlations between scores before and two years after transfer	P scores	.342^{+}		.558^{+++}	
	M scores	.267$^{\triangle}$	* *	.484^{+++}	$\triangle$
Correlations between scores one and two years after transfer	P scores	.714^{+++}	* *	.727^{+++}	*
	M scores	.634^{+++}		.699^{+++}	

Significance levels for correlations (two-tailed) $^{\triangle}p < .10$, $^{+}p < .05$, $^{+++}p < .001$
Significance levels for differences between correlations $^{\triangle}p < .10$, $^{*}p < .05$, $^{**}p < .01$

TABLE 94. Stability and Change in Leadership Behavior for Transferred and Nontransferred Leaders Bank C

			Managers Transferred to:		
			Different Branches		
	All Transferred Managers (N = 202)	All Nontransferred Managers (N = 158)	Same Kind of Department (N = 51)	Different Kind of Department (N = 39)	Same Branch, Different Kind of Department (N = 51)
P scores	.286^{++++}	.652^{++++}	.445^{++++}	.268^{+}	.262^{+}
Difference (All Transferred vs. All Nontransferred)	* * * *				
Difference (All Nontransferred vs. Same Kind of Department)		* * *			
Difference (All Nontransferred vs. Different Kind of Department)		*			
Difference (All Nontransferred vs. Same Branch, Different Kind of Department)		* *			
M scores	.351^{++++}	.534^{++++}	.343^{+++}	.235	.570^{++++}
Difference (All Transferred vs. All Nontransferred)	* *				
Difference (All Nontransferred vs. Different Kind of Department)		*			
Difference (Different Kind of Department vs. Same Branch, Different Kind of Department)				*	

Note: The number of "All Transferred Managers" is greater than the sum of the number of managers in the three specific categories of transfers because data concerning the nature of the transfer were unavailable for some managers.

Significance levels for correlations (two-tailed) $^{+}p < .10$, $^{+++}p < .01$, $^{++++}p < .001$

Significance levels for differences between correlations (two-tailed) $^{*}p < .10$, $^{**}p < .05$, $^{***}p < .01$, $^{****}p < .001$

TABLE 95. Stability and Change in Leadership Behavior for Transferred and Nontransferred Leaders Bank D

	All Transferred Managers ($N = 121$)	All Nontransferred Managers ($N = 525$)	Managers Transferred to: Different Branches, Same Kind of Department ($N = 67$)	Managers Transferred to: Different Branches, Different Kind of Department ($N = 23$)	Managers Transferred to: Same Branch, Different Kind of Department ($N = 19$)
P scores	.478^{++++}	.682^{++++}	.564^{++++}	.097	.589^{+++}
	****(All Transferred vs. All Nontransferred)		**(Same Kind vs. Different Kind); ***(All Nontransferred vs. Different Kind)		*(Different Kind vs. Same Branch)
M scores	.378^{++++}	.543^{++++}	.418^{++++}	−.012	.651^{+++}
	**(All Transferred vs. All Nontransferred)		*(Same Kind vs. Different Kind); ***(All Nontransferred vs. Different Kind)		**(Different Kind vs. Same Branch)

Note: The number of "All Transferred Managers" is greater than the sum of the number of managers in the three specific categories of transfers because data concerning the nature of the transfer were unavailable for some managers.

Significance levels for correlations (two-tailed) $^{+}p < .10$, $^{+++}p < .01$, $^{++++}p < .001$

Significance levels for differences between correlations (two-tailed) $^{*}p < .10$, $^{**}p < .05$, $^{***}p < .01$, $^{****}p < .001$

than if they were assigned to a different kind of department. Apparently, when leaders are thoroughly familiar with the kind of work being done in their new position, they are able to demonstrate the same kind of P-oriented leadership as previously even though other aspects of their surroundings were changed. Transfers to different kinds of departments within the same branch results in more stable M scores than do transfers to different kinds of departments in a different branch. However, the P score correlations for this latter group differ considerably between the two banks. Thus although conclusions concerning P leadership are uncertain for within-branch transfers, perhaps the presence of the same immediate superiors and peers as before, and the proximity of previous subordinates, encourages a leader to keep a stable maintenance orientation despite an interdepartmental transfer. For people who were not transferred, correlations between their scores before and after a one-year period show greater stability than in the cases of transfer.

Overall, the configuration of results indicates that leadership behavior tends to change as a result of personnel transfers to the extent that the new position differs from the old position with respect to work content and social context. Still, the ranking of the PM types in relation to various criteria in the banks studied, as in studies previously discussed, does not change over time.

Taken together, these findings supporting the cross-situational validity of the PM types and the potential for changing a leader's PM type have encouraged the kind of PM training and development programs that will be described in chapter 15.

Causal Relationship between Leader Behavior and Subordinates' Work Attitudes

Several researchers have pointed out the ambiguity in the appropriate causal interpretation of correlational results found in leadership field research (e.g., Kerr and Schriesheim 1974; Korman 1966; Lowin and Craig 1968). A few longitudinal (Franklin 1975*a,* 1975*b*) and field experimental studies (Mitchell and Wood 1980) have begun to address the causal relationship issue in the United States. In addition to the laboratory experiments conducted as part of the PM research program to establish general causal relationships, the longitudinal nature of some of the PM field surveys allows causal hypotheses to be tested in some specific field settings. One such study uses statistical techniques for analyzing panel data (Campbell and Stanley 1963; Heise 1975; Pelz and Andrews 1961; Vroom 1966; Yee and Gage 1968) to test hypotheses concerning the effects that prior subordinate morale and performance have on subsequent leader behavior.

A number of studies have identified particular effects of a subordinate's performance on leader behavior (see Peterson 1981). Herold (1977) established situations in which a subordinate's behavior was manipulated and a supervisor's response was studied as well as situations in which a leader's behavior was manipulated and a subordinate's response was studied. The results indicated that the leader's behavior is affected by subordinate performance and that subordinates' behavior varied according to the supportive or punitive contents of the leader's communications to them. However, subordinate performance affected leader behavior more than leader behavior affected subordinate performance.

Greene (1973, 1975) conducted three surveys of leadership behavior and subordinate satisfaction at one-month intervals for first-line supervisors in three companies. Two subordinates under each supervisor described their supervisor's levels of consideration and initiating structure. The criteria consisted of two other co-workers' evaluations of each respondent's performance and the respondents' self-report of job satisfaction. Cross-lagged correlations indicated that leader consideration was positively related to subsequent subordinate satisfaction after both one- and two-month intervals. Leader initiating structure had no relationship to subsequent subordinate satisfaction. Subordinate performance affected subsequent leader behavior such that good performance was followed by an increase in leader consideration and a decrease in leader initiating structure after both one- and two-month intervals. However, a similar study by Downey, Sheridan, and Slocum (1976) involving two surveys at a one-year interval gave different results. It showed a more uniform reciprocal causal relationship indicating that leader behavior affected subordinate performance and satisfaction to a similar degree that subordinate performance affected leader behavior.

Greene (1974, 1979*a*) used a longitudinal approach to test the hypothesized causal relationship postulated in the path-goal leadership theory. He conducted two surveys at a three-month interval. The results indicated that a leader's instrumental behavior clarifies the role and enhances the satisfaction of people experiencing low task structure. For people experiencing high task structure, supportive leader behavior enhances subordinates' satisfaction. Reciprocally, when subordinate performance is poor, a leader's instrumental behavior increases, and supportive behavior decreases. Greene (1979*b*) conducted another study based on the path-goal model testing the assumption that objective task structure is low for people shortly after they are assigned a new job. He found the same causal relation between the leader's behavior toward the subordinate and both subordinate performance and task satisfaction noted above.

Sims (1977) and Szilagyi (1980) have carried out longitudinal tests of a leadership model based on contingent reinforcement theory. Causal relationships between a leader's reward behavior (positive, punitive, and advancement reward) and subordinate performance were assessed using two surveys at a six-month interval. Sims reported that the positive reward and the advancement reward behaviors tended to increase subordinates' performance. On the other hand, high subordinate performance significantly reduced positive reward behavior while low performance tended to increase it slightly. Szilagyi collected two waves of survey data at a three-month interval and reported similar results. That is, a leader's positive reward behavior enhances subordinate satisfaction while punitive behavior tends to increase dissatisfaction. Reciprocally, low subordinate performance and high absenteeism tend to increase punitive behavior.

Sims and Szilagyi (1979) compared the data obtained in pairs of surveys carried out at three-, six-, nine-, eighteen-, and twenty-seven-month intervals. Cross-lagged correlations were calculated between leadership scores in the first survey and subordinates' performance in the second, and between subordinates' performance in the first and leadership in the second for each pair of surveys. They found that cross-lagged correlations for surveys carried out at the three-month interval were the highest. The cross-lagged correlations decreased as the interval between each pair of surveys increased.

In summary, leader consideration, supportive behavior, and positive reward behavior enhance subordinate satisfaction. Conversely, high subordinate performance increases leader consideration and supportive behavior, while low performance tends to increase leader initiating structure, instrumental behavior, and punitive reward behaviors.

A Long-Term Study of Bank Employees

Data were collected from a bank which has branches throughout Okinawa (Misumi and Mannari 1982). A PM leadership survey was carried out in this bank five times between November 1975 and November 1980 at about fifteen-month intervals. The questionnaire items for leader behavior and work attitudes are identical to those described in chapter 3. All bank employees described their immediate supervisor and their own work attitudes. The number of respondents and supervisors differs from year to year, but an average of 1,325 subordinates described 303 superiors each time.

The purpose of the study was to determine the causal relation between the P and M behavior of leaders and subordinates' attitudes. In the bank studied, personnel changes occurred frequently so that more than half of all the subordinate groups changed supervisors between each pair of surveys. Consequently, changes between the pairs of survey waves were assessed separately for those groups which experienced no supervisory personnel change and for those which did experience a supervisory change. Comparison of changes between these two types of groups permits the latter to serve as a field analogue of a nonequivalent control group (Campbell and Stanley 1963).

Data Analysis

P and M scores for each leader were calculated by taking the average of their subordinates' descriptions. Measures of the eight work attitude variables were also measured using the average score for each work group. In the present analysis, "morale" scores correspond to the average score for the eight work attitude variables. Because group data based on only one or two subordinates are unstable, only groups with three or more subordinates were used. Data from all five survey administrations were converted to standard scores. Data from the first survey for every work group were compared with data from the survey conducted fifteen months later, the second survey wave was compared with the third wave, the third was compared with the fourth, and the fourth with the fifth. Data were analyzed separately for those groups where a supervisor was brought in between the previous and following survey, and for those groups where the supervisor did not change. There were a total of 287 groups for which the supervisor changed and 159 groups for which the supervisor did not change. The average size of each work group, including the supervisor, was seven people.

Results

Figure 29 presents the correlations between leadership and employee attitude scores in the previous year and those in the following year both for groups which did and those which did not experience supervisor changes. There is no significant correlation in the cases of supervisory transfers between the former supervisors' and their successors' P-oriented scores or M-oriented scores. In the groups which did not change supervisor, there is a high correlation between the previous and the following year's scores for both P-oriented and M-oriented behavior. The difference between the groups where the supervisor was changed and those where he was not is significant at the 0.1 percent level for both P-oriented and M-oriented scores. There was a similar trend in the correlation between the work attitude scores in each pair of survey waves. The correlation is low for the groups which experienced a supervisor change, but tends to be somewhat higher for the groups which did not change their supervisor. The difference is statistically significant ($p < .05$). Overall, only when the supervisor was not replaced was there consistency both in leadership behavior and in the morale of work groups between the previous and the following year surveys.

Table 96 concerns the relation between leader behavior changes and subordinate attitude changes over time. For the groups which changed their

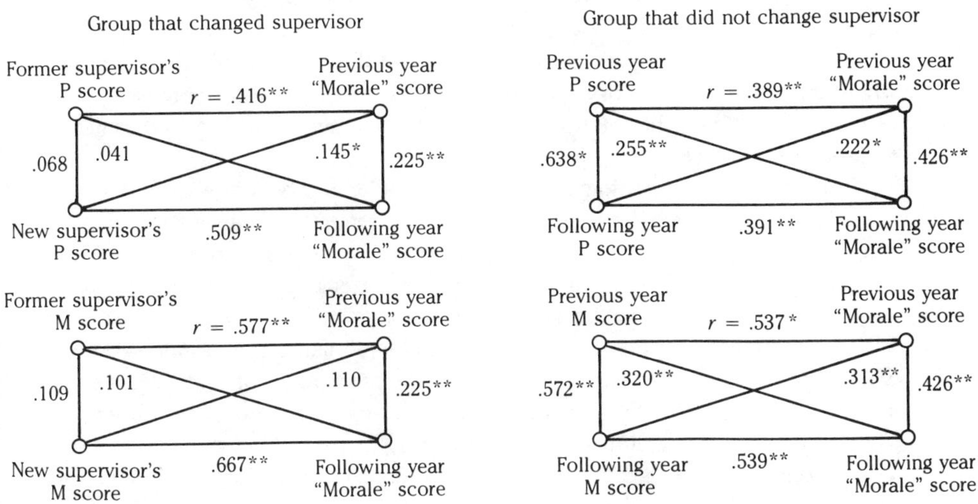

Fig. 29. Correlation between leadership and ''morale'' scores of previous year and those of following year. Test of significance (two-tailed test): $*p < .05$; $**p < .01$.

TABLE 96. Correlation between Leadership Score and "Morale" Score Changes

	Group That Changed Supervisor (N = 287)		Group That Did Not Change Supervisor (N = 159)	
Degree of P score change	.496*	++	.343*	+
Degree of M score change	.667*		.481*	

Note: Correlations are calculated according to Vroom's (1966) Corrected Dynamic Correlation method.

Test of correlation significance (two-tailed) $*p < .001$

Test of the difference between correlations $^{+}p < .05$, $^{++}p < .001$

supervisor, there is a positive correlation between the degree of change in perceived leadership scores and subordinates' work attitudes. For instance, when the successor supervisor's P and M leadership scores is much higher than his predecessor's, the work group's morale score also rises substantially. Conversely, when the successor supervisor's leadership score is lower than the former's, work group morale scores also tend to fall. The correlation between the degree of M score change and morale score change is particularly high. On the other hand, in the group which did not change their supervisor, there is little correlation between the degree of leadership score change and morale score change between the previous and the following years. That is, where there is no change of supervisor, leadership and morale scores are both relatively stable and the relation between any changes occurring in these two variables is positive.

The results suggest that a supervisor's leadership behavior affects work group morale to a greater extent than work group morale affects a supervisor's leadership behavior. However, can we say that the work group morale which developed under a former supervisor has no effect on a new supervisor's leadership behavior or on the group's subsequent morale?

A multiple regression analysis was conducted using the morale score of the following year as a criterion and using the previous year's morale scores and the new supervisor's leadership behavior scores as predictor variables. The results indicated that the new supervisor's M-oriented behavior (standardized partial coefficient: $\beta = .545$), the new supervisor's P-oriented behavior ($\beta = .207$) and the previous year morale ($\beta = .135$) together explain 49.92 percent of the total variation in the morale score of the following year. Therefore, the effect of the morale developed under a former supervisor appears weak compared to that of the new supervisor's behavior.

TABLE 97. New Supervisor's Leadership Score in Low and High "Morale" Groups of the Previous Year

Morale Score the Previous Year	*N*	P-score of the New Supervisor Mean	P-score of the New Supervisor SD	M-score of the New Supervisor Mean	M-score of the New Supervisor SD
High	142	.008	.83 ⌉ *	−.093	.80
Low	145	−.187	.82 ⌋	−.165	.77

Note: Significance level for t-test (two-tailed) $*p < .05$

Table 97 shows mean differences (t-tests) in the new supervisor's leadership score for groups showing above average and below average morale in the previous year. Significant differences in the new supervisor's leadership scores are found for P-oriented leadership, but not for M-oriented leadership. For those groups in which the previous year's morale score was higher than the average, the new supervisor's P-oriented score tends to be high.

Table 98 indicates the relation between the previous and following year morale scores and the new supervisor's PM leadership type. This cross tabulation shows that for groups whose previous year morale is above the average and whose new supervisor shows either pm- or P-type leadership behavior, morale tends to become low in the following year. Conversely, in groups

TABLE 98. Work Group Morale of the Previous and Following Year and the Supervisor's PM Leadership Type

Previous Year Morale	Following Year Morale		PM	M	P	pm	Total (All PM Types)
High	High	N	53	13	10	6	82
(*N* = 142)		(%)	(37.4)	(9.2)	(7.0)	(4.2)	
	Low	N	7	4	19	30	60
		(%)	(4.9)	(2.8)	(13.4)	(21.1)	
Low	High	N	30	18	4	12	64
(*N* = 145)		(%)	(20.7)	(12.4)	(2.8)	(8.3)	
	Low	N	12	14	9	46	81
		(%)	(8.3)	(9.9)	(6.2)	(31.6)	
Total		N	102	49	42	94	287

Note: Numbers in parentheses represent the percentage of high (or low) morale work groups in the previous year.

whose previous year's morale is below average, when a new supervisor shows either PM- or M-type leadership behavior, the group's morale in the following year tends to increase.

A Log-Linear Model (LLM) was applied to analyze the relation among the three variables shown in table 98. This model allows the expected value logarithm to be predicted for every cell using a linear combination of several predictors. For three variables, the following formula represents the saturated model.

$$\text{Log } F_{ijk} = U + U1(i) + U2(j) + U3(k) + U12(ij) + U13(ik) + U23(jk) + U123(ijk)$$

F_{ijk} : Theory frequency

The LLM is similar to the analysis of variance model and is described using similar terms. U is the "Grand mean effect," $U1(i)$ is the "Main effect" of the i category of variable 1, $U2(j)$ and $U3(k)$ express respectively the j category of variable 2 and the k category of variable 3. $U12(ij)$ is the first order interaction effect between the i category of variable 1 and the j category of variable 2. $U13(ik)$ and $U23(jk)$ also express first-order interaction effects. $U123$ (ijk) expresses the quadratic interaction effect of the i category of variable 1, the j category of variable 2, and the k category of variable 3.

The estimates of all parameters to which the saturated model was applied are indicated in table 99. Goodman (1971) showed that the standardized values obtained by dividing parameter estimates by the standard error approximates the standard normal distribution. Thus, the significance of each parameter's effect can be statistically tested, and a standardized effect value of ± 1.96 is significant at the $p < .05$ level.

In the Log-Linear Model, the main effect statistics reflect only the number of cases falling within each category of a single predictor (e.g., the number of high morale and low morale groups). Only the first- and second-order interaction effects in a Log-Linear Model indicate the kind of relationships among variables that are useful for testing the hypotheses of the present study.

Tests for first-degree interactions (table 99) show a strong relationship between the new supervisor's leadership behavior type and the following year's morale. A smaller relationship is found between the new supervisor's leadership behavior type and the previous year's morale. This latter finding suggests that work group morale tends to affect a supervisor's leadership behavior type. However, the magnitude of this effect is clearly less than that exerted by leadership behavior on morale. On the other hand, there is no relationship between the work groups' previous and following year morale scores. Neither is there any second-degree interaction among these three main factors.

TABLE 99. Parameter Estimates and Standardized Values According to the Saturated Model

Parameter	Effect	Standard Error	Standardized Value
Grand mean effect	2.601		
1 New supervisor's leadership behavior type			
PM	0.349	0.121	2.875*
M	−0.231	0.142	−1.624
P	−0.394	0.149	−2.647*
pm	0.275	0.125	2.205*
2 Following year morale	−0.002	0.078	−0.028
3 Previous year morale	−0.063	0.078	−0.807
1 & 2 PM	0.737	0.121	6.070*
M	0.360	0.142	2.528*
P	−0.361	0.149	−2.428*
pm	−0.736	0.125	−5.895*
1 & 3 PM	0.070	0.121	0.579
M	−0.332	0.142	−2.331*
P	0.479	0.149	3.219*
pm	−0.217	0.125	−1.740
2 & 3	0.121	0.078	1.557
1 & 2 & 3 PM	0.156	0.121	1.283
M	0.111	0.142	0.778
P	−0.079	0.149	−0.531
pm	−0.188	0.125	−1.502

*$p < .05$

The effects of the four leadership behavior types of new supervisors were also analyzed. First considered was the interaction effect between work groups' previous year morale and the new supervisor's leadership type. The results indicated that P-type leadership is associated with high morale during the previous year. M- and pm-type leadership correspond with low morale during the previous year. When morale in the prior year is high, the frequent presence of P-type supervision coincides with the t-test results. PM-type supervisors appear almost at random rather than in response to either high or low morale. Also, high morale in the following year corresponds with PM- and M-type behavior by the new leaders, while low morale corresponds with the pm and P types. Both the positive relation between the PM type and morale and the negative one between the pm type and morale are particularly strong. Of particular interest is the finding that the M type, which has a negative relation with morale in the previous year, has a positive relation with morale in the following year. Conversely, the P type, which is positively related to morale in the previous year, is negatively associated with it in the following year. These results suggest that P-type supervision tends to appear in response to high morale and to decrease the groups' morale. Conversely, M-type supervision tends to appear in low morale groups and to increase the groups' morale. PM-type supervisors appear with little relation to work groups' morale in the previous year, and strongly tend to increase morale. The pm-type supervisor appears frequently in low morale groups and tends to further decrease morale.

Discussion

In summary, subordinates' morale in the bank studied tends to affect leadership behavior, but the force of leadership behavior on subordinates' morale is much stronger. These results are consistent with the findings of studies conducted in the United States and leave open the possibility that subordinates' performance may be a stronger determinant of leadership than are their attitudes. Comparing these results with other field studies and laboratory experiments based on PM leadership theory, this finding suggests that the influence exerted on subordinates' morale by leadership behavior is higher than that exerted by subordinates' morale on leadership behavior style. Moreover, the Log-Linear Model analysis shows that PM- and M-type leadership increase work group morale while P- and pm-type leadership tend to decrease it. Therefore, when displayed with M behavior, P-oriented leadership behavior appears likely to increase work group morale.

CHAPTER 15

The Planned Change of Leadership Behavior

A program of leadership development and training has been devised on the basis of the PM leadership theory. This program is also called PM sensitivity training for reasons to be given below. However, others working in the leadership field have raised the question, can leadership really be nurtured and developed by education and training? Several studies have led some researchers to answer this question negatively. One of these is a study of leadership training conducted at Ohio State University. Fleishmann and Harris (1962) examined the effect of leadership training carried out at the International Harvester Company and found that the effect of leadership training designed to promote considerate behavior was opposite to that which was intended—it contributed to an increased emphasis on initiating structure. In other research, Fiedler (1972*a*, 1972*b*) argues that leadership training does not change a leader's Least Preferred Coworker (LPC) score and that LPC is the main determinant of leadership effectiveness. He applies this research by arguing that the right man should be placed in the right position or that situations be changed to fit a leader instead of expecting a uniformly positive effect of training.

Before discussing the approach taken in PM leadership training, the conceptual issue of whether or not leadership can be changed and developed by training, education, or any other external influences must be addressed. If leadership behavior is determined by a leader's personality, any change in leadership requires a change in personality. Although reviews of personality influences on leadership indicate that personality does play a role in leadership behavior (Stogdill 1974), personality is typically identified as only one of many behavior determinants in recent research (Peterson 1981). From this body of research, it follows that leadership involves behavior that is changeable by other means than by personality change. Research in personality and child development indicates that a person's fundamental personality is built in from childhood, particularly characteristics pertaining to inborn temperament, and that it changes relatively little under external influences. The more leadership behavior is dominated by personality factors, the less substantial the results one can expect from any training. However, recent leadership theories have downplayed the dependence of leadership on temperament and personality. Although some research concerning the influence of personality traits on leadership behavior continues (Fiedler 1967), a functional or situational approach has emerged. Thus, the determining factors in leadership behavior are not so much those of a leader's inborn characteristics but include the overall situation in which concrete behaviors are enacted.

It is difficult to change behavior which has become habitual. In a study of group decision making carried out under Lewin's guidance, however, eating habits, which are usually difficult to change, were modified using a procedure which first involved acquiring new knowledge and information. Similar changes were confirmed in Japan in studies by Misumi and Haraoka (1958, 1960). Behavior can be changed at three levels—cognitive, motivational, and behavioral. The PM-style leadership development training is characterized primarily by the introduction of shock on the cognitive level.

Cognitive Discrepancies in Leadership Ratings

Studies conducted at Ohio State University showed cognitive discrepancies between the self-descriptions of leadership by a supervisor and ratings by his subordinates when both were measured using the same questionnaire. Leadership ratings by subordinates were also found to correlate more highly with group performance and group member satisfaction and motivation than were leaders' own self-ratings. Similar results were obtained in the studies of PM leadership types in Japan as shown in table 100. This table shows the correspondence between self-ratings by the foremen of the Kurume factory of the

TABLE 100. Self-ratings and Subordinate Ratings of PM Leadership Behavior

PM Type Based on Ratings by Subordinates	Number of Leaders	P-behavior			M-behavior		
		Self-rating	Subordinate Rating	Difference	Self-rating	Subordinate Rating	Difference
PM	10	31.7	29.8	1.9*	31.4	30.2	1.2
P	10	31.3	30.3	1.0	31.6	25.8	5.8**
M	12	30.7	25.9	4.8*	31.4	29.2	2.2
pm	9	32.3	26.9	5.4**	31.7	25.9	5.8**

$*p < .05$, $**p < .01$

Bridgestone Tire Manufacturing Co., Ltd. and the ratings of their leadership by their subordinates using the same PM questionnaire. Clear differences (cognitive discrepancies) are evident in the table between self-ratings and ratings by subordinates. Ratings by subordinates indicate that these foremen can be divided into the four PM types—PM, P, M, and pm. According to the foremen's self-ratings, however, they all fall into the PM category. The differences between the ratings by subordinates and the self-ratings are the greatest for pm-type foremen. For foremen described as M-type leaders, great differences are found in P scores, while for those of the P type, great differences are found in M scores.

Similar comparisons were also made between self-ratings and follower ratings in a study of school teachers. According to ratings by pupils, 25 percent of the teachers were of the PM type, 25 percent the P type, 18 percent the M type, and 31 percent the pm type. According to self-ratings by teachers themselves, however, 66 percent were of the PM type—by far the majority—followed by the M type with 19 percent, the pm type with 10 percent, and the P type with only 5 percent. Great discrepancies were found between the ratings by pupils and teacher self-ratings. This tendency, found between supervisors and subordinates and between teachers and pupils, was also found between supervisors and subordinates in government and in other organizations.

The higher self-ratings compared to ratings by subordinates for both P and M leadership may result from conscious or subconscious self-justification or self-rationalization by a leader. When cognitive discrepancies between self-ratings and ratings by subordinates are due to unconscious self-justification, ways of making a leader aware of such unconsicous processes without causing a loss of self-esteem may be quite helpful in carrying out leadership training. The portion of PM-style leadership training which focuses on constructively exposing the unconscious aspect of cognition is referred to as PM-style sensitivity training.

''Sensitivity'' implies, for example, that in approaching pupils, a teacher predicts as accurately as possible how they will react and selects an appropriate action to cope with their anticipated reaction. The intent of such a sensitive response is to advance students' school work, increase their social consciousness, and change them in the direction of what is anticipated and desired. In other words, sensitivity in this case means the teacher's ability to exercise leadership in this overall situation.

Sensitivity can also be viewed from the perspective of social interaction as an ability or skill. When a teacher approaches a class, the teacher can seek to arouse within himself or herself the same reaction that is aroused among the pupils. The teacher can then respond to the reaction that has been aroused. The teacher's behavior is then simultaneously a reaction vis-à-vis his pupils and also vis-à-vis what has been aroused within himself. The extent to which a teacher can accurately empathize with or arouse within himself the same reaction that has been evoked among his pupils and properly respond to the reaction aroused within himself is an important aspect of sensitivity.

According to G. H. Mead (1934), the "self" involves the whole process of invoking in oneself other people's reactions to behaviors one might take before the behaviors are actualized. In accordance with Mead's theory of the self, an operational definition of the nuclear part of sensitivity was developed for PM training. It was in Bethel, Maine, that sensitivity training (ST) first started in 1947. Thereafter, ST, also known as T-group or group dynamics training, spread throughout the world. A PM-style ST has been developed in Japan which involves a different system from the original Bethel approach. What makes it different from the nonstructured Bethel approach, known also as the NTL or National Training Laboratory approach, is that a particular emphasis is placed on the P and M aspects of behavior among all kinds of interpersonal behavior which appear in group situations.

The first step in PM-style ST is for each individual to become conscious of the degree of cognitive discrepancy between ratings by subordinates and self-ratings. The second step is to try to bring self-ratings as close to ratings by subordinates as possible. The third step is to endeavor to move each person's P and M scores toward the PM type. However, in cases where subordinate descriptions are difficult to obtain, ratings by other people whose positions and roles are similar to the person being described are used. In most of the training programs described in the discussion that follows, both ratings by others and self-ratings are used.

PM-style Leadership Training and Its Evaluation

The PM-style leadership training method was first developed to train foremen at the Kurume factory of the Bridgestone Tire Manufacturing Co., Ltd. The first training program was held in April, 1967, at Bridgestone's Training Center located in the hotspring town of Amagase, an hour train ride from the Kurume factory. Amagase was picked as the site for this program because the town is relatively isolated from civilization.

The PM-style training program was divided into two courses—the preliminary and main parts—both of which were built around case studies. Incident-process cases were provided to make it easy for the participants to take part in the program as actively as possible.

Preliminary Course

The purpose of the preliminary course was to prepare the participants for the activities to be carried out in the main course and to motivate them for the main course. The preliminary course was held in a quiet room of an employees' club house adjacent to the factory for two hours each day after work for six days. Each group was made up of nine foremen selected from each section of the factory.

On the first day, an orientation session was given describing incident process analysis. Examples of case studies were shown to the trainees using a manual published for training use. From the second day on, the incident process was used based on cases which had actually occurred in the factory. Those section chiefs or officers in charge who were personally involved in the actual cases served as the leaders for the case studies. The case study began with the presentation of an incident to the participants. The leader then invited the participants to ask questions. The leader answered these questions to provide additional information and data concerning the case. While it was left up to the leader to decide how long the question and answer session should last, the leaders were encouraged to wrap it up before questions had been exhausted, and while the participants were still motivated to think about the case.

Upon the completion of the question and answer session, group discussions among the participants began. The groups discussed such things as where the problems in each case lay and how these problems should be handled. Prior to beginning the discussion session, the leader instructed the participants to make suggestions about handling problem situations based on their own beliefs about leadership and management. When the discussion session had continued for an hour or so, the session was brought to a close. Upon closing the session, each participant was asked to decide individually how the case should be handled. All participants were instructed to submit whatever decision they reached in writing, stating the reasons why they reached that decision.

For six days from Monday through Saturday, the participants dealt with one case each day. After resting on Sunday, they moved into the main course on Monday of the following week. During the entire period of the main course, everyone remained in the training center, an "island" culturally isolated from the outside world.

Main Training Program

The main training program lasted four days and three nights. A specific example of a training schedule is shown in table 101. PMT (PM training) constituted the nucleus of the training schedule consisting of seven sessions. During the orientation session on the first day, the schedule of the training program was explained and the Yatabe-Guilford Self-diagnosis Test was given.

The PM training program is made up of the following components:

TABLE 101. Training Schedule

Time of day	First day	Second day	Third day	Fourth day
7–8		exercise breakfast	exercise breakfast	exercise breakfast
8–10		group discussion (II)	group discussion (IV)	group discussion (VI)
10–12		group discussion (III)	group discussion (V)	group discussion (VII)
12–1	lunch	lunch	lunch	lunch
1–2	orientation	group guidance technique	human relations technique	lecture
2–5	group discussion (I)			final summation
5–7	supper group guidance technique	supper group guidance technique	supper human relations technique	

(1) group discussion built around case studies, (2) self-ratings and ratings by others concerning PM behavior after a discussion session, and (3) feedback on self-ratings and ratings by others.

Group Discussion of Case Studies

The cases prepared during the preliminary sessions in the preceding week were discussed again. Group discussions were conducted without any leader. Prior to beginning the discussions, the paper each participant had submitted upon completion of the preliminary course stating his decision about the case involved and the reasons for the decision was returned to him. The trainer then asked the participants to proceed with the discussion in such a way that they, as a group, came to a decision which would be agreed upon by everyone after one and a half hours of group discussion. Misumi served as the trainer and one case was used for each PMT session. Since each participant did his own decision making and provided his own rationale during the preliminary course, the groups invariably ended up having a heated debate before they could reach any consensus as a group. The resolution of initially diverging opinions is one of the most important aims of the PMT. Ego involvement is enhanced through the conflicting pressures of commitment to an initial position and identity with a group having diverging opinions. Time pressures further enhance ego involvement. Thus the chance of expressing the subconscious in behavior during the debate is increased. Observers kept a record of what group members said and how often they spoke. The trainer neither led nor participated in the discussion.

Self-Rating/Rating by Others

After the one-and-a-half-hour group discussion was over, the participants began the process of self-rating and rating others. Rating forms were distributed to all group members. The behavior of those group members who said or did something during the one-and-a-half-hour discussion session was rated according to the PM behavior rating scale prepared beforehand. First, self-ratings were completed. After describing their own behavior, participants rated each of the other group members. In groups of nine members, this process took twenty to thirty minutes. The average values of the self-ratings and ratings by others were summed up, plotted on a graph, and diagrammed.

Feedback

Immediately before the next PMT session began, the trainer reported to the group members the results of the diagram and the summation of the frequencies of statements group members made during the discussion. The data for each member was kept anonymous and identified by a code known only to the member it represented. Figure 30 shows an example of the method used to provide feedback. In the case of A, his self-rated M score is higher and his P score is lower than in the ratings given by others. If ratings by others are regarded as the best estimate of actual behavior, then M levels are overestimated and P levels are underestimated by A. In the case of B, the levels of both P and M behavior are overestimated. The discussion, rating, and feedback procedures were repeated for the first through the fourth cases. Therefore, the results of the overestimation and underestimation were fed back to the group members seven times. Thus, each member was clearly shown the differences between self-ratings and ratings by others and was able to see the relative place of his own leadership compared with that of the other eight

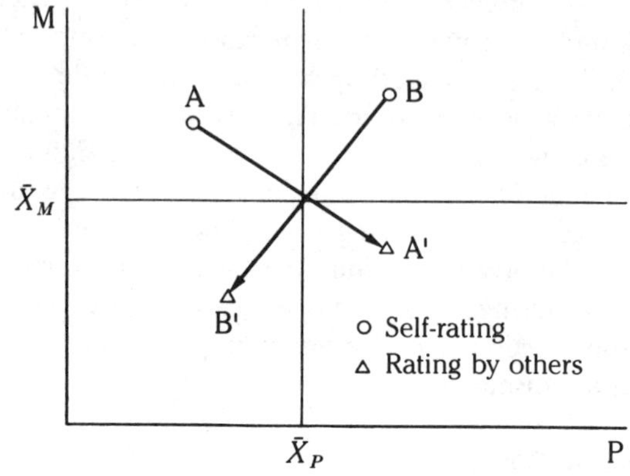

Fig. 30. An example of feedback

members. The trainer analyzed the differences between self-ratings and ratings by others and emphasized the importance of using ratings by others as a "mirror" to revise their self-ratings in a realistic way.

While the PMT sessions constituted the nucleus of the training course, lectures on human organization and human relations included in the schedule reinforced this nucleus. Also included in the schedule were lectures concerning the theory of group dynamics, group discussion, technical guidance for role playing, group decision making, and guidance in interview methods for counseling. The final summation of the program had several components. First, the details of the seven sessions of PMT were made available for the participants' information and possible later use. The results of a PM survey based on ratings by subordinates also covering general morale which was conducted during one week in the latter part of November, 1966, were distributed to each participant. The survey results included data reflecting each person's own scores and morale scores of the work group for which he was responsible as well as scores for the whole factory. The session ended with a discussion of what the participants gained from the training program, the results of which were reported by their representative. Participants were also instructed to decide what they should do when they went back to their workplace. They were urged to make a note of whatever actions they decided to take and take it back with them. In other words, they did the kind of group decision making and public commitment which Lewin had found effective in changing behavior.

Training programs following the same format were conducted nine times during the period from April, 1967, to February, 1969. Eighteen senior officers and 135 foremen in the company participated. With the exception of a few newly appointed officers and foremen, all eligible persons from the Bridgestone Kurume factory took part. While the curriculum underwent slight changes at different points along the line, the PMT formula remained the same throughout.

Evaluation of the Effects of Training Programs

While various kinds of training programs have been carried out in many organizations, comparatively few studies have been designed to determine the effectiveness of these programs. To examine the effects of the training, differences between self-ratings and ratings by others were checked at the time of the first and the last PMT session. Table 102 shows the results of this examination. The table indicates that cognitive discrepancies were smaller for both P and M behavior at the time of the last PMT than at the time of the first PMT. The cognitive discrepancies with regard to P behavior narrow down most strikingly ($p < .01$). Examining the change in cognitive discrepancies by leadership type, significant reductions were found in the M type and the pm type, both of which are weak in P-oriented behavior. The discrepancies for M behavior were reduced, but not to any significant degree.

While the above results are important in shedding light on the goal of reducing discrepancies, whether or not the effects of training are reflected in PM ratings by subordinates is even more important. A major assumption of the training program was that narrowing the cognitive discrepancies between self-ratings and ratings by others would cause a change in a leader's behavior which would be reflected in ratings by subordinates. To test this assumption, the results of the survey conducted in November, 1966, were compared with those of the PM survey carried out in November, 1967. The control group used consisted of those foremen who had not undergone the training by that time. The outcome of the comparison is shown in table 103. At the time of the first PM survey, eighteen of the people who had participated in the training program were pm-type leaders and seven were PM-type leaders. By the second survey, the number of PM-type leaders increased to ten and the number of pm-type leaders decreased to thirteen. For the nonparticipants, the number of pm-type leaders increased from five to eight, while the number of PM-type leaders decreased from thirteen to eight. These results show diametrically different tendencies between PMT participants and nonparticipants.

Due to a sharp increase in newly recruited employees and environmental changes in and around the company, the morale among the employees gener-

TABLE 102. Changes in the Discrepancy between Self-ratings and Ratings by Others

	Total (N = 63)			PM (N = 8)			P (N = 11)			M (N = 16)			pm (N = 15)		
	T$\bar{X}$I	T$\bar{X}$VI	significance	PM$\bar{X}$I	PM$\bar{X}$VI	significance	P$\bar{X}$I	P$\bar{X}$VI	significance	M$\bar{X}$I	M$\bar{X}$VI	significance	pm$\bar{X}$I	pm$\bar{X}$VI	significance
P behavior	5.4	3.8	*	5.8	4.6		5.4	4.0		5.6	3.4	*	5.7	3.9	*
M behavior	4.2	4.0		5.2	4.8		4.3	3.7		3.4	3.2		4.1	3.7	

T$\bar{X}$I indicates the average discrepancy between self-rating and rating by others in group session I, while T$\bar{X}$VI indicates that of session VI.

$\bar{X}$ is calculated by first determining the average difference between each member's self-rating and his ratings by others in his group. The overall $\bar{X}$ is calculated by averaging all members' discrepancy scores.

*$p < .01$

TABLE 103. Differences in Leadership Changes between Training Participants and Nonparticipants

	Participants				Nonparticipants			
	PM	P	M	pm	PM	P	M	pm
PM survey before training	7	11	15	18	13	5	8	5
PM survey after training	10	14	14	13	8	8	7	8
Change	3	3	−1	−5	−5	3	−1	3

ally deteriorated and the company-wide average P and M scores dropped in 1967. Although this tendency was reflected in the nonparticipants, it did not affect the participants at all. Leadership among the participants improved. This result further demonstrates the effectiveness of PMT as a means of leadership development in the company. Table 104 shows the results of a questionnaire distributed to the senior officers who were the superiors of the foremen. The answers further indicate that the participants benefited from the training.

Even though many studies of PMT have shown results similar to these, these results alone are not enough to justify any unambiguous conclusions about what specifically brought about leadership changes. These are nothing more than data to be used for reference. The most important data which have been used to evaluate this study involve a comparison between two surveys conducted in 1966 and 1967. The problem in identifying the specific effects of PMT training is the lack of data about how studies other than this study of PMT have been evaluated. The process of decreasing cognitive discrepancies between self-ratings and ratings by others is important, but to evaluate the effects of PMT alone, it would be necessary to control the effects of the decision-making sessions and other curricula included in the training course. In most action research programs, however, some uncontrollable factors are inevitably involved. In conducting action research, research controls may need to begin with a liberal control which is made increasingly systematic as the research progresses.

TABLE 104. Ratings of Training Participants by Their Superiors

Very substantial improvement	6
Considerable improvement	50
Can't judge at present	6
No change	9
Worse than before	0

The training model initiated at the Bridgestone Kurume factory was used subsequently in a series of action research projects conducted at Tokyo Denki Kagaku (TDK), Asahi Denka, and other companies. The first sensitivity development (SD) seminar was held at the Manpower Development Center located at the foot of Mt. Fuji for five days from August 22 through 26, 1970, assembling leaders from all over the country. The SD seminar is a combination of Bethel-style ST and PMT.

Action Research on PM-style Sensitivity Training—the First SD Seminar

As mentioned before, PM-style sensitivity training (hereafter referred to as ST) is based on PM leadership theory. It differs from the traditional NTL-style sensitivity training begun at Bethel, Maine, in many ways. The most important difference is that while Bethel tended to use ST in unstructured situations, SD is more structured in that it uses case studies. At the first SD seminar held under the auspices of the Institute for Group Dynamics, the following experiment was conducted using PM-style ST and NTL-style ST. Group A was given an NTL-style ST in the first half of the program and a PM-style ST in the second half. Group B was given the two kinds of training in reverse order. The purpose of this experiment was to determine which of the two training approaches would be more effective. Our hypotheses in this experiment were as follows:

1. Group A, which underwent an NTL-style ST during the first half of the program, will show smaller cognitive discrepancies between self-ratings and ratings by others concerning PM behavior during case study discussions than will Group B with no ST before the case study discussion.
2. Group A will show a greater increase in the experienced attractiveness of the meeting than will Group B.

Method and Procedure

The twenty-four male participants were rank and file employees and middle-echelon managers from various industries who had not met one another before. Four of them were in their twenties, fourteen in their thirties, and six in their forties. In forming two groups of twelve members each, matched pairs were placed in different groups taking into consideration age, position, and location of their workplace so that the composition of the two groups was similar. Each group participated in ten training sessions. For Group A, the first five sessions involved NTL-style ST and the latter five sessions involved PM-style ST. For Group B the first five sessions were based on PM-style ST and the second five sessions were based on NTL-style ST. There were two trainers, one a psychiatrist and the other a psychologist. Table 105 shows the schedules of the meetings of the two groups.

The meetings were conducted and evaluated as follows. A series of case studies were used in the PM-style ST sessions. The five cases given were entitled "Hidden Errors," "Acting Arbitrarily on His Own Authority," "Analysis of Organizational Climate," "Leadership Evaluation," and "Personnel Department in a Research and Development Organization." Each discussion lasted ninety minutes and self-ratings and ratings of others were done for each member's behavior at the end of each case discussion period. Ratings were done using a PM rating scale consisting of ten items to measure P behavior and ten items to measure M behavior. Ratings of the attractiveness of the meeting (one item) and other ratings concerning the training experience were done during a period of thirty minutes following the discussion. Self-ratings, ratings of meeting atmosphere, and ratings of meeting attractiveness were done by each of the twelve members of the group. Rating of others was done for five members picked at random beforehand from among the eleven members not including "me." That is, each member was rated by five other members of the same group. Each member was confidentially provided with the results of their self-rating, the rating by others, and the discrepancy between the two ratings immediately before the second group meeting started. Each member attended the second meeting knowing about the discrepancies.

The following items were used for the PM ratings of behavior during the case discussions (Misumi, Seki, and Shinohara 1969). Items 1 through 10 are M items and 11 through 20 are P items.

1. To what extent did you perceive a friendly attitude on the part of each group member during the last discussion period?
2. To what extent did you perceive bright and pleasant feelings from each group member during the last discussion period?
3. To what extent did you perceive cooperative feelings from each group member during the last discussion period?
4. Generally speaking, did each group member try to listen to other members?
5. Was each group member considerate of the feelings of other members?
6. Did each group member try to create a friendly atmosphere during the discussion?
7. To what extent did each group member show kindness toward other members?
8. Did each group member try to remove unpleasant feelings among other members?
9. Did each group member try to make other members feel comfortable?
10. Did each group member try to maintain unity among group members?
11. To what extent did each group member try to encourage other members to speak up?
12. To what extent did each group member try to correct other members if they had wrong opinions?
13. To what extent did each group member offer new views or solutions?
14. To what extent did each group member try to reconcile group members' opinions?

TABLE 105. Schedule of the First SD Seminar

	Morning		Afternoon		Night	
First day			opening ceremony	A1 B1	A2	free time
					B2	film
Second day	A3	theory	A4	theory	A5	theory
	B3	session	B4	session	B5	session
Third day	B1	film	B2	theory	B3	free time
	A1	free time	A2	session	A3	free time
Fourth day	B4	theory	B5	feedback	mutual rating of PM leadership (both groups)	
	A4	session	A5	session		
Fifth day	mutual rating of PM leadership (both groups)	theory session (both groups)	theory session (both groups)	overall evaluation of seminar (both groups)	ending ceremony (both groups)	

15. To what extent did each group member try to get all the members to concentrate their efforts on common goals?
16. To what extent did each group member try to obtain opinions and ideas from other members in order to solve their problems?
17. To what extent did each group member try to steer discussion back to the main theme when necessary?
18. To what extent did each group member try to get his idea across to other members?
19. To what extent did each group member try to positively develop other members' pertinent opinions?
20. To what extent did each group member try to solve a given problem through consensus of all the members?

The response to each of these questions was rated on a five-point Likert-type scale, giving 5 to the most affirmative response and 1 to the most negative. The total scores on each of the P and M dimensions could range from 10 to 50.

In the case of NTL-style ST, unlike the PM-style ST, no problem solving concerning a case is involved, so that there is no fixed subject of discussion. The group meeting began with the trainer's instruction to the effect that ''We have no particular subject to discuss in this session which sets this session apart from other regular meetings. There isn't anything that you have to discuss or that you are not supposed to discuss. So, you can talk about anything right off the top of your head. Now, let us proceed with free discussion.'' The sessions lasted ninety minutes, as in the PM-style ST. Like the PM-style ST, all members were instructed to rate meeting attractiveness and to submit comments about the session in writing. Thirty minutes was set aside for these activities.

Results and Discussion

The discrepancies between self-ratings and ratings by others with regard to PM behavior during case study discussions in the PM-style ST were smaller in Group A than in Group B. There were greater discrepancies in P behavior than in M behavior as the sessions progressed. It was also reported in the aforementioned study of PM-style ST by Misumi, Seki, and Shinohara (1969) that the discrepancies between self-ratings and ratings by others significantly decreased for P behavior from the first session to the final session. However, a study by Fujita (1975*b*) indicated that discrepancies in M behavior as well as P behavior decreased between the first session and the final session.

According to table 106, the discrepancies between the two ratings of P

TABLE 106. Mean Discrepancies between Self-ratings and Ratings by Others of Leadership Behavior

	Session					
	1	2	3	4	5	Total
Discrepancies in P behavior						
Group A	4.72	2.29	2.85	1.97	0.97	2.56
Group B	5.50	5.49	3.33	3.92	3.96	4.45
Total	5.13	3.88	3.09	2.94	2.46	3.50
Discrepancies in M behavior						
Group A	4.17	2.10	3.15	2.45	1.68	2.71
Group B	3.40	2.32	2.18	2.97	3.81	2.94
Total	3.78	2.21	2.67	2.71	2.75	2.82
Discrepancies in P and M together						
Group A	4.44	2.20	3.00	2.21	1.33	2.63
Group B	4.48	3.89	2.76	3.44	3.88	3.69
Total	4.46	3.04	2.88	2.83	2.60	3.16

behavior in Group A decreased as the sessions advanced. In Group B, however, the discrepancies decreased during the earlier sessions, but the discrepancies in both P and M behavior increased in the fourth and fifth sessions. Comparing the results obtained from Group A and B, however, the discrepancies between ratings of P and M behavior gradually decreased from the first session through the fifth session.

No significant differences were found between the discrepancies in M behavior in Group A and those in Group B. With regard to P behavior, however, the discrepancies in Group B were significantly greater than they were in Group A. This indicates that, as far as ratings of M behavior are concerned, no effects of the presence or absence of prior experience in NTL-style ST were found. Differences between the groups were found, however, in cognitive discrepancies in P behavior.

Ratings of the Attractiveness of the Meeting

Figure 31 shows average scores for the attractiveness of the NTL-style ST and PM-style ST meetings. Table 107 shows the results of an analysis of variance conducted using a three-factor mixed model. Table 108 shows the average scores of attractiveness for the two kinds of meetings.

Table 107 shows no significant differences according to whether NTL-style ST or PM-style ST is experienced first. Thus there is no difference between Group A and Group B in overall attractiveness of the meetings. Since the main effects comparing NTL-style ST and PM-style ST show significant

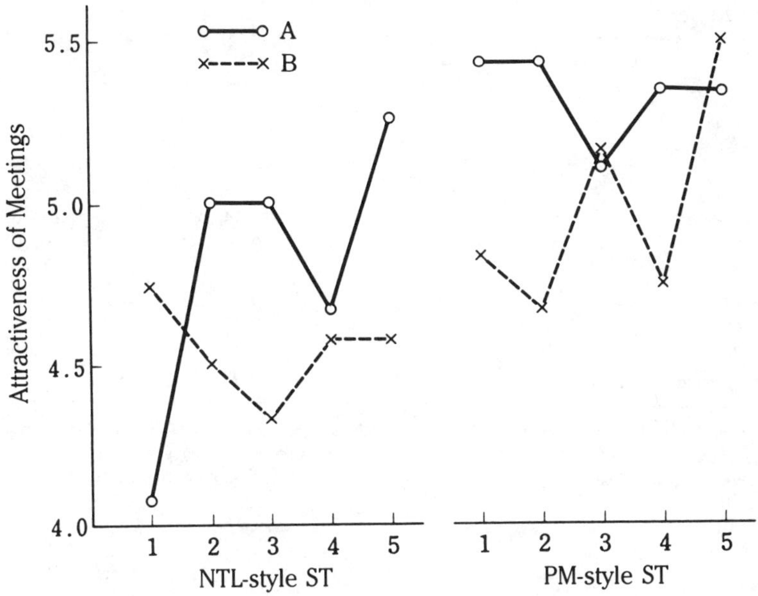

Fig. 31. Average scores on attractiveness of the meetings in NTL-style ST and PM-style ST

differences between them (F = 13.76, df = 1/198, $p < .01$), the overall attractiveness of meetings for the PM-style ST (average score 5.15) is greater than that of the NTL-style ST (average score 4.68). Figure 31 indicates that in NTL-style ST, meeting attractiveness in Group A shows an upward trend while it shows a downward trend in Group B. In PM-style ST, meeting attractiveness for Group A shows a generally high level, even though it declines slightly. Meeting attractiveness for Group B begins at a low level, but shows an upward trend.

To recapitulate, meeting attractiveness in Group A gradually increases in NTL-style ST and shows a generally high level in PM-style ST. In Group B, attractiveness did not maintain a consistent level in PM-style ST, and shows a downward trend in NTL-style ST. No difference is found between Groups A and B in overall meeting attractiveness throughout the ten sessions of group experience. From the point of view of group development, Group A, in which meeting attractiveness begins at a low level and gradually increases, may be more effective for the group members than is Group B in which meeting

TABLE 107. Analysis of Variance (Three-factor) Concerning the Attractiveness of Meetings for NTL-style ST and PM-style ST

	df	MS	F
Between subjects	23		
Group (A)	1	5.11	1.08
Error	22	4.73	
Within subjects	216		
ST versus PMT (B)	1	13.54	13.76**
A × B	1	0.10	0.10
Session C	4	1.10	1.12
A × C	4	0.68	0.69
B × C	4	0.28	0.28
A × B × C	4	2.32	2.36*
Error pooled	198	0.98	

Note: According to the result of the test of homogeneity about three error variances, it was not significant at 5 percent level ($X^2 = 5.86$, df = 2, $p < .10$) so they were pooled. A test of the homogeneity of the three error variances showed no significant differences ($X^2 = 5.86$, df = 2, $p < .10$) so they were pooled.

*$p < .10$

**$p < .01$

TABLE 108. The Mean Scores of Attractiveness of Meetings for NTL-style ST and PM-style ST

	Session					
Group	1	2	3	4	5	Total
In NTL-style ST sessions						
A	4.08	5.00	5.00	4.67	5.25	4.80
B	4.75	4.50	4.33	4.58	4.58	4.55
Total	4.42	4.75	4.67	4.63	4.92	4.68
In PM-style ST sessions						
A	5.42	5.42	5.08	5.33	5.33	5.32
B	4.83	4.67	5.17	4.75	5.50	4.98
Total	5.13	5.04	5.13	5.04	5.42	5.15
In NTL-style ST and PM-style ST together						
A	4.75	5.21	5.04	5.00	5.29	5.06
B	4.79	4.58	4.75	4.67	5.04	4.77
Total	4.77	4.90	4.90	4.83	5.17	4.91

attractiveness shows a downward trend. However, the attractiveness of a training group experience may not reflect its subsequent practical usefulness. As an old saying goes, "a good medicine tastes bitter." A positive experience in ST may not be correlated with the attractiveness of the meeting.

PM Training in Local Government Organizations

PM leadership training programs have also been conducted for section chiefs and subsection chiefs in prefectural and city government offices using the same method developed for industrial organizations. These programs have been conducted at government training centers usually over a period of three nights and four days.

Table 109 shows how many of the thirty participants come within one standard score in the difference between self-ratings and ratings by others in P and M behaviors after the case study discussions. Figures for each session are given. The standard score is set at 3, and is set according to the ratings obtained from all previous leadership training programs. Table 109 shows the number of participants whose discrepancies between self-ratings and ratings by others are less than 3 as well as the number of participants having discrepancies above 3. Table 109 shows a tendency for the differences between self-ratings and ratings by others to decrease for both P and M behavior as the sessions progress.

Table 110 shows the relationship between the four PM leadership types before and after each participant is given feedback about their self-ratings and ratings by others. For all PM types combined, 44 percent (39 of 88) participants were described as showing the same behavior pattern before and after the feedback. Fifty percent of the 26 participants who initially showed PM-

TABLE 109. Discrepancies between Self-ratings and Ratings by Others

	Session			
	1	2	3	4
M behavior				
Within the standard score	15	16	20	22
Over the standard score	15	14	10	6
P behavior				
Within the standard score	18	17	20	24
Over the standard score	12	13	10	4

Note: In the fourth session, only twenty-eight people participated in the discussion because two had been involved in other private business.

TABLE 110. Changes in PM Type Shown in Peer Ratings Based on Group Discussion Process

	After Session				
Before Session	PM	P	M	pm	Total
PM	13	1	5	7	26
P	3	4	2	2	11
M	9	0	2	6	17
pm	5	4	5	20	34
Total	30	9	14	35	88

type behavior were described similarly after the feedback. Four of the 11 people who initially showed P behavior continued to do so (36 percent). Two of the 17 people (12 percent) initially rated as showing M-type behavior continued to be rated similarly. Fifty-nine percent (20 of 34) who initially showed pm behavior continued to do so.

Fifty-six percent of the 88 participants were rated differently after the feedback than they were before. Of the 26 participants initially identified as showing PM-type behavior, 7 (27 percent) changed to pm, 5 (19 percent) changed to M, and 1 (4 percent) changed to P. Of the 17 people who initially showed M behavior, 9 (53 percent) subsequently changed to PM, and 6 (35 percent) changed to pm, but none changed to P. The percentage of initially P and pm people who changed to another leadership type was approximately equal for each other leadership type. In general, the data show no clear pattern of change to or away from any particular PM type. Inoue (1974) has been pursuing a line of research to determine if a useful way to change to PM from other types of behavior is to go through M.

At present, leadership behavior changes and training have been limited to a few specific organizational settings. A variety of experimental hypotheses concerning planned behavioral changes are currently being tested. Because the change programs designed so far have been oriented toward behavioral issues in a few specific settings, studies evaluating their effects are best considered to be studies of specific behavioral dynamics at the present time.

Promoting the Use of PM Leadership in Problem Solving

An important component of the studies of specific PM dynamics has been the initial testing of programs designed to increase the use of the PM type of leadership. When managers become aware of a deficiency in leadership, an obvious recourse is to provide leadership training. Although the behavior of formal and informal leaders is certainly affected by a broad variety of personal and organizational variables which can interact or interfere with training (Peterson 1981), leadership training certainly has the potential to contribute to organization development programs.

Leadership can also be promoted by several structural means. One method of promoting informal leadership is to develop representative participation schemes. By singling out informal leaders for participation in collaborative problem identification or decision making, an informal leader can be provided with further information, influence, and skill in promoting adequate work group problem solving. Quality of Work Life programs have used this approach to some extent (e.g., Macy and Peterson 1981). It is also used implicitly when union stewards are elected to serve a representative function.

Formal leadership is most typically promoted by appointing formal supervisors and providing them with the skills, information, and other resources they need to handle the organizational problems of their subordinates which are not dealt with by formal organizational rules or other problem-solving modes. Other kinds of formal leadership might also be employed. ''Clinical educators,'' for example, are specialists in health care systems who can be assigned to improve staff resources and promote staff integration in one or a few departments. In other organizations, staff personnel managers and corporate ombudsmen can play similar formal leadership roles. Formal leadership can also be encouraged through several of the lateral linking arrangements suggested by Galbraith (1973) for promoting interdepartmental communication.

Training to improve leadership clearly ranks among the central concerns of organizational development consultants and personnel managers (Neider 1980). Recent leadership theory has progressed considerably in identifying situational contingencies which trainers should encourage their clients to consider when trying to learn how to provide appropriate leadership (Hersey and Blanchard 1969; Vroom and Yetton 1973). Managers who want to improve their leadership need also to be aware of the context in which they are providing leadership. Leadership is not provided in a vacuum in which no other methods of organizational control are available.

PART VI

Conclusion

CHAPTER 16

The Science of Leadership Behavior

The present book develops a Performance-Maintenance (PM) theory of leadership designed to describe and explain leadership behavior according to two basic group functions. The performance or P function involves leadership directed toward promoting goal achievement while the maintenance or M function involves leadership directed toward maintaining social stability. The PM leadership theory was developed because prior, traditional distinctions between such leadership types as democratic/autocratic, authoritarian/liberal, dovish/hawkish, and conservative/progressive were found to be conceptually equivocal and difficult to operationally define. They are value-laden and not objective concepts because they are colored—often intentionally—by social desirability. Any attempt to use these types scientifically is difficult because of the need to base research on scientifically oriented "functional" concepts rather than descriptive concepts which refer to specific historical events or conditions. Traditional leadership typologies also make multidimensional analysis difficult because they typically emphasize a single dimension. For these reasons, traditionally accepted leadership types fail to meet the requirements of scientific concepts. Thus a new typology was developed in Japan while other scientific approaches to leadership were being developed in the United States.

Without dismissing traditional leadership concepts as wholly meaningless or inadequate for daily use, it is important to transform them into concepts that fulfill the requirements of scientific inquiry. In order to accomplish this conceptual transformation, an empirical program of research into leadership behavior has been pursued. This research program has relied equally on experimental laboratory methods and field methods to develop and test functional concepts which can be operationally defined.

The Behavioral Science of Leadership

Only since the beginning of the present century have laboratory studies of leadership behavior been conducted anywhere in the world. The most classic early study of leadership was conducted by Lippitt and White (1943) in the United States. Toki (1935) also undertook an important leadership study in Japan several years before the study by Lippitt and White. Many correlational studies concerning leaders' individual traits were also conducted during the first half of the century (Stogdill 1948). Both Gibb (1969) and Stogdill (1974; Bass 1981) point out that the results of studies based on the traits approach show only limited consistency. Gibb concludes with the now prevailing opinion that the requirements for leadership vary according to both characteristics of leaders and their surroundings. A laboratory study by Misumi and Seki (1971) also demonstrated that the effects of leadership can be affected by the context of leadership.

Bales and the University of Michigan group were the first to deductively use the concept of group performance and maintenance functions to describe leadership behavior patterns. By contrast, the Ohio State group inductively identified similar group functions by using factor analysis to identify patterns of leadership behavior. These studies form a background which is helpful for understanding the PM theory of leadership.

Barnard (1938), in his book *The Functions of the Executive,* cited promoting effectiveness and efficiency as two fundamental managerial functions. These concepts are also related to leadership functions, although they were not proposed for the particular purpose of operationally describing leadership behavior. Bales (1953, 1955) conducted a number of studies in which the basic concepts of group functions were employed for measuring leadership behavior and studying its consequences. Bales studied two behavioral types, task leader and emotional leader, in his empirical study of group discussion processes. From the perspective of the PM leadership theory, task leadership appears to correspond to P leadership and emotional leadership appears to correspond to M leadership. However, Bales's analysis conceptually emphasized only the P type and M type used in PM leadership theory while the PM type and pm type tended to be omitted. Because these two latter types are deemphasized, it is somewhat unclear whether the task leader in Bales's scheme actually corresponds to the P or PM type and whether the emotional leader actually corresponds to the M or PM type. In studies designed to test the PM theory of leadership it has been found useful to manipulate or measure the intensity of P or p separately from M or m. By treating these functions in different combinations, the interactive effect of a combined emphasis on P and M behavior is suggested.

Bales also suggested that different leadership functions could be fulfilled by different group members. Especially in an unstructured group situation, leadership is not limited to the role behavior of a particular person holding a specific position, but may move from one group member to another. One member may assume task-oriented leadership, while another exercises group maintenance–oriented leadership. Thus, the two leadership functions can be shared among a number of persons. However, as a group becomes hierarchically structured, leadership becomes concentrated in a specific leadership position in the hierarchy, thus becoming "fixed." "Leadership" in a hierarchical organization usually refers to the role behavior of managers and supervisors at various levels of a hierarchy. Group members, at least in Japan, typically expect task-oriented leadership and group maintenance–oriented leadership to be exercised by every leader in formal organizations.

Empirical tests of the leadership theories of Bales (1955) and Hachiya (1967) indicated that in an unstructured group situation, one type of leadership often tends to dominate the other to so great an extent that the two sometimes seem mutually exclusive. Under some circumstances, however, the two types of leadership can be compatible and even complementary in the long run. In early studies of P and M leadership, before the PM leadership theory was first proposed (Sato 1960), P and M were treated as mutually exclusive leadership types. In one early study, a first-line supervisor and a second-line supervisor were experimentally simulated in a task situation. Four sets of leadership conditions were arranged in which different combinations of P and M leadership were provided by the two leaders. The four leadership situations were the P-P combination (first-level P leader and second-level P leader), P-M combination, M-P combination, and M-M combination. The experimental hypothesis tested was that the P-M and M-P combinations would produce more complementary effects than would P-P or M-M, and that the group's end results would be better under P-M or M-P than under P-P or M-M. However, these hypotheses were not supported. Three experiments were conducted in which the tasks were changed and the leaders' training was increased, but the results were not what had been anticipated. From these experiments, it was determined that when the P and M leadership functions are fulfilled by different persons, the constructive effects of the PM type of leadership studied in the PM leadership theory do not tend to occur. To sum up, one of the most important differences between the studies by Bales and the PM leadership theory lies in the fact that the former are based on a dichotomous (either P or M) conception of leadership, while the PM leadership theory does not dichotomize P and M.

Another relevant series of studies concerning leadership in hierarchical organizations has been carried out by the University of Michigan group. At the Institute for Social Research (ISR) of the University of Michigan, empirical studies concerning the types of supervisory behavior in industrial organizations were conducted by R. Likert, D. Katz, S. Seashore, R. Kahn, F. Mann, and D. G. Bowers based on a conceptualization of group functions. The PM leadership theory was influenced more by the Michigan studies than by any other single research program. In fact, the PM concept has been taken from the theory of group functions proposed by Cartwright and Zander (1968) in *Group Dynamics*. However, the perspective on group functions taken in the PM theory is not identical to the perspective taken in many of the Michigan studies. For example, the correspondence between the four leadership functions proposed by Bowers and Seashore (1966) and those proposed in the PM theory is uncertain. Two of the Bowers and Seashore dimensions—"support" and "interaction facilitation"—may correspond to M behavior, while the other two—"goal emphasis" and "work facilitation"—may correspond to P behavior. However, even if these four dimensions actually correspond to the leadership behavior provided by group members and even if these dimensions are quantified, the classification of leadership types based on these four dimensions is not complete. Because particular combinations of high and low levels of each dimension are not identified or discussed by Bowers and Seashore, the interactive hypothesis proposed in the PM leadership theory has not been tested by four-factor researchers.

Another prominent and appropriately influential set of studies has been undertaken following a group at Ohio State. As is well known, A. W. Halpin and B. J. Winer (1957) identified two main leadership factors by applying factor analysis to a large number of questionnaire items. The two major factors were labeled "consideration" and "initiating structure." The former may well correspond to an M behavior emphasis and the latter to a P behavior emphasis. Subsequently, numerous studies of these two factors have been conducted. Among the most important theories integrating much of this work is the path-goal theory proposed by R. J. House (1971). House followed in the footsteps of M. G. Evans (1970), who applied the expectancy theory of work motivation (Georgopoulos, Mahoney, and Jones 1957; Vroom 1964) to the study of leadership. The path-goal theory is designed to explain varying results of field surveys by suggesting that the effects of leadership depend on situational variables, particularly task structure. The idea that the effects of leadership are contingent on task structure, even though important, is not the most significant contribution of path-goal theory (these effects had been demonstrated previously in experimental studies by Misumi and his colleagues). More significantly, the path-goal theory introduced a conceptual link between leadership and the expectancy theory of motivation that gives a psychological meaning to task structure. However, path-goal theory has faced the obstacle of inconsistent results concerning the leadership behavior of initiating structure. Furukawa (1975) suggests that this may be due to the inconsistencies involved in the methods of measuring both leadership behavior and task structure.

Avenues for continuing work based on the path-goal theory may be seen by approaching it from the perspective of the PM theory. The leadership conditions studied in path-goal theory are based on the two main factors of the

Ohio State studies. However, these factors are studied in such a way that the four PM types cannot be clearly identified. In addition, like all studies based on survey measures developed on the basis of similarities in respondents' answers, the leadership measures used are limited for testing theory-based hypotheses and conceptual models. This limitation occurs because naming factors obtained by factor analysis is done by inductively classifying and consolidating "data" that respondents subjectively collect in the course of day-to-day living. This data is necessarily influenced by the particularities of everyday language. Factors are named on a factor-by-factor basis individually, independently, and directly on a day-to-day commonsense level. Fundamentally, relations among factors are conceptually arbitrary and are consequently difficult to interpret. There is often no systematic theoretical consistency among groups of factors.

In our studies of the PM theory, scales were developed to measure leadership behavior using multivariate analysis or factor analysis procedures similar to the procedures used in the Ohio State studies. However, the PM concept was developed in advance for theoretical reasons and was subsequently applied to interpret groups of factors. The measures have been developed to test the theory in field settings; the field measures do not dominate the theory. The question may be raised of how such a process is carried out.

The PM concept has been formed around a conceptualization of basic group functions. The PM leadership theory suggests that leadership behaviors performed by specific group members having leadership roles are particularly important to fulfilling these functions. Because a leader's behavior is directed toward fulfilling group functions, any concrete action by a leader can be assumed to involve some degree of emphasis on both performance and group maintenance. Based on this assumption, the PM leadership concept has been developed deductively from the definition of leadership. This deductive approach to the basic PM concept differs from the inductive approach implicit in research beginning from factor analytically derived survey measures. Each questionnaire item used in survey research identifies concrete examples of behavior reflecting varying degrees of P and M emphasis. However, no questionnaire item can precisely and exclusively reflect the abstract meaning of P or M behavior. When statistical rather than conceptual conventions govern the factors extracted and labeled in factor analysis, the resulting concepts are necessarily difficult to link to a theoretical system. However, in the PM leadership theory, factors identified in field surveys are interpreted on the basis of the generality, universality, and systematic logical consistency of the PM concept. The PM concept is a construct that links together statistically derived phenomenological islands lying in conceptual isolation from one another and gives them a specific theoretical order.

The Behavioral Morphology of PM Leadership

Table 111 shows the dimensions identified by developing items with particular applicability to specific field settings and applying factor analysis to the resulting data. Some factors found in different field settings can be interpreted as almost identical while other factors clearly differ depending on special characteristics of each setting. However, all of the factors identified can be conceptually classified as primarily reflecting some form of either P behavior or M behavior.

The results of studies designed to assess the validity of the four PM types are shown in table 112. This table shows the ranking of the four PM types in the order of their association with several criterion variables. Presented in this table are only the results of analyses in business or industrial organizations. Both objective criterion variables and cognitive criterion variables were selected to serve as value-based standards for judging the validity of the four PM types.

TABLE 111. Factor Obtained as a Result of Factor Analysis on Leadership Behavior Items

Kind of Organization or Group	Factors Pertaining to P Behavior	Factors Pertaining to M Behavior	References
Private enterprises (first-line supervisors)	*Planning *Pressure	*Group Maintenance	Chapter 7
Local government offices (subsection chiefs)	*Execution Plans *Discipline Guidance *Observance	*Group Maintenance	Chapter 5
Local government offices (section chiefs)	*Planning and Coordination *Discipline Guidance and Execution Plans *Observance	*Group Maintenance	Chapter 5
Classroom (teachers of fifth or sixth grade students)	*Discipline and Training Concerning Life and Learning *Discipline and Training Concerning the Sense of Community and Morality	*Consideration of Pupils *Friendliness toward Pupils *Easing Tension in the Class	Chapter 7
Family (parents of sixth grade students)	*Performance	*Maintenance	Chapter 8
Sports groups (college students' sports clubs)	*Control *Rigidity of Training	*Consideration *Club Maintenance	Chapter 9

TABLE 112. Rank Order of Effectiveness among Four PM Types

	Leadership Type			
	PM	M	P	pm
Objective criterion variables				
Field studies of achievement (long term)	1	2	3	4
Laboratory studies of achievement (short-term)				
Subjects having low task motivation	2	4	1	3
Subjects having high task motivation	1	3	2	4
Accident rate	1	2	3	4
Turnover	1	2	3	4
Cognitive criterion variables				
Willingness to work	1	2	3	4
Satisfaction with salary	1	2	3	4
Satisfaction with company	1	2	3	4
Teamwork	1	2	3	4
Meeting quality	1	2	3	4
Communication adequacy	1	2	3	4
Mental health	1	2	3	4
Performance norm	1	3	2	4

Productivity, accident rate, and turnover rate were selected to serve as objective criterion variables in several studies. Since these variables have been selected to judge what effects the four PM types produce, it is necessary to control extraneous variables to equalize all conditions other than leadership conditions. It is not always easy to extract objective achievement indices for use in judging the effects of leadership conditions. Evaluations of achievement by the leader's superior or other human evaluators is subjective. In order to avoid such subjectivity, objective achievement indices were obtained from several industrial organizations, among them a coal mine. Objective achievement indices were also obtained in laboratory studies. In the case of the bus driver accident rate criterion, the measure used only includes those accidents which were blamed on the drivers involved. Turnover rate was used as a criterion in a study conducted at the Yokohama factory of the Bridgestone Tire Manufacturing Company in 1960 when the Japanese economy was growing rapidly. In this study, statistically significant differences in employee turnover rate were found among leaders exhibiting the four PM types.

The results for objective criterion variables which involve achievement differ somewhat between laboratory and field studies. In the field surveys, PM-type leadership is typically associated with the highest achievement levels followed by M, P, and pm leadership. In laboratory studies, however, PM ranks first for those subjects whose need for achievement is high, followed by

P, M, and finally pm. A different pattern is found for those subjects whose need for achievement is low. In laboratory studies of such people, P leadership is associated with the highest achievement levels followed by PM, pm, and M. The difference between the results of the field studies and those of the laboratory studies probably reflects the difference between long-term and short-term effects of leadership. The causal explanation for the difference between laboratory and field results will be discussed in the section concerning behavioral dynamics.

The field results concerning accident rates show differences between the short-term and long-term effects of P and M leadership. In the short term just after an accident occurs, P is superior to M in reducing subsequent accident rates. In the long term, however, M leadership proved to produce lower accident rates than P leadership.

The cognitive criterion variables studied were the willingness of followers (subordinates) to work, their satisfaction with salary, sense of belonging to the company, teamwork, meeting quality, communication adequacy, mental health, and performance norms. The results indicate that the PM type ordinarily ranks first, followed by M, P, and pm for all but the measures of performance norms. For performance norms, PM comes first, followed by P, M, and pm.

It is even more difficult to obtain objective criterion variables for studying leadership in government offices, schools, and family groups than it is in industry. If similar tendencies can be found in these settings using cognitive criterion variables similar to those found in laboratory and industrial organization studies, then limited confirmation can be inferred for the generalizability of the PM leadership theory. One reason that interdisciplinary studies are instrumental for advancing research is that even when practical limitations are encountered in the research methods used to introduce a concept into one area, the concept's validity can still be inferred if stronger research methods have clearly demonstrated its validity in another field. In this way, progress can be made despite initial obstacles. A similar logic has traditionally been followed in using laboratory research in artificial settings to establish causal relationships and determining generalizability to field settings using methods that are less than optimal for causal inferences.

Cognitive criterion variables as well as objective criteria were used in examining the validity of the four PM types. Because leadership was also rated by the same subordinates who provide criterion measures, the design of many field studies raises the possibility that subordinates' attitudes may bias their rating of their superior's leadership behavior. Thus, their satisfaction with various workplace conditions may affect their leadership ratings. The argument that pervasive response biases account for the relationships found using cognitive criteria is inconsistent with the experimental manipulation checks used in several laboratory studies. The four PM types were first proposed as experimental conditions and thus, as independent variables. However, using behavioral stimuli as experimental conditions does not involve simple physical manipulations like the manipulations used in experiments on perception. Instead, they involve behavior simulation. In order to check the adequacy of the manipulations, observers were used to determine whether or not the experimental conditions were set as intended.

In studies such as the first experimental study at the Kyushu Postal Administration Research Center (Misumi and Shirakashi 1966), the study of the contingent effects of the four PM types depending on the subjects' need for achievement (Misumi and Seki 1968), and the study in which the effects of experimenters' leadership on learning recall was analyzed (Misumi and Sato 1968), the four PM types were shown to be successfully induced as experimental conditions on the basis of both observers' reports and subjects' perceptions. Subjects' perceptions of leadership and the objective conditions (the observers' results) were nearly identical. These findings imply that achievement indices and subjects' satisfaction with their task situation legitimately can be used as experimental dependent variable measures. Even if the halo effect of the subjects' satisfaction affected their experiences of the experimental conditions, there have been no instances in which it disturbed the results of any experiments. The findings which show a convergence between experimental leadership conditions, observers' reports, and subjects' reports have implications for the validity of field studies of the PM leadership types.

Michigan's Institute for Social Research group conducted a number of studies during the 1950s and 1960s concerning the correlations between satisfaction with work (morale) and productivity. Kahn (1960) concluded after reviewing many studies that, with the exception of pride in a small group, there is no correlation between achievement and attitudinal variables such as satisfaction with job, wages, promotions, or sense of belonging to the company. Misumi and Sato (1966) also conducted a survey similar to those done by Katz and Kahn in conjunction with the PM leadership surveys. The study provided little support for the proposition that attitudes about work situations and achievement are highly correlated.

Thus there does not seem to be excessive confounding between the attitudinal and behavioral outcomes studied in relation to the PM leadership types either. The relationships between PM leadership types and both objective and cognitive criterion variables show a clear rank order of PM types. However, since the correlation between work attitudes and objective achievement is generally not high, the differences in the effects of the four PM types can hardly be interpreted as being the halo effect of subordinates' satisfaction with their work conditions.

The Behavioral Dynamics of Leadership

The task of determining the behavioral dynamics of PM leadership requires that questions such as the following be answered. What causal laws make the PM type of leadership more effective than any of the other three types? Why is it that pm is consistently found to be the least effective of the four styles in field studies? How can one explain the fact that P and M are found to be intermediate between PM and pm in effectiveness in field studies? Why does the relative effectiveness of the four PM types in laboratory studies vary according to the subjects' need for achievement, and why does the rank order in laboratory studies differ from the rank order found in field studies? To what causal law can these differences be attributed?

Although the work attitudes measured in the Japanese PM studies do not appear to intervene between leadership and performance, one study indicates that attitudes are causally dependent on leadership, at least when a new supervisor is appointed in a department. Misumi and Mannari's (1984) longitudinal study indicates that the perceived leadership type of a new supervisor predicts morale one year later better than morale predicts the new supervisor's subsequent leadership. In particular, high morale tends especially to follow PM-type leadership and secondarily M-type leadership, while low morale follows P- and pm-type leadership. To a smaller degree, high morale tends to precede increased P- and pm-type leadership and reduced M-type leadership.

The Effectiveness of the P Leadership Type

The conclusions of behavioral dynamics research can be reviewed by considering first the effectiveness of the P leadership type. In one study, a simple and insignificant perceptual-motor job was given to the subjects. In the early stages of the experimental sessions, the largest amount of work was achieved under the P type of leadership. In another experimental study where teams of three subjects were given the job of counting the number of holes in a computer punch card, the largest amount of work was achieved under PM leadership, followed by P leadership. Even in this case, however, if the subjects' need for achievement was controlled, the largest amount of work was achieved under the P type of leadership in the early stages of the experiment for those groups of subjects with a low need for achievement. Even when a monotonous, insignificant job is given to subjects who have a low need for achievement, the P leadership condition was the most effective. This result may be attributable to the factor of pressure being part of P leadership. The presence of P leadership may serve as an external pressure which forces the subjects to perform the task they are given. Compared with the other three types of leadership the pressure produced by P leadership is the most intense. The presence of considerable pressure was confirmed by Misumi and Shirakashi (1964) and Misumi and Sato (1968). These researchers reported that observers found P behavior to occur more often in the experimental P leadership condition than in the PM condition. External pressure may, however, arouse psychological resistance among the subjects. If this psychological resistance grows to the point where it matches the external pressure, it will negate the effect of pressure from the leader. As long as nothing weakens the psychological resistance to external pressure, only the effect of the pressure of P leadership will be reflected, however temporarily, in performance during the early stages of the work process.

Other factors have been found in field studies of P leadership behavior besides pressure. The interpretation of these factors will be discussed later. Generally speaking, the early stage of the P type of leadership mainly involves the factor of pressure.

The Effectiveness of the M Leadership Type

The main component of the M leadership type appears to be similar to the Ohio State factor of consideration. M behavior does not provide subordinates with direction toward task accomplishment, nor does it put pressure on the subjects. Rather, it plays a role in making it more comfortable for subordinates to move in the direction they are already headed.

The results of experiments by Misumi and Seki (1968) indicated that the performance of a group of subjects with a high need for achievement under M leadership ranked third after the PM and P leadership types in the early stages of the experiment, but later exceeded the P type to eventually rank second after PM leadership. However, this effect occurred for a group of subjects who spontaneously had a high need for achievement. For subjects with a low need for achievement, M-type leadership showed the lowest performance toward the end of the experiment. This indicates that maintenance-oriented behavior when not accompanied by performance-oriented leadership does not have any direct effect in accelerating task performance and goal achievement. In a group of subjects with a low need for achievement, the effectiveness of the pm type of leadership exceeded that of the M type.

The M type of leadership also produced the lowest performance in a perceptual-motor learning task in which subjects were given the difficult task of copying inverted Japanese alphabet characters. In this case, the effectiveness of pm leadership exceeded that of M-type leadership. How can the finding be explained that pm leadership exceeds M leadership in its effect on performance under some laboratory conditions?

The Effectiveness of the pm Leadership Type

The mind-set that subjects bring to laboratory situations is relevant to the comparative effects of pm and M leadership. Subjects usually accept the fact that they will be required to perform some task even when they know only vaguely what the task will be. However, compared with subjects in field studies, the subjects in laboratory studies were clearly not highly motivated because of the insignificance, monotony, nonselectivity, and vagueness of the tasks used in the experiments. Thus, the subjects in these experimental situations are likely to have some degree of "expectancy anxiety"—anxiety associated with the anticipation of instructions from the experimenter. Those leaders (experimenters) who neither give any instructions to their subjects nor say anything to assuage their expectancy anxiety may well increase, not decrease, the subjects' tension and misgivings. Furthermore, experimental situations have an inherent task-oriented norm. Therefore, the pm leadership condition may have the effect of giving subjects an air of "silent coercion." Thus, a "quasi-P" type of pressure factor may be produced, although it is probably not as strong as that of P leadership itself.

The quasi-P pressure may explain the fact that pm leadership has a more positive effect on performance than M-type leadership in some laboratory situations. A similar kind of quasi-P pressure could hypothetically be present in field settings, especially in work organizations. Kerr and Jermier (1978) argue that organizational and task characteristics can "substitute" for leadership. In the field studies conducted thus far, however, the pm type invariably shows the lowest effectiveness in terms of both objective criteria and cognitive criteria. Subjects' motivation in field situations is generally higher than that in laboratory situations. Consequently, field subjects tend to respond to leadership in a way similar to more motivated laboratory subjects. For those field subjects who have a relatively high motivation level, pm leadership may show effects different from the effects found in laboratory situations. This point implies that the PM leadership theory must take into account the total leadership situation including both individuals and their environment because the effects of leadership have the potential to be contingent on characteristics of a given situation.

The Effectiveness of the PM Leadership Type

It was found in many laboratory studies that the PM-type leader exhibits P behavior less frequently than does the P-type leader during the process of experiments. M behavior, too, is shown less frequently in the PM than in the M condition, and thus M scores are lower (Fujita 1975*a;* Misumi and Seki 1971; Sato 1968). However, the effects of PM-type leadership are more positive than those of either the P type or the M type. Therefore, laboratory studies and field surveys were conducted to test the hypothesis that the effects of PM-type leadership are not just the sum of the effect of the P and M components, but include the interactive effect of their combination. With regard to the effect of P and of P $\times$ M, as explained in the previous discussion of the effect of P-type leadership, the effect of P in promoting performance during the early stages of an experiment is due to the presence of pressure. However, M behavior can eventually assuage and dispel the psychological resistance aroused among followers by leader pressure.

As long as the psychological resistance that pressure from a leader produces among followers continues, the followers' motivation keeps decreasing. But once resistance is assuaged by M behavior, followers' motivation eventually stops decreasing, and may even increase, depending on the level of motivation in the absence of leader pressure. If the followers' motivation not only stops decreasing but also increases because of the interaction of P and M behavior, then the pressure component of P behavior undergoes a qualitative change and is no longer experienced as "pressure" in the literal sense of the term.

The label "pressure" can only be applied to a component of P behavior in situations where it arouses psychological resistance and tension among the followers and, typically, decreases their motivation as a result. If the followers' motivation increases and goal achievement and problem solving are accelerated, the factor of pressure is no longer the motivating factor in P behavior. Instead, P behavior takes on the quality of, say, the factor of "planning" or the factor of "expertise" which have been found in addition to the factor of pressure in field settings. Even P leadership involving planning and expertise is immediately transformed into pressure-oriented P behavior if planning and expertise are forcefully displayed without any consideration for the followers. One implication is that it is likely that other aspects of P behavior besides the factor of pressure are included in the initiating structure concept proposed by the Ohio State studies. These other factors probably reflect a certain amount of consideration as well as direction to followers. Needless to say, the consideration component is conceptually similar to the concept of M behavior. Even when P behavior contains the factor of pressure, some degree of maintenance behavior, however small, coexists with it. When P behavior contains the factors of planning and expertise, sufficient M behavior must also be present to minimize the presence of pressure.

Because P behavior does not contain the factor of pressure when it coexists with M behavior, M behavior may be said to have a catalytic or complementary effect on P behavior. Studies of the relationship between the PM types and social power support the above interpretation.

An analysis of available material indicates that coercive power and reward power are reflected much more strongly in P-type leadership than in the other leadership types. By contrast, in PM-type leadership expert power is much more evident than in the other leadership types. In M-type leadership, referent power is stronger than in the other types, while in pm-type leadership, legitimate power is much stronger than in the other types. The use of expert power in PM-type leadership is far greater than the average amount of expert power typically used in P-type and M-type leadership. Reward, coercive, legitimate, and referent power are qualitatively different from one another. Therefore, the effect of the PM leadership type cannot be considered the result of a sum of several power bases, but is instead a result of the interaction between the effect of single P and the effect of single M. Thus, its effect differs qualitatively from the effect of either single P or single M.

Fujita's study (1975*a*) concerning the effects of experimenter behavior on the Einstellung (fixed mind-set) of learners in productive thinking and creative problem-solving tasks further supported the hypothesis of an interactive effect of combining P and M leadership. As is well known in the field of learning psychology, a fixed habitual set stands in the way of creative thinking. Fujita studied the effects that an experimenter's approach to instructing subjects had on the subjects' Einstellung in problem solving. He adopted the perspective that the interpersonal relationship between experimenters and subjects in a laboratory study is basically a relationship between a leader and followers. Under which of the four PM leadership types is such a fixed habitual set or overdependency on a habitual solution present to the smallest extent? The results indicated that a fixed set involving a habituated but inefficient solution is readily aroused under P-type leadership. For those subjects who do not have a high degree of manifest anxiety, a fixed habitual set was more evident under P-type and M-type leadership than under PM-type. This suggests that the effect of PM leadership is not the summation of the effects of the P and M types, but an interactive combination of the emphasis on both performance and maintenance functions. For anxious subjects in a laboratory situation, the habitual set decreases through the provision of M behavior.

The Einstellung experiments support the proposition that PM-type leadership is an appropriate leadership strategy for minimizing fixed habitual sets. In this form of leadership, performance-oriented behavior externally arouses motivation in those followers who do not have strong situational anxiety. Maintenance-oriented behavior optimally reduces any tension due to either P-oriented behavior or tension from other internal or situational sources.

The conclusions of the Einstellung studies are supported by the results of a study concerning escape from an emergency situation. When subjects believed that failure to escape from a maze would result in a substantial shock, fixated escape behavior occurred less under PM-type leadership than under M-type or, especially, P-type leadership. The study also indicates that the perception of pressure-oriented P behavior depends on whether or not it is accompanied by M behavior. When combined with M-oriented behavior, pressure-oriented P is described as planning P. Only when not combined with M leadership is it experienced as pressure P.

Followers' Need for Achievement and the Effects of the Four PM Types

Assume that there is a group of followers who have a high need for achievement and are thus already motivated toward achieving a specific goal. Which of the four PM types is likely to be the most effective for this kind of follower? First of all, since the followers have a high need for achievement and are already motivated toward achieving a specific goal, P behavior is not necessary. Some people might think that M behavior alone would suffice. However, it is possible to predict that not only P behavior but even M behavior would be unnecessary, and thus that pm behavior would suffice.

Based on the results of field surveys, neither M nor pm leadership is optimal. Even when followers are highly motivated, PM-type leadership proved the most effective. How can this finding be explained? A reasonable interpretation is that the high motivation and aspiration level of the followers (subjects) means that they are not satisifed with their own individual achievement potential. They are motivated to achieve more than they are currently able to achieve.

Those people who have a high aspiration level and high need for achievement may tend to seek leadership which will help them exceed their personal limitations. If they seek leadership which will help them reach higher levels of achievement, it should be performance-oriented P leadership. However, since these followers have a strong internal motivation, they may show a psychological resistance against external sources of pressure (House and Mitchell 1974). Therefore, a kind of P-type leadership which contains not only the factor of pressure but also the factors of expertise and planning may be best suited for followers who have a high level of internal motivation. However, even this kind of P leadership may arouse some psychological resistance among followers. Consequently, M-type leadership which serves to assuage and reduce psychological resistance becomes important to optimally guide people with a high need for achievement. Thus, the most appropriate leadership type for those followers whose internal motivation is high is neither pm nor M, but PM leadership.

Relationship of the PM Theory to the "Managerial Grid" Theory

Blake and Mouton's (1964) ''Managerial Grid'' theory is based on the assumption that there is a certain consistent pattern in managerial behavior. The concrete details of an individual's behavior change endlessly according to situations faced. However, since a general pattern can be found in a leader's behavior that changes only in its details in response to situations, managerial behavior can be predicted.

Blake and Mouton have used ''concern for production'' as a horizontal axis and ''concern for people'' as a vertical axis in their grid and divided each axis into nine parts, thus creating eighty-one managerial types. They proposed five basic managerial types—1-1, 9-9, 1-9, 9-1, and 5-5. These styles superficially resemble the PM styles. Blake and Mouton stated that they created such grid styles based on the results of studies in the behavioral sciences which were being conducted at the time their theory was formed. However, they report little subsequent research designed specifically to test their own hypotheses apart from the opinions of managers (Blake and Mouton 1982).

The scales used to measure the leadership types of the grid theory are based on self-descriptions of leadership. In PM theory, however, PM scores in field settings are obtained from ratings by subordintes because the validity of the PM scores obtained based on self-ratings was found to be extremely low. The difference between the grid theory and the PM theory in the method of measurement has important implications. First, leaders' self-description on Blake and Mouton's grid style is likely to bear little or no relationship to their leadership as conceptualized and measured according to PM theory. Second, a PM-type leader, for example, may only be moderately above average on the P and M dimensions, not necessarily at the extreme conceptually reflected by Blake and Mouton's 9-9 concept. As a matter of fact, it is nearly impossible to use ratings by subordinates to identify leaders who could be classified as 9-9, 1-9, 9-1, or 1-1 leaders because these extremes are rarely found. Consequently, these grid types do not correspond to measurement scores but are hypothetical rather than operational. The measurement differences mean that grid theory and PM theory deal with completely different leadership phenomena even though both are rooted in similar social science concepts.

In general, the Blake and Mouton model, being primarily a guide for organizational interventions, has not been tested empirically to the extent the PM model has been studied. This empirical limitation as well as the other limitations hinder their response to the charge that high ''concern for people'' and high ''concern for production'' reflect mistaken belief in a ''myth'' (Larson, Hunt, and Osborn 1976). By contrast, tests of the PM theory provide considerable support for the contention that leader behavior reflecting an emphasis on both the performance and maintenance functions has generally constructive consequences over a broad range of social settings in Japan.

Relationship of the PM Theory to Fiedler's Contingency Theory

The leadership theory based on Fiedler's Least Preferred Coworker (LPC) measure bears some resemblance to trait approaches to leadership (Fiedler 1967). However, unlike earlier trait theorists, Fiedler does not take the position that LPC scores, as an index of leaders' personality traits, produce the same behavior in all situations. He proposed a "Contingency Model" that systematically identifies behaviors which should correspond to certain combinations of a leader's LPC score and situational factors. Fiedler also makes conceptual links between the contingency model and the dimensions of leadership identified in the Ohio State studies. Fiedler initially proposed that low LPC levels correspond to the task-oriented leadership style and high LPC levels to the relationship-oriented leadership style. However, because of considerable uncertainty and ambiguity in the meaning of the LPC measure itself, little consistency has been found in the results of studies reporting the relationship of LPC scores and behavior according to specific situational variables (Peterson 1981; Rice 1978). The LPC theory is also of limited value in guiding field research because the method of measuring situational variables including leader-member relations, task structure, and position power is unclear in field settings and there is little clear correspondence between laboratory and field measures of these variables. But the most fundamental problem with the LPC theory is the vagueness involved in the LPC measure itself. For instance, there is some doubt about how many behavioral dimensions are associated with the scale used to measure LPC scores. Studies of the relationship between LPC and the PM leadership types have indicated that people having intermediate LPC scores—scores between low LPC and high LPC—did not show the qualities intermediate between high LPC and low LPC leaders, but showed some heterogenous qualities. Whether or not the LPC measure meets the necessary and sufficient requirements of a measure to predict specific leadership behavioral tendencies is questionable. In other words, if the LPC measure is an adequate index for predicting the effectiveness of leadership, it should have clearly produced more consistent results than it has even if there was some degree of ambiguity in the way situational variables are combined. To make the contingency model simpler and more interpretable, the LPC measure itself should be replaced. However, the PM theory of leadership has benefited considerably by the issues raised by the contingency theory, as it has by the grid theory and the prior Ohio State and Michigan studies.

Speculations Concerning the Applicability of Japanese Leadership Research to Western Cultures

Child (1981) suggests that comparing research carried out in different national settings requires a consideration of possible differences in culture, contingencies affecting typical organization design, and national economic-political structure. Thus, although many studies in the PM leadership program were designed to identify the general morphology or understand the general dynamics of leadership, they might be viewed by some as specific studies from the perspective of the generalizability of their results outside Japan. One next step in the PM leadership research program will be to determine whether or not its results can be applied to non-Japanese cultures. Arrangements are now being made to conduct PM studies in the United States, Europe, and China, and additional research sites are being actively sought.

Some research programs and theoretical perspectives on leadership originating outside of Japan encourage the belief that the basic morphology and dynamics of leadership in Japan may be similar to those elsewhere. Although most leadership research conducted outside Japan has tended to abstract performance-oriented leadership from maintenance-oriented leadership by treating them as separate, noninteracting dimensions, ideas conceptually similar to these basic dimensions are evident in research programs with conceptual and methodological roots in Bales's (1953) research or in the Michigan and Ohio State studies (Katz, Maccoby, and Morse 1950; Stogdill and Coons 1957). The idea that the two dimensions may be best combined to represent types is incorporated to some extent in the normative leadership model proposed by Blake and Mouton (1964). However, as already noted, the Blake and Mouton model does not unambiguously indicate the applicability of the PM leadership research findings even within the limited range of settings in the United States to which the model is most often applied.

Despite a small amount of field research in the West that does not support an interactive hypothesis similar to the PM hypothesis (Larson, Hunt, and Osborn 1976), there are many reasons to believe that the conclusions of the PM leadership theory will be applicable to some settings in the West. Japan has been "Westernized," "democratized," and "industrialized" to a considerable degree since World War II. Broadly speaking, the culture of Japan has much in common with that of the Western world even though its unique Oriental heritage also produces noticeable differences. Also, as Ouchi (1981) argues, what might be considered the "subcultures" within large organizations in Japan (e.g., lifetime employment, participative mechanism quite similar to those of some organizations in the United States.

Conclusion

We have tried to summarize the PM leadership theory, but our summary covers only what we have found thus far. Needless to say, the PM leadership theory has many more questions to resolve. We decided to consolidate all our data into this book in order to make known our interdisciplinary approach to the leadership phenomenon from the viewpoint of modern behavioral science. It is not easy to create a new academic system of scientific knowledge based on interdisciplinary studies. In the course of our interdisciplinary studies of leadership we realized that there are limits to the possibility of developing an interdisciplinary approach to leadership by conducting research within the framework of the existing classification of the social sciences. Thus, we propose a new paradigm to define an academic field that extends beyond the existing classification of the social sciences in the interest of systematizing the science of leadership. The new system that we propose covers four areas: general behavioral morphology of leadership behavior, specific behavioral morphology (or behavioral ecology), general behavioral dynamics, and specific behavioral dynamics. These areas provide a framework for developing a descriptive science and an explanatory science to use in analyzing leadership behavior as a factual phenomenon.

Finally, does this paradigm suffice to cover leadership behavior? As far as the knowledge system of leadership goes, it is our position that this paradigm does suffice. However, our research thus far leaves open the question of what method, training, treatment, and strategy should be employed to put the knowledge system of leadership into practice and thus obtain desirable leadership. A leadership development system which can be used to apply and practice the systematized knowledge about leadership remains to be refined. While we have discussed a few of the development strategies we have used, it remains for future studies to systematize the technical and practical leadership science centering around this kind of leadership development system. An adequate theoretical and practical leadership science will be established if and when the scientific study of leadership behavior that we have developed in this book is integrated with technical and practical strategies for changing leadership.

APPENDIX

Hayashi's Quantification III

Quantification on Response Pattern: Factor Analytic Method for Qualitative Data

(We may call this "Principal components analysis in the qualitative case.")

This is one method of classification of individuals based on the similarity of responses to questions having several categories. This method is especially important here as no other method exists for classification.

The response pattern of individuals is shown in the following table or chart. We assume that individuals are interviewed with L questions and give only one response to each question.

In order that individuals with similar response patterns may be listed in a certain order in the chart, so that they are located in roughly the same area of the chart as well as in categories having similar characteristics, we want to classify individuals and categories simultaneously.

From this, we can find the configuration of both the individuals and response categories in multidimensional Euclidean space, in order to be able to make inferences from them.

Inferences can be made easily, if we have these configurations in one-dimensional space. This means that we can summarize the information on similarity among the individuals and among response categories on one axis. If the configurations cannot be summarized on one axis, we shall have to interpret configurations in multidimensional space. So, first, we will start our interpretation in one-dimensional space and then continue to multidimensional space.

We define $\delta_i(j)$ as

$$\delta_i(j) = \begin{cases} 1, & \text{if the } i\text{-th individual (or type) selects the } j\text{-th response category} \\ 0, & \text{otherwise} \end{cases}$$

Reprinted from Hayashi 1956.

where $i = 1, 2, \cdots, Q$ and $j = 1, 2, \cdots, R$ and

$$R = \sum_{j=1}^{L} K_j;\ K_j \text{ is the number of response categories in the } j\text{-th item}$$

$$l_i = \sum_{j=1}^{R} \delta_i(j);$$

$$n = \sum_{i=1}^{Q} s_i;\ \bar{l} = \frac{1}{n} \sum_{i-1}^{Q} l_i s_i$$

where L is the number of items, s_i is the number of respondents that fall into the i-th type and n is sample size.

We want to quantify types (individuals) and categories by assigning numerical values to them that will maximize the correlation coefficient between individuals and categories. This is the idea of the simultaneous grouping of individuals and categories and also is considered to be one method of taxonomy of individuals and categories based on response pattern (see table A1).

So, let the types be 1, 2, . . . , Q and response categories be $1(C_{11})$, . . . , $K_1\ (C_{1K_1})$, $K_1 + 1(C_{21})$, . . . , $R(C_{LK_1})$. Then we require $y_1, y_2, \ldots,$ y_Q given to types and $x_1, x_2, \ldots, x_R$ given to categories to maximize the correlation coefficient ${}^1\rho$ between x and y,

TABLE A1. Spatial Representation of Individuals (Types) and Response Categories in Question Items Based on the Information of Response Pattern

		A	1				2			···	L		
		B	1	2	···	K_1	$K_1 + 1$	···		···		···	R
D	E	F C	C_{11}	C_{13}	···	C_{1K_1}	C_{21}	···	C_{2K_2}	···	C_{L_1}	···	C_{LK_L}
l_1	s_1	1	V					V					V
l_2	s_2	2	V				V						V
l_3	s_3	3		V					V		V		
·	·	·											
·	·	·											
·	·	·											
l_Q	s_Q	Q	V						V				V

Note: V sign shows the response category of individual. The categories contain neither D.K. nor "other" responses. Those who select D.K. or "other" mentioned above show no sign. Thus the number l's of responses in the question items of types are generally different.

A = item (question); B = consecutive number; C = category; D = total of sign; E = frequency; F = response type (individuals).

where: ${}^1\rho = C_{xy}/\sigma_x\sigma_y$

$$\sigma_x^2 = \sum_{i=1}^{Q}\sum_{j=1}^{R}\delta_i(j)s_ix_j^2/(\bar{l}n) - \left\{\sum_{i=1}^{Q}\sum_{j=1}^{R}\delta_i(j)s_ix_j/(\bar{l}n)\right\}^2$$

$$\sigma_y^2 = \sum_{i=1}^{Q}s_il_iy_i^2/(\bar{l}n) - \left\{\sum_{i=1}^{Q}s_il_iy_i/(\bar{l}n)\right\}^2$$

$$C_{xy} = \sum_{i=1}^{Q}\sum_{j=1}^{R}\delta_i(j)s_ix_jy_i/(\bar{l}n) - \left\{\sum_{i=1}^{Q}\sum_{j=1}^{R}\delta_i(j)s_ix_j/(\bar{l}n)\right\}\left\{\sum_{i=1}^{Q}s_il_iy_i/(\bar{l}n)\right\}.$$

And in order to maximize ${}^1\rho$, it is to solve

$$\frac{\partial\,{}^1\rho}{\partial x_k} = 0, \qquad \frac{\partial\,{}^1\rho}{\partial y_e} = 0 \qquad (k = 1, 2, \cdots, R;\ e = 1, 2, \cdots, Q)$$

which implies

$$\sum_{j=1}^{R}h_{jk}x_i = {}^1\rho^2\sum_{j=1}^{R}f_{jk}x_j \qquad (k = 1, 2, \cdots, R)$$

where: $f_{jk} = \begin{cases} -b_{jk}; & (j \neq k) \\ d_k - b_{jk}; & (j = k) \end{cases}$

$$h_{jk} = a_{jk} - b_{jk}$$

$$a_{jh} = \sum_{i=1}^{Q}\frac{\delta_i(j)\delta_i(k)}{l_i}s_i$$

$$b_{jk} = \frac{1}{\bar{l}n}\left\{\sum_{i=1}^{Q}\delta_i(j)s_i\right\}\left\{\sum_{i=1}^{Q}\delta_i(k)s_i\right\}$$

$$d_k = \sum_{i=1}^{Q}s_i\delta_i(k).$$

For further convenience, the matrix representation

$$HX = {}^1\rho^2FX$$

will be used in the following discussion, where the elements of the matrix H are h_{jk}, those of the matrix F are f_{jk}, and X is a column vector. Then calculate the latent vector corresponding to the maximum latent root of ${}^1\rho^2$, where we can set $\bar{x} = \frac{1}{\bar{l}n}\sum_{j}^{R}\sum_{i}^{Q}\delta_i(j)s_ix_j = 0$ and $\sigma_x^2 = 1$ without loss of generality.

And we obtain

$$y_e = \frac{1}{{}^1\rho}\frac{\sigma_x}{\sigma_y}\left(\frac{1}{l_e}\sum_{j=1}^{R} x_j \delta_e(j)\right), \qquad (e = 1, 2, \cdots, Q)$$

which implies

$$y_e = \frac{1}{l_e}\sum_{j=1}^{R} x_j \delta_e(j) \text{ in case of } \frac{1}{{}^1\rho}\frac{\sigma_x}{\sigma_y} = 1.$$

This method is equivalent to that of maximizing $\eta^2 = \sigma_b^2/\sigma^2$, where σ_b^2 is between individual (type) variance and σ^2 is total variance (σ_w^2 is variance within individual (type) and is equal to $\sigma^2 - \sigma_b^2$).

We generalize this idea to multidimensional quantification. We want to quantify types (individuals) or categories by assigning numerical vectors to them to minimize the within generalized variance, $|W|$, with the total variance being constant. In other words, it is to minimize $|W|/|VT|$, where $|VT|$ is generalized total variance with respect to vector ${}^sX_i$ (or ${}^sY_j$) for $s = 1, 2, \cdots, S$ and for all i (or j), and S is the number of dimension of the space.

The process mentioned above is described in detail below. We consider to maximize $1 - |W|/|VT|$ under the reasonable condition that the nondiagonal elements in matrix W vanish, and this means to maximize $1 - |\tilde{W}|/|VT|$ where $\tilde{W}$ is the diagonal matrix of W. As $|\tilde{W}|/|VT| \geqq |\tilde{W}|/|\tilde{VT}|$ and $|VT| \leqq |\tilde{VT}|$ hold, $1 - |\tilde{W}|/|\tilde{VT}| \geqq 1 - |\tilde{W}|/|\tilde{VT}|$, where $\tilde{VT}$ is the diagonal matrix of VT. Thus, it is desirable to quantify the individuals and the categories, (in other words, to require vector x_i [or y_j] for all i [or j], so as to minimize $|\tilde{W}|/|\tilde{VT}|$, or to maximize $1 - |\tilde{W}|/|\tilde{VT}|$. This reduces to the maximizing of $\prod_s^S {}^s\eta^2$ for ${}^s\eta^2$ which is the correlation ratio with respect to ${}^sx_i$ for all i, and which is equivalent to maximizing $\prod_s^S {}^s\rho^2$ where ${}^s\rho$ is the correlation coefficient between ${}^sx_i$ and ${}^sx_j$ for all i and j.

Thus, it leads us to solve the latent equation $HX = p^2FX$, and ${}^sX$ is the latent vector corresponding to the s-th largest latent root of H. Generally speaking, the smaller S is the more desirable (for example S being at most three). However, we do require that the minimum dimension, or minimum S, makes ${}^s\rho^2$ small.

In some cases, we make $\sigma_{sx}^2 = {}^s\eta^2$, where $s = 1, 2, \cdots, S$, without loss of generality, and when this assumption holds, it is also useful to describe some concentration elipsoids and to classify the individuals and categories into several groups. In the classification, some methods of statistical numerical taxonomy are available with computer programs.

In order to visualize the result of the above calculations, we would like to represent it in the following two-dimensional Euclidean spaces. In doing so, we take the two-dimensional vector $({}^1X, {}^2X)$, for ${}^1X$ and ${}^2X$ are the corresponding latent vectors to the maximum latent root, ${}^1\rho^2$, and the second maximum latent root, ${}^2\rho^2$ respectively.

In the two-dimensional spaces, the nearer the points are, the closer it shows that the relations of the categories to be. That is to say, figure A3, categories *A* and *B* have very close relation while *A* and *C* do not. Those who select category *A*(*B*) have a strong tendency to select category *B*(*A*) and not category *C*. So the distance (far and near) between points corresponds to the similarity of categories in responses (see figs. A1, A2, and A3).

In figures A1 and A2, the response categories *A, B, C, D, E, F, G, H* have the same relative positions in two-dimensional space and show the same configuration. And the counterclockwise rotation of axis of figure A3 by ninety degrees coincides with figure A2, where ${}^1X$ in figure A3 corresponds to ${}^2X$ in figure A2 and ${}^2X$ in figure A2 corresponds to ${}^1X$ in figure A3.

However, this meaning is different, because ${}^1X$ is more powerful in expression of correlation of responses than ${}^2X$ in both figures. That is to say, the discriminant power on ${}^1X$ is larger than on ${}^2X$ since the latent root, or correlation ratio, is larger on ${}^1X$ than ${}^2X$. More precisely, for the group of respondents from which the figure A2 is obtained, those who select the response categories (*D, H*) will less possibly select (*E, F*) than those who select (*A, B*) are to select (*C, G*), while for the group of respondents from which figure A3 is formed, those who select (*A, B*) have less possibility of selecting (*C, G*) than those who select (*D, H*) to select (*E, F*). Thus, between these two groups of respondents, we can observe some differences in their way of thinking, that is the difference of concept which is commonly shared in each alternative response categories is viewed differently in both groups of respondents.

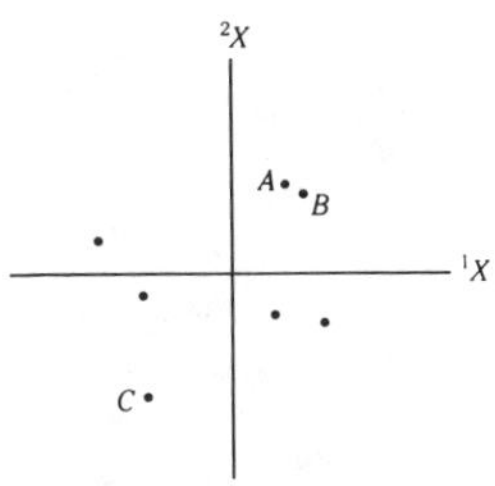

Fig. A1

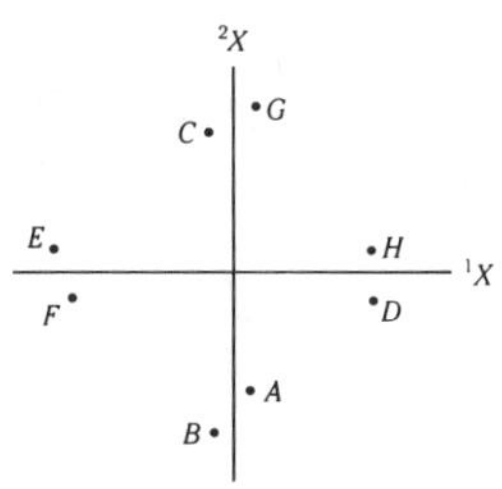

Fig. A2

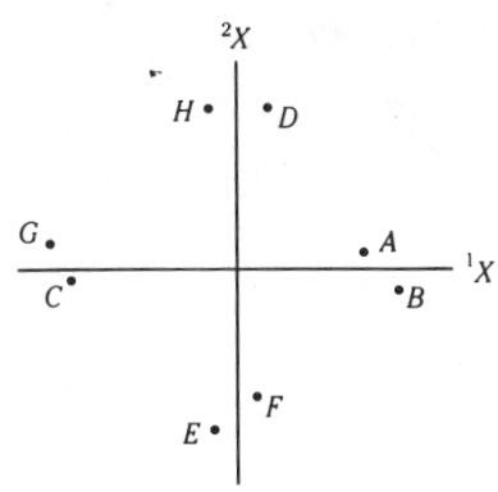

Fig. A3

References

Abe, K. 1978. *Collective behavior* (in Japanese). Tokyo: Tokyo University Press.

Akune, M. 1973. A factor analytic study of teachers' leadership behavior (in Japanese). *Bulletin of the Faculty of Education, Kyushu University* 17:25–34.

Alper, T. G. 1948. Task-orientation and ego-orientation as factors in reminiscence. *Journal of Experimental Psychology* 38:224–38.

Amidon, E., and Flanders, N. A. 1961. The effects of direct and indirect teacher influence on dependent-prone students learning geometry. *Journal of Educational Psychology* 52:286–91.

Ammons, R. B. 1950. Acquisition of motor skill: III. Effect of initially distributed practice on rotary pursuit performance. *Journal of Experimental Psychology* 40:777–87.

Anderson, H. H., and Brewer, H. M. 1945. Studies of teachers' classroom personalities. Vol. 1, Dominative and socially integrative behaviors of kindergarten teachers. *Applied Psychological Monograph,* no. 6.

Archer, E. J. 1954. Post rest performance in motor learning as a function of prerest degree of distribution. *Journal of Experimental Psychology* 47:47–51.

Asch, M. J. 1951. Nondirective teaching in psychology. *Psychological Monograph* 65 (4).

Atkinson, J. W. 1958. *Motives in fantasy, action, and society.* Princeton: Van Nostrand.

Bales, R. F. 1953. The equilibrium problem in small groups. In *Working papers in the theory of action,* ed. T. Parsons, R. F. Bales, and E. A. Shils. Glencoe, Ill.: Free Press.

———. 1955. The equilibrium problem in small groups. In *Small group: Studies in social interaction,* ed. P. Hare, E. F. Borgatta, and R. F. Bales. New York: Knopf.

Bales, R. F., and Isenberg, D. J. 1982. SYMLOG and leadership theory. In *Leadership: Beyond establishment views,* ed. J. G. Hunt, U. Sekaran, and C. A. Schriesheim. Carbondale: Southern Illinois University Press.

Ballard, P. B. 1913. *Obliviscence and reminiscence.* Cambridge: Cambridge University Press.

Barnard, C. 1938. *The functions of the executive.* Cambridge, Mass.: Harvard University Press.

Bass, B. M. 1981. *Stogdill's handbook of leadership.* New York: Free Press.

Berkowitz, L. 1954. Group standards, cohesiveness, and productivity. *Human Relations* 7:509–19.

Blake, R. R., and Mouton, J. S. 1964. *The managerial grid.* Houston: Gulf.

———. 1982. Theory and research for developing a science of leadership. *Journal of Applied Behavioral Science* 18:275–91.

Bons, P. M., and Fiedler, F. E. 1976. Changes in organizational leadership and the behavior of relationship and task motivated leaders. *Administrative Science Quarterly* 21:453–73.

Bowers, D. G., and Seashore, S. E. 1966. Predicting organizational effectiveness with a four factor theory of leadership. *Administrative Science Quarterly* 11:238–63.

Calder, B. J. 1977. An attribution theory of leadership. In *New directions in organizational behavior,* ed. B. Staw and G. Salancik. Chicago: St. Clair Press.

Cammann, C.; Fichman, M.; Jenkins, G. D.; and Klesh, J. 1983. Michigan organizational assessment questionnaire. In *Observing and measuring organizational change: A guide to field practice,* ed. S. E. Seashore, E. E. Lawler, P. H. Mirvis, and C. Cammann. New York: Wiley-Interscience.

Campbell, D. T., and Stanley, J. C. 1963. Experimental and quasi-experimental designs for research on teaching. In *Handbook of research on teaching,* ed. N. L. Gage. Chicago: Rand McNally.

Carlyle, T. 1841. *The hero and hero-worship.* Boston: Adams (1907).

Cartwright, D., and Zander, A., eds. 1953. *Group dynamics—research and theory.* New York: Harper and Row.

———. 1968. *Group dynamics—research and theory.* 3d ed. New York: Harper and Row.

Cattell, R. B. 1949. "γ_p" and other coefficients of pattern similarity. *Psychometrica* 14:279–98.

Child, J. 1981. Culture, contingency and capitalism in the cross-national study of organizations. In vol. 3 of *Research in organizational behavior,* ed. L. L. Cummings and B. M. Staw, 303–56. Greenwich, Conn.: JAI Press.

Coch, L., and French, J. R. P. 1948. Overcoming resistance to change. *Human Relations* 1:512–32.

Collins, B. E., and Raven, B. H. 1969. Group structure: Attraction, coalitions, communication and power. In *The handbook of social psychology,* ed. G. Lindzey and E. Aronson, 4:102–204. Reading, Mass.: Addison-Wesley.

Cowen, E. L. 1952*a*. The influence of varying degree of psychological stress on problem-solving rigidity. *Journal of Abnormal and Social Psychology* 47:512–19.

———. 1952*b*. Stress reduction and problem-solving ridigity. *Journal of Consulting and Clinical Psychology* 16:425–28.

Dansereau, F.; Alutto, J. A.; Markham, S. E.; and Dumas, M. 1982. Multiplexed supervision and leadership: An application of within and between analysis. In *Leadership: Beyond establishment views,* ed. J. G. Hunt, U. Sekaran, and C. A. Schriesheim, 81–103. Carbondale: Southern Illinois University Press.

Downey, H. K.; Sheridan, J. E.; and Slocum, J. W., Jr. 1976. The path-goal theory of leadership: A longitudinal analysis. *Organizational Behavior and Human Performance* 16:156–76.

Ebbinghaus, H. 1885. *Uber das Gedachtnis.* Leipzig: Dunker and Humbolt.

Eden, D., and Leviatan, U. 1975. Implicit leadership theory as determinant of the factor structure underlying supervisory behavior scales. *Journal of Applied Psychology* 60:736–41.

Eglash, A. 1954. A group-discussion method of teaching psychology. *Journal of Educational Psychology* 45:257–67.

Emerson, R. 1850. *Representative men: Seven lectures.* Boston: Phillips, Sampson.

English, H. B., and English, A. C. 1958. *A comprehensive dictionary of psychological and psychoanalytical terms.* New York: Longman.

Evans, M. G. 1970. The effects of supervisory behavior on the path-goal relationship. *Organizational Behavior and Human Performance* 5:277–98.

Eysenck, H. J., ed. 1964. *Experiments in motivation.* Oxford: Pergamon.

Eysenck, H. J., and Maxwell, A. E. 1961. Reminiscence as a function of drive. *British Journal of Psychology* 52:43–52.

Eysenck, H. J., and Willett, R. A. 1961. The measurement of motivation through the use of objective indices. *Journal of Mental Science* 107:961–68.

Farris, G. F., and Lim, F. G., Jr. 1969. Effect of performance on leadership, cohesiveness, influence, satisfaction and subsequent performance. *Journal of Applied Psychology* 53:485–97.

Feldman, H. 1937. *Problems in labor relations.* New York: Macmillan.

Fiedler, F. E. 1967. *A theory of leadership effectiveness.* New York: McGraw-Hill.

———. 1972*a*. Predicting the effects of leadership training and experience from the contingency model. *Journal of Applied Psychology* 56:114–19.

———. 1972*b*. The effects of leadership training and experience: A contingency model interpretation. *Administrative Science Quarterly* 17:453–70.

Flanders, N. A. 1951. Personal-social anxiety as a factor in experimental learning situations. *Journal of Educational Research* 45:100–110.

———. 1960. *Teacher influence, pupil attitudes and achievement.* Minneapolis University Office of Education Cooperation Research Project, no. 397.

Fleishmann, E. A. 1953. The measurement of leadership in industry. *Journal of Applied Psychology* 37:153–58.

Fleishmann, E. A., and Harris, E. F. 1962. Patterns of leadership behavior related to employee grievances and turnover. *Personnel Psychology* 15:43–56.

Franklin, J. L. 1975*a*. Down the organization: Influence processes across levels of hierarchy. *Administrative Science Quarterly* 20:153–64.

———. 1975*b*. Relations among four social-psychological aspects of organizations. *Administrative Science Quarterly* 20:422–33.

Fujita, M. 1970. The influence of PM leadership types on concept formation (in Japanese). Unpublished masters thesis, Kyushu University.

———. 1975*a*. The influences of PM leadership types on Einstellung effect in problem solving process (in Japanese with English abstract). *Japanese Journal of Experimental Social Psychology* 15:116–28.

———. 1975*b*. PM sensitivity training: Training for organizational change (in Japanese). In *Organizational Change and PM Leadership Theory,* ed. Japan Institute for Group Dynamics, 72–98. Tokyo: Daiyamondo-sha.

Furukawa, A. 1970. Methodology for measurement of parent and child relations (in Japanese). Unpublished masters thesis, Kyushu University.

Furukawa, A.; Misumi, J.; and Shinohara, H. 1969. Measurement of PM parental leaderships (in Japanese). Proceedings in the 33d Annual Meeting of Japanese Psychological Association, 293.

Furukawa, H. 1972. The effect of success or failure evaluation upon follower's morale and perception of leadership function (in Japanese with English abstract). *Japanese Journal of Experimental Social Psychology* 11:133–47.

———. 1975. Management of motivation of employees in a hierarchical organization: A development by the expectancy theory (in Japanese). *Bulletin of the Research Institute of National Railroad* 29:101–13.

Galbraith, J. 1973. *Designing complex organizations.* Reading, Mass.: Addison-Wesley.

Galton, F. 1870. *Hereditary genius.* New York: Appleton.

Georgopoulos, B. S.; Mahoney, G. M.; and Jones, N. W. 1957. A path-goal approach to productivity. *Journal of Applied Psychology* 41:345–53.

Gibb, C. A. 1969. Leadership. In *Handbook of social psychology,* ed. G. Lindzey and E. Aronson. 2d ed. Vol. 4, *Reading.* New York: Addison-Wesley.

Goldin, P. C. 1969. A review of children's reports of parental behaviors. *Psychological Bulletin* 71:222–36.

Goodman, L. A. 1971. The analysis of multidimensional contingency tables: Stepwise procedures and direct estimation method for building model for multiple classifications. *Technometrics* 13:33–61.

Greene, C. N. 1973. A longitudinal analysis of relationships among leader behavior and subordinate performance and satisfaction. Proceedings of the 33d Annual Meeting of the Academy of Management.

———. 1974. The path-goal theory of leadership: A replication and an analysis of causality. Proceedings of the 34th Annual Meeting of the Academy of Management.

———. 1975. The reciprocal nature of influence between leader and subordinate. *Journal of Applied Psychology* 60:187–93.

———. 1979*a*. Questions of causation in the path-goal theory of leadership. *Academy of Management Journal* 22:22–41.

———. 1979*b*. A longitudinal investigation of modifications to a situational model of leadership effectiveness. Proceedings of the 39th Annual Meeting of the Academy of Management.

Greene, S. G., and Mitchell, T. R. 1979. Attributional processes of leaders in leader-member interactions. *Organizational Behavior and Human Performance* 23:429–58.

Guetzkow, H. 1951. *Groups, leadership, and men: Research in human relations.* Pittsburgh: Carnegie Press.

Guttman, L. 1950. Chaps. 2, 3, 6, and 8. In *Measurement and prediction,* ed. S. Stouffer. Princeton: Princeton University Press.

Hachiya, Y. 1967. A study in the relationship between group task motivation and the conflict of two functional roles (in Japanese with English abstract). *The Japanese Annals of Social Psychology* 8:193–203.

Halpin, A. W. 1957. The observed leader behavior and ideal leader behavior of aircraft commanders and school superintendents. In *Leader behavior: Its descrip-*

tion and measurement, ed. R. M. Stogdill and A. E. Coons. Columbus: Ohio State University Press.

Halpin, A. W., and Winer, B. J. 1957. A factorial study of the leader behavior description. In *Leader behavior: Its description and measurement,* ed. R. M. Stogdill and A. E. Coons. Columbus: Ohio State University Press.

Haraoka, K., and Shinohara, S. 1975. Studies on teachers' leadership I, II (in Japanese). Proceedings of the 17th Annual Meeting of the Japanese Educational Psychological Association, 368–71.

Harary, F. 1959. Status and contrastatus. *Sociometry* 22:23–43.

Hayashi, C. 1956. Theory and examples of quantification (II), *Proceedings of the Institute of Statistics and Mathematics* 4:19–30.

Hayashi, C.; Higuchi, I.; and Komazawa, T. 1970. *Information processing and statistical mathematics* (in Japanese). Tokyo: Sangyo-Tosho.

Hayashi, T. 1963. Effects of distributed and massed learning IV: An experimental test of the nature of reactive inhibition (in Japanese with English abstracts). *Japanese Journal of Psychology* 34:211–17.

Heise, D. R. 1975. *Causal analysis*. New York: Wiley.

Hemphill, J. K. 1957. Leader behavior associated with the administrative reputations of college departments. In *Leader behavior: Its description and measurement,* ed. R. M. Stogdill and A. E. Coons. Columbus: Ohio State University Press.

Herold, D. M. 1974. Two-way influence processes in leader-follower dyads. *Academy of Management Journal* 20:224–37.

Hersey, P., and Blanchard, K. H. 1969. Life cycle theory of leadership. *Training and Development Journal* 23:26–34.

Herzberg, F.; Mausner, B.; Peterson, R. O.; and Capwell, D. F. 1957. *Job attitudes: Review of research and opinion.* Pittsburgh: Psychological Services of Pittsburgh.

Heyer, A. W., Jr., and O'Kelly, L. I. 1949. Studies in motivation and retention II, retention of nonsense syllables learned under different degrees of motivation. *Journal of Psychology* 27:143–52.

Hilgard, E. R. 1962. *Introduction to psychology*. 3d ed. New York: Harcourt, Brace & World.

Hollander, E. P. 1958. Conformity, status, and idiosyncracy credit. *Psychological Review* 65:117–27.

House, R. J. 1971. A path-goal theory of leader effectiveness. *Administrative Science Quarterly* 16:321–38.

House, R. J., and Mitchell, T. R. 1974. Path-goal theory of leadership. *Journal of Contemporary Business* 3:81–97.

Hovland, C. I. 1938. Experimental studies in role-learning theory: I. Reminiscence following learning by massed and by distributed practice. *Journal of Experimental Psychology* 22:201–24.

Hull, C. L. 1943. *Principles of behavior*. New York: Appleton, Century, Crofts.

Hurley, J. L., and Cattell, R. C. 1962. The Procrustes program producing direct rotation to test a hypothesized factor structure. *Behavioral Science* 1:258–62.

Inoue, S. 1974. An experimental study upon the effect of PM leadership change (in Japanese). *Bulletin of the Faculty of Education, Kyushu University* 18:75–85.

Ishiguro, S. 1955. *An experimental study of the effect of group learning*. Vol. 3 of *Educational psychology*, ed. Department of Psychology, Tokyo Educational College (in Japanese).

———. 1963. The influence of motivation on memory and its retention (in Japanese). *Bulletin of the Faculty of Liberal Arts, Gifu University* 1:59–74.

Ishiguro, T., and Fujiwara, K. 1954. Dotage, negligence and autocracy (in Japanese). *Child Psychology* 8:34–87.

Jackson, J. M. 1953. The effect of changing the leadership of small work groups. *Human Relations* 6:25–44.

———. 1960. Structural characteristics of norms. In *Dynamics of instructional groups*, ed. G. E. Jensen. Chicago: University of Chicago Press.

Jsujioka, B.; Shinohara, T.; and Yatabe, T. 1957. A factorial study of the temperament of Japanese college male students by the Yatabe-Guilford Personality Inventory. *Psychologia* 1:110–19.

Kahn, R. L. 1960. Productivity and job satisfaction. *Personnel Psychology* 13:275–87.

Kamitake, S. 1939*a*. A study of leadership psychology: Quasi conditional-genetic study of children's group as its prerequisites, Part I, no. 1 (in Japanese with English abstract). *Japanese Journal of Educational Psychology* 14:370–88.

———. 1939*b*. A study of leadership psychology: Quasi conditional-genetic study of children's group as its prerequisites, Part I, no. 2 (in Japanese with English abstract). *Japanese Journal of Educational Psychology* 14:471–84.

———. 1939*c*. A study of leadership psychology: Quasi conditional-genetic study of children's group as its prerequisites, Part I, no. 3 (in Japanese with English abstract). *Japanese Journal of Educational Psychology* 14:944–71.

Kano, S. 1970. An interaction between group structure and leadership upon group effectiveness and group morale (in Japanese). *Japanese Journal of Education and Social Psychology* 9:127–44.

Kashiwagi, S. 1965. Geometric vector orthogonal rotation method in multiple factor analysis. *Psychometrica* 30:515–30.

Kato, T. 1975. Problems of administrative managers (in Japanese). *Jickikenshu* 181:27–43.

Katz, D., and Kahn, R. L. 1978. *The social psychology of organizations*. 2d ed. New York: Wiley.

Katz, D.; Maccoby, N.; and Morse, Nancy C. 1950. *Productivity, supervision, and morale in an office situation*. Ann Arbor: University of Michigan, Institute for Social Research.

Kawakita, J. 1967. *How to come up with ideas* (in Japanese). Tokyo: Chuokoron-sha.

Kawazu, Y.; Misumi, J.; and Ogawa, N. 1972. A psychophysiological study of the features P, M, and PM type leader behaviors in the PM leadership theory (V) (in Japanese with English abstract). *Japanese Journal of Experimental Social Psychology* 12:11–19.

Kawazu, Y.; Misumi, J.; Ogawa, N.; Osato, E.; and Miyamoto, M. 1973. The interaction between the placebo effects and the leadership effects (in Japanese with English abstract). *Japanese Journal of Experimental Social Psychology* 13:22–30.

Kawazu, Y.; Ogawa, H.; and Misumi, J. 1974. *A psychophysiological study on leadership condition: The interaction between the placebo effects and the leadership effects* (in Japanese). Proceedings of the 38th Annual Meeting of the Japanese Psychological Association, 816–17.

Kelley, H. H. 1967. Attribution theory in social psychology. In vol. 15 of *Nebraska symposium on motivation,* ed. D. Levine. Lincoln: University of Nebraska Press.

______. 1972. Causal schemata and the attribution process. In *Attribution: Perceiving the causes of behavior,* ed. E. Jones, D. Kanouse, H. Kelley, R. Nisbett, S. Valins, and B. Weiner. Morristown, N.J.: General Learning Press.

______. 1973. The processes of causal attribution. *American Psychologist* 28:107–28.

Kerlinger, F. N. 1956. The attitude structure of the individual: A Q-study of the educational attitudes of professors and laymen. *Genetic Psychological Monograph* 53:283–329.

Kerr, S., and Jermier, J. M. 1978. Substitutes for leadership: Their meaning and measurement. *Organizational Behavior and Human Performance* 22:375–403.

Kerr, S., and Schriesheim, C. A. 1974. Consideration, initiating structure, and organizational criteria—an update of Korman's 1966 review. *Personnel Psychology* 27:555–68.

Kerr, W. A. 1957. Contemporary theories of safety psychology. *Journal of Psychology* 45:3–9.

Kidosaki, M. 1973. The influence of need for achievement to supervisory methods and group performance norms (in Japanese with English abstract). *Japanese Journal of Experimental Social Psychology* 12:108–12.

Kimble, G. A. 1949*a*. An experimental test of a two-factor theory of inhibition. *Journal of Experimental Psychology* 39:15–23.

______. 1949*b*. Performance and reminiscence in motor learning as a function of the degree of distribution of practice. *Journal of Experimental Psychology* 39:500–510.

______. 1950. Evidence for the role of motivation in determining the amount of reminiscence in pursuit motor learning. *Journal of Experimental Psychology* 40:248–53.

Kishida, M. 1958. A study of the human relationships between pupil and teacher (1) (in Japanese with English abstract). *Japanese Journal of Educational Psychology* 5:87–95.

______. 1959. A study of the human relationships between pupil and teacher (2) (in Japanese with English abstract). *Japanese Journal of Educational Psychology* 7:67–78.

Kojima, H. 1968. Children's report on their parent's attitude and behavior (in Japanese). *Bulletin of the Faculty of Education, Kanazawa University* 16:47–61.

______. 1970. A study of the parental behavior inventory: Balanced scale (in Japanese). *Bulletin of the Faculty of Education, Kanazawa University* 19:129–44.

______. 1973. Maternal behavior and attitude and elementary school children's academic achievement: An exploratory research (in Japanese). *Bulletin of the Faculty of Education, Kanazawa University* 22:73–88.

Komuro, S. 1955. The influence of learning method upon social behavior of children (in Japanese with English abstract). *Japanese Journal of Educational Psychology* 2:217–23.

———. 1956. The influence of learning method upon social behavior of children (II) (in Japanese with English abstract). *Japanese Journal of Educational Psychology* 3:157–63.

Korman, A. K. 1966. "Consideration," "initiating structure," and organizational criteria—a review. *Personnel Psychology* 19:349–61.

Krech, D.; Crutchfield, R. S.; and Ballachey, E. L. 1962. *Individual in society*. New York: McGraw-Hill.

Kugihara, N., and Misumi, J. 1984. An experimental study of the effect of leadership type on follower's escaping behavior in a fearful emergency maze-situation (in Japanese with English abstract). *Japanese Journal of Psychology* 55:14–21.

Kugihara, N.; Misumi, J.; and Sato, S. 1980. Experimental study of escape behavior in a simulated panic situation (in Japanese with English abstract). *Japanese Journal of Experimental Social Psychology* 20:55–66.

Kugihara, N.; Misumi, J.; Sato, S., and Shigeoka, K. 1982. Experimental study of escape behavior in a simulated panic situation II: Leadership in emergency situation (in Japanese with English abstract). *Japanese Journal of Experimental Social Psychology* 21:159–66.

Larson, L. L.; Hunt, J. G.; and Osborn, R. N. 1976. The great hi-hi leader behavior myth: A lesson from Occam's razor. *Academy of Management Journal* 19:628–41.

Lewin, K. 1939. Experiments in social space. *Harvard Educational Review* 9:21–32.

Lewin, K.; Lippitt, R.; and White, R. K. 1939. Patterns of aggressive behavior in experimentally created climates. *Journal of Social Psychology* 10:271–99.

Likert, R. 1967. *The human organization: Its management and value*. New York: McGraw-Hill.

Lippitt, R., and White, R. K. 1943. The social climate of children's groups. In *Child behavior and development,* ed. R. G. Barker, J. S. Kornin, and H. F. Wright. New York: McGraw-Hill.

Lowin, A., and Craig, J. R. 1968. The influence of level of performance on managerial style: An experimental object-lesson in the ambiguity of correlational data. *Organizational Behavior and Human Performance* 3:440–58.

Luchins, A. S. 1942. Mechanization in problem-solving. *Psychological Monograph* 54:1–95.

———. 1945. Social influence on perception of complex drawing. *Journal of Social Psychology* 21:257–73.

———. 1951. On recent usage of the Einstellung effect as a test of rigidity. *Journal of Consulting and Clinical Psychology* 15:89–94.

———. 1961*a*. Social influence on impressions of personality. *Journal of Social Psychology* 54:111–25.

———. 1961*b*. On conformity with judgement of a majority or an authority. *Journal of Social Psychology* 53:303–16.

Luchins, A. S., and Luchins, E. H. 1955. Previous experience with ambiguous and non-ambiguous perceptual stimuli under various social influence. *Journal of Social Psychology* 42:249–70.

———. 1959. *Rigidity of behavior*. Eugene: University of Oregon Press.

______. 1966. Consequences for agreeing with another's wrong judgement. *Journal of Social Psychology* 68:275–90.

Lyle, J. 1961. Communication, group atmosphere, productivity, and morale in small groups. *Human Relations* 14:369–79.

McClelland, D. C.; Atkinson, J. W.; Clark, R. W.; and Lowell, E. L. 1953. *The achievement motive*. New York: Appleton.

Macy, B. A., and Peterson, M. F. 1981. Evaluating change in a longitudinal quality of work life intervention. Paper presented at the annual meeting of the Academy of Management, San Diego.

Maeda, H.; Kojima, S.; and Nakashima, S. 1962. An experimental study of relationship between cohesiveness and productivity (in Japanese). *Japanese Journal of Educational and Social Psychology* 3:39–50.

Maeda, H.; Kojima, S.; and Noma, K. 1960. An experimental study on group cohesiveness and productivity I: When attraction to group members is manipulated (in Japanese). *Japanese Journal of Educational and Social Psychology* 1:164–73.

Malzman, I.; Fox, J.; and Marrisett, L. T. 1953. Some effects of manifest anxiety on mental set. *Journal of Experimental Psychology* 46:50–54.

Markus, H. 1977. Self-schemata and processing information about the self. *Journal of Personality and Social Psychology* 35:63–78.

Martinko, M. J., and Gardner, W. L. 1982. The observation of high performing education managers. Paper presented at the International Symposium on Managerial Behaviour and Leadership Research, Oxford.

Mead, G. H. 1934. *Mind, self and society*. Chicago: University of Chicago Press.

______. 1936. *Movements of thought in the nineteenth century*. Chicago: University of Chicago Press.

Mintzberg, H. 1973. *The nature of managerial work*. New York: Harper and Row.

______. 1979. *The structuring of organizations*. Englewood Cliffs, N.J.: Prentice-Hall.

Misumi, J. 1972. *Leadership* (in Japanese). Vol. 7 of Modern business administration series, ed. S. Takamiya. Tokyo: Daiyamondo-sha.

______. 1975. Action research on the development of leadership, decision-making processes and organizational performance in a Japanese shipyard. *Psychologia* 18:187–93.

______. 1978. The effects of organizational climate variables, particularly leadership variables and group decision, on accident prevention. Paper presented at the 19th International Congress of Applied Psychology, Munich.

______. 1982. What is leadership? (in Japanese). *Psychology* 25:12–19.

______. 1983. Decision-making in Japanese groups and organizations. In *International yearbook of organizational democracy,* ed. B. Wilpert and A. Sorge. London: John Wiley and Sons, 525–39.

Misumi, J., and Haraoka, K. 1958. An experimental study on group decision II (in Japanese). *Bulletin of the Faculty of Education, Kyushu University* 5:61–81.

______. 1960. An experimental study on group decision III (in Japanese). *Japanese Journal of Educational and Social Psychology* 1:136–53.

Misumi, J.; Ikeda, S.; and Yamaguchi, H. 1971. A psychological study of the experimenter effect on memory learning (in Japanese). Proceedings of the 35th Annual Meeting of Japanese Psychological Association, 467–68.

Misumi, J., and Kawazu, Y. 1970. A psychophysiological study of the features of P and M type leader behavior in PM leadership theory (in Japanese). *Japanese Journal of Educational and Social Psychology* 9:79–86.

Misumi, J.; Kurokawa, M.; and Shinohara, H. 1973. Studies on the validity of 16 patterns of PM leadership (I) (II) (III) (in Japanese). Proceedings of the 37th Annual Meeting of Japanese Psychological Association, 32–37.

Misumi, J., and Mannari, N. 1982. The empirical study concerning the validity of the measurement for the leadership behavior in industrial organizations. Proceedings of the Conference of the Japanese Organizational Science Association.

Misumi, J., and Nakano, S. 1960*a*. A cross-cultural study of the effect of democratic, authoritarian and laissez-faire atmospheres in children's groups II (in Japanese). *Japanese Journal of Educational and Social Psychology* 1:10–22.

———. 1960*b*. A cross-cultural study of the effect of democratic, authoritarian and laissez-faire atmospheres in children's groups III (in Japanese). *Japanese Journal of Educational and Social Psychology* 1:119–35.

Misumi, J.; Ogawa, N.; and Kawazu, Y. 1971. A psychophysiological study of the features of P and PM leader behaviors in the PM leadership theory (in Japanese). *Japanese Journal of Educational and Social Psychology* 10:1–9.

Misumi, J., and Sako, H. 1982. An experimental study of the effect of leadership behavior on followers' behavior of following the leader in a simulated emergency situation (in Japanese with English abstract). *Japanese Journal of Experimental Social Psychology* 22:49–59.

Misumi, J., and Sato, S. 1966. Validity of morale survey. *Japanese Psychological Review* 8:15–26.

———. 1968. An experimental study of the effects of PM patterns-leadership upon task performance and its reminiscence processes (in Japanese). *Japanese Journal of Educational and Social Psychology* 8:12–23.

Misumi, J., and Seki, F. 1968. An experimental study on the effect of the conditions achievement motive upon the effectiveness of PM patterns-leadership (in Japanese). *Japanese Journal of Educational and Social Psychology* 8:25–33.

———. 1971. Effects of achievement motivation on the effectiveness of leadership patterns. *Administrative Science Quarterly* 16:51–59.

Misumi, J.; Seki, F.; and Shinohara, H. 1969. An attempt to prepare scales for rating PM functions in discussion groups (in Japanese). *Japanese Journal of Educational and Social Psychology* 8:173–91.

———. 1974. Reanalysis of measurement scale of the PM-leadership pattern (in Japanese with English abstract). *Japanese Journal of Experimental Social Psychology* 14:21–30.

Misumi, J., and Shinohara, H. 1967. The atmosphere of work space and accidents (in Japanese). In *Psychology of accident and rehabilitation,* ed. Y. Tsujimura and J. Misumi, 35–64. Tokyo: Asakurashoten.

Misumi, J., and Shirakashi, S. 1963. An experimental study of the effects of supervisory behavior on productivity and morale in a hierarchical organization (in Japanese). *Japanese Journal of Educational and Social Psychology* 4:115–27.

———. 1966. An experimental study of the effects of supervisory behavior on productivity and morale in a hierarchical organization. *Human Relations* 19:297–307.

Misumi, J.; Shirakashi, S.; Takeda, T.; Shinohara, H.; and Seki, F. 1970. Studies on leadership behavior in organization (in Japanese). *Japanese Annals of Social Psychology* 11:63–90.

Misumi, J.; Takeda, T.; and Seki, F. 1967. An empirical study of the effects of managerial and supervisory behavior of PM pattern on productivity and morale, particularly need for achievement, in a hierarchical organization (in Japanese). *Japanese Journal of Educational and Social Psychology* 7:27–42.

Misumi, J., and Tasaki, T. 1965. A study on the effectiveness of supervisory patterns in a Japanese hierarchical organization (in Japanese). *Japanese Journal of Educational and Social Psychology* 5:1–13.

Misumi, J.; Yoshida, M.; and Sato, S. 1969. The effect of PM-pattern leadership upon performance and reminiscence in perceptual-motor learning (II): The experimental study in distributed learning (in Japanese). *Japanese Journal of Educational and Social Psychology* 8:147–58.

Mitchell, T. R., and Wood, R. E. 1980. Supervisor's responses to subordinate poor performance: A test of an attributional model. *Organizational Behavior and Human Performance* 25:123–38.

Nagasawa, M. 1958. A study on learning effect (in Japanese). *Japanese Educational Review* 4:1–5.

Neider, L. 1980. An experimental field investigation utilizing an expectancy theory view of participation. *Organizational Behavior and Human Performance* 26:425–42.

Nietzsche, F. W. 1885. *Thus Spoke Zarathustra*. Leipzig: A. Keöner.

Nystrom, P. C. 1978. Managers and the hi-hi leadership myth. *Academy of Management Journal* 21:325–31.

Osato, E.; Ogawa, N.; Misumi, J.; and Nishino, I. 1971. A differential effect of experimenter verbal instructions based on PM leadership theory on subject's psychomotor performance and blood pressure (in Japanese with English abstract). *Japanese Journal of Experimental Social Psychology* 11:57–66.

Osuga, T. 1959. *Labor groups* (in Japanese). Applied Social Psychology Series 3:258–301. Tokyo: Kobun-sha.

Ouchi, W. 1981. *Theory* Z. Reading, Mass: Addison-Wesley.

Patchen, M. 1962. Supervisory methods and group performance. *Administrative Science Quarterly* 7:275–94.

Pelz, D. C., and Andrews, F. M. 1961. Detecting causal priorities in panel study data. *American Sociological Review* 29:836–48.

Peterson, M. F. 1981. A model of problem-appropriate leadership applied to leadership behavior antecedents. *Journal Supplement Abstract Service Catalogue of Selected Documents in Psychology.*

______. 1982. Leadership: A mode of managing organizational problems. Paper presented at the annual meeting of the Academy of Management, New York.

Renson, G. J.; Schaefer, E. S.; and Levy, B. I. 1968. Cross national validity of a spherical conceptual model for parent behavior. *Child Development* 39:1229–35.

Rice, R. W. 1978. Construct validity of the least preferred coworker score. *Psychological Bulletin* 85:1199–1237.

Roethlisberger, F. J., and Dickson, W. J. 1939. *Management and the worker*. Cambridge: Harvard University Press.

Rush, M. C., and Beauvais, L. L. 1981. A critical analysis of format-induced versus subject-imposed bias in leadership ratings. *Journal of Applied Psychology* 66:722–27.

Rush, M. C.; Thomas, J. C.; and Lord, R. G. 1977. Implicit leadership theory: A potential threat to the internal validity of leader behavior questionnaires. *Organizational Behavior and Human Performance* 20:93–110.

Sakamaki, Y. 1974. The effects of the factors of group structure and the degree of task performance on group members' perceptions of leadership functions (in Japanese with English abstract). *The Japanese Journal of Experimental Social Psychology* 14:139–46.

Salancik, G. R., and Pfeffer, J. 1978. A social information processing approach to job attitudes and task design. *Administrative Science Quarterly* 23:224–53.

Sarason, I. G. 1957. Effects of anxiety and two kinds of motivating instructions on verbal learning. *Journal of Abnormal and Social Psychology* 54:166–71.

Sasaki, K., and Yamaguchi, M. 1971. An experimental study of the effect of leadership on the formation of group norms (in Japanese). *Bulletin of the Faculty of Sociology, Kansei Gakuin University* 22:209–26.

Sato, S. 1960. An experimental study on leadership functions in a hierarchical organization (in Japanese). Unpublished masters thesis, Kyushu University.

———. 1968. The effect of motivation on performance and reminiscence: The effect of supervisory behavior of PM type (in Japanese). *Japanese Journal of Educational and Social Psychology* 7:159–67.

———. 1972. The effects of experimenter's supervisory behavior patterns upon performance and reminiscence in perceptual-motor learning. *Japanese Psychological Research* 14:120–32.

Schachter, S.; Ellerton, N.; McBridge, D.; and Gregory, D. 1951. An experimental study of cohesiveness and productivity. *Human Relations* 4:229–38.

Schaefer, E. S. 1965. A cofiguration analysis of children's report of parent behavior. *Journal of Consulting Psychology* 29:552–57.

Schriesheim, C. A., and Stogdill, R. M. 1975. Differences in factor structure across three versions of the Ohio State leadership scales. *Personnel Psychology* 28:189–206.

Seashore, S. E. 1954. Group cohesiveness in the industrial work group. Ann Arbor: University of Michigan, Institute for Social Research.

Seeman, M. 1957. A comparison of general and specific leader behavior descriptions. In *Leader behavior: Its description and measurement*, ed. R. M. Stogdill and A. E. Coons. Columbus: Ohio State University Press.

Shaw, M. E. 1955. A comparison of two types of leadership in various communication nets. *Journal of Abnormal and Social Psychology* 50:127–34.

———. 1959. Acceptance of authority, group structure and the effectiveness of small groups. *Journal of Personality* 27:196–210.

Shiba, S. 1967. *Correlation analysis methods in behavioral sciences* (in Japanese). Tokyo: University of Tokyo Press.

Siegelman, M. 1965. Evaluation of Bronfenbrenner's questionnaire for children concerning parental behavior. *Child Development* 36:164–74.

Simon, H. A. 1969. *The science of the artificial.* Boston: MIT Press.

Sims, H. P. 1977. The leader as a manager of reinforcement contingencies: An empirical example and a model. In *Leadership: The cutting edge,* ed. J. C. Hunt and L. L. Larson. Carbondale: Southern Illinois University Press.

Sims, H. P., and Szilagyi, A. D. 1979. Time lags in leadership research. *Journal of Applied Psychology* 64:66–72.

Smelser, N. J. 1963. *Theory of collective behavior.* New York: Free Press.

Snedecor, G. W., and Cochran, W. G. 1980. *Statistical methods.* 7th ed. Ames: Iowa State University Press.

Spence, K. W.; Farber, I. E.; and McFann, H. H. 1956. The relation of anxiety (drive) level of performance in competitional and non-competitional paired-associates learning. *Journal of Experimental Psychology* 52:296–305.

Spence, K. W.; Taylor, J.; and Ketchel, R. 1956. Anxiety (drive) level and degree of competition in paired-associates learning. *Journal of Experimental Psychology* 52:306–10.

Stephenson, W. 1953. *The study of behavior: Q-technique and its methodology.* Chicago: University of Chicago Press.

Stogdill, R. M. 1948. Personal factors associated with leadership. *Journal of Psychology* 25:35–71.

______. 1963. *Manual for the leader behavior description questionnaire—Form XII.* Columbus: Ohio State University, Bureau of Business Research.

______. 1969. Validity of leader behavior descriptions. *Personnel Psychology* 22:153–58.

______. 1972. Group productivity, drive, and cohesiveness. *Organizational Behavior and Human Performance* 8:26–43.

______. 1974. *Handbook of leadership: A survey of theory and research.* New York: Free Press.

Stogdill, R. M., and Coons, A. E., eds. 1957. *Leader behavior: Its description and measurement.* Columbus: Ohio State University, Bureau of Business Research.

Strauss, A. L. 1944. The literature on panic. *Journal of Abnormal and Social Psychology* 39:317–28.

Symonds, P. M. 1939. The psychology of parent-child relationship. *American Journal of Psychology* 50:195–206.

Szilagyi, A. D. 1980. Causal interference between leader reward behavior and subordinate performance, absenteeism, and work satisfaction. *Journal of Occupational Psychology* 53:195–204.

Takeuchi, T., and Yabuki, S. 1961. A Q-technique study of the types of elementary school teachers I (in Japanese with English abstract). *Japanese Journal of Educational Psychology* 9:189–99.

Tasaki, T., and Misumi, J. 1976. A study of the effect of leadership behavior on group norms in job situation of industrial organization (in Japanese with English abstract). *Japanese Journal of Experimental Social Psychology* 16:1–7.

Taylor, J. C., and Bowers, D. G. 1972. *Survey of organizations.* Ann Arbor: University of Michigan, Institute for Social Research.

Toki, K. 1935. The leader-follower structure in school classes (in Japanese with English abstract). *Japanese Journal of Psychology* 10:27–56.

Tokuda, Y. 1962. A Q-study of the educational attitudes of teachers (in Japanese with English abstract). *Japanese Journal of Educational Psychology* 10:90–98.

Uchida, U. 1951. *Uchida-Kraepelin psychodiagnostic test.* Tokyo: Institute of Psychological Engineering.

Umemoto, T.; Morikawa, Y.; and Ibuki, M. 1955. The non-association values and meaningfulness of 1892 Japanese two-letter syllables and words. *Japanese Journal of Psychology* 26:148–55.

Van de Geer, J. P. 1957. *A psychological study of problem solving.* Haarlem: Uitgeverig De Toorts.

Vroom, V. H. 1964. *Work and motivation.* New York: Wiley.

———. 1966. A comparison of static and dynamic correlational method in the study of organizations. *Organizational Behavior and Human Performance* 1:55–70.

Vroom, V. H., and Yetton, P. W. 1973. *Leadership and decision making.* Pittsburgh: University of Pittsburgh Press.

Ward, L. B. 1937. Reminiscence and role learning. *Psychological Monograph* 49, no. 220.

Wasserman, H. N. 1951. The effect of motivation and amount of pre-rest practice upon inhibitory potential in motor learning. *Journal of Experimental Psychology* 42:162–72.

Weber, M. 1947. *The theory of social and economic organization.* New York: Oxford University Press.

Wertheimer, M. 1943. *Productive thinking.* New York: Harper and Brothers.

White, R. K., and Lippitt, R. 1960. *Autocracy and democracy: An experimental inquiry.* New York: Harper.

Whitehead, A. N. 1925. *Science and the modern world.* New York: Macmillan.

Willett, R. A., and Eysenck, H. J.1962. An experimental study of human motivation. *Life Science* 4:119–27.

Williams, O. 1926. A study of the phenomenon of reminiscense. *Journal of Experimental Psychology* 9:368–87.

Winer, B. J. 1962. *Statistical principles in experimental design.* New York: McGraw-Hill.

Wispe, L. G. 1951. Evaluating section teaching methods in introductory course. *Journal of Educational Research* 45:161–86.

Withall, J. 1949. The development of a technique for the measurement of social emotional climate in classroom. *Journal of Experimental Education* 17, no. 3.

———. 1952. Assessment of the social emotional climates experienced by a group of seventh graders as they moved from class to class. *Educational Psychology Measurement* 12:440–51.

Wyndham, C. H., and Cooke, H. M. 1964. The influence of the quality of supervision on the production of men engaged on moderately hard physical work. *Ergonomics* 7:139–49.

Yamauchi, M., and Yamaguchi, H. 1973. The effects of anxiety (drive) level, task difficulty and experimenter's supervisory behavior patterns on paired-associates learning (in Japanese). *Bulletin of the Faculty of Education, Kyushu University* 17:9–17.

Yatabe, T. 1949. *Psychology of thinking* (2) (in Japanese). Tokyo: Baihukan.

______. 1954. Construction of the Yatabe-Guilford personality inventory (in Japanese). Research Report of the Faculty of Literature in Kyoto University, no. 3.

Yee, A. H., and Gage, N. L. 1968. Techniques for estimating the source and direction of causal influence in panel data. *Psychological Bulletin* 70:115–26.

Yukl, G. A. 1971. Toward behavioral theory of leadership. *Organizational Behavior and Human Performance* 6:414–40.

______. 1981. *Leadership.* Englewood Cliffs, N.J.: Prentice-Hall.

Yukl, G. A., and Nemeroff, W. 1979. Identification and measurement of specific categories of leadership behavior: A progress report. In *Crosscurrents in leadership,* ed. J. G. Hunt and L. L. Larson. Carbondale: Southern Illinois University.

Zajonc, R. B. 1965. Social facilitation. *Science* 149:269–74.

Subject Index

Author Index